China's Silent Army

JUAN PABLO CARDENAL
and HERIBERTO ARAÚJO

China's Silent Army

The Pioneers, Traders, Fixers and Workers Who Are Remaking the World in Beijing's Image

Translated by Catherine Mansfield

Photographs by Luis de las Alas

ALLEN LANE
an imprint of
PENGUIN BOOKS

ALLEN LANE

Published by the Penguin Group

Penguin Books Ltd, 80 Strand, London WC2R ORL, England

Penguin Group (USA) Inc., 375 Hudson Street, New York, New York 10014, USA

Penguin Group (Canada), 90 Eglinton Avenue East, Suite 700, Toronto, Ontario, Canada M4P 2Y3
(a division of Pearson Penguin Canada Inc.)

Penguin Ireland, 25 St Stephen's Green, Dublin 2, Ireland (a division of Penguin Books Ltd)

Penguin Group (Australia), 707 Collins Street, Melbourne, Victoria 3008, Australia
(a division of Pearson Australia Group Pty Ltd)

Penguin Books India Pvt Ltd; 11 Community Centre, Panchsheel Park, New Delhi – 110 017, India

Penguin Group (NZ), 67 Apollo Drive, Rosedale, Auckland 0632, New Zealand
(a division of Pearson New Zealand Ltd)

Penguin Books (South Africa) (Pty) Ltd, Block D, Rosebank Office Park,
181 Jan Smuts Avenue, Parktown North, Gauteng 2193, South Africa

Penguin Books Ltd, Registered Offices: 80 Strand, London WC2R ORL, England

www.penguin.com

First published 2013
001

Copyright © Juan Pablo Cardenal and Heriberto Araújo, 2011, 2013
Translation copyright © Catherine Mansfield, 2013
First published in Spanish as *La silenciosa conquista china* by Editorial Crítica, 2011

The moral right of the authors and translator has been asserted

Set in 10.5/14 pt Sabon LT Std
Typeset by Jouve (UK), Milton Keynes
Printed in Great Britain by Clays Ltd, St Ives plc

ISBN: 978-1-846-14539-1

www.greenpenguin.co.uk

Penguin Books is committed to a sustainable
future for our business, our readers and our planet.
This book is made from Forest Stewardship
Council™ certified paper.

ALWAYS LEARNING   PEARSON

Heriberto:

For my mother, father and sister, and *to Julie C. and the rest of the Calderón Gómez family.*

Juan Pablo:

To my wife and children, Cristina, Jimena and Bosco.

'Observe and analyse calmly, secure our position, tackle changes patiently, hide our abilities and wait for the right moment, keep a low profile, never claim leadership, carry out business modestly.'

The strategy announced by Deng Xiaoping in early 1990 – shortly after the Tiananmen massacre – as a way of managing the changes taking place at that time. Largely, continues to dominate China's international strategy to this day.

Contents

Illustrations

1. Chinese and Sudanese agricultural workers outside Khartoum, Sudan (photograph by Luis de las Alas, who formed part of the project throughout the investigation in Africa)
2. Chinese and Mozambican workers in Xai-Xai, Mozambique (photograph: Luis de las Alas)
3. A Chinese entrepreneur and his client in Khartoum (photograph: Luis de las Alas)
4. Lodgings of a Chinese worker in Luanda, Angola (photograph: Luis de las Alas)
5. Employees of the Chinese state-owned company Anhui Wai Jing in Maputo, Mozambique (photograph: Luis de las Alas)
6. Workers on a Chinese construction project in Luanda, Angola (photograph: Luis de las Alas)
7. Chinese workers at the construction of the Merowe dam, Sudan (photograph: Luis de las Alas)
8. *Shanta sini*, the Chinese street vendors in Cairo, Egypt (photograph: Luis de las Alas)
9. A Chinese entrepreneur at his timber warehouse in Beira, Mozambique (photograph: Luis de las Alas)
10. Anatoly Lebedev, a prominent campaigner for the survival of the Siberian forests – in Dalnerechensk, the Russian Far East (photograph: Anatoly Petrov)
11. A Turkmen worker at the base camp of Chinese oil company CNPC, in Karakum Desert, Turkmenistan (photograph: Heriberto Araújo)
12. A Chinese engineer constructing a major road in Tehran (photograph: Zohreh Soleimani)

13. A mural in Marcona, Peru, condemning the Chinese mining company Shougang Hierro Peru (photograph: Marco Garro)
14. Cubans practising the Chinese art of *tai chi* in Havana, Cuba (photograph: Juan Pablo Cardenal)
15. A Burmese worker at a Chinese-owned gold mine in Myitkyina, Burma (photograph: Juan Pablo Cardenal)
16. A Chinese hairdressing salon in Vladivostok, Russia (photograph: Heriberto Araújo)

Acknowledgements

This book would not have been possible without the help and support of Keiko Aoki, Gustavo Ayala, Ombretta Borgia, Lito Cardenal, Angelo Carella, Ricardo Córdido, José Luis Díaz, Jesús Egusquiza, João Feijó, Montserrat Galdo, Alicia García Herrero, Antonio Hidalgo, Ainur Kulzhanova, Rosana Lake, Anatoly Lebedev, Iván Máñez, Eduardo Morcillo, Gamble Nelkin, Awad Nubia, Mark O'Neill, Christian Phong, Hkanhpa Sadan, Luis Tolosa, Jason G. Tower, Aliya Tshai, Mariano Turzi, Harry Verhoeven and Jumpei Yoshioka. We would like to say a big thank you to all of them for the invaluable help, logistic support, enthusiasm and time they have invested in this project.

Maddalena Simoncelli deserves a very special mention for her patience, hard work, support and kindness. We will never forget it.

We would also like to thank Liu Guijin, the Chinese government's Special Representative for African Affairs, for his good-natured willingness to grant us an interview. Ambassador Liu has been the friendliest face of a government that we have otherwise turned to time and time again in search of answers without much success.

Our gratitude also goes out to the 500 people, approximately, who were interviewed for this book, and to the many more anonymous people across the world who unselfishly agreed to tell us their stories, helping our investigations by giving us the key to understanding what was happening on the ground; nor should we forget all the people who have contributed to our knowledge of China's reality over the last few years. We would also like to give a special mention to the hundreds of Chinese people, both in the twenty-five countries we visited and in China itself, who welcomed us into their lives and helped us understand the inner workings of the Chinese world.

We also thank Félix Balanzó, Nicholas Bequelin, Madhu Bhalla, Enrique Criado, Geoffrey Crothall, Michael Elleman, Ángeles Espinosa, Josh Gordon, Fraser Howie, Guaicaipuro Lameda, Irene Jay Lui, Susana Moreira, William Nee, Alek Nomi, Pál Nyíri, Nicolás de Pedro, Xulio Ríos, José Manuel Seage, Ian J. Storey, José Toro Hardy and Víctor Torres for all of their comments, corrections and suggestions when revising these chapters. Their contribution has been invaluable and the responsibility for any errors found here rests entirely with us.

We would like to show our appreciation, too, for our colleagues at *Notimex* and *El Economista* for being so understanding when the posts of Beijing Correspondent and Hong Kong Correspondent were left empty while we were carrying out part of this project. We would like to give a special mention to Sergio Uzeta, Miguel Ángel Sola and Salvador Borja, as well as to Alejandro Valente, Alexandra Pineda and all the outstanding professionals working at the Spanish-language office of *Radio France Internationale*.

We would also like to say a big thank you to our editor, Simon Winder, for his belief in this project from day one, to our agent, Felicity Bryan, for making this book go global, and to our translator, Catherine Mansfield.

A very special mention goes to our friend, the great photographer Luis de las Alas, who joined us on our 'paradisiacal' journey through Africa. Part of this project also belongs to him.

Finally, our warmest thanks go to Wu Ye for her matchless efforts spent arranging paperwork, organizing interviews with Chinese people, translating, sorting out logistics and generally righting the wrongs that took place during the more thankless parts of our journalistic investigation from China. The same can be said for our friend and great adventurer H. S., who played a vital role in gaining access to Chinese projects and to the Chinese emigrants who are silently conquering the world. Thanks to him, we got much further on the ground than we ever could have done alone. It is a great shame that we have had to omit their real names here because of the reprisals they might otherwise face in China.

Note to the English Edition

Writing a book about a phenomenon as dynamic and complex as China's international expansion carries definite risks. The emergence of the new Asian giant has such wide-ranging implications that, as you will see for yourselves over the course of the following pages, these inevitably create both light and shadow. A thin line often separates the positive from the negative, and this must be understood if we are to get to the essence of a phenomenon that is changing the world.

The playing out of events over the year since publication of this book's original Spanish edition – with such abrupt changes as the global repercussions of the Arab Spring and the internal evolution of the Chinese regime itself, now moving somewhat turbulently through the first changes in the highest ranks of its leadership in a decade – could have made what we describe in this book obsolete. As it turns out, this has very much not been the case.

To the contrary, everything described in these pages has become further validated by the passage of time. This is not only because none of the phenomena explored in *China's Silent Army* have lost their relevance, but also because the book's principle thesis and conclusions have been reinforced. From Tehran to San Juan de Marcona in Peru, from Luanda to Hanoi, the rise of the giant is happening on an overwhelming scale, although still concealed by the lack of transparency typical of Chinese initiatives in the developing world.

China's arrival in Africa, Asia, the Middle East and Latin America is the theme of the book in your hands, which has been fully updated for Anglophone readers. In it, we draw on countless human stories and over 500 interviews to describe how China is guaranteeing its future supply of natural resources, opening new markets and creating strong alliances. China is setting itself up as an autocratic superpower without any interference from the usual counterweights which might otherwise submit its world conquest to international scrutiny. We also examine the consequences of all this activity for the countries currently receiving investment, money and support from China.

The intensification of the financial crisis in 2012, whose painful effects have become particularly visible in Europe, has strengthened the hypothesis that we gradually developed over the two years of active research needed to write this book: that China's expansion is inexorable, has a global scope and is driven by the depression in the West. Furthermore, the crisis has not only boosted China's presence in the developing world, but has also already led the Asian giant to come knocking on the door of the West, which because of the economic turmoil itself currently offers some mouth-watering opportunities, particularly in Europe.

China's conquest of the planet has therefore entered its second phase: a gradual entry into Western markets. This is done with the help of the indisputable power of its state capitalism, including its endless supplies of cash, its influential and seductive diplomacy, an army of tireless entrepreneurs and the sheer force of Chinese products, which are becoming ever more difficult to compete with. There is no doubt that we are witnessing the start of a long-distance offensive, which, however discreet and tactful, is nonetheless happening unstoppably – in the West as in the developing world.

If you are a lover of Bordeaux wine, for example, it may surprise you to hear that Chinese investors have engaged in the largest wave of investments at the world centre of premium wine between 2010 and 2012, acquiring dozens of *chateaux* and properties. If you are interested in the world of high fashion, you may know that wealthy Chinese dressmaking companies based in Tuscany have already made a name for themselves in the 'Made in Italy' market. Alternatively, you may have heard how Chinese millionaires are targeting the property market in the United Kingdom and United States.

And that is not all. The crisis has given the Chinese state the opportunity to acquire shares in the control of strategic assets abroad, something that was always closed to them in the past. Now, thanks to the depth of their pockets and the West's pressing need for investments to help create short-term employment, China can easily sweep away the obstacles that have impeded their access to Western markets. They now have a clear road towards the West's most valuable assets and technology, essential if China is to take a further leap forwards in terms of quality and innovation.

Perhaps the most important example – although by no means the only one – is Europe's first 'Chinese' port, the Port of Piraeus in Greece. This infrastructure of unique geostrategic importance has been managed by the Chinese state-owned company Cosco since 2009 and for the next thirty years, after the company paid out over 3 billion euros for the privilege. Similarly, Chinese state-owned businesses have landed at the heart of the Portuguese electricity sector, while a Chinese sovereign fund has acquired 8.68 per cent of the British water company Thames Water. The expansion has even reached as far as powerful Germany, where China has become the largest foreign investor in terms of the number of operations, overtaking the United States for the first time in history.

There is no doubt whatsoever that this irruption – from Africa, Latin America, the Middle East and Asia to Europe, the United States and Australia – has set a momentous tectonic shift in motion, suggesting a new world order. Now is the time, for example, when the developing world will find out whether the Chinese recipe for success really is the best option for its development; when Brussels will continue manoeuvring in an almost desperate attempt to realign its relationship with Beijing, a relationship which seems to be getting more asymmetric by the day; or when the United States will make a serious attempt to understand the nature of its co-existence with a new world power.

At the same time, in domestic terms we are witnessing the transfer of power to a new generation of leaders in the upper levels of Chinese politics. This transition process began in November 2012 with the meeting of the Communist Party of China (CPC) and will culminate in the spring of 2013. It came as no surprise that the XVIII Congress of the CPC, which will put an end to Hu Jintao's decade of power and establish Xi Jinping as the new strongman of the regime, has been shrouded in the usual veil of secrecy. What *was* a surprise, on the other hand, was the fact that the date of the congress was announced several weeks late as a result of the scandal unleashed by the so-called 'Bo Xilai case'.

Bo Xilai was arguably China's most charismatic politician, and the aura of success emitted both by his revolutionary heritage and his expeditious approach to politics had led him to be summoned as a new member of the next Politburo Standing Committee of the CPC. This is the country's most powerful organism, which in practice decides the destiny of China's 1.35 billion inhabitants. The role would have placed him in a privileged position to eventually reach the pinnacle of power, even giving him the opportunity to defy the established order.

All this probably would have happened if Bo hadn't fallen from grace following China's biggest political scandal to be made public in decades. The plot was thick with corruption, nepotism, betrayal and illicit million-dollar business deals overseas. Like some action-packed detective novel, it included the murder of a British business consultant and the attempted defection of Bo's closest collaborator, the 'super-cop' Wang Lijun. The regime attempted to plug the open wound in the reputation of both China's political elite and the Party itself with Bo's immediate expulsion from the CPC, as well as severe prison sentences for everyone involved.

The 'Bo Xilai case' has once again shown how difficult it is to unite wills and reach a consensus at the heart of the Party, where balancing the influence of the various factions – from the military to the directors of the biggest state-owned companies, from the descendants of revolutionary leaders to the organizational heads of the Party – requires intense negotiations in order to make decisions and share power. With the downfall of Bo Xilai, the next president, Xi Jinping, is free of one of his biggest political rivals, and can now take up his new role with greater internal support than his immediate predecessors.

With his revolutionary blood and strong connections in the upper echelons of the military, Xi stands out for his pragmatic and technocratic approach to politics. However, it is difficult to judge how he will govern the most populated country on Earth, or what type of relationship he will establish with his regional neighbours, the West and rest of the world. We must wait to see whether he will incline towards continuing with the political reforms expected from

Hu Jintao, or opt for the gradualism that has prevailed in high-level Chinese politics since the death of Mao Zedong.

Whatever happens, the future direction of global affairs depends on his sensitivity in terms of governing and how he will choose to wield his power during his decade-long mandate, during which time we will see China becoming the most powerful economy in the world. And, of course, his hand will hold the baton which will direct – in one way or another – the orchestra that will play to the sound of China's expansion across the planet.

As we already mentioned, this international offensive is taking place in the West, where it is still in the early stages but going strong, and in Africa, Latin America and Asia, where it has played an important role for over a decade and is described in detail in this book. Both campaigns run parallel to one another and complement each other, underlining an *unstoppable and silent world conquest* that is set to change the course of human history.

1 October 2012

Introduction

'The Chinese can't be seen . . . but they're everywhere.'
An Egyptian shopkeeper in Cairo commenting
on Chinese immigrants in the city

For most people, this date perhaps no longer means anything at all, but at exactly 8.08 p.m. on 8 August 2008 history changed its course.[1] That moment marked the beginning of the opening ceremony of the Beijing Olympic Games, the first event of its kind to take place in a developing country. It was an event that came shrouded in controversy and doubt. As well as the uncertainty caused by the organizers' lack of experience there were concerns over the politicization of the sporting contest, a consequence of the latest of countless suppressed uprisings in Tibet that had occurred just months before and, more generally, of the dictatorial nature of China's regime.

However, eighteen days later the Games came to an end with another spectacular display to match the one with which they began. China had passed the final test: the organization was outstanding and for the first time the country had become the sporting power to beat, overtaking the United States in the medal table. However, the greatest victory of all was not hammered out on the athletics track at the mighty Bird's Nest stadium or in the cube-shaped Olympic swimming pool. The real triumph took place on the television sets of over 2 billion people who watched the event on the small screen and witnessed the fresh and likeable image of a modern country confident in its own abilities: the image of twenty-first-century China.

Beijing 2008 represented a priceless PR campaign for the Chinese regime. Not only did the event serve to legitimize the regime in the eyes of its own people, but it also showed China to be worthy of a level of international prestige which immediately wiped away the tragic memory of the tanks of Tiananmen Square, the blood spilt in Tibet, and the daily trampling of human rights. Heads of State and of governments who just months before had threatened to boycott the Games now showered their Chinese counterparts with more tributes than ever before. In the press, China was now only of interest from an economic perspective, while social stories of injustice or repression were pushed, surprisingly, to the sidelines. Overnight it seemed that China had become 'one of us'.

For those of us who lived in China and, from our journalistic vantage point, were daily witnesses to the abuse, excesses and horrors of the regime, this *sterilization* of the world's biggest dictatorship was something we looked on with a mixture of astonishment and distress. It was a trend that would only increase in the months that followed: the cheering from the Olympic Games that had put the Asian giant on a pedestal had scarcely died away when Lehman Brothers, the fourth biggest investment bank in the United States, declared bankruptcy; 15 September 2008, just three weeks after the end of the Olympics, marked the beginning of the crisis which threatened the downfall of the Western financial system.

The chaos caused by the financial collapse in the United States and Europe, including the bailouts of banks, the mass closure of businesses and the dismissal of millions of workers, is not only still clearly visible today but many more years will have to go by before these wounds really heal. In China, however, the crisis passed by almost unnoticed, thanks to state intervention in the financial system, which helped to prevent contagion, and Beijing's quick reaction to side-step the recession. Furthermore, while the world was falling apart around it, the Asian giant – with its growing demand and infinite reserves of foreign currency – emerged as a lifesaver amid the wreckage of the West, buying debt and giving out loans here, there and everywhere. In a little less than a year, China's prestige and position in the rest of the world had taken a 180-degree turn, from treacherous dictatorship to saviour of the world's economy.

It was clear that the balance of world power had begun to swing towards the East. In November 2009 we watched in astonishment as Hu Jintao and Barack Obama appeared together during the president's first official visit to China. The American leader's low profile when tackling traditionally uncomfortable issues for Beijing – such as human rights – which had always played a prominent role in the diplomatic agenda of his predecessors, was a sure sign of China's emergence and growing influence on the world stage. Just weeks before, the new incumbent of the White House had approached China with the idea of creating a G2, a Washington–Beijing axis to take the lead in world affairs. Beijing had said no. Why should it form an alliance with the United States when world leadership was already within its grasp?

With full pockets and renewed prestige, the giant felt strong. And so, in the midst of the opportunities offered by the financial disruption, China began to spread its net wide. Investments worth millions of dollars, long-term supply contracts for raw materials, and the acquisition of assets across the planet offered ample proof that the Chinese world conquest had become a reality which, from where we sat in our Beijing office, seemed indisputable. We soon became fascinated with the magnitude of the phenomenon: what was the nature of China's expansion across the planet, an expansion based on the silence of money rather than the military might used by other world powers? Was the Asian country actually colonizing Africa? How close were the military, economic and nuclear ties between Beijing and Tehran? Was the colossus really sweeping away forests in Mozambique? How was neighbouring Russia digesting China's intrusion? Had China's tentacles already reached as far as Latin America?

One by one, these questions sharpened our curiosity, unable as we were to come up with any answers based on facts. Meanwhile, writing on a daily basis about GDP and other variables of Chinese macroeconomics was becoming an almost unbearable routine when we could see that history was changing its course right in front of our eyes, in the oil wells of Angola, the iron mines of Peru and the 'Made in China' markets of Central Asia. 'Let's get back to some real journalism and start sticking our noses into this business,' we told each other, convinced that this book would only make sense if we carried out our investigation on the ground. We would have to go to where the giant's footprint was most visible – in the developing world. In other words, it was time to travel to Asia, Africa and Latin America, to see, touch and taste for ourselves how China is becoming a global power.

The summer of 2009 was already coming to a close when we began an investigation that would take two years of total dedication. Understanding this 'new Chinese world' started off as a bet but soon became a passion, complete with email exchanges full of mostly hare-brained ideas at ungodly hours of the night. As we moved forwards and began to understand the key issues and secrets of the phenomenon, the investigation grew into an obsession. Fortunately, we weren't the only ones determined to find out more: the American media analysis company Global Language Monitor announced in December 2009 that 'the emergence of China' was the most closely followed story in newspapers, radio, television and the internet since the beginning of the century, bigger even than 9/11 or the election of President Obama. For one pair of journalists, there could be nothing more exciting than setting off in pursuit of the 'news of the decade'.

This increasing global interest in the new China is a direct consequence of the country's growing influence in the developing world, where it is able to spread quickly and easily. However, China's longer-term vocation is genuinely without limits. There is no doubt that we are witnessing a phenomenon that will sooner or later lead China to storm Western markets, where it is already buying sovereign debt, building new infrastructure in Eastern Europe, acquiring controlling stakes in strategic assets such as ports, utilities and power companies, taking over German technology firms, and rescuing Western brands from the brink of collapse. We are therefore facing a slow but steady conquest destined to change the lives of every one of us and which is most likely already laying the foundations for the new world order of the twenty-first century: a world under China's leadership.

The challenge of investigating this phenomenon demanded meticulous preparation; we would have to look into all of the million-dollar projects announcing the emergence of China that were spewing out of the office teletype machines on a daily basis. Where to go? Which countries to choose? Who to interview? Which leads to follow? These were the questions we asked ourselves when faced with the evidence that there was not a single corner of the planet which China had not yet reached. Months of intensive research followed, with countless interviews with experts in Beijing and endless hours spent checking and classifying the information available to us. It gave us a global vision of a phenomenon which we would soon have the opportunity to confirm on the ground: the new Chinese world is already here. All the figures point to this fact: between 2005 and July 2012, Chinese companies invested US$460 billion across the globe, $340 billion of which (74 per cent of the total amount) was spent in the developing world.[2]

What is happening is crystal clear. While the West suffers the consequences of the 2008 crisis, China goes from strength to strength. From a contract for $6 billion in the Democratic Republic of Congo using a 'minerals for infrastructures' formula to China's invaluable contribution to the motorization of Castro's Cuba, a country that was suffering from shortages of salt, powdered milk and rice when we visited the island; from the sale of satellites to Venezuela to an unprecedented offensive on the part of China's state corporations to guarantee their supply of 'black gold', including the investment of $48 billion in oil assets between 2009 and 2010.[3] And let us not forget the matchless flow of exports that has been forged over the last decade, since China became a member of the World Trade Organization (WTO). In just ten years the country has multiplied its trade with the rest of the world six times, with an increase from $510 billion in 2001 to $2.97 trillion in 2010.[4]

While there is no doubt that the crisis provided a powerful boost to China's spread of influence across the world, it is impossible to separate the country's expansion from the abilities of the Chinese people or the strength of its state and financial system. To begin with, China's expansion would not be what it is today without the support of millions of anonymous people who brave prejudice and uncertainty to set up businesses in the most unlikely places around the planet. China benefits from an army of astonishing human beings with a limitless capacity for self-sacrifice, who venture out into the world driven only by their dreams of success and who go on to conquer impossible markets which Westerners never dared to tackle – or if they did, they failed.

As well as the drive of its private sector, it is important to take into account the efficiency of China's economic model, which uses its astonishing financial clout to serve the country's national strategic objectives. The practically unlimited funds offered by policy banks such as the Export Import Bank (China Exim) and the China Development Bank (CDB) represent an incalculable advantage in an era otherwise dominated by empty coffers and a dwindling cash flow. Firstly, these loans allow state-run businesses working in the extractive sector to buy strategic assets, secure long-term supply contracts and develop projects to exploit natural resources. Furthermore, these limitless funds allow Chinese construction companies to bid for international projects with the most tempting financial packages on the market.

Many times they don't even go through public biddings. The recurrent funds offered by China Exim and the CDB also allow China to grant millions of dollars' worth of credit to countries such as Iran, Ecuador, Venezuela, Angola and Kazakhstan, among countless others. These loans are almost always backed with oil and are usually made under conditions classified as confidential. Despite the global crisis, in 2009–10 Beijing overtook the World Bank as the biggest lender on the planet, granting over $110 billion in credit in that period alone. This provides China with a lethal financial weapon: being the 'world's banker' not only underpins China's international diplomacy and global influence, but it also gives 'China Inc.' – the triumvirate formed by the party-state, the banks and the state-owned businesses – the ammunition needed to blow their competitors out of the water, as we ourselves have been able to confirm in country after country. And they can do all this without being accountable to anyone.

This issue wouldn't let us rest. Where do the Exim Bank and the CDB get their unlimited resources? How is a developing country like China able to become such a financial heavyweight when the rest of the world is going through economic turmoil? What is China's magic formula? The answer to this mystery is found right at the heart of the dictatorial regime: in short, it is the Chinese people who pay for the dreams and ambitions of the Chinese state, whether they like it or not. Why is this? On the one hand, the Exim Bank and the CDB finance themselves with bond issues bought by Chinese commercial banks, an expenditure backed by the deposits of 1.3 billion Chinese savers. As there is no welfare state, the Chinese people save over 40 per cent of their earnings, which represents the highest rate of savings in the world. On the other hand, this huge quantity of deposits is combined with what economists call 'financial repression', which under the Chinese system means that depositors are forced to lose money with their savings. This is because savers receive negative returns on their deposits, a consequence of interest rates which are often lower than the rate of inflation. Most importantly, despite the value loss of their savings, depositors are prevented from leaving the system to look for better deals elsewhere because of strict controls on capital outflow. Domestic investment options are limited and strict capital controls prevent savers from investing their money in more profitable options abroad. Therefore, the financial losses suffered by the Chinese people fit perfectly with the needs of 'China Inc.', which uses this money (on which it pays de facto zero interest) to provide state-owned companies with cheap financing to carry out their global conquest. If the restrictions were to be lifted, these savings would leave the system by being moved to other investment options abroad, thereby cutting off the flow of cheap capital. Therefore the magic wand of limitless funding is paid for at great expense by Chinese savers while, at the same time, China's commercial competitors complain that this capacity for preferential credit is unfair.

At any rate, this strategy has allowed China to launch an international offensive that is primarily aimed at the developing world. It is in these countries that China can find the raw materials required to fuel its economy, as well as untapped markets with little competition for Chinese products. China's expansion in Africa, Asia and Latin America is therefore a strategic issue that should be interpreted from the point of view of domestic policy: China needs to achieve at least 8 per cent annual growth to maintain social stability, and therefore a constant supply of raw materials is needed to keep the 'factory of the world' and China's urbanization – two of the country's driving economic forces – from stagnating. For Beijing, there is simply too much at stake to leave such matters in the hands of the market.

At a local level, China's expansion is causing dramatic transformations. The effects are arguably most visible in Africa thanks to its

chronic lack of infrastructure, despite quality concerns.[5] In this continent alone, China has contributed to the construction of
2,000 kilometres of railway tracks, 3,000 kilometres of roads, dozens
of football stadiums and 160 schools and hospitals, among other
projects. But we should not forget the 300 dams that China is building or financing across the world; the thousands of kilometres of
strategic oil and gas pipelines in places such as Sudan, Kazakhstan
and Burma; the construction of housing in war-torn countries such as
Angola; or its railway projects in Argentina and Venezuela. Furthermore, China's plans to change the world include long-term aspirations:
Beijing has proposed the construction of a 200-kilometre 'dry canal'
across Colombia as an alternative to the Panama Canal, and Chinese
companies have also shown interest in a similar infrastructure project
which will unite the Pacific and Atlantic oceans via the Amazon River.

We were able to get a sense of China's growing power on our first
journey in November 2009, when we flew out to the Egyptian seaside
resort of Sharm el-Sheikh to test the waters at the most recent – at the
time – China–Africa summit. Among the usual speeches singing the
praises of Sino-African friendship, China's Prime Minister Wen Jiabao
announced that China would be granting the continent $10 billion in
concessional loans, a figure to which China added another $20 billion
during the July 2012 China–Africa summit held in Beijing. The real
revelation in the 2009 summit, however, occurred at the end of the
press conference given by China's government number two. Wen stood
in the room packed with over fifty African and Chinese journalists
like a triumphant bullfighter, smiling to the crowd in the midst of a
standing ovation and having his photo taken with the reporters, who
were falling over themselves to shake hands with the new Messiah.
We couldn't believe what we were seeing: journalists applauding the
authorities! 'Can China really be doing so well in Africa?' we asked
ourselves. From what we had just seen, the answer seemed to be a
resounding yes.

And so we began our travels, setting out on a fabulous and dangerous adventure through over twenty-five counties to find out whether
all this applause was really justified. Our aim was to understand how
China is carrying out its current expansion and what impact this is
having at a local and regional level. From the copper mines of the

Democratic Republic of Congo to Turkmenistan's gas-rich deserts, and from the Siberian forests to Ecuador's Amazonian dams, our philosophy was always the same: to witness what was happening with our own eyes, to give a voice to the main actors in this drama, and to use our years of experience as journalists in China to help explain this new reality. The decision to fund the project ourselves was completely insane in financial terms, but worth it to maintain our journalistic independence.

We carried out extensive fieldwork to avoid falling into the trap of anecdote. We boarded eighty planes to fly across 235,000 kilometres; we crossed eleven land borders and put our lives at risk over the course of the 15,000 kilometres covered on dangerous roads and dirt tracks. One date in particular stands out from our safari through the Chinese world because it highlights some of the more demanding aspects of the journey: 22 August 2010. At six o'clock that morning we flew from Luanda to Cabinda, a small Angolan enclave on the border with the Democratic Republic of Congo; the night before we had spent several hours checking in at an airport with no computers, caught up in the drama of a general power cut. Crossing one of the most dangerous borders in Africa was particularly stressful that day because the checkpoint was closed for a public holiday and many of the soldiers guarding it were high on drink and drugs. It also didn't help that we were carrying four laptops, seven cameras and five hard disks – all of them loaded with the work of several weeks.

Once we reached Muanda, the lawless, poverty-stricken Congolese town closest to the border, we were detained for several hours before the Spanish Embassy rescued us from the grasp of the local chief of police, who was rubbing his hands with glee at the thought of getting hold of a substantial bribe. Next we travelled the 400 kilometres to Kinshasa, the Congolese capital, on a hellish journey along a narrow road full of potholes, with wrecked cars lining the ditches and lorries driving towards us at full speed with no headlights. It was gone midnight when we finally arrived at the hotel in Kinshasa, where the most eclectic bunch of people imaginable came together after dark, united by alcohol, ear-shattering music and firearms. At 100 euros per night, internet access and running water were luxuries we could only dream of. Meanwhile, sleeping was a constant battle with the mosquitoes. Day after day it went on like this, living on a knife-edge.

Some of the 500 interviews we carried out for this project also took place under difficult circumstances, particularly in countries which are less than friendly, journalistically speaking, such as Hugo Chávez's Venezuela or Iran under the ayatollahs. In military-run Burma, for instance, we failed in our first visit as a result of the constant vigilance of the authorities. What is more, our presence was beginning to put our sources at risk and so we decided to leave the country to keep them out of danger. We were investigating the trade in jade in the volatile Kachin state in the north of the country, where Chinese businessmen have teamed up with the Burmese military junta to plunder the region's natural resources, with dramatic social and environmental consequences. Under these circumstances, we couldn't just throw in the towel. We made contact with dozens of journalists, academics, activists and all kinds of experts with knowledge of Burma, both inside and outside the country. Ten months later, all our hard work began to pay off when we received a message from our contact outside the country: 'We've been in touch with our people on the inside and they're willing to help you. They'll wait for you in Myitkyina [the capital of Kachin state] during the Manao Festival, the festival of the Kachin people. Act like tourists. Stay in Hotel *** and wait until they contact you. They will come and find you.' A year after our first failed attempt, we finally reached our destination, taking a train from Mandalay to help us arrive unnoticed. Our aim was to interview the businessmen involved with jade mining, and the heroin-addicted miners and prostitutes, as well as priests, local leaders and activists. The drama being played out in that forgotten corner of the world – for which China clearly holds some responsibility – would never have been captured in this book if we had not been able to get there and see it for ourselves.

Finding a way to overcome these obstacles and keep on going was essential so that hundreds of people would let us into their lives and show us, from the point of view of their own small experiences, the subtle details of China's expansion across the planet. We met Chinese entrepreneurs who had left their country and families behind them for the chance to become millionaires, emigrants and their descendants who safeguard their Chinese DNA like a precious treasure, and workers at Chinese state-owned companies who – in exchange for massive pay rises – work day in and day out on infrastructure projects in the most inhospitable corners of the world. We also met the bosses who undertake these same projects out of loyalty to their company and to China, victims of the environmental and workplace abuse which goes hand in hand with any Chinese investment, and politicians, activists and academics who have tried to unravel the true nature of China's loans or to find evidence to support their suspicions of corruption.

Chinese people often agreed to meet us to talk about their businesses and projects or to share details of the titanic efforts they have made in impossible countries. Some were keen to show us that even the most senior local representative of a Chinese state-run company sleeps in a pokey room containing little more than a bunk covered with a mosquito net. Most of all, they welcomed us because of their impressive sense of hospitality, as in the case of Fan Hui Fang, a businessman from Shandong who produces 1,400 tons of vegetables each year on an arable farm on the outskirts of Khartoum, the capital of Sudan. These meetings almost always resulted in new revelations, phrases or details which perfectly reflect how the Chinese people see their arrival in the 'new world'. Our previous experience in China was very useful when it came to creating the atmosphere of trust needed for these confessions to come about, as on a summer's night in Khartoum in 2010.

'Courtesy of the Chinese embassy,' Fan told us, brandishing a bottle of rice wine (baijiou), a rare luxury in the Islamic country, as we sat down to the delicious meal he was hosting for us at his home. His friend Gong, a logistics manager at a Sinopec oil refinery on the outskirts of Khartoum who was joining us for the meal, looked almost ecstatic as he took his first sip. After making toast after toast, the conversation began to take a more serious turn.

'I am very proud that China is developing Sudan,' Fan told us, solemnly. 'If we weren't here, the Sudanese people would have no future.'

'When we arrived in Khartoum eight years ago, the tallest building was only three floors high,' Gong added, exhaling a long cloud of cigarette smoke.

'Yes, I've seen how the country has developed in recent years,' Fan agreed. 'They used to have nothing. No roads or cars. China has played a decisive role in that change.'

'The Sudanese wanted to develop their country and they asked the West for help, but they refused. And so we helped them. Now the West is jealous of China because they see the benefits we're getting from it,' said Gong, accusingly.

Fan instinctively followed Gong's lead. 'While the Americans come here to drop bombs,' he said, referring to the American missile attack on a Sudanese laboratory in 1998, 'we are in Sudan to build roads, buildings and hospitals. We are here to bring happiness to the Sudanese people.'

There is much truth in Fan's comments about the benefits of the Asian giant's expansion for developing countries. However, in many cases China's actions are debatable to say the least, if not openly controversial. In fact, once you go beyond Beijing's official party line, which generally trumpets its undoubtedly legitimate international interest wrapped up in 'win-win' situation rhetoric, many of China's projects in these countries lack any solid explanation. Not only is the chronic lack of transparency emanating from the very heart of China's political system a strategic error in terms of public relations, but we also encountered opaqueness at every turn whenever we tried to get to the bottom of issues such as contractual information, the impact of China's projects on the environment or the state of workplace conditions.

From the very beginning of our investigation we agreed to follow one fundamental rule: as well as listening to all the other actors, we would prioritize the voice of the various levels of the Chinese state, of the people who are pulling the strings behind China's expansion. We hoped that official China would explain the logic and motivation behind its actions. We wanted it to give us a formal answer to the questions that gave rise to this book: how does China secure its oil supply? What are the environmental consequences of its investments? Why does Beijing support dictatorships around the world? What is the country's diplomatic strategy? How is China's private sector conquering impossible markets? What is the scale of emigration from the most populated country on the planet? What is the real motivation behind the football stadiums, roads and dams that China is building all over the world? Who is really benefiting from the opportunities offered by Chinese investments? What is the global impact of the Asian giant's emergence?

Unfortunately, the complete lack of co-operation and the deeply engrained secretiveness shown by the official side of China made it difficult for us to keep our promise to give the Chinese authorities the right of reply. China's embassies rarely answered our calls, while its biggest oil companies – CNPC, Sinopec, CNOOC – refused to grant us interviews, whether in Beijing or elsewhere in the world. China's ministries either evaded our questions or declined to answer them at all. However, thanks to the perseverance and invaluable support of our Chinese assistants – experts in the art of *guanxi*, or building those personal relationships so vital to life and business in China – we were able to fill these gaps wherever possible with information gathered first-hand on the ground, as was the case, for example, in Turkmenistan and Argentina.

There were, of course, some exceptions to this official lack of transparency. One example was our meeting with Liu Guijin, a highly respected diplomat and China's special representative for African affairs. His interview showed us that even within the Chinese authorities there are frank and open people who ask themselves questions and fight to make things better. However, even when people did volunteer to tell us the Chinese version of events – whether they were diplomats, academics, in-country managers of state-owned companies or experts working closely with the authorities – we often found that they chose to stick closely to Beijing's official party line.

For example, things seemed to be looking up on 9 October 2010 when we were finally granted an interview with China Exim Bank, one of China's financial bodies that are key players in the country's international strategy. We had been preparing the ground work for a whole year, sending dozens of faxes in Mandarin and making over fifty phone calls before we finally found ourselves sitting in the Exim Bank's headquarters in Beijing's financial district. However, our initial enthusiasm didn't last long. The three executives with a technical background who met us in an imposing meeting room spent the whole hour-long interview finding ways to dodge our questions. The situation became more and more surreal, such as when the leader of the delegation leant over to whisper loudly like a school-boy in his colleague's ear, telling him not to reveal what kind of assets and natural resources China is buying in the developing world, as if it were a state secret that Beijing is buying oil and minerals. He then went on to deny the existence of any overarching statistic describing the total amount of credit that the bank is granting to other countries or their businesses.

Things really came to a head in the final round of questions, when our tense-looking interviewee began to answer all of our enquiries with nothing but a forced smile, which was fixed to his face for several minutes. Naively, we thought that he simply didn't understand our questions. Refusing to budge, he dodged his way around the conversation with a string of 'I don't know's as his only response. Astonished, we asked ourselves why he was wasting this opportunity to tell us about the bank's indisputable contributions to development in Asia, Latin America and Africa. Did the bank have something to hide? After a whole hour he had not given us a single useful piece of information, but the interview was extremely revealing in terms of the importance that Beijing gives to the transparency of its overseas projects.

Maybe our questions were somewhat difficult to answer, based as they were on our real-life experiences over the course of our travels. Or maybe our questions were simply 'not balanced', as one Western expert in China's relations with Africa unexpectedly suggested to us. While China is a constant source of heated debate, many observers of the country's international offensive tend to concentrate on its positive aspects, downplaying or even ignoring any wrongdoings, as well as the side effects of the phenomenon. Our aim, on the other hand, was to reveal every aspect of China's silent conquest of our planet, with all of its highs and lows. After all, we have never forgotten that our duty as journalists is not to put a torch under the spotlight, but instead to throw light into the darkest corners. The result is a book based not on idle rumours and theories but on real human stories and facts.

I

The *Mingongs** Take on the World

'If a Chinese man were to set out to compete in a cycling competition like the Tour de France he'd end up coming last. Do you know why? Because he'd spend the whole race looking around him at the villages and towns along the road, thinking to himself: where would be a good place to set up a business?'

Chinese businessman in San José, Costa Rica

Winding her way among the women in *niqab* and the tradesmen selling lamb and tea, Lan Xing's pale figure emerges from the crowd like a kind of apparition. Energetic and determined, she leaves a trail behind her as she drags her jerky cart along the sandy roads of the Ain Shams district in northern Cairo. It's Friday, a holy day and a day of rest. The local people have headed into the streets to smoke *shisha* outside bars and relax as they watch the world go by. Men watch football on portable televisions set up outside. Young men, soaked in sweat, brandish blowtorches as they try to fix old-fashioned cars from another era which have inevitably broken down thanks to the heat and constant traffic jams. Bakers display rows of date *brioches* and sesame bread straight from the oven, and the smell of freshly baked pastry mingles with the humidity and pollution in the air.

Lan was brought here in a black taxi which has seen better days and which will come back in the small hours of the night to take her home to the flat she shares with four compatriots. If something goes wrong, she'll turn to the scrap of paper with her address written on it

* Migrant workers (literally, 'worker from the countryside').

15

in Arabic which she keeps hidden in her pocket like a precious treasure. That scrap of paper represents her only lifeline between the hubbub of Arabic around her and the world she understands, between the reality all about her and her own reality. With her long hair uncovered and her almond-shaped eyes, Lan is clearly a foreigner in this busy, traditional corner of old Cairo. Her arrival in this country was an 8,000-kilometre leap into the unknown, an attempt to start life anew after her fortieth birthday. With her relentless drive to succeed, this was nothing that Lan couldn't handle.

Lan and her husband both come from Liaoning, a province bordering North Korea in north-east China. They arrived in Egypt seventeen months ago, hoping to make their fortune overseas. They left behind them a fourteen-year-old son who now lives with his grandparents, although Lan herself describes him as 'a difficult teenager'. Ever since arriving in Egypt, Lan has been taking her cart loaded with 25 kilos' worth of all types of clothing, from pyjamas to *hijabs*, and wandering through the streets of Cairo in search of customers; this has become her obsession. She dedicates around ten hours each day to her task, dragging her cart up and down staircases in old, dark buildings, knocking on doors in the hope of walking away with a handful of Egyptian pounds in exchange for a cotton dressing gown or some sheets made of fake silk.

Lan is one of the many thousands of Chinese men and women who make up the group known as the *shanta sini*, or 'Chinese bag-people' in Egyptian Arabic. This army of migrants from the poorest areas of China, many living in the country illegally on expired visas, has managed to conquer Egypt's retail textile market with nothing but their go-getting attitude and determination to escape from poverty.[1] Together they personify the virtues that have made Chinese migrants the most enterprising on the planet for at least the last three centuries: a capacity for self-sacrifice, a good nose for business, the ability to adapt to their surroundings and a talent for cutting costs. A tendency to save money, a discreet nature and an exclusive web of intra-Chinese contacts also provide invaluable help. Today the army of the *shanti sini* can be seen everywhere where they arrive with just a bundle of belongings on their backs in search of potential consumers.

Yu, a young woman aged around twenty, is playing with her hair in a fashionable café opposite the American University in Cairo. Looking at this sharp, beautiful woman, anyone would expect her to be completely oblivious to the sufferings of the *shanti sini*. In fact, she's an expert. 'They get off the plane today and tomorrow they're out on the streets of Cairo selling goods from door to door. They don't speak a word of Arabic,' says the niece of one of the Chinese pioneers who identified a gap in the market over a decade ago and who has since gone on to make a fortune worth over 4 million euros. That uneducated emigrant who fled poverty in China is now a successful businessman with eight factories and sixty warehouses across the country. Yu says that, in order to understand how the Chinese have managed to carve out a niche for themselves in a country which has a long textile tradition and exports cotton to the whole of Europe, we must embark on a journey across the thousands of kilometres back to Canton, at the industrial heart of China.

It is there, right at the mouth of the Pearl River, where Chinese entrepreneurs buy the fabric and begin a cycle of business that they end up controlling from the top down. Silk, polyester and wool are shipped in containers to Libya, a country that shares a border and a customs agreement with Egypt. Chinese entrepreneurs understand that to start an empire in a globalized world, it's important to be able to squeeze the margins. Not only is this something they have been doing for centuries, but the ability seems to be engraved into the genetic code of the Chinese people. As Yu explains, this is why they export the fabric to Libya rather than to Egypt, as the country puts comparatively less tax on Chinese textiles. Once on African soil, the fabric is exported again to Egypt with the help of an Egyptian middleman, before going on to fuel the underground workshops that have been set up in apartments on the outskirts of Cairo.

It is not easy to get access to one of these small, secret factories. We failed completely on our first trip to the Egyptian capital, when one businessman agreed to a date and then refused to let us in, while a second only let us get as far as the front door. It was just as difficult on our second visit to Cairo, despite being accompanied by several Chinese workers from the sector. We failed because of the distrust that is caused by the sight of a foreigner poking his nose into their business practices, especially when these are propped up by various illegalities that help them to topple the local competition. In fact, lack of transparency was one of the elements we encountered most regularly throughout our journey through the Chinese universe.

However, the presence of a Chinese friend finally paid off when Ding Tao, a modest businessman with ten years' experience in the country, welcomed us right into his centre of operations: a makeshift workshop in a four-room apartment in a suburb full of rundown buildings and vandalized cars left on street corners. Inside the apartment, different tasks were organized by room: in one room, a young man and two women, both dressed in *hijabs*, cut out material and use six sewing machines to make the clothing; in another room, the clothes are ironed and packed into boxes; meanwhile, a fifth employee works on number crunching in the office.

Despite the Chinese entrepreneurs' preference for employing their fellow countrymen, who they consider to be more disciplined workers, the owners of the workshop use Egyptian tailors because they are cheaper. 'If they were Chinese we would have to pay them twice as much, as they would be much more productive. That's the price of the market,' explains Ding Tao's wife, who can speak basic Arabic. Each month they pay their employees between 250 and 300 euros to work for ten hours a day, six days a week. Minimal salaries and an extremely low production quality guarantee a product that can be sold at an unbeatable price. As well as the miserable salary, the workers suffer from severe job insecurity, as there are no contracts or medical insurance, leading to a constant turnover of staff. This is a similar situation to the one seen in China's manufacturing hubs, such as Wenzhou or Shenzhen, where a factory can easily renew its entire workforce in just two years. The Egyptian workers reject the possibility of demanding better working conditions, since they are sure that the police know about the underground workshops but tolerate them in exchange for bribes. In an economically stagnated country where 16.7 per cent of the population lives below the poverty line,[2] and which is suffering from the aftermath of a revolution that overthrew the tyranny that had been clinging on to power for the last three decades, their choice is simple: it's either this or nothing.

But why would the Egyptian people want to buy clothes at home when they can easily go out and buy them in traditional shops? Yu, who talks as if she's telling us a story, soon clears up this mystery. 'In Egypt, women eat lots of sweets and many of them are very fat, and so they prefer to buy clothes at home. That way, they avoid the shame of having to display their bodies outside their own houses.' In other words, in order to spare their customers a hard time at the shops, emigrants such as Lan set out through the Egyptian twilight after evening prayers to tackle their customers in the doorways of their own homes. '*Aiz haga?*' ('Do you want anything?'), they blurt out from the landing. Sometimes the only answer is a door slammed in their faces. On other occasions they get lucky and sell a piece of clothing, or the lady of the house asks them to take her measurements for a dressing gown which the *shanta sini* will bring back to her home a few days later.

One day, this miserable, frugal life of braving the heat and loneliness to roam the streets of Cairo will finally come to an end. The Chinese emigrant, who is typically uneducated and exploited by his employer but shrewd and good at saving, will one day decide to take a step up in the production chain. He will stop distributing goods and, after investing months' or years' worth of savings, will instead become a producer and businessman in his own right. Starting off with a workshop and just one area of distribution, he will go on to expand his network, often while also embarking on other business opportunities. With business practices bordering on the illegal – or even crossing the line completely in terms of silencing the Egyptian authorities – it is possible to expand very quickly. They are helped on their way by an extensive web of Chinese contacts, who serve both to point them towards new opportunities and to act as an invaluable safety net. In fact, time and time again agreements between the importer and the textile factory, or between the workshop and the distributor, are made between Chinese nationals. The Chinese people's tendency to stick together goes beyond a national level. In fact, transactions between Chinese emigrants in all the countries we visited – not just Egypt – were often restricted to people from one particular village or region. This is partly because of the great variety of different ethnic groups and languages spoken in China and partly due to the importance of family ties. Sharing a language and a birthplace creates a strong sense of trust and guarantees loyalty to the company. As a result, Chinese businesses ranging from private enterprises to state-run companies operating overseas regularly import their entire Chinese workforce from just one area.

'If all the workers on a construction site come from the same town or village, they are much more easily controlled and they don't go against the law or their bosses. Their colleagues and friends, sometimes with family ties, are also watching. And no Chinese person wants his family to lose face at home, or to be accused of being lazy or a thief.' The words of a young Chinese worker who has spent several years living in Africa sound like an echo of the Maoist era, when tens of millions of Chinese people were sent to labour camps where they lived in a constant state of paranoia. Workers were obliged to carry out the duties of a 'good comrade', both guarding their co-workers and being guarded, informing on them and being informed on, whether in the factory or in the camp, at school or in the apparent privacy of their own homes. Nobody could escape the all-seeing eye of the authorities.

A SHADY BUSINESS

Under these circumstances, some entrepreneurs have been quick to launch new business ventures offering all kinds of highly profitable and ethically unsound services to this growing influx of emigrants. After expanding their textile network across Egypt, Yu's family has embarked on a new enterprise – bringing Chinese emigrants to Egypt. The family takes advantage of the lack of controls on immigration and the siren call of a better life, a message that strikes a deep chord in the areas of China which have not yet jumped on the train of progress and where opportunities are few and far between. Yu tells us that her family uses the company's licence, which can easily be obtained by the use of bribes, to apply for visas which they sell for around 5,000 yuan (520 euros), although this price varies depending on whether the applicant is a friend or relative. Family members and friends spread the word in their home towns and villages, especially in China's north-east provinces, where the privatization of heavy industries inherited from the Maoist era has caused unemployment to rise to between 30 and 40 million people in little over a decade.[3] This 'pull effect' spreads like wildfire in the areas where the opening up of China's economy resulted in the dismantling of the unproductive Maoist factories at the end of the last century, taking away the livelihood of millions of families and causing serious damage, the effects of which can still be seen today. 'People aren't dying of hunger, but there are hardly any opportunities to get ahead,' Yu tells us in justification.

This situation has forced China to break with its centuries-old tradition of reluctance to allow its nationals to leave the country. In fact, the state is now facilitating emigration – and even actively encouraging it[4] – as an escape route for its unemployed workers. 'China has distanced itself from the task of controlling the migration of its nationals and has transferred responsibility for this on to the receiving countries. Some of these are weaker states, such as some African countries where corruption and a lack of administration make it relatively easy for Chinese people to enter the country,' explains Antoine Kernan, an expert in Chinese migration at the University of Lausanne in Switzerland.[5] 'It is much easier for Chinese migration to happen today than it was in the past,' adds Kernan, who has followed this phenomenon both in China and in Francophone countries in Africa.

This is a winning strategy for Beijing and China's local governments: emigration helps to combat unemployment, alleviating the social tensions thriving in the areas that have been struck the hardest by lay-offs. What is more, the problem tends not to reappear once the emigrant finishes his or her time abroad. Workers usually come home with a significant amount of capital to invest in the education of their children or in business opportunities which offer a greater level of financial security than they ever could have enjoyed before leaving China.[6] In a way, it could be said that China is exporting labour in return for capital to be reinvested in the country, generating economic growth (and jobs) within China itself.

Seen from this perspective, the door-to-door textile business carried out by the *shanti sini* is little more than the repetition in Egypt of what has been happening continuously over the last three decades of China's miraculous expansion: the success of some rests on the shoulders of others. Over those three decades, the 'factory of the world' has always been fuelled by an enormous contingent of emigrants who work for up to fourteen hours each day for a miserable salary, and the Egyptian textile business is fed by the sacrifices of those same poor emigrants. At the end of the day, the efforts of these individuals contribute to the collective success of the Chinese people. The reason why Chinese emigrants nowadays choose to settle in the Democratic Republic of Congo or Venezuela instead of Spain or Canada is essentially because the developing world is still comparatively unexplored and therefore offers many more opportunities to emigrants than the West, with its strict regulations and more competitive markets. Yu estimates that there are 15,000 Chinese people making a living by selling door-to-door in Egypt, far more than the 5,000 suggested by the Chinese embassy in Cairo. 'There's not a corner of Egypt which the *shanti sini* hasn't yet reached,' Yu assures us. The Egyptian press has gone even further, estimating that the army of 'Chinese bag-people' is made up of between 60,000 and 100,000 emigrants,[7] while the Chinese media has placed this figure at somewhere between 20,000 and 30,000.[8]

The business opportunities on offer go beyond bringing Chinese emigrants into Egypt; in fact, many of them actually arrive from Thailand on a tourist visa and end up staying in the country for several months. Some opportunists have also profited from the everyday needs of the new arrivals. When the emigrants arrive in Cairo, these businesses hire an apartment for them, show them how the industry works, advise them on which areas of the city to cover and explain the inner workings of the Egyptian pound. They also take them to the warehouses to buy merchandise, for which the intermediaries receive a small commission. This 'gold fever' leads some people, such as Mrs Lan Jie, to try their hand at even shadier activities, such as procuring prostitutes. This is another very profitable business, although it is not without its risks. Apparently oblivious to any offence this might cause in a highly traditional country where 90 per cent of the 80 million inhabitants are faithful to Sunni Islam, Mrs Lan is looking into opening a brothel in the Egyptian capital. She wants to diversify her business dealings, which are slowing down in the textile industry and her underground dealings with emigrants. 'There's too much competition now. There are lots of *shanti sini* and they don't earn as much as they did before,' she tells us in a Chinese restaurant in Cairo. And so she has decided to start importing beautiful Chinese prostitutes.

In fact, she has already started trialling the project: over the course of our dinner she receives a call from a client, which she answers with 'the girl is not at home today'. Completely unashamed and without any scruples, Mrs Lan is perfectly happy sharing details of her business with us. 'Each time a client goes with a girl, he pays 600 Egyptian pounds [around 75 euros]. My commission is 200 Egyptian pounds,' she explains. With guaranteed supply and demand, her only concern is that the police are still not on her payroll, a key factor in a business of this kind. 'Do you know how to bribe the police?' she asks our Chinese friend, who confesses that he knows nothing about the subject. She doesn't give up that easily. 'If you come over to our house you might change your mind,' she insists, giggling mischievously.

Lan Jie is not the only Chinese expat to set out to run a prostitution business outside China, a country bursting with all kinds of brothels, from luxury karaoke bars where prostitutes sing in the nude to dingy massage parlours with pink neon lights where massages always finish with a 'happy ending'. Sometimes the same pattern is re-created abroad. The spread of Chinese businesses and expats across the world has stimulated demand for a variety of services, from Chinese restaurants and clinics specializing in traditional Chinese medicine to acupuncture and massage parlours. Although it cannot be attributed to the Chinese alone, prostitution is always one of the star businesses.

Hidden behind karaoke bars, massage parlours and hairdressers' shops, prostitution in Africa led to the first act of international intervention by China's special police unit, which was set up by the Ministry of Public Security in 2007 to combat the trafficking of women. In November 2010, ten Chinese police officers landed in Kinshasa in the Democratic Republic of Congo with orders to dismantle a prostitution network trafficking women from the poverty-stricken region of Sichuan in western China, who were supposedly being forced to work as prostitutes in the Congolese capital. According to the Chinese press, the drama came to an end when the women surprised the police officers by refusing to leave the country. After all, in Kinshasa they could earn US$50 a time, a small fortune compared to a monthly salary equivalent to just $300 back in Sichuan.[9]

FEAR AND DEPENDENCY IN NEIGHBOURING RUSSIA

The night train pulls out of Beijing and within a few hours is making its way through the heart of a far less charming side of China. Despite the geographical proximity of the Russian Far East, getting to Vladivostok by land is no laughing matter. Manchuria, a region that has suffered all kinds of cruelty and hardship (whether at the hands of the Japanese, Russians or Chinese), opens up ahead of us with its blunt manners and barren landscapes. In the morning we arrive in Suifenhe, a city of 100,000 inhabitants close to the Russian border. It is the first stop in our journey of discovery on the trail of the Chinese emigrant through a region that has been frequented by Asian merchants since the fifteenth century, when they used to exchange surplus tea and soya for fresh supplies of fish and ginseng. To our surprise, Jiou Peng is waiting for us at the station in a Porsche Cayenne. Good natured and slightly built, Jiou came to meet us on the orders of his boss, Liu Desheng, who we first met in Beijing and would soon see again in Russia. Following Liu's instructions, Jiou is going to help us with the logistics of getting to Vladivostok. He invites us to have breakfast with him in the city's flagship hotel, after first taking us for a drive around this fast-growing metropolis which has made its fortune from a logging industry fed by the vast Siberian forests.

The city has the same manic pace of life and typical aesthetics of any fast-growing Chinese metropolis. The shopping malls, where Chinese turbo-pop blurts out of loudspeakers, are packed from morning to night. Russian tourists pile into the shops and supermarkets to buy everything that they can't get on the other side of the border, or to buy items they can get at home but at a fraction of the price. In the Holiday Inn, Russian couples tuck into generous breakfasts after a busy weekend of shopping and relaxation. 'I have a VIP card. There's no need to pay,' Jiou Peng insists when we attempt to foot the bill. As well as his Porsche Cayenne, Jiou's Birkenstock trainers, Jeep polo shirt, Cartier watch and white gold Bulgari ring all announce that life is good. He is the perfect example of Chinese new money: self-made millionaires who have made their fortune in less than a decade and who live in new-built towns with no sense of glamour or luxury and throw their money away on the last word in Western fashion. These are all status symbols in a hierarchical society where it pays to mark the difference between yourself and the lower classes.

Once we have a Russian stamp on our passports, we set off on our journey to Vladivostok along roads which take us back to another era and another world. We are struck by the almost clinical division at the border in terms of race, as if sliced down the middle with a scalpel: the coarse facial features of northern China give way suddenly to the slender figures, pale skin and blond hair of the Caucasian race. Crossing from one country to another is also a leap back into the past: the dual carriageways, bridges and skyscrapers of the Chinese side give way to a poor, rural and ancient landscape. Time has frozen here in the shadows of the Soviet era.

Liu Desheng is waiting for us in a café in central Vladivostok. We first met him at a lunch in Beijing which he attended as a representative of Chinese businessmen working in Russia's most important Pacific port. He told us about the difficulties faced by investors in a region wracked by endemic corruption. 'For the first few years, a Chinese man doing business with a Russian has to hand over almost all of his takings to the Russian. That's what we mean when we talk about the mafia. The mafia isn't some separate, autonomous entity. It's everywhere. But once you've established a relationship of trust, everything gets better.' Born in 1973, Liu personifies the Chinese version of the American dream. In 1995 he decided to give up his job as a cook and to go into business with his two brothers selling Chinese products in the retail market in Vladivostok.

His two older brothers were the pioneers. They first travelled to the Russian city in 1992 to work in the construction industry for a monthly wage equivalent to 120 euros. After six months, they returned to their village to convince their family to start trading in Chinese products after identifying a powerful business opportunity. Brought up in a poor rural family, Liu's only education came from primary school and a cookery course. He earned his living first in a restaurant and then in a brewery, and he didn't hesitate for a moment in leaving it all behind to join his brothers in their new business venture.

'I first crossed the border with Russia on 28 October 1995,' he tells us, sitting between his assistant and his chauffeur at a café in a five-star hotel. Earlier that day his chauffeur had picked us up in one of the few modern Mercedes to be seen in Vladivostok. 'I began by selling boots made in Heilongjiang. Fifty-eight days later I'd made my first fortune: 24,000 roubles, or about 500 euros,' he recalls, smiling. 'Back then I slept in the same place where I kept my merchandise to save money, while my brother was in charge of supplying the business with new stock. We started to grow and we set up our first shop. Then we acquired the place next door, and we knocked down a wall to widen the business,' continues Liu, a father of three children aged eleven, six and three. Family and friends played an important role, he assures us. Today over 120 people from his circle of acquaintances are involved in a business which extends across the whole of Russia and employs thousands of people. The company now owns four shopping centres in Vladivostok, two in Khabarovsk and several shops in Moscow.

With his piercing gaze and muscular build, Liu confidently plays the traditional Chinese role of head of the clan or, in his case, leader of his enterprising compatriots. 'My family is one of the most influential in Vladivostok,' he tells us. 'If you have any kind of problem here, just show my card to a Chinese person in any bus or in the street and they will help you. They know who I am.' To gain his trust, we met him several times in Chinese restaurants where the staff hurried to give us their best private rooms. We toasted Sino-Spanish friendship, showed off our chopstick skills, and recommended some favourite dishes from northern China by memory in Mandarin. Not for the first time, we found that the dinner table is the best possible place when it comes to breaking down Chinese reserve.

'Russia puts a 50 per cent tax on products imported from China,' he tells us, 'so some people decide to bring them in illegally. They drive a truck to the border and bribe the Russian customs officers. Once the truck is over the border, they need to avoid taking main roads or making any suspicious movements, because if they get stopped at another checkpoint the price of the merchandise goes up, since they will have to pay another bribe.' In between toasts with rice wine and mouthfuls of sweet and sour pork, Liu offers us his observations on the secrets of success for Chinese businesses in Russia. Little by little, we are drawn into the heart of the phenomenon of Chinese migration in the country and we begin to understand the fear that this inspires in the local people. 'If the Russians don't want us to bring illegal merchandise into the country, they should lower their customs duties on our products,' he tells us.[10]

Russian officials later tell us that these taxes are applied to protect the failing local industry, but this sounds outrageous to Liu: 'The Russians can't live without Chinese products. When the police make trouble for Chinese businessmen, declaring their businesses illegal and trying to shut them down, the businessmen come to me and say we should leave and stop selling things to them. Let's see how they would manage then!' Liu concludes, referring to eastern Russia's dependency on China for agricultural supplies and consumer goods.[11]

The extent of this dependency becomes strikingly clear when we visit the biggest market in Vladivostok, which belongs to Liu. At 4,000 square metres, the market is an impressive visual spectacle which houses a thousand shops with 2,000 employees. In the covered area of the market, businesses are arranged according to the birthplace of the Chinese shopkeepers, who run almost all of the businesses in the market. The aisle for 'shoemakers from Yunnan' is next to the one for 'tailors from Jilin', while tradesmen from Hebei sell knick-knacks, toys and cheap jewellery. In the open-air area we find an enormous street market where shipping containers have been converted into market stalls. Russian, Vietnamese, Central Asian and, most of all, Chinese traders fall over each other to sell spices, torches, T-shirts, bread, sweets, tinned food and anything else you can imagine. Over 80 per cent of the products on sale come from China and – to the anger of the local people – there has been very little impact on local job creation as two out of every three salespeople are Chinese. The same trend can be seen throughout Russia: 83 per cent of foreign workers in Siberian markets are Chinese, and when we consider the situation in the whole of the country the figure is 61 per cent.[12]

The success of the thousands of Chinese traders working in Siberia contrasts sharply with the decline of the former Soviet State, which is now on its guard against its neighbour's miraculous expansion. While Chinese border towns such as Suifenhe are developing at full speed without ever looking back, the atmosphere when we got off the

Trans-Siberian Railway in Khabarovsk was one of gentle decline and nostalgia for another age. During our stay in this city, where most people still drive old Lada cars which refuse to give up the ghost, the townspeople held a lively party to celebrate Khabarovsk's 152nd anniversary. Whole families had piled out into the streets, from grandparents and grandchildren dressed in their Sunday best to sailors holding hands with retro-looking girls in high heels. They all crammed onto the path alongside the river, welcoming the first rays of spring sunlight after a long, hard winter and enjoying themselves at a funfair that looked like something out of a Cold War spy film. The comparison is inevitable. On this side of the Amur River people sing, dance, drink and celebrate, apparently oblivious to how their neighbours on the opposite bank are developing at a breakneck speed.

China and Russia are old acquaintances who have spent centuries waging war on one another, each taking chunks out of territory that boasts an enormous store of natural resources, from gold and oil to fresh water and rare wood. Chinese migration has become a very sensitive issue in Russia, a country which now lives in fear of a silent Chinese invasion.[13] As we confirmed over the course of our travels, China is also expanding into neighbouring Central Asia, a region which once formed part of the Soviet Union and which, despite its current state of decline, remains to a great extent under Moscow's control.[14] Russia has not forgotten that, back before the Revolution, Chinese merchants made up 13 per cent of the local population in their eastern territories, a strategic region for Moscow.[15] Experts and politicians view the situation with some concern, particularly because of its future implications: the four provinces in northern China which share a border with Russia (Inner Mongolia, Heilongjiang, Jilin and Liaoning) boast a population of 132 million people[16] as well as increasingly rare natural resources such as water, wood, oil and fertile land. On the other side of the Amur River, a vast territory stretching from Irkutsk to Vladivostok is home to just 6 million people and contains the natural resources and raw materials that China needs. There is also the psychological impact of the fact that China – a symbol of poverty just three decades ago in the midst of the ending of Maoism – is now a rich country. As a proud nation used to holding a position of power and looking down its nose at its poor neighbour, it is not easy for Russia to come to terms with the idea that times have changed. Whether the Russians like it or not, China's moment has finally arrived.

Despite the anxiety that the thought of a silent invasion causes in Siberia, many people see Beijing as the only alternative in a developing region which has been neglected by Moscow and has been hit by a steady population decline. 'We don't have a choice here. The population in the Russian Far East will decrease from 6 million to 4 million by 2050. We already don't have an adequate workforce and we will have less in the future. We will then be dependent on Chinese trade, investments and workers,' argues Vladimir Kucheryavenko, a researcher at the Russian Academy of Sciences at Khabarovsk's Institute of Economic Research.

Other experts, such as Mikhail Tersky, director of the Pacific Centre of Strategic Development at the University of Vladivostok, have thrown in the towel altogether, insisting that Russia's destiny lies in collaboration with China. 'We have no future unless it is with China. It would be crazy to stand in the way of a hurricane. If China considers us its enemy it will be much worse for Russia, so it would be better for us to work together. Now it is just a question of finding ways of minimizing our losses.'

HISTORY REPEATS ITSELF

By exploring the business practices of the *shanti sini* and wandering through Liu's Russian markets we can gain some insight into the strategy of Chinese emigrants, their need to abandon their country for economic reasons and, most importantly, the significant regional impact of their expansion across the planet. This impact is first felt by local businesses, which can only stand by and watch as they lose territory to competition which is both better organized and able to sell goods at unbeatable prices.[17] We will later see how this emigration also transports Chinese environmental and labour standards across the world. However, it is impossible to understand the Chinese diaspora across the planet without taking into account the migratory flow that has been taking place for decades within China itself. Since the beginning of the opening of China's economy, at least 200 million people have abandoned rural areas in search of new opportunities in the towns and cities. Experts predict that another 300 million people will undertake the same journey over the course of the next few years. While population mobility is increasing within China itself, spurred on by economic growth, a great flow of emigrants is also setting off in search of new opportunities outside China, conquering international markets everywhere, from Nigeria to Argentina and from Papua New Guinea to Canada. Here we see the acceleration of a trend that began centuries ago but which is now greater, faster, broader and more decisive than ever before.

The Chinese people have been emigrating for hundreds of years, fleeing from hunger, war, repression (even before the Communists came to power) and social conflict. All of these factors have contributed to China having one of the largest emigrant populations in history, with around 35 million citizens of Chinese ethnicity – mostly from the Han[18] ethnic group – scattered across the planet.[19] In some Asian regions, Chinese migration dates back to the twelfth century, when the Chinese empire was just beginning to transform itself into the naval powerhouse which it became in the fifteenth century at the hands of Admiral Zheng He, who is known by some as the Chinese Christopher Columbus. Zheng captained several expeditions on the orders of the Yongle Emperor of the Ming dynasty and took China as far as the Gulf of Aden on the coast of present-day Somalia. The seven naval missions that he led between 1405 and his death in 1433 were all aimed at extending the tax and tribute system of a nation which at that time had no equal in terms of modern technology and control of the seas.

With vessels four times larger than the *Santa Maria* which Columbus sailed to the West Indies, the voyages of Zheng He – a eunuch of Muslim origin who won the respect of the Ming emperors through his courage in battle – managed to transport up to 27,000 men on several different ships.[20] His voyages marked the beginning of the golden age of trade in South-East Asia, promoting trade in spices and handicrafts and giving ports such as Malacca the importance they still enjoy today on modern shipping routes.[21] Driven by improvements in navigation, trade became the real springboard for the gradual migration of millions of Chinese people throughout Asia. Their descendants today make up the greater part of the population of various countries in the region: the Chinese Academy of Social Sciences estimates that there are 28 million people of Chinese ethnicity scattered throughout Asia, constituting a significant part of the population in countries such as Singapore, Malaysia, Thailand and Indonesia.[22]

Human trafficking also played a part in the arrival of small numbers of Chinese slaves in Western colonies in America and Africa. However, it was not until the abolition of the trade over the course of the nineteenth century that Chinese emigration really began to go global. At this point Chinese emigrants started to appear in the farms of Peru, the mines of South Africa, and even on First World War battlefields, where Great Britain, France and Russia employed up to 150,000 Chinese workers for tasks such as digging trenches and burying the war dead in exchange for pitiful wages.[23] During these decades, China was effectively falling apart. Political unrest, economic hardship and generalized chaos culminated in bloody civil war and Japanese invasion, creating the conditions which laid the groundwork for the process of modern migration before the foundation of the People's Republic in 1949. Waves of Chinese emigrants from provinces such as Fujian and Canton did not hesitate for a moment in piling themselves with debt in order to get hold of the boat ticket that would take them far away from hardship and foreign invasion and carry them to a new land of opportunities.

What happened to them? Did they achieve their goals? To do so, they had to face extreme hardship, even worse than that experienced by the modern-day *shanta sini*. However, for many of them the rewards for their efforts are still clearly visible today, as is the case for some of the people we met on our travels. They left China in order to succeed in life and they made their fortunes and never went back. Today, their children, grandchildren and great-grandchildren are no longer emigrants. Instead they make up the new generations of Chinese overseas.

For Fung Xi Mao, for example, leaving his native Canton in 1947 meant he would never see his father again. He was barely eighteen years old when he set off on the journey that would take him to the promised land – Venezuela – where he finally arrived after a week spent crossing the Pacific, from Hong Kong to Manila and Honolulu and then on to San Francisco, Managua and Caracas. To see him sitting in his office in Maracay, 110 kilometres west of the Venezuelan capital, nobody would ever guess that for the first few years after his arrival in the country he had to sleep in the coffee bar where he worked twelve-hour days in return for just 100 bolivars per month, the equivalent of around 15 euros. The walls of the company's headquarters from which he and his sons manage his small empire are covered in prizes given in recognition of his business achievements. There are also rows of photos showing him shaking hands with old friends, such as the ex-presidents of Venezuela, Carlos Andrés Pérez and Rafael Caldera, among others. However, he tells us, back at the beginning of his difficult journey he never would have believed that he would one day be rubbing shoulders with the great and the good of Venezuela.

'I settled in Maracay in 1957. Back then there were only 3.5 million people living in Venezuela. It was a land of opportunities,' he recalls.[24] He speaks slowly, in a South American Spanish under which can still be heard some of the phonetic traces which betray his true origin. Like Liu, the entrepreneur who runs the markets in Russian Siberia, Fung Xi Mao got ahead in business on the strength of his ambitious personality, his capacity to make sacrifices and his audacity in the face of risks. He was also helped by the financial support of his fellow countrymen, all of whom also came from his hometown, Enping. 'A friend lent me 12,000 bolivars [nearly 2,000 euros by the current rate of exchange]. I used that money to set up an ironmonger's and then later a wholesaler for Chinese merchandise. There was no competition. I imported a hundred containers each year from Hong Kong and my margin was 30 per cent.' His earnings skyrocketed. He used them first to open a toy factory and then a chain of supermarkets. He was the director of a bank for ten years. He founded a television channel and a newspaper, and invested in the lucrative construction industry. In other words, the once poor immigrant is now a millionaire.

Many of his compatriots followed in his footsteps. The proof can be seen in the network of bustling streets in central Maracay which today has been literally taken over by Chinese businesses. There is no shop selling household products, hardware, electronic devices or any type of ironmongery that is not under the control of emigrants from Enping, as is shown by the name 'Fung' – typical of that region – which hangs over the entrance of most of these businesses. Fung Xi Mao, the respected head of the clan, has played a decisive role in this expansion. Ever since he made his fortune, he has worked tirelessly to help his fellow countrymen to succeed in business. 'Over the years many Chinese people have asked me to lend them money to help them start up their own businesses. They always return it – not a single one has let me down. They only have to give me their word. In China, giving your word is as good as signing a document,' he tells us.

It is estimated that between 3 and 7 million Chinese people like Fung Xi Mao left their country from the seventeenth century onwards, in search of new opportunities abroad.[25] Others left to escape from repression or were caught up in the ideological struggles of the Cold War.[26] This silent, gradual diaspora across the world has left a permanent mark on many countries, mainly in South-East Asia but also in Africa.[27] In fact, people of Chinese ethnicity make up the biggest ethnic group in countries such as Singapore (76.8 per cent), and form a significant part of the social composition of Malaysia (25.6 per cent), Thailand (11 per cent) and Brunei (29.3 per cent).[28] The factor that makes these communities so important in their receiving societies is, without a doubt, their economic power. This is clear from the extent of the participation of these communities in the domestic economies, which ranges from 4.5 per cent of the GDP in Vietnam to 80 per cent in Singapore. Even in countries such as Indonesia, where people of Chinese descent make up just 3 per cent of the total population, the group plays a significant role in the domestic economy. Some estimates even try to put a highly speculative figure on the fortune amassed by Chinese people living overseas across the centuries: an incredible $1.5 trillion.[29]

As we saw earlier, this immense wealth is largely down to the idiosyncratic personality of the Chinese people. Their capacity for hard work and saving money, as well as their sharp business sense, are passed down from generation to generation, as if embedded in their genes. However, this is not the only factor at work. The success of Chinese emigrants can also be explained by the network of connections created by the 'great Chinese lodge':[30] wherever there is a Chinese person keen to set up a business, there will always be a compatriot ready to lend him or her money or provide help with getting a visa or a permit, whether out of family or racial ties. 'This characteristic is particular to Chinese emigrants. While some other countries with a culture of Confucianism also demonstrate similar behaviour, the sense of solidarity is much stronger in Chinese overseas communities,' explains the migration expert Zhuang Guotu. Zhuang emphasizes that as well as resulting from the 'group feeling' typical of Eastern cultures (in comparison with 'Western individualism'), this behaviour is largely influenced by the fact that for centuries a large proportion of Chinese emigrants have come from the same coastal areas of China (e.g. Fujian and Canton). 'The power of family cohesion and regionalism is very important to Chinese people living overseas.'

As such, intra-Chinese ties are reinforced among emigrants after leaving their country of origin: in Great China[31] people keep it in the family. This strong attachment to Chinese customs, language and culture no doubt explains the initial lack of interest shown by these groups in integrating or even adapting to their receiving societies. Chinese emigrants tend to keep a low social profile and have very little contact with local people, other than business transactions.[32] While this sense of belonging to a peer group is often diluted to some extent in the children and grandchildren of emigrants, the consciousness of carrying a legacy and certain values which must be passed down to future generations stays very much alive. Language and marriage within the community guarantee the survival of a cultural heritage which keeps these future generations anchored to their Chinese roots.

'During the time of my grandfather, things were very rigid in the sense that you had to marry people from your own village, not just your own race. Things aren't as rigid now as they were in my grandfather's time, but there's still the feeling among the younger generation that they should marry their own kind,' explains Bonnie Pon, the grandson of a Cantonese emigrant who arrived in South Africa at the end of the nineteenth century. Bonnie's family still runs the business set up by his grandfather over a hundred years ago in the heart of Johannesburg's so-called 'First Chinatown'. He now forms part of a family tree which currently has fifty-six members spread throughout

South Africa, and which has also branched out as far as Canada, Australia, New Zealand and Singapore. 'All except two of those fifty-six married people of Chinese descent,' he tells us. As well as the traditional mentality stemming from the 'old Chinese society', which caused Bonnie's grandfather to reject mixed marriages, this trend was also affected by racial segregation in South Africa, where Chinese people were considered 'not white', and therefore effectively 'black'. 'Living in South Africa, we were constantly reminded of race. It was natural for us to marry our own kind.'

Long after the ending of apartheid, Bonnie's son Erwin is continuing the family tradition. he is married to a Taiwanese woman who has recently given birth to a daughter who, Bonnie assures us, will learn the official languages at school – English and Afrikaans – and Cantonese and Mandarin at home. 'We were fortunate that our parents insisted that we retained our mother tongue,' he adds. Bonnie, who was born in South Africa and recognizes that he is 'Westernized in many ways', gives great importance to his Chinese roots and heritage; at the same time he distances himself from the values emerging from modern-day China. 'When I look in the mirror I see a Chinese face. However, we were born in South Africa and we have been here all our lives. I go to China once a year to buy goods, but I'm not used to the way of life in China. It's not home to me, in the sense that I'm not comfortable with the way they do things. Our family is more traditional in some ways than the modern Communist youngsters,' he concludes. In a family that has lived for five generations in South Africa, the country with the most people of Chinese origin in Africa,[33] Bonnie and his clan guard their Chinese DNA like a small treasure. For them, it is the code that tells them who they are and where they come from.

DESCENDANTS OF SUN YAT-SEN IN ECUADOR

With his slim figure, lightly almond-shaped eyes and fine moustache skimming his upper lip, it isn't hard to see the Chinese ancestry in Harry Sun Soria. However, the tale of this former mayor of Guayaquil, the economic capital of Ecuador, differs from those of other Peruvians, Brazilians and Ecuadorians whose grandparents or great-grandparents arrived in South America to help build railways or to work on nineteenth-century sugar plantations. Harry Sun is a member of the family of Sun Yat-Sen, the first president of China who founded the Republic of China in 1911. The blood running through his veins comes from the same stock that helped put an end to millennia of Imperial rule in China.

Harry Sun speaks in the measured, almost hypnotic tones typical of educated people blessed with the gift of talking to the masses. As well as his role as mayor, this ability helped him to become a national member of parliament in 2002. The architect and father of two daughters is now partially retired from business and spends his fortune and time running the Ecuadorian Sun Yat-Sen Foundation, of which he is president. Although four generations separate him from his great-grandfather, Sun Kun Sang, the sibling of the founder of modern China, he is still unshakeably loyal to his origins. 'I feel Chinese,' he tells us in his office in an upmarket area of Guayaquil. 'I love the Ecuadorian people and I respect them. They gave us an identity which we didn't have before. But I feel Chinese.' Just looking at him is enough to believe what he says: he is wearing a traditional Chinese suit made of brown Cantonese silk with black embroidery which stands out a mile in this city built on the shores of the eastern Pacific Ocean.

Harry Sun's great-grandfather arrived in Ecuador in 1881, fleeing from the chaos that was striking China at that time. 'He came from a rural family. He started out as an agricultural labourer and then later set up his own businesses, such as exporting cocoa beans and coffee,' he recalls. 'At the beginning of the century, the emperor issued a death sentence against him and his family because of the activities they had carried out to put an end to the empire. This is what led Sun Yat-Sen to visit Ecuador in 1907, for example.' His great-grandfather married an Ecuadorian woman, which led the Sun family to put down roots in the country without ever breaking their ties with the 'motherland'. 'I've been travelling to China for twenty-seven years. My daughter has been studying in Beijing for three years. She has a commitment: over a hundred years since our family fled China, we're going back.

It's important to teach all descendants of Chinese people to love China,' he tells us.

'I can identify with the revolutions led by Sun Yat-Sen and Mao Zedong,' Harry Sun continues. 'Why? Because before then we [referring to China] were nothing. All the world powers invaded us. They took control of China and used us as a political prize. They taught Chinese people to consume opium to make up the balance of business, because China was flooding their markets with porcelain, silk and inventions . . . They corrupted the Chinese people with that drug. France and England kept themselves rich at the cost of Chinese blood. Why wouldn't I support a revolution?'[34] Harry Sun looks us straight in the eyes as he repeats, almost word for word, the Communist Party of China's official line regarding the scars left on China by the greedy West. This is the basis on which Harry Sun has built his philosophy of identity and the value of being Chinese.

In his own words, his foundation aims 'to show Ecuador that we have a 5,000-year-old culture. To put an end to the myth that Chinese people are just shoe and textile salesmen,' he insists, always using the first-person plural. Apart from its didactic function, the foundation also offers support to Chinese people living in the city, a group which has grown exponentially as a result of illegal immigration and corruption among Ecuador's immigration services. 'We give refuge to Chinese people. If they need help with their businesses, either financially or spiritually, we give it to them. Whenever a Chinese person ends up in prison we make sure they have someone by their side.' Harry Sun personifies a characteristic typical of the Chinese overseas community, an attitude seen everywhere from Mozambique to Cuba and from South Africa to Ecuador: attachment to the motherland. While they are officially citizens of the receiving country, these communities maintain close ties with China despite the fact that their parents or grandparents were forced to flee from Maoist repression or from the hardship of the Imperial era.

This sense of belonging to China and pride in feeling Chinese despite being born in another country also explains the impressive quantity of donations given to China by its overseas community over the course of the twentieth century. In the 1920s and 1930s, Chinese expats financed the construction of roads, bridges, universities and

railways such as the Xinning Railway, which bridges the 138 kilometres between the Cantonese town of Enping and the Pearl River. This
is a habit that continues to this day. The umpteenth example, which is
also perhaps the most archetypal, was motivated by the Beijing Olympic Games in 2008. The voluntary donations of 350,000 Chinese
people living in 102 countries across the world helped to pay a significant chunk of the 100 million euros needed to build the Olympic
swimming pool known as the 'Water Cube'. 'We did it to send a message to the world: we are also part of China,' explains Sun, who
contributed some of his fortune to help turn the emblematic building
into a reality. Even so, these donations form just a small part of the
fabulous contribution that the Chinese overseas community has made
to the resurgence of the People's Republic of China.

In fact, this community has provided the main source of financial
support for Chinese industrial development since the beginning of the
economic opening up and reform in 1979, when the 'Little Helms-
man' Deng Xiaoping successfully steered China out of the state of
chaos in which Maoism had left it. It is estimated that 65 per cent of
the $500 billion accumulated in direct foreign investment (DFI) up
until 2003 came from the Chinese overseas community, particularly
in Hong Kong, Taiwan and South-East Asia.[35] Conscious of the value
of having a culturally like-minded community with bountiful resources
spread across the world, the Communist government – which treated
its overseas citizens with particular contempt during the Cultural
Revolution[36] – has been working hard since the 1980s to repair its ties
with this group. While Beijing effectively disowned its overseas citizens for a good part of the twentieth century, the government has now
turned to the Chinese diaspora to help rebuild the country, even passing laws granting them greater tax privileges than other foreign
investors.[37] As part of its 'go out' and 'bring back in' policies (走出
去-引进来), Beijing has sent thousands of representatives across the
world to attract capital and court foreign investors of Chinese origin.
In Fuqing alone, a city of around a million inhabitants situated in
Fujian Province, it is estimated that the Chinese overseas community
has donated over 140 million euros, invested in around 900 businesses and contributed over $4 billion in DFI.[38]

Today, a form of cross-border nationalism has evolved for millions of citizens who, despite living at opposite ends of the world, find a cohesive element in China's homeland and culture, albeit to varying degrees. In the eyes of Westerners used to understanding the world from the perspective of the nation-state model, this characteristic behaviour of the Chinese people can appear surprising or, in the worst case, frightening. For example, a Spanish, British or Italian national feels an attachment to his or her country that is defined by measurable borders and characterized by a common language and culture. When he or she emigrates and puts down roots, for instance in Mexico, Australia or the United States, these ties gradually disappear from generation to generation as their children quickly identify with the receiving country and its customs. In other words, the son of a Spanish migrant is no longer 'Spanish'; he is Mexican.

This is not usually the case with Chinese emigrants. The journalist and academic Martin Jacques argues that this is due to the very nature of China as a country: rather than a nation-state, China is a civilization-state. As such, the sense of belonging to a culture, a tradition and a history that officially dates back over 5,000 years does not disappear after an individual emigrates, regardless of the fact that he or she is inhabiting another territory and living in a different social and cultural reality. Civilization is the cohesive element, the thread that holds together the string of pearls formed by the great Chinese community overseas. The Chinese national, whether inside or outside Chinese borders, is immersed in this great tide of civilization where traditions, beliefs, language, customs and culture are passed down from parent to child. In other words, you never stop being Chinese, however far you are from China.

Throughout the years, the Chinese state has always played the part of guarantor for this ancient civilization. First the empire, with its elite of mandarins and high-ranking officials, and later the Communist government took up the role of guardian and agent of this precious heritage, bringing together everything from the philosophy of Confucius to a sense of respect for one's ancestors and family. In the modern era, this has led to a distinct sense of nationalism which has an important role to play. Particularly since the collapse of Maoism, which left the regime without an ideological anchor, Beijing has worked hard to promote a nationalist discourse based not only on trust in China's own strengths, but also on subliminal anti-Western and openly anti-Japanese messages. When Mao was in power, nationalism was used to fight capitalism and bourgeois beliefs, a similar technique to the one used by North Korea today. However, throughout China's economic opening up and during the present-day emergence of 'red capitalism', a type of nationalism which uses an ad hoc discourse to touch the hearts of the population is being used to diffuse any possibility of China adopting a Western-style liberal democracy.[39]

Perhaps the most telling recent example took place during the world tour of the Olympic flame in the run up to the 2008 Beijing Games. During the tour, many young Chinese people took to the streets of Buenos Aires, Paris, London and Sydney to counteract demonstrations in support of Tibetan independence and human rights. Although there is no denying that Chinese embassies played a role in orchestrating these protests, the initiative shown by the students themselves in hitting the streets to protect the Olympic flame from Western saboteurs must not be underestimated.[40]

This sense of nationalism which Beijing promotes among its population and which at times becomes very deeply entrenched has spread beyond Chinese borders and filtered through to the overseas community. There is no shortage of examples of Chinese expats such as Harry Sun who are prepared to fight tooth and nail to defend the motherland on behalf of Chinese people overseas. This does not mean that the Chinese diaspora forms part of some monolithic entity that is following the lead of the Chinese party-state to unite against their Western rivals. That would be an oversimplification of the facts. However, it is clear that the Chinese overseas community has benefited from its economic alliance with Beijing's regime, making money and taking advantage of China's arrival in the international economic system. In this current climate, full of opportunities for business and investment and rapid economic and geopolitical growth, forcing political change is not exactly a priority for the Chinese global community. As such, pressure to put an end to the hegemony of the Communist Party, or even to encourage the regime to become more open, has been forgotten. Only time will tell whether this situation is temporary or if it is here to stay.

2

The New Silk Road

'Annam is adjacent to Champa and the hundred barbarians, with all of whom frontiers should be maintained, so that there are no encroachments or transgressions. Likewise, neither civilians nor soldiers should be permitted to cross the frontier, or privately go on the seas and trade with barbarian countries.'
Emperor Zhu Di (1403–24), 1407 edict aimed at limiting China's contact with other countries.[1]

After fourteen tortuous hours spent lying on a filthy bunk, the long-distance bus from Urumqi is finally making its way along Horgos's semi-deserted main avenue. As we step off the bus, the air is filled with the smell of lamb's brain boiling in a nearby pot – how long it has been there is anyone's guess. Women and children pester travellers with baskets of fruit, sweets, pickled chicken feet and other local delicacies suitable only for the more daring palate. The bearded faces topped with traditional *doppa*, the colourful hats worn by the Uighur minority, easily locate us in the remote and troubled Xinjiang Province, whose name means 'the new frontier' in Mandarin. With its strong Muslim roots, this immense region, dominated by imposing mountains and deserts, stretches across a sixth of China's total territory. The province boasts 25 per cent of China's oil and gas reserves, as well as 40 per cent of its coal reserves and mineral deposits. Xinjiang welcomes us with the fiercely intense blue sky typical of Central Asia and a magnificent quality of light, something rarely seen now in industrialized China with its sad skies and shades of metallic grey.

The street signs and posters in both Mandarin and Uighur, with its alphabet derived from Arabic, highlight the dramatic coexistence of two cultures – Chinese and Uighur – which have been clashing constantly ever since the expansionist Qing dynasty seized control of the region in the eighteenth century.[2] Here we see the meeting of two very different worlds: that of the Uighur culture, with its deeply entrenched traditions and Muslim roots dating back to the tenth century, and the Chinese world, hungry for economic development and with the Communist Party's values as its only creed. The clash between these two worlds has led to mutual distrust, hostility, repression and bloodshed. Today, the two ethnic groups live very separate lives: one lives to the south of the treacherous Taklamakan desert and practises Sunni Islam in mosques – an activity looked on with suspicion by Beijing – while the other lives mainly in the urban hubs to the north of the region, where they use bulldozers and pass new regulations fuelling the destruction of historic districts in order to make room for banks, shopping centres and karaoke bars housed in striking glass buildings. The scene is set for the struggle between tradition and modernity that is taking place in this historic enclave on the old Silk Road, which is now being used as a springboard to further China's strategic objectives in Central Asia.

As such, Horgos has been called to play a decisive role: to act as a gateway into Central Asia. Close to the border with Kazakhstan, today it is little more than a quiet, unwelcoming town with barely 20,000 inhabitants in the middle of nowhere. However, the future is already being built at breakneck speed. 'Come back in ten or fifteen years and Horgos will be full of hotels and skyscrapers,' warns Wang Yanjiang, an entrepreneur and vice-president of the local business association. As he drives his 4x4, Wang proudly explains that the town has been officially listed as a Special Economic Zone (SEZ),[3] guaranteeing it a wave of new infrastructure building and an enticing legal framework to attract investors. The aim: to transform the town into a first-class manufacturing and logistics centre. 'Over the next decade, the population of Horgos will multiply by ten to 200,000 inhabitants. The same will happen with businesses, whose number will reach 10,000,' Wang assures us.

Looking at the important role that the SEZs have played in China's spectacular economic development over the last thirty years, there is no doubt about the effectiveness of these zones and China's capacity to carry out projects on such a grand scale. Selling land in Horgos at affordable prices, or even giving it away, and facilitating credit and earnings exemptions from certain taxes, Beijing is hoping to recreate the runaway success seen in Shenzhen.[4] Once a small fishing town close to Hong Kong, Shenzhen was selected as one of China's first SEZs. Just three decades later it is now a dazzling city of 15 million inhabitants, brimming with skyscrapers and wide, endless avenues. Thanks to enormous investments in new infrastructure, Shenzhen is now the second richest city in China, giving birth to a new urban middle class that has filled the city with shopping centres, golf courses, luxury cars and smart residential districts. While in the past China prioritized its eastern and south-east regions, it is now using the exact same model to develop its impoverished 'Great West'.

As we drive towards the border, Wang points out the three large shopping centres lining the road, where hundreds of small shops are displaying everything from washing machines and electrical appliances to knick-knacks, *matryoshka* dolls and soft toys. When we reach the border we are able to see for ourselves how Horgos is preparing to become the next Shenzhen. Busloads of potential Chinese investors from other provinces travel across the 5.2 square kilometre area authorized by China and Kazakhstan to house the future Free Trade Zone. Free from the shackles of bureaucracy and the current tax rates, the zone will pave the way for Chinese products to be exported throughout the markets of Central Asia and perhaps even beyond into European territory. Beijing's plan for the economic development of its 'rebel province' has brought the historic Silk Road back to life, and it is now showing the same startling vitality that it once boasted all those centuries ago.[5]

A plentiful supply of cheap labour also provides China with a powerful advantage when it comes to conquering the Central Asian markets. 'Producing something in Kazakhstan costs five times more than in China because of taxes and salaries. A Chinese employee in Horgos earns an annual salary of around 18,000 yuan (2,000 euros), while a Kazakh worker expects 1,200 euros each month. This has caused many Kazakh businesses to lose sectors and market share,' Wang explains. Crossing the border at Horgos is enough to give us an idea of the power of Chinese products in the region. An army of lorries loaded with Chinese tea, DVD players, crockery, electrical appliances and bicycles is queuing to be inspected by the Kazakh customs control. The lorry drivers, mostly hefty-looking Central Asians, leave their vehicles and kill time by playing cards, drinking and smoking, flashing the gold teeth typical of the people of the former Soviet Union every time they laugh. The customs officials arrogantly measure, weigh and take note of the products, confident in the sense of authority granted by their grey uniforms. 'It costs 20,000 dollars to take a lorry across the border,' Wang tells us, referring to the exorbitant customs duties imposed on Chinese products in a vain attempt to fend off an invasion that is unstoppable in the face of such vast differences in production costs: once we arrive in Kazakh territory we count almost 300 empty lorries queuing for several kilometres at the side of the road to get back to China to stock up on supplies. Here, as in so many other places, taxes are powerless against the pull of Chinese products.[6]

The pedestrian border crossing also defies any kind of common sense. A multi-ethnic mob of around 200 thieves, soldiers and men loaded down with gigantic bundles and boxes crams into a space measuring just a few square metres at the gates of a narrow passage lined with iron railings. At the end of the passage, one Chinese soldier is waiting to carry out the preliminary passport check. The sweaty, noisy crowd mercilessly pushes each other out of the way. The only law here is the law of the jungle; the most forceful surge forward without paying any attention to the hopeless cries of the people they trample on their way. The strongest and most impatient applicants are the first to cross the border in this cut-throat place where the philosophy is always 'me first, you later'. The rest of the horde, mostly made up of chubby women and old men with silvery beards, waits its turn: this is natural selection in its purest form. Meanwhile, the Chinese find opportunities amidst the chaos, with the shopping-mad Kazakhs as their potential customers. They sell them passport covers and other useless items, or offer the use of wheelbarrows to carry their great piles of shopping – plasma televisions, dryers, clothing – across the border in exchange for just a few dollars. All these items can be sold in Kazakhstan for several times their original price.

Crossing the 350 kilometres between the Chinese border and

Almaty, the economic capital of Kazakhstan, means taking a road that has no dividing lines between lanes and is full of potholes: a world away from the spotless G-312 motorway that took us from Urumqi, Xinjiang's provincial capital, to Horgos on the Chinese side of the border. The dangerous second-hand Audis and Mercedes imported from Germany after being retired by their European owners can barely make their way through the potholes on a precarious road that shows just how little interest Kazakhstan has in increasing its overland trade. This is the complete opposite of what is happening on the other side of the border. The reason for this is that the little that Kazakhstan sells to China – mainly oil and gas – is generally not transported on this road but through underground pipelines. The only effect of improving overland transport would be to promote the arrival of more Chinese products into Kazakh markets.[7]

This sense of crossing through time as well as space – of taking a leap back into the past – is a familiar feeling whenever we leave China by land. This contrast is mostly a result of the country's recent revolution in new infrastructure building.[8] Enormous bridges that defy all the rules of logic, perfect motorways which cut across mountain ranges, and railway lines connecting the four cardinal points of the country make up the new landscape of a state which has always understood the importance of investing in its transport networks in order to strengthen its governance.[9] In the past, the mandarins made their way to the furthest corners of their territory to ensure control of their dominion. Today, the creation of new infrastructure serves the same purpose as it did in the Imperial era: to improve links and trade between Chinese urban centres located thousands of kilometres away from Beijing. However, the modern-day transport links also play a role that was restricted or even openly opposed by the Imperial governments – the expansion of Chinese trade outside its own borders.[10]

As such, China has broken with centuries of isolation and aversion to having any contact with the outside world – even in questions of trade – out of fear of the potential consequences that this might have on a domestic level. One example of Imperial China's reluctance – or even outright opposition – to dealing with the rest of the world is seen in the experience of the first British trade envoy sent to China by George III in September 1792. The group of diplomats, merchants, soldiers, scientists and painters led by Lord George Macartney travelled to Macao in the hope of persuading the Emperor Qianlong to allow Great Britain access to Chinese ports and to encourage Beijing to lower its custom duties on its products. In order to impress the holder of the 'Mandate of Heaven', the delegation carefully carried telescopes, barometers and clocks on their four-month journey across the entire length of the country from the southern city of Canton – the only port authorized for foreign use – to the northern Forbidden City in Beijing. After a brief encounter with the Emperor, Lord Macartney came away with just a short and disheartening response from the Son of Heaven:

> We have never valued ingenious articles, nor do we have the slightest need of your country's manufactures. Therefore, O King, as regards your request to send someone to remain at the [Chinese] capital, while it is not in harmony with the regulations of the Celestial Empire we also feel very much that it is of no advantage to your country.[11]

ALL ROADS LEAD TO CENTRAL ASIA

The Chinese government is anticipating an influx of millions of dollars in investment over the next five years to help develop infrastructure in Xinjiang: in May 2010 it approved a project budget of between $17 billion and $22 billion – the equivalent of Bolivia's entire GDP in 2009 – a figure which will enable the amount of road in the province to increase from the current 15,000 kilometres to 80,000 kilometres by 2016.[12] There is also an ambitious plan in place to extend the country's rail network, including its high-speed railway.[13] Improving the efficiency of transport links in the region will not only increase the number of routes available for exporting Chinese products into Central Asia. Coinciding with China's rapid process of urbanization, the improved transport links will also facilitate the development of 'cluster-towns', important logistical and production centres such as the one that is quickly becoming a reality in Horgos.

Given the scale of the development planned for the region on China's north-west border, one question cannot be ignored: what are the aims behind this immense deployment of resources? From a domestic perspective it is clear that Beijing understands perfectly the potential impact that economic development may have on its strategy to stabilize the turbulent Xinjiang province at any cost. This has become even more urgent since 2009, when the region became the site of the worst outbreak of violence in the country since the 1989 protests in Tiananmen Square: inter-ethnic violence left 197 people dead and over 1,700 injured.

At the same time, the new infrastructure will create endless opportunities for trade both in Central Asia and beyond. Xin Guangcheng, an expert in Central Asia at the Chinese Academy of Social Sciences, drew our attention to both factors: 'The government wants to create a new Shanghai in Xinjiang. It aims to take advantage of the province's geographical position, since over 70 per cent of trade between Central Asia and China passes through this region. The biggest challenge it faces in order to do this is to attract human capital and investments,' he explained during a two-hour interview in Beijing which was meticulously transcribed by a civil servant so that it could later be submitted to the Communist Party's commissioners for review.

Xin Guangcheng is hinting here at the prospect of a massive influx of people of Han Chinese ethnicity moving to the Muslim province, attracted by the new opportunities that are bound to emerge from the immense government investment and favourable tax conditions. The arrival of thousands of Han traders, investors and workers will have one inevitable and obvious consequence: the dilution of the Uighurs' dominance within Xinjiang's ethnographic panorama.[14] This would be nothing new in the history of a country whose central government – whether Imperial or republican – has regularly used population displacement as a tool to support the territorial and ethnic conquest of the Han people.[15] The Communists made extensive use of this practice from the moment they came to power, submitting the unruly provinces of Xinjiang and Tibet to a gradual, silent process of ethnic and cultural assimilation. This is still taking place today with the arrival of waves of Han Chinese emigrants from other regions in the country.[16] There is therefore little doubt that the economic development plan outlined for the region has a carefully calculated dual

purpose: to weaken Uighur resistance by encouraging ethnic assimilation, and to use the region as a springboard for conquering new
foreign markets.

The consequences of this development are crystal clear for Xinjiang
and the Uighurs, but what mark will the flood of Chinese products
leave on China's neighbours? On the other side of the border, China's
plans for expansion are looked on with a mix of anxiety, distrust and
resignation. Kazakhstan, the most important of the ex-Soviet republic
countries in Central Asia, is already suffering the real-life consequences of this Chinese 'invasion'. While it is difficult to get hold of
any reliable data on the number of Chinese products flooding the
Kazakh markets,[17] some experts place the figure at between 70 and
80 per cent of the total.[18] The merchandise itself ranges from basic
necessities such as food to machinery, construction materials and electronic devices. Competition from Chinese products has not just caused
the deterioration of Kazakh industry; it has brought it to its knees.
When Kazakhstan achieved independence in 1991, it inherited a grim
industrial landscape made up of obsolete technology and unproductive factories – when there were factories at all. At the same time,
China was being flooded with foreign investment, thus modernizing
its production systems and becoming the industrial power that it is
today. And so, the law of logic prevailed: out of the two countries,
China won hands down.

Kazakhstan is now to some extent in the hands of its Chinese neighbour, which it relies on for its supplies. 'We have no alternative. If we
were to eliminate Chinese products we would end up facing a severe
deficit of products in the market,' explains Konstantin Syroezhkin, a
leading expert in Sino-Kazakh relations at the Kazakhstan Institute of
Strategic Studies in Almaty. There is not even a dilemma, he tells us. 'If
we restrict trade with China, we will end up doing ourselves serious
harm. There are 2.5 million small businesses in this country, and over
50 per cent of them have business dealings with China,' he points out,
making it clear that the survival of a significant sector of the Kazakh
economy depends on trade with China remaining wide open.[19] 'It is
better for us to be good friends with China. What else can we do if we
have no productive industry in our country?' he concludes. With several years to go before Horgos – the next Shenzhen – becomes a new

bridgehead to Eastern Europe, it seems that China's checkmate has already been played.

A stroll through Almaty's main bazaar is enough to tell the story. With its complete lack of indigenous produce, Kazakhstan now appears to be in a state of total dependency on China, which supplies the country with every imaginable type of product. The official name of the premises is *baraholka* (Russian for 'market') but it might be truer to reality to use the Chinese term, *shichang*. While the majority of traders are Kazakh, Russian, Uighur or Turkish, the vast majority of merchandise was made in factories belonging to China. 'Eighty per cent of products here come from China,' says Igor, the manager of one of over twenty companies who rent trading space in the gigantic market. The bazaar houses aisle after aisle of shipping containers – thousands of them – which have been given a quick coat of paint and converted into market stalls. To give us an idea of the magnitude of the market, which acts as a link in a distribution chain which spreads throughout Kazakhstan and the rest of the region as well as providing a space for retail sales, Igor tells us that 'around thirty lorries with forty-ton containers arrive every day'; and that is in his area of the market alone. In other words, at a rough estimate we could be talking about thousands of tons of goods arriving throughout the market, almost all of them from China.

This is why some sectors of Kazakh civil society and the media openly doubt the ability of the autocratic government run by Kazakhstan's first (and only) president, Nursultan Nazarbayev, to deal with China's growing influence in the country. They hold the government responsible for selling Kazakhstan's mineral wealth without laying the foundations for a sustainable economic policy for future generations. 'The whole economy of Kazakhstan is based on producing crude oil, selling it for US dollars and using these dollars to buy cheap Chinese products. There is no industry in this country apart from the extractive industry. Nobody understands that in twenty years there will be no more oil in this country and then there will be nothing left. Oil is our curse. We would be happier people without it,' says Serikzhan Mambetalin, the then vice-president of Kazakhstan's Chamber of Commerce and Industry and secretary-general of the country's Green Party. The relentless arrival of imported goods, China's growing influence in the Kazakh energy sector and the millions of dollars' worth of credit that Beijing has granted to the country are all striking real fear into some areas of Kazakh society, who believe that China's next move will be territorial.[20]

Driven on by its own commercial power and huge demand for raw materials, China has burst decisively into Central Asia, a strategic region that has historically been under Russian influence.[21] Beijing first started moving into the region after the collapse of the Soviet Union, when it quickly recognized the potential of the former Soviet republics. China was able to take advantage of the gap left by Russia, which was busy weathering the storm of its own delicate domestic situation. This allowed China to move stealthily into the Kazakh energy sector, which contains a modest but valuable 1 per cent of the world's gas reserves and 2 per cent of its oil reserves.[22] Fifteen years later, academics agree that Beijing has played a decisive role in terms of stability in the region, mostly because China considers Central Asia as being key to its own national security. The 3,300 kilometres of border that China shares with countries in this region, as well as the proximity of the hornets' nests of Afghanistan and Pakistan, provide powerful enough reasons for this belief.

'Without the co-operation of Central Asian countries, the situation in Xinjiang would be much more difficult to control,' admits Xin Guangcheng of the Chinese Academy of Social Sciences, under the watchful eye of the official scribe who oversaw our interview. Xin is referring to the creation in 2001 of the Shanghai Co-operation Organization (SCO), a body set up by Beijing to boost military co-operation and the exchange of information between regional secret services.[23] With its growing influence in the region, China has used the SCO to impose control both within and outside its own territory. The aim is to strengthen a porous border that could potentially offer great manoeuvrability to Xinjiang's Muslim separatists. As such, China has managed to stifle any support which the Uighur secessionist movement may have otherwise gathered abroad from Uighur communities in Kazakhstan and other countries.[24] Using the pretext of the fight against terrorism, Beijing has forged a new geopolitical landscape that not only endangers the rights and freedom of the Uighur community abroad,[25] but also poses a real threat to its survival.

BUSINESS BETWEEN MANDARINS AND AYATOLLAHS

We cross from Turkmenistan into Iran in the blink of an eye, thanks to the immigration officials' complete lack of interest, a short, rowdy queue of lorry drivers and a quick chat about the Spanish football team. As we cross the border, our national side looks down at us from a full colour poster which shares a wall with portraits of Ayatollahs Khomeini and Khamenei. Getting to Tehran from the border town of Bajgiran involves travelling along a thousand kilometres of isolated roads through a mountainous desert, passing remote towns and villages where women walk by wrapped in their *chador* in the scorching heat of the sun. One of these places is the remote city of Sabzevar, which was rumoured to have served as a hiding place for Osama bin Laden for a few years. We are travelling from Central Asia, and as we plunge further and further into a recognizably Middle Eastern landscape, we are curious as to whether Iran – which has the world's fourth biggest oil reserves – has also fallen for China's commercial charms.

The Islamic Republic is *a priori* an attractive market, thanks to its 75 million inhabitants and average annual income of $6,360 in 2011.[26] However, the market is also fraught with difficulties, due to the international sanctions imposed on Iran since the Islamic Revolution in 1979.[27] While trade between China and Iran was practically non-existent at the end of the twentieth century, the amount of trade between the two countries now approaches $50 billion, according to Iranian officials. This has been achieved despite the difficulties involved in even opening a letter of credit in the country[28] and the risks inherent in a market with a less than favourable operating environment for businesses.[29] As we will see in Chapter 4 in the case of the oil sector, China's role in Iran is to fill the gap left by Western businesses. Bound by law and prompted either by fear of compromising their interests in the United States or by simple risk avoidance, Western corporations have suspended all forbidden trade with the Islamic country.

China is playing a dangerous game, trying to safeguard a responsible image in the diplomatic arena while also taking advantage of the business opportunities offered by trading with the Iranian regime. As such, it is selling every imaginable product to Iran, from consumer goods, electronic devices, textiles and food to various types of machinery, cement, plastics, vehicles and electrical components. This trade is stimulated almost entirely by agreements made between the two governments, since participation from the private sector has fallen to a mere 20 per cent of the total.[30] One striking example of this growing commercial relationship, which is based more on politics than on business terms, is the Tehran metro system, an exact replica of the one in Shanghai. The platforms, trains and signals are all identical; the only real difference is the 'female-only' carriages filled with women dressed in black from head to toe. Another less visible but perhaps more substantial example is seen in the close ties between the state-run Chinese companies and the Guardians of the Islamic Revolution, who dominate much of the Iranian economy.

Our arrival in Tehran in the middle of June 2010 coincides with the first anniversary of the violent street protests against President Mahmoud Ahmadinejad's regime in 2009. We also arrive in the midst of an atmosphere of heated relations between Tehran and Beijing: certain media sectors and figures close to the Iranian authorities are reacting with outrage and disappointment to a recent act of 'betrayal' on the part of their Chinese friends. Just two weeks earlier, Beijing had given its support to UN Resolution 1929, despite its veto power as a Security Council member.[31] The new resolution enforces a fourth round of sanctions against the Iranian regime, cranking Iran's economic strangulation up a notch in an attempt to force Tehran to abandon its nuclear programme.

Mehdi Fakheri, vice-president of the Iran Chamber of Commerce, Industry and Mines, alludes to these events as he offers us tea and pistachio nuts in his office in central Tehran. After China's recent actions, which he describes as going 'behind our backs', he explains that 'there is now a certain amount of concern about whether it is convenient to have all of our eggs in one basket. What would happen if China were to side with the United States and Europe on the subject of sanctions on Iran?' he argues in perfect Spanish. 'Many people in the government as well as in the private sector are now asking themselves if it wouldn't be wise to review our relationship with China. China enjoys optimum business conditions in Iran for political reasons. However, now we feel betrayed. Therefore, if economic and trade relations can be expanded for political reasons, they can also be hindered and limited.' Even so, the truth is that Tehran has very little room to man-oeuvre, and even less so after the latest round of sanctions taken by the United States and the EU in 2012 to limit Iranian oil exports, which ultimately might lead to the financial collapse of the Islamic regime. On the one hand, it relies on China for supplies, and this dependence is growing all the time. On the other hand, no other country in the world has shown such staunch opposition to the unilateral sanctions – different from those of the UN – imposed on Iran by the United States and Europe, which China considers inadmissible for reasons of extraterritoriality. With some reservations, China's support undoubtedly provides Iran with a vital lifeline, particularly in terms of its all-important energy sector.

This growing dependency on China has not gone unnoticed by Asa-dollah Asgaroladi, president of the Sino-Iranian Chamber of Commerce, who is giving his support to a plan to increase trade between the two countries by strengthening political relations. 'When I went to the World Expo 2010 in Shanghai I met with Prime Minister Wen Jiabao. I told him that bilateral trade will increase by 50 per cent over the next five years. We can achieve that objective as long as political rela-tions are good,' he warned, sitting in his office in Tehran, the walls of which were dominated by portraits of the leaders of both autocra-cies.[32] To demonstrate the weaknesses in the new embargo, Asgaroladi assures us that '40 per cent of the 15 billion dollars generated in bilat-eral trade between Iran and the United Arab Emirates is actually trade with China. That means 6 billion extra dollars.' As well as trade, he points out, China is investing in various different sectors. At this point the conversation takes an interesting turn, as Asgaroladi seems tempted to broach the impenetrable world of Chinese investments in Iran. However, when we push him on the subject he concludes by saying 'I'll only say that there is a lot of Chinese investment in the mining sector, but I won't give you any details or tell you where, because I don't want to end up seeing it in the newspapers and putting Chinese businesses in the firing line of the United States.'

Asgaroladi, a businessman sympathetic to the regime who made his

fortune exporting pistachios, cumin, prawns and caviar and importing sugar and electrical appliances, among other things,[33] shifts
uncomfortably in his seat as the interview develops, particularly when
we delve further into the thorny subject of the embargo. From his
obvious nerves and some of the things he says it is clear that he is
dying to deliver a very tough message to these two Western journalists, but is working hard to control his emotions. Inevitably, the
interview finally strays into the extremes of anti-Western discourse. It
is when we ask him about the effects of the embargo that he finally
snaps.

'America is foolish! We want relations with the West, but the West
is now completely foolish!' he shouts, angrily, in English. Through the
open door of his office, the serious tone of his outburst can apparently
be heard throughout the Chamber of Commerce.

'How much harm are the sanctions doing?' we push him, adding
fuel to the fire.

'The sanctions are not effective. They only make business more
expensive. I can say that Iran annually imports goods worth 60 billion
dollars and that [figure] increases year on year. But I am not going to
say how! America is foolish!'

'And what is China's role in all this . . . ?'

'I'm not going to give you any details. I'll only tell you that the relationship with China is very good . . .'

Asgaroladi goes on and on with his attack against the Western
world. His shouted tirade of abuse echoes all around the room. Suddenly the telephone rings. Asgaroladi picks it up, listens and responds
with monosyllables. A minute later he hangs up. It seems he has been
given instructions. He looks us straight in the eyes and stands up.

'That's enough for today!' he exclaims, making it clear that the
interview is over.

'Mr Asgaroladi, we're here to find out what China is doing in Iran
and to reflect the Iranian point of view about . . .'

'The relationship with China is very good. The West is foolish! That
German woman in Berlin [referring to Angela Merkel] and Sarkozy
are two fools!'

'Mr Asgaroladi, we're not here representing any government . . .'

'This conversation is over!'

We leave the Sino-Iranian Chamber of Commerce with complimentary boxes of pistachios under our arms, a good telling off and a kick up the backside. But one little gem emerged from our thirty-minute conversation with the disgruntled president: the magic number – $6 billion – for China's trade with Iran via the United Arab Emirates. Almost unconsciously, Asgaroladi had let slip a vital piece of information when he was talking about the sanctions, as he more or less officially confirmed that China chooses to carry out part of its trade with the ayatollahs' regime via a third country rather than directly with Iran. This of course raises the question, why?

CHINA AND THE IRANIAN NUCLEAR PROGRAMME

It is not difficult to see the effects of the embargo at Tehran's Mehrabad airport, where rickety Boeing 727s and ancient Airbuses trundle along the runway. Most common of all are the terrifying Russian Tupolevs, a type of plane which is easily purchased by the Iranian regime but which has a terrible record of accidents inside the country. Landing in Bandar Abbas, Iran's second city and main gateway into the country, places us right at the heart of the illegal trade route that enters Iran via the Strait of Hormuz. Stepping out onto the tarmac feels like standing under a giant hairdryer before walking right into a sauna. The pounding heat of the desert and the humidity coming off the ocean wrap the city in a thick, nebulous haze, giving it a somewhat ghostly appearance. The empty streets covered with patches of sand reveal low, ochre-coloured houses, shops that will not open until five in the evening, and branches of banks which swell the ranks of the financial 'blacklist' issued by Washington and Brussels. The thermometer has risen to 45 degrees. The heat is unbearable and there is no sign of life in Bandar Abbas.

Standing on the jetty outside the Homa hotel, supposedly one of the best in the city despite its out-moded design, we can make out the slow, distant traffic of oil tankers which line up one by one to tackle the Strait of Hormuz on their way in or out of the world's richest oil zone. In the middle distance, smaller boats with deep drafts and outboard motors fly over the waves in the direction of the coast. These boats carry many types of merchandise, all of it brought in illegally from Dubai. The moment they reach the beaches, a crowd of people suddenly materialize and quickly unload the cargo, which disappears in a matter of minutes: from the boat into vehicles and from there on to the streets and shops across Iran. Almost a quarter of Dubai's population have links with Iran and it is home to 5,000 registered Iranian companies, which have acted for many years as a conduit through which all kinds of merchandise enter the land of the ayatollahs.

According to the president of the Sino-Iranian Chamber of Commerce, not much has changed. However, things are not in fact as straightforward as they were in previous years, when Dubai was the nerve-centre for trade – including the illegal kind – for the whole of the Middle East. Since 2007, and particularly since the least orthodox of the Persian Gulf emirates found itself in need of a financial bailout from Abu Dhabi after the explosion of its housing bubble, the emirate – which lacks any significant oil resources – has increased co-operation with the United States and tightened control of its ports. This has led Tehran to set its sights on the East in order to guarantee supplies. Here Iran can find business partners with no qualms about getting involved in the forbidden trade which the embargo and the sanctions have done their best to bury: the trafficking of arms and nuclear technology. North Korea is one of them, according to a report issued by the UN in May 2011.[34] The other is China. The underground side of the Silk Road secretly branches out into the very heart of Iran's atomic programme.

Is Beijing playing a double game? While it may seem contradictory, China's position in respect to Iran is in fact carefully calculated. On the one hand, China questions American dominance in the Middle East and does not feel itself to be bound by the unilateral sanctions imposed by Washington. Beijing interprets the application of American law outside United States territory not only as a sign of an arrogant and hegemonic mentality, but also as a modern variant of the extra-territorial behaviour that humiliated China over the course of the century after the Opium Wars.[35] On the other hand, Beijing has given its support to the United States' aim to stop Iran developing a nuclear arsenal, in order to convince Washington that it is a responsible international business partner. Beijing is conscious of the fact that it cannot openly defy the United States in the Middle East without this having a very negative impact on bilateral relations and, by extension, its domestic economic development.[36] This explains both Beijing's backing of the UN sanctions and the fact that this support is in no way unconditional. As we have seen, China supports the sanctions, but only after delaying and diluting them as much as possible.[37]

With its diplomatic flank covered, how does China behave in practice? To begin with, a glance at the arms trade confirms that China overtook Russia in 2007 as Iran's primary arms supplier.[38] Furthermore, analysis carried out by Western intelligence services suggests that in recent years China has played an 'important supporting role' in Tehran's ambitions to develop a medium-range ballistic missile capable of carrying a nuclear warhead and reaching Israel.[39] This is backed up by evidence which shows that Chinese companies are continuing to supply Iran with components, materials and chemicals for its ballistic programme, despite the enforcement of international sanctions.[40] At the end of 2010, for example, months after the approval of UN Resolution 1929, both Singapore and South Korea stopped and searched boats found in their waters which were heading to Iran. In both cases the boats were carrying aluminium powder and phosphor bronze, materials which can be used for military purposes and are forbidden by the sanctions. Both cargoes came from Chinese companies. Soon afterwards, in May 2011, an internal report for the use of the UN Security Council confirmed that trade in missile technology between North Korea and Iran is carried out via a 'neighbouring third country'. In a telephone interview, a high-ranking UN diplomat connected to the committee supervising the sanctions against Iran identified the country for us on the condition that he would remain anonymous: it was China.[41]

At the same time, Hong Kong – with one of the busiest ports on the planet – was offering itself to Iran as a re-export centre every bit as attractive as Dubai was in its heyday. Some twenty Iranian shipping companies – essential for getting round the embargo – have been operating for years in the ex-British colony, which is now subject to Chinese sovereignty under the 'one country, two systems' formula. This so-called 'ghost fleet' is able to do this after reflagging and renaming their

blacklisted ships, and also thanks to the amount of room for man-
oeuvre allowed by the generous guarantees granted by Hong Kong law
as well as the island authorities' apparent slackness when implement-
ing the Resolution 1929 sanctions regime.[42] This issue is particularly
significant because Hong Kong is able to import American dual-use
technology thanks to bilateral agreements signed during the British
colonial era. This technology cannot be bought by countries that
Washington considers to be less than rigorous in their control proce-
dures – including mainland China.[43] The paradoxical consequence of
all this is that sensitive American technology could have made its way
into Iran's ports thanks to the triangulation with Hong Kong.[44]

The involvement of the Chinese state in this illegal trade is certainly
mysterious. Is it a deliberate, strategic decision on the part of the government? Are we seeing a form of tacit approval? Or are the giant
state-run companies in the Chinese arms industry trading on their
own account, without the support of the government and outside its
control? In short, how much effort and resources are the Chinese government prepared to use in order to rein in the illegal trade? At the
moment there are no answers to these questions, although the aforementioned UN diplomat did confirm that 'Chinese-made weapons
and other merchandise have been discovered in this type of trade'.[45]
What we do know, warns Michael Elleman, an expert in international
security at the International Institute of Strategic Studies in Bahrain,
is that 'this trade exists, it continues to exist and [China has] been
unable or unwilling to stop that trade. China appears to be unwilling
to make it a strategic priority to stop exports that would help Iran's
missiles programme. The evidence is quite clear on that.' As such,
beyond the half-hearted diplomatic support given by China at the UN
against the rise of Iran's nuclear programme, in practice its position is
notoriously ambiguous. 'China is one of the biggest problems when it
comes to the proliferation of weapons of mass destruction, without a
doubt,' Elleman concludes.

Night has already fallen by the time the *Iran Hormuz 14* ferry sets
sail from Bandar Abbas. The passengers mostly consist of traders and
casual labourers on their way to build skyscrapers in Dubai, as well
as entire families led by women in *niqab*. After a vigorous separation
by gender at immigration control, and then again after boarding the

boat, it is time for the nightmare journey to begin. Crossing the 100 nautical miles between the Iranian port and Dubai via the Strait of Hormuz involves spending fourteen miserable hours on board a slow, rickety and uncomfortable boat filled with a strong smell of gas oil. Meanwhile, another promised land for Chinese products awaits us on the other side of the Persian Gulf.

THE DRAGON'S POWER IN THE HEART OF THE MIDDLE EAST

'Where do we go, m'dam?'

'Shop. Speed.'

The mumbled words have barely left Fei Zhen Xu's mouth when the Porsche Cayenne roars into life and is soon cruising at 140 kilometres per hour along Dubai's sandy motorway. *Siji*, as Fei calls her Indian chauffeur, grasps the vanilla-coloured leather steering wheel with one hand and uses the other to tune into some music on the local radio stations. The enormity of Dubai with its inhuman glass architectural forms is reflected in Fei's sunglasses as we talk. Bristling with energy, she is busy with her two mobile phones, handing out a constant stream of instructions to her employees as she looks out at the swarm of skyscrapers through the tinted windows of the Porsche. 'Business good in Dubai,' she says, leaning back in her seat. With her husky voice and broken English, Fei has spent a decade doing business in an emirate that has made up for its poor oil reserves by making the most of its strategic position and legal and political stability, positioning itself as a key financial and logistical centre.

Seen from the sky, the Dragon Mart – which Fei insists on referring to as 'shop' – lives up to its name, forming the silhouette of a gigantic reptile. Its dozen or so silver hangars, with roofs representing the creature's scales, are arranged in an S-shape leading to the main entrance in the shape of the dragon's head. Measuring 1.2 kilometres in length and covering an area measuring 150,000 square metres (or three times the size of London's Wembley stadium), the Dragon Mart is the biggest market for Chinese goods outside China. This building houses 4,000 Chinese shops selling every imaginable kind of product, from reproductions of the Bible or Koran in the form of a key-ring to artificial lawns to combat the ochre desert that Dubai is built on. Opposite the main entrance, a statue demonstrates the role that is expected of China here: a ferocious dragon wrapped around a golden globe.

Fei moves through this 'Chinese world' like a fish through water. She runs a shoe shop, a shop selling bags and jewellery, and a restaurant on one of the market's busiest walkways. 'Take whatever you want. For your mother or your girlfriend,' she says, generously, in her strong accent from the city of Wenzhou, the birthplace of some of China's most brilliant entrepreneurs.[46] The building is a temple to business: aisles arranged by product, signs in various different languages, currency exchange bureaus and air conditioning on full blast. The products, businessmen and women and the majority of employees are all Chinese. If it wasn't for the Emirati couples dressed in predictable clothing – the women in black *niqab*, the men in startling white *dishdasha* – anyone would think that the Dragon Mart is simply an extension of China in the Middle East.

Fei came to Dubai in search of new opportunities. When the Dragon Mart opened in 2004, she decided to invest in this strategically placed site mid-way between Asia and Africa. 'Dubai is a great place for business because it's easy to get a visa and there are very low taxes,' she tells us. Customs duty is just 5 per cent on imports if the product is to be sold in the Emirates, or tax-free if it is going to be re-exported. Forty years old, Fei lives alone and far away from her son, who is studying engineering in the United Kingdom, and her husband, who is in charge of running the family's factories back in Wenzhou. This town is the global capital of footwear, cigarette lighters and sunglasses, as over 70 per cent of the worldwide total of these goods are made in the area. She travels back to China just twice a year. 'Once for Chinese New Year and once to monitor the factories and buy merchandise,' she tells us in her office, where we find a print showing the god of fortune and a green and grey jade statue. Given the success of her businesses, we wonder why she doesn't delegate the work to others so that she could enjoy a wealthy life or spending time with her son. 'I start work at eight in the morning and finish at night. I never take a day off. My calling is a professional one: I'm fascinated by making money. And it's also about contributing to the success of our country,' she adds.

The creative brain behind this experiment called Dragon Mart – which other countries such as Mexico are working hard to reproduce – is Abdullah Lootah.[47] In 2004, this elegant, clean-shaven Dubai-born businessman, who speaks perfect English with a slight lisp and boasts two decades of experience in business dealings with China, began the process of setting up this distribution centre which gives buyers from the Middle East and east Africa access to Chinese products. Traders can therefore avoid going to Yiwu, the world's biggest wholesale market situated in eastern China, where at least 200,000 Arab traders travel each year to stock up their businesses.[48] Lootah told us how he started with an idea about how to divert trade in products between the Middle East, Africa and China to make it pass through Dubai. 'We thought about just having a general warehouse or a big distribution centre, but we later decided to have a market as well. The Chinese Deputy Prime Minister Wu Yi visited Dubai in 2003 and told us that she liked the idea and that the Chinese government would be supporting it. We set up a group of two Arabs and a hundred and twenty Chinese people. And that is how it all started,' Lootah recalls, amidst the constant beeping of his Blackberry.

Around 2,000 businesses – 'all of them Chinese. That's imperative' – and 6,000 Chinese workers and entrepreneurs share in the rewards offered by this distribution centre which helps deliver Chinese products to the furthest corners of the region. 'People come here from Iran, Iraq, Oman, the Arab states, African countries ... They come to the Dragon Mart because it is a convenient market place for products. Location plays a major role, as well as language, because they don't need a translator,' Lootah continues.

The property of Dubai's government via the investment company Dubai World and its subsidiary Nakheel, the Dragon Mart took barely ten months to build. Less than a year later it had sold every inch of its available space for exhibitors and traders. 'By nature, the Chinese like to control every aspect of the business. This was very challenging. Groups of Chinese people were coming and trying to get control of things, but this really did not work here. We told them that we would be treating them all the same and that the process would be transparent. They wanted to do things like in Kazakhstan, for example, where the Chinese have bought the shops, but we are the landlords here and we have the power. We have established limits,' Lootah explains. The government has therefore managed to attract Chinese traders and products without having to relinquish control of the business. Each seller must contribute a minimum rent of $1,500 dollars per square metre in order to display their products. On top of this they pay for a variety of other services, such as water, light, accommodation, visa processing and business licences, the proceeds of which also go towards the sovereign fund. The world's second largest shipping company, the Chinese state-run COSCO,[49] has taken charge of transporting the merchandise to the final client from the giant warehouse measuring 40,000 square metres – another Wembley Stadium – located alongside the Dragon Mart.

Many different types of traders are brought together in this commercial centre, from those who have spent their life savings on setting up a shop to millionaires who control every aspect of their business from the production phase to the arrival of the merchandise in Dubai. Lootah, who refuses to give us any figures regarding the volume of business generated by the Dragon Mart, does however tell us that all of the Chinese entrepreneurs begin trading in the same way. 'When he opens his business, the Chinese man is the owner, porter, cashier, driver and salesman ... He is a one-man company. Why does he do this? So that he can understand exactly how the business works, so that when he hires someone, that person can't cheat him.'

The Dragon Mart and the thousands of Chinese people who live, invest and work in Dubai are not the only indication of China's growing power in this strategically important region of vast oil reserves. On the shores of the Persian Gulf, an artificial island created 280 metres from the coast of Dubai is home to the most emblematic hotel in the region: the seven-star Burj Al Arab, considered by many to be the world's most luxurious hotel. With its 310-metre-high shimmering glass structure in the shape of a ship's sail, the hotel boasts its own heliport, an entire fleet of Rolls-Royces and 202 duplex suites (there is no other type of room in the hotel). In kitsch surroundings dominated by gold leaf and plasma TVs, guests can enjoy a Jacuzzi made of Italian marble, the most sumptuous Arab carpets and the most elegant French perfumes; in other words, luxury by the bucketful – if not sophistication – for the new Asian millionaire.

Getting into this iconic Dubai building – 'the Eiffel Tower of the Emirates', in the words of one of its promoters – is no easy task. An initial control point 250 metres away from the building blocks the arrival of any visitors who have not been invited to this private party. Access to the hotel is only possible if you have booked a room in advance or, if the aim is only to enjoy the hotel's gastronomic offering, an advanced payment of $100 per person is required. In the reception, a team of hostesses, porters and waiters move into position with the harmony of a Russian ballet, serving tea and dried fruit to welcome their guests. Classical music echoes through the immense entrance hall where spurts of water shoot out of a fountain in time to Bach or Mozart. To our surprise, a group of Chinese guests were having their photo taken in reception before climbing into their waiting limousine. 'The Chinese have become the hotel's most important customers. Not long ago a Chinese group reserved fifty rooms here,' explains a slender Shanghainese woman who works as a hostess at the hotel.

The economic crisis of 2008 put an abrupt end to the extravagance of wealthy British and American visitors, who up until then were the hotel's biggest customers. 'Three years ago Chinese customers barely made up 4 per cent of the hotel's business figures. In 2011 this shot up to 26 per cent and we are hoping this will rise to 29 per cent by the end of 2012,' explains David Loiseau, the Frenchman who devised the Chinese commercial strategy adopted by the Jumeirah Hotel Group, the owner of the Burj Al Arab. During Chinese holiday seasons such as Chinese New Year, the hotel's new emperors can make up 60 per cent of its guests. 'About fifteen thousand Chinese customers visited the establishment in 2011, mostly from Canton, Shanghai and Beijing. We have a strategy in place to develop the rest of the big cities in the west of the country. This is a powerful market that is only just emerging and which should lead to 100 million Chinese people travelling abroad each year by 2020,' Loiseau tells us, mentioning a figure of mythical dimensions which would be a dream come true for the tourism sector.

Depending on the season, each Chinese guest pays between $2,200 and $4,000 on accommodation alone to spend just one or two nights in this monument to luxury and excess. In the face of growing demand, the hotel has been forced to respond to this change in the profile of its clientele by making some adjustments, such as training Mandarin-speaking staff and hiring chefs who can master Cantonese or Sichuanese cuisine. The onslaught of Chinese consumers into the luxury sector can be seen as the prelude to what may take place in the near future: Chinese exports will become more sophisticated until one day the Asian giant's products will take pride of place in the dreams of the world's wealthy classes.

THE ZHANG FAMILY ARRIVES IN AFRICA

It takes two chaser telephone calls before Zhang Qi finally arrives, slightly late, to our appointment at Club Belge in Kinshasa. 'Sorry for the delay. I was following the Hong Kong stock exchange and only got two hours sleep,' he explains as he settles his bulky figure into a chair on the terrace of this small oasis aimed at the Congolese capital's wealthy classes. His presence instantly causes a certain amount of interest and attracts several of the customers who are enjoying the club's swimming pool or sipping a gin and tonic at the garden bar. The staff also come over to greet him. '*Comment vas-tu, mon pote?*' he asks the waiter, just before going to greet the mayor of the Congolese capital. 'A good friend of mine,' Zhang explains.

The fact is that Zhang Qi is something of an institution in both the Chinese and non-Chinese world of the Democratic Republic of Congo (DRC), probably the country with the most turbulent colonial past in Africa as well as some of the world's greatest reserves of natural resources. Originally from Ningbo, Zhang Qi has lived for twenty-five years in this country where, he remembers, he arrived 'at twenty-three years of age, single, with a master's degree in finance and without a single word of French'. At that time, only around a hundred of his compatriots lived in the country, most of them either embassy staff or doctors sent by Beijing as part of the aid package that China has offered to the continent since 1960.[50] Zhang recalls that in those days Zaire – as the country was then known – was, as it still is today, a hostile place for businesses, with a labyrinthine bureaucracy and extremely strict laws. This is why his uncle – the only member of the Zhang family who managed to emigrate to Hong Kong with part of the family's fortune before the Communists took it all away in 1949 – had sent him to open a saucepan factory in the capital in 1986. His task was to control production and sales both in the local market and in neighbouring Congo-Brazzaville.

'My uncle was the investor, but he was never here. In twenty years of production, I only remember him coming here once or twice. I took care of everything. We employed 750 local workers and 28 Chinese workers, who were the technicians and the cook. We stayed open 24 hours a day and made 150,000 dollars per year,' he recalls as he fiddles with his three mobile phones, which keep going off throughout the course of the meeting. 'To begin with I knew nothing about business. I had to work twenty-hour days, seven days a week. I lost seven kilos in barely three months. In just under half a year I spoke a bit of French and began to understand how things work in this country.'

Understanding the world of business in the Congo means, for example, that it is impossible to make any kind of profit without the involvement of the authorities. 'We had to give part of our shares to one of the men closest to the president, because in the 1990s the law was extremely complicated and strict. It was practically impossible to make a profit through the legal route. In other businesses we even went into partnership with the president. They didn't do anything, of course: they made no contribution either in terms of capital or experience. But we gave them a percentage and that helped us,' explains Zhang. A *guanxi* – the Chinese term used to refer to networks of relationships – continues to this day which, he tells us, has helped him to become 'more important than the Chinese ambassador here'. 'When the Chinese embassy has a problem they call me. I know everyone here, all of the generals. I'm different because I'm always talking to the top people here. When I talk to one particular business partner it's like I'm talking to the president. And I have a good relationship with the president's son. We're close friends: we go to China together; we go to the nightclub together. I feel so free.'

In 1991, after five years in the country, Zhang got married. It was then that he and his wife – his greatest business ally – set out to conquer the Congolese market. In September 1991 they took advantage of the opportunity that arose in the aftermath of the economic collapse caused by looting soldiers in Kinshasa and the country's other major towns.[51] 'It was very dangerous. People were going to all the white people's houses to take things. I have never seen the Congolese people so hard or so strong. They destroyed shops and homes and brutalized white women. They attacked everyone who wasn't black: Chinese, Indians, Westerners,' he recalls. 'By then I already knew everyone in the country. I asked a Chinese friend to lend me 250,000 dollars and I brought fifty-two shipping containers into the Congo: fifty of them were filled with shoes and trainers, with a total of 3 million pairs. The other two contained textile products, mostly dresses for women.' All these products came from the 'factory of the world'.

The small Belgian and French investors had left the country after their supermarkets and shops were looted, and Zhang took advantage of the gap they left in order to win a share of the market. It was a chance to become the 'Number One' in the retail sector, he recalls. He began travelling more frequently to China to buy directly from footwear factories and organize the logistics of the business, and he soon began to make his fortune. In just three months he was able to return the money he had borrowed – 'it was 250,000 US dollars, which at that time was worth the equivalent of 2 million dollars today' – and he continued to expand his economic activities throughout the country. In less than a year his business had doubled and he began to import 100 containers at a time. He also created a network of shops alongside Indian and Portuguese business partners to distribute his goods throughout the DRC, from Lubumbashi in the far south to Kananga in the centre of the country. 'I opened four shops in Kinshasa. I began to import more goods and I became the principal supplier of merchandise for other businesses as well. Some factories in China were producing goods just for me. Soon the other Chinese people in the country began to copy me and tried to flood the market. But I reacted quickly by changing my products and looking for goods with a greater profit margin.'

In no time at all he had opened around fifteen shops throughout all the major urban centres and was managing to keep them fully stocked with a constant supply of goods, an immense challenge in the world's twelfth largest country where the roads and other infrastructure are in a disastrous state of disrepair. To control his empire he flew the entire length of the country in a light aircraft, miraculously surviving an accident in the north. 'I make sure that there is a Chinese worker in every shop to take control of my money. I know that they cheat me and steal some of the earnings, and that they increase the price that I've marked on products and don't give me everything they owe. They also tamper with the sales figures, but it doesn't bother me. They live in remote areas with no television, electricity or social life. Life is very hard there and my only choice is to accept it. I make a lot of profit, so does it really matter if you lose 5,000 dollars when you make 100,000?'

With his personal courage and extensive web of contacts, Zhang prides himself on being 'a very strong guy', having stayed in the country during successive outbursts of violence. This includes even the nightmarish summer of 1991. 'I sent all my Chinese workers to Hong Kong, but I didn't have any choice: I had to stay. The factory belonged to my uncle and I had to take care of it. I locked myself inside the factory along with the Chinese cook to protect it. The soldiers came to my factory but I had eight soldiers with me and we did everything we could to shut them out. We managed to get rid of them right at the last minute. I was lucky, because two months before the looting I had the feeling that something was going to happen and so I ordered soldiers from the presidential guard to protect us.'

Today, aged forty-eight, Zhang is a millionaire. His import-export business for Chinese products is still going strong. The range of products he brings in from China has risen to 2,000 items and his distribution network reaches the four corners of the immense national territory. 'My fortune is large enough for me and the next generation of my family to have a good life,' he admits, laughing. He has also diversified his investments into various different industries (mining, timber, property, energy) and has 'secured' his fortune, as he puts it, to avoid any repeat of the events of 1949. 'Chinese people don't trust the government. Nobody knows whether at some point in the future they'll do what the Communists did in 1949. That's why my money is in Hong Kong.' He has also risen in terms of status, with a daughter studying at Columbia University and working in her spare time for the American business magnate Warren Buffett. However, Zhang's passion for business, inherited from his ancestors,[52] prevents any thoughts of retiring. 'That is the question: I don't know when I should retire. Because I think that there are still a lot of business opportunities out there and so I try to keep on working hard.'

REPRODUCING THE ECONOMIC
MODEL OF COLONIAL EUROPE

Stories such as Zhang's help illustrate a phenomenon that is clearly visible to any traveller who now happens to set foot in Africa: the arrival of Chinese goods in every corner of the continent, from Cape Verde to South Africa via Senegal, Chad or Mozambique. In all these places, a good proportion of the 750,000 Chinese people officially living in Africa[53] have gone into the retail business, setting up shops in all the urban hubs and conquering a sector which until recently was generally dominated by local businessmen or more traditional immigrants.

A good example can be seen in Dakar, where Chinese traders have taken over the main thoroughfare of the Senegalese capital with boutiques selling every imaginable kind of Chinese product, imported from China itself. The *Dakaroises* joke – with a certain amount of bitterness – about the *Allée du Centenaire*, which some of them refer to as *Boulevard Mao* since local and Lebanese retailers have found themselves forced out of the sector by 'red' entrepreneurs, whose prices are simply unbeatable.[54] Dakar's over 2 million inhabitants represent a considerable target for Chinese traders, who began to arrive in the country two decades ago. However, the strength shown by the Chinese when it comes to setting up businesses has also led them to countries with less of a market, such as Cape Verde, the quiet former Portuguese colony which today is one of the most stable countries in Africa. In just fifteen years Chinese immigrants have opened over fifty shops in the eight habitable islands of the archipelago, which are home to barely half a million inhabitants.[55]

There is little doubt that the arrival of Chinese products in Africa – spurred on by China's acceptance into the World Trade Organization

(WTO) in 2001[56] – has had positive effects on the African people, who now have access to low-cost Chinese goods that they would otherwise not be able to afford. China's improved tariff conditions, a consequence of its entry into the WTO, have played a decisive role in the worldwide invasion of Chinese products, but it is not the only factor at play: China has also made effective use of its newly acquired WTO legal protection when it has been targeted by protectionist measures imposed on it by third-party countries. The United States was a driving force behind the negotiations because it hoped to flood China with its own products, since the Asian giant had no major businesses at that time and its competitiveness appeared limited. In fact, the opposite of what the Americans expected has now taken place: 'Made in China' products have taken over world markets.

The macroeconomic figures clearly demonstrate this explosion in trade between Africa and China, which has now become the continent's first trade partner, generating over $166 billion in 2011, sixteen times higher than it was in 2000, despite the economic impact on North African economies of the turmoil in countries such as Libya and Egypt. The Asian giant turns to Africa for supplies of oil, minerals, timber and other raw materials, while also taking advantage of African markets to off-load its manufactured goods. As such, the raw materials acquired by China in Africa serve as fuel for the factories and workshops which, along with the added value contributed by millions of available workers, create the finished products that China sells throughout the region.

Beijing draws on the 'complementarity' of its economic dealings with Africa, Central Asia and Latin America as a justification for these economic relations. However, in reality the formula 'my finished products for your raw materials' on which China bases its commercial ties with these regions inevitably brings to mind the colonial system that was formerly used by the West in order to establish its hegemony.[57] This system was invented by the United Kingdom in the nineteenth century, when the Industrial Revolution transformed the country into the leading world power of the age. Adapted by Beijing today, the British model was based on the use of colonies both as suppliers of natural resources, such as cotton, and as a market for the products that were flying out of Manchester's textile mills, the production of which greatly exceeded national demand.[58] Unlike the British Empire in that era or twentieth-century Japan, China has no military control overseas. However, its objectives in Latin America and Africa are the same: to guarantee its supply of raw materials, to ensure new markets for its products, and to build its trade relations on this foundation. As Osvaldo Rosales, a senior official at the Economic Commission for Latin America and the Caribbean (ECLAC), convincingly told the Mexican news agency Notimex, 'We are tied to China, the hub of economic development in the twenty-first century, with an export structure taken from the nineteenth century, fundamentally using basic products.' The director of ECLAC's International Trade and Integration Division was criticizing the fact that 90 per cent of Latin America's exports to China are unprocessed or barely processed natural resources, while their imports are processed products. 'The relationship is basically inter-industrial; in other words, we export raw materials and import manufactured goods. Furthermore, we export much less to China than we export to the rest of the world,' Rosales added. In 2011, the balance of trade between China and Latin America was $46 billion in China's favour.

Some voices from within the Chinese government openly acknowledge the disadvantageous nature of this situation. During an interview in Beijing with Liu Guijin, China's special representative for African affairs, Liu acknowledged the problematic effects of this economic structure, particularly in Africa, from which '85 per cent of imports to China are natural resources'. 'We cannot remain as we are in terms of trade with Africa. Along with our partners in the United States and Europe [who also import mostly natural resources], we need to do something to address the problem, to diversify the trade structure . . . However, the greatest part of the responsibility rests with African countries, with their companies and governments. They need to use the revenues from the expanded trade with China properly in order to diversify their economy, to support small and medium-sized industries . . . They have to follow the Chinese model for development,' he told us, referring to the 1980s and 1990s, when China exported resources and used the income to create added value within its own domestic economy.

Although a brief overview of the situation shows that Chinese

demand for natural resources has doubtlessly caused economic benefits for the region, China's arrival as a business partner in Africa has
also had inevitable side effects, as it has done elsewhere on the planet.
This can be seen in countries with a certain level of industrial infrastructure in place – such as Morocco, Lesotho, South Africa and
Nigeria – where the arrival of extremely competitive Chinese products has led to the collapse of some industries. This not only
represents a loss of sales in the domestic market but also on an international level.

The classic example is seen in the case of the textile sector. The end
of the Multi-Fibre Arrangement (MFA) in 2005, which imposed quotas to prevent countries such as China from flooding world markets
with cheap textiles and unbeatable competitiveness, had grave consequences for African clothing producers, three-quarters of whose
exports overseas went to the United States and Europe. Thousands of
small, medium and large producers were forced to close their businesses, and hundreds of thousands of jobs were lost throughout the
continent, from Swaziland to Kenya and Ethiopia, after these markets were taken over by China's much larger and more competitive
industry from 2005 onwards.[59] A similar situation has arisen in
Latin America, where exports from the region to the United States fell
by 13.1 per cent between 2001 and 2006 as a result of Chinese
competition.[60]

Everything suggests that this trend will continue in the future, particularly when China begins to export products with a greater added
value without losing its dominant position in highly labour-intensive
industries.[61] This means that China will not only continue to export
cheap electrical goods, footwear, textiles and toys, but will also
compete – as it is in fact already doing – in the markets for high-quality
electronic appliances, machinery and renewable energies. An example
of this is seen in the automobile sector, which is being developed at great
speed in China. As well as aiming to compete with German, American
and Japanese companies for the Chinese domestic market, where over
12 million cars are sold each year (the biggest market in the world),
Chinese firms have thrown themselves into the task of exporting vehicles
to Africa, the top destination – even ahead of Asia – for Chinese cars.[62]
Furthermore, China is breaking into hi-tech sectors previously reserved

for the United States and Europe, such as aviation, electric vehicles and telecommunications.[63] One undisputable example is that of the Chinese company Huawei, the world's second largest producer of telecommunications products, which earns around 20 per cent of its sales revenues in Africa.[64]

CHINESE SUPERMARKETS IN ARGENTINA

A decade after the financial crisis that swept away Argentina's former wealth, Buenos Aires is still a marvellous city with an appearance somewhere between Madrid and the 5th *arrondisement* in Paris. With cafés, bookshops and theatres on every street corner, the city has held on to the sense of glamour that guarantees the traveller to fall in love at first sight, despite the evidence of economic decline.

Here, Chinese immigrants are carrying out a successful strategy to take control of another form of selling Chinese products: the lucrative supermarket sector. The Chinese immigrant community in Argentina – estimated at around 75,000 people – began arriving in the 1990s, when it started to create what has become a modern-day phenomenon. These emigrants arrived in Argentina without two coins to rub together in search of new opportunities. The majority hailed from Fujian in south-east China, a province which is famous for being the origin of many emigrant communities that have settled all over the world. As tends to happen in the case of overseas Chinese communities, the new immigrants arrived in Argentina with the support of their compatriots already living in the country, who helped to arrange paperwork, provided financial support and helped them find jobs. In other words, the new arrival was quickly taken under the wing of his own people.

The same process continues to this day. The result has been the creation of an empire of over 8,900 supermarkets throughout Argentinian territory. These local shops have replaced the convenience stores that were controlled decades ago by Spanish or Italian immigrants. 'We open twenty-two new shops every month,' explains Miguel Angel Calvete, secretary general of the Chamber of Shops and Supermarkets

Owned by Chinese Residents (Casrech), which represents 7,000 of these supermarkets and has become an important lobby group within the country.

Casrech's website includes photos of the organization's senior executives at the Casa Rosada, Buenos Aires' presidential palace, posing enthusiastically alongside President Cristina Kirchner, who they accompany on her visits to China. And with good reason: Casrech now controls 30 per cent of the supermarket sector and competes with all the major distributors, such as the French giant Carrefour and the American company Wal-Mart, who have already received several battle scars as a result of the competition. The Casrech supermarkets employ over 19,000 people and, according to Calvete, can make a combined annual turnover of 8.3 billion euros.[65] Furthermore, Casrech has begun to expand, launching its own brands and developing every aspect of the business. This mammoth organization has managed to trump the competition thanks to its centralized purchasing system. This allows Casrech's supermarkets to offer customers each of the fifty basic products of domestic consumption at between 5 and 15 per cent less than their competitors. This impressive margin wins over the customer and wipes out the competition.

'The Chinese overseas community is like a giant Masonic lodge,' says Calvete to explain the rapid and well-organized progression of Chinese supermarkets in Argentina. This is a reference to the fundamental importance of 'being Chinese' in terms of joining the business. As a result of their Chinese blood and place in the social order, new arrivals receive financing, advice and support in order to set up their own shop, where they will never be the outright owners. 'Normally various Chinese people have shares in every supermarket. The person who puts the most money in will control the business, but ownership is always shared,' says Calvete. 'In fact, twelve Chinese families control the whole business. They were the first ones to arrive here and they have shares – however small – in all the supermarkets.' He tells us that Casrech is already functioning in the same way in Bolivia, Chile and Ecuador and plans to export products to Peru using the network of *chifas* (Chinese restaurants in the country).

The press and some politicians have warned against the business practices used by the supermarkets' Chinese owners, who they accuse of evading taxes, having links with the Chinese mafia, and not respecting the country's hygiene legislation. 'Casrech is extensively lobbying the Argentinian government. This is how they avoid paying some taxes,' explains Gustavo A. Cardozo of the National University of Tres de Febrero. 'The reason for the low profit margin of the business could be that it is [an instrument] for money laundering,' he points out. Despite the criticism, the Chinese proprietors do not shy away from demonstrating their ownership of the supermarkets: they can be seen sitting in the doorways, watching over their territory, while Bolivian immigrants work at the butcher's counter or stack shelves and Argentinian customers make their way to the till, providing an endless supply of fuel for the business.

3

Chinese Mines in the New Wild West

*'Everything under the Heavens belongs to the Emperor: every-
one who lives in this territory is the Emperor's subject.'*
From The Book of Odes, western
Zhou dynasty (1046–771 @A)

Weighed down by twice as many passengers as its capacity or common sense allows, the minibus jerks its way along the narrow gravel
road which ploughs, bend by bend, through the Hengduan Mountains towards the town of Zhangfeng in China's Yunnan province.
The roar of the motor echoes through the bodywork, competing with
the 'turbo-pop' which is spouting out of a Chinese radio station and
adding a layer of surrealism to the tobacco smoke-filled air inside the
vehicle. The bus is packed with a jumble of workers, women, children
and all kinds of bits and bobs, condemning the traveller to a hellish
journey along the China–Burma border. Soon nausea gives way to
outright retching on the part of weaker travellers, culminating in little
puddles of vomit appearing inside the bus. Despite the horror show
occurring inside his vehicle, the driver impassively follows his route
until he reaches his final destination.

The journey to Zhangfeng reminds the traveller that China is still a
developing country and that the mirages of Beijing and Shanghai are
really no more than that: oases of abundance among a general framework of poverty. Phyu Phyu Win,[1] a Burmese environmental activist
from Kachin Development Networking, a group active on both sides
of the border, has arranged to meet us in a mediocre hotel on the outskirts of this small Chinese urban hub. After a long conversation in

75

the hotel lounge, she offers to guide us through one of the dramas that has struck this region: deforestation.[2] We set off along the dusty roads which unite Tengchong, Yingjiang and Ruili, three Yunnan Province towns on the route of a significant amount of the country's cross-border trade, to witness the environmental disaster taking place here.

Pointing towards the bare Burmese mountains on the horizon, Phyu Phyu Win assures us that these forests have been literally wiped off the map. 'Two hours away from the border on the Burmese side there is practically nothing left,' she tells us. The mining industry has been out of control now for several decades, she explains, and the mining companies are destroying the forests in order to facilitate the extraction of gold and jade. 'Chinese companies are responsible for the damage. But the Burmese government allows the destruction to happen.' The situation is not as brazen as it was a few years ago, but the constant trickle of lorries coming from the Burmese border carrying enormous tree trunks in broad daylight is more than enough proof that business is still going strong. On the outskirts of Yingjiang, the lorries drive in and out of open-air warehouses at the side of the road, where tons of logs can be seen waiting in piles to be processed.

The official in charge of exports at the state-owned Ruili City Yasen Wood Industry Company backed this up. 'It doesn't matter what type of wood or how much, or whether it's rare wood or not; we can supply as much Burmese timber as necessary,' he told us while we were posing as European buyers of parquet flooring material. The company's premises are filled with the relentless sound of cutting machines and cranes lifting tree trunks. Hanging on the walls of his office we find more evidence to support his words: maps of the company's forestry concessions in the neighbouring country, and photographs of the company's Chinese owners posing alongside Burmese generals. A report published by the British NGO Global Witness pinned a devastating statistic on the illegal logging trade between the two countries: every seven minutes over each and every day in 2005, a truck loaded with 15 tons of illegally logged Burmese timber crossed a border post with China.[3]

In other words, a million cubic metres' worth of timber disappeared every year from Burmese forests at that time, gobbled up by Chinese demand. The evidence of this forestry genocide must have jolted some consciences in Rangoon,[4] Kunming and Beijing in the run up to the 2008 Olympic Games, as new restrictions imposed on the logging trade following the highly critical report caused a 70 per cent fall in illegal trade, according to Chinese customs data gathered as part of a new Global Witness study in 2009.[5] However, Phyu Phyu Win confirms that business had picked up again in 2010 in Kachin, Burma's northernmost state. 'Every night dozens of trucks loaded with timber cross into China,' she tells us. Burma's great wealth of forests and biodiversity – among the largest in the world – along with its vast reserves of gold and jade, have caused China to extend its tentacles into Kachin, fiercely exploiting its mineral deposits and forests. For China's companies and entrepreneurs, such vast natural treasures represent a business opportunity that is too good to miss, particularly as there are no restrictions or any competition from the domestic market.

After Burma gained its independence from the United Kingdom in 1948, Kachin suffered decades of armed conflict as a result of its separatist aspirations until 1994, when the Rangoon-based government and the ethnic guerrilla groups agreed to a ceasefire that paved the way for a fragile peace that lasted until mid-2011, when hostilities resumed between the Burmese Army and the Kachin Independent Army (KIA).[6] Until then, the territory had for seventeen years come under the more or less effective control of the Burmese ruling military junta, as it remains to this day. The only exception is seen in certain areas close to the border where the ethnic groups have maintained their military and administrative structure.[7] However, in reality it hardly matters who controls which part of the territory: China and its companies play a decisive role either way. The country's limitless funds allow it to offer both sides the financing they need. The usual formula applies: the Burmese offer concessions to exploit natural resources to the highest bidder while the Chinese hand over the money and don't ask questions. The first side becomes obscenely rich while the second carries off the jade, gold and timber. The only losers are the region's over 1 million mostly impoverished inhabitants, who have seen no improvement in their living conditions despite the brutal ransacking of their national heritage.

It was China's role in deforestation in northern Burma that brought us to the region, but we soon realized that this was just the tip of the iceberg of a phenomenon that stretches across the entire mining sector (including the exploitation of forests). Although China has no military control, its activities in Burma demonstrate some of the classic signs of a savage act of plundering committed by a neo-colonizer. This can be seen clearly in the act of looting natural resources without creating any added value at a local level. The wave of Chinese migrants arriving in northern Burma – estimated at somewhere between 1 and 2 million people[8] – contributes to this impression. Or at least that was how Phyu Phyu Win and the other activists and experts we spoke to in both Burma and China described this process. Therefore, Kachin and, by extension, Hpakant, the centre of the imperial jade extraction industry, became the next stop on our journey.

AN EXPLOSIVE COCKTAIL: JADE, HEROIN, PROSTITUTION AND AIDS

The slow, incessant jolting eases up little by little until the train finally grinds to a halt in the middle of the track. It is past five o'clock in the morning but there is still not even a crack of light in the sky. The cool wintry air of South-East Asian mornings is coming in through the window. For a while silence reigns in the darkness, but, as the new day dawns, passengers begin to leave their cabins and the word starts spreading through the train. Several kilometres ahead of us on the route between Mandalay and Myitkyina, the capital of Kachin State, a train has gone off the rails. The adventure of travelling on a Burmese railway is beginning to follow the expected pattern; in fact, the first hour on board was enough to get a sense of the dangers involved. Along with the usual horizontal jolting typical of any narrow-gauge railway there was also a far more worrying vertical jumping motion. With every jolt of the train, dozing passengers woke up and were forced to seek comfort in exchanging conspiratorial glances with their fellow travellers. Faced with a derelict railway dating back to the colonial period, it is a miracle that this story does not end more often in tragedy.

Inside our compartment, the tedium of long hours spent waiting around is interrupted only by the ear-shatteringly loud music coming from the restaurant carriage, together with thick smoke and the smell of fried rice. The first-class area of the train hardly stands out for its creature comforts, but at least it is relatively sheltered from the end-less movement of people and there is more precious personal space than in the crammed standard-class carriages. Sitting on the two lower bunks, the pair of Chinese travellers sharing our cabin have already reached for their cigarette packets and are smoking away non-stop. The usual feast is waiting on the built-in table under the window: various types of fruit, little cakes, packets of dried fruit and other Chinese snacks, along with a cheap bottle of whisky and a Ther-mos of tea for each of them. After the first few drinks, our companions break the ice.

Unlike his more reticent colleague, Xiang is in the mood for talking and he soon begins to tell us more about himself. He is thirty-six years old and comes from Harbin in northern China. Roughly twice a year he travels from Shanghai to Burma to stock up on supplies of jade which he then resells in his own country. He has been doing this for the last decade and has found that acting as the link between the high-est quality jade in the world and the market most prepared to spend money on it offers some fantastic opportunities. To illustrate this, he opens a small suitcase that he had been keeping under his bunk and from the pocket of a perfectly folded waistcoat he carefully takes out a silver ring crowned with the greenish-coloured stone. He smiles proudly as he shows it off, holding it delicately between his thumb and forefinger. 'I paid 600 US dollars for this in Rangoon; in China I can sell it for 3,000 dollars,' he tells us, quietly. The gleam in his eyes gives away the satisfaction that comes from knowing that he is in pos-session of a wonderful treasure.

Ten years' experience in the business has helped Xiang to optimize his earnings, as he has gradually managed to cut out the network of middlemen who originally gave him access to the highly desirable stone. The recipe for success is all about having the right contacts in order to buy the jade directly on site. 'I've known the owners of the mines for many years now and so I can buy jade at a price that is *100 times* better than what they would give to a stranger. The key question is whether you are inside or outside the business.' Xiang insists that in order to be inside you have to travel, as he is doing, to

Hpakant, a remote mining enclave in the heart of Kachin State. The bleak mining settlement of Hpakant and its emerald-green gems that have seduced the Chinese people since time immemorial were also our motivation for spending the last twenty-three hours travelling from Mandalay to Myitkyina on board this ancient Burmese train.

The train finally starts up again and sets off through a spectacular landscape. Outside the window we can see the fierce natural beauty of tropical Asia, as well as the poverty of the villages where children play barefoot while their mothers wash clothes in rivers full of rubble. At this slow and weary pace, the train will not arrive in Myitkyina until two o'clock in the morning. There, Xiang explains, another logistic obstacle awaits us before we can get to Hpakant: a hundred kilometres and a seven-hour journey minimum during the dry season. When we start dropping hints, Xiang quickly puts an end to any possibility that we might be able to accompany him to the home of the jade. 'It's a dangerous place. There are fights, thieves and violence. You need to take protection,' he tells us immediately. 'Foreigners are not allowed into the territory,' he adds, insisting that with our Caucasian features we will have no chance of crossing the three military checkpoints that have turned the mining settlement into an impregnable fortress. For many years, nobody has been able to get in without the required permits. Nobody, as we will soon see, apart from the Chinese.

Hidden in a remote jungle in the foothills of the Himalayas and isolated for several months of the year by the heavy rains of the monsoon season, Hpakant has become the epicentre of the world's jade extraction industry, its mountains and subsoil harbouring the only significant jadeite reserves on the planet.[9] The purity and intense colour of the so-called 'imperial jade', as well as its association with immortality and perfection, have caused the stone to be revered as a talisman in China for centuries. In recent years this has become an outright craze: at a Christie's auction in 2010, a Burmese jade necklace was bought for $7.2 million, the third most expensive piece of jewellery sold in the international world of auction houses that year. However, it is unlikely that anybody attending the auction that day in glamorous Hong Kong would ever have suspected that the reality behind the celestial luxury so characteristic of China is in fact a modern-day hell.

The Burmese military regime and Chinese companies share responsibility for this particular underworld. Phyu Phyu Win, the environmental activist we met in Yunnan, described Hpakant as a medieval, inhuman place where thousands of young men are exploited in mines in return for miserable wages; an enclave where people fight cruelty and desperation by injecting themselves with heroin; a place where people share hardships, syringes and prostitutes who travel there from all over the country; a mining community rife with Aids, endemic malaria and casinos; the home of destitution, violence, abuse and death. 'It's a social catastrophe,' she concluded. Her story revealed the sinister heart of a business that causes widespread marginalization and suffering while one of the world's worst dictatorships and its Chinese comrades make fortunes thanks to the desire of Beijing's and Shanghai's millionaires to flaunt their new-found wealth.

It is therefore hardly surprising that there is a very strong military presence in Hpakant. The Burmese generals and their like-minded business magnates have invested in the mines, and these investments produce significant dividends. The territory is also politically sensitive, not only because it was under the control of ethnic groups up until the 1994 ceasefire, but also because a Russian mining company is supposedly extracting uranium in the area.[10] However, most of all it is in the interests of the regime to keep Hpakant cloaked in secrecy in order to hide the social chaos and the legal and ethical violations which take place there on a daily basis. This excessive behaviour is the result of a savage production schedule, according to a teacher who spent several months in the area. He tells us that the thundering of heavy machinery belonging to the concessionary companies, most of which are Chinese,[11] can be heard twenty-four hours a day, seven days a week. Blast after blast, the extraction process has caused the demolition of entire mountains, whose soil is then removed inch by inch in order to dig up rocks of jade.

This work is carried out by hand by employees of the Chinese concessionary companies, who earn a basic monthly salary of between US$60 and $240 as well as a small bonus based on productivity.[12] The majority of them are young men, physically tough and with a clinical eye for detecting jade. 'Miners work in life-threatening conditions without protection', stated the report Blood Jade in 2008.[13]

Meanwhile, a steady stream of lorries carry the excavated earth spoil outside the concessions. This soil accumulates, ton by ton, forming enormous artificial mountains. For the residents of Hpakant who are not employed in the mines, the new mountain forms are at once a possible lifeline and a death trap. Winding their way on motorbikes through the dense traffic of heavy vehicles and the bosses' luxury cars, they head to the stone and earth dumping sites with no tools other than a hammer, a torch and their own hands. They spend endless hours searching for leftover pieces of jade which might have escaped the eyes of the companies' workers, while middlemen hover around in case of a find.

Kyaw Min Tun is one of the *yemase*, as these stone collectors are known in the local language. He spends hours scrabbling around among the rubble, climbing up and down the mountains day and night, come rain or shine, vying for the best spaces with the other hundreds or even thousands of aggressive jade pickers like himself. Their lives are often at risk: every now and again, landslides bury people alive, while floods regularly sweep away everything in their path.[14] Only very occasionally will a stroke of luck reward them with a precious green translucent stone like the one Kyaw Min Tun shows us when we meet him in Myitkyina. 'I can sell this for 1,000 dollars,' he assures us, naming the market price for a piece of jade the size of a mobile phone. Kyaw Min Tun, who is forty-two years old and lives in Hpakant, has dedicated half his life to this profession. Two decades ago, he points out, the extraction of jade was a local business, providing a fundamental means of support to the local people. Back then, the small scale of the industry and the lack of technology meant that the impact on the environment was limited.

However, everything changed with the arrival of the new concessions system, which helped to forge the alliance between the Burmese generals and the Chinese businessmen. This led to the arbitrary confiscation of thousands of people's land, forcing them to move. The local people were left with nothing but crumbs. 'The Chinese won all of the auctions. They bribed the civil servants because they could afford to pay much more than the local businessmen,' Kyaw Min Tun recalls. The local residents lament the fact that – among so much greed – they were given no share of the riches. 'The mountains have disappeared. It's all flat now. None of the best quality imperial jade is left anymore. We've lost everything and we're still poor.' Since the diggers have been working day and night on an enormous scale for over a decade, the reserves of the best jade in the world are diminishing at an unstoppable pace. The total depletion of the gem is now just around the corner. 'I am quite sure that in less than ten years all this activity will have to stop. There will be nothing left,' he predicts. 'Agriculture will be the only means of survival left to us.' All these years of exploitation have not even served to develop a jade processing industry in the region to create added value and local jobs. All of the processing is currently carried out in China.

While this colossal process of exploitation with overtones of institutionalized plundering continues,[15] Hpakant is also living through an intense social drama. Faced with a terrible job market and severe social problems, as well as fierce competition between the *yemase* themselves, the majority of the 100,000 *yemase* working in Hpakant earn the bare minimum needed to survive. 'It's a very tough job. Many *yemase* are addicted to heroin. The majority of young miners are hooked on drugs,' Kyaw Min Tun assures us. At six dollars a dose, opium boosts levels of concentration to help detect jade, increases physical resistance and relieves pain. The cheap alternative is to inject heroin directly into the blood, at just two dollars a fix. As Hpakant borders on the 'Golden Triangle', where the cultivation of opium is widespread, access to the white or brown powder is both easy and affordable. Unsurprisingly, opium is very closely linked to jade culture.[16]

For Myo Hlaing, thirty-six years old and a father of three, it took just two weeks for him to become addicted. That was eight years ago. 'It's impossible to do this job without heroin,' he tells us. Dark skinned and weighing barely 48 kilos as a result of the poison that is killing him a little more every day, he wears the traditional Burmese sarong, or *longyi*, wrapped around his waist. He speaks slowly but clearly as he explains that he and his friends collect jade, drink beer and inject themselves in groups. 'At least fifteen of my friends are addicts. Another five died from overdoses,' he tells us.

Inside the Chinese mines it seems that things are not so different. Ye Myint Oo became addicted to heroin several years ago while he was working for the Chinese mining company Shwe Gaung Gaung. He is still hooked today. 'The companies couldn't care less who takes what. The only thing they care about is increasing production. It's easy for anyone to get hold of the drug,' he insists. A group made up of Christian priests working in the heart of Kachin and an NGO volunteer, who agreed to talk to us on condition that they would remain anonymous, also confirm that the drug has spread like wildfire through the Chinese gold and jade mines.[17] A report by Kachin News Group[18] goes even further, directly linking the Chinese companies to the drug trade in the area: 'All opium sold in Hpakant is distributed by only two Chinese companies who are also involved in [jade] mining', it states.[19]

While there are no official statistics on the subject, there are many indications of the enormous scale of the social catastrophe that has struck Hpakant. In 2008, a local priest stated that over 100,000 young people under the age of forty had died in Kachin between 1997 and 2007 as a direct consequence of the drug. In 2009, over 2.5 million syringes were distributed in Hpakant alone.[20] The aforementioned activist working in the area assured us that over 100,000 people are affected by drug addiction in the home of jade. Out of these, between 50 and 75 per cent are also infected with HIV. Death is spread, shot by shot, through used syringes or an uncontrollable prostitution industry that takes place in makeshift karaoke bars and bamboo dens especially made for the purpose. This trade is carried out by young people such as Myo Mi Mi, a young woman brought up in extreme poverty who got hooked on heroin as a teenager and who now, at barely twenty years of age, plays a daily game of Russian roulette with Aids in exchange for little more than a few dollars a time. The combination is lethal: an effective killing machine.

THE BEST IMPERIAL JADE ENTERS THE ILLEGAL CIRCUIT

Days after meeting Xiang on the train to Myitkyina, we see him again in the city's central Pan Tsun hotel, where he is putting together the final preparations for his journey towards the great opportunities in

Hpakant. He is standing with his calculator in hand and several wads of American dollars spread out on the counter of the hotel reception in front of him, enough to grease several palms over the course of his journey. To start with, he needs $1,500 just to get to Hpakant. After that, it will cost several thousand more to ease his merchandise's journey across the border to Shanghai. With a 30 per cent tax on products it is impossible to do business legally, he assures us, completely unabashed. Therefore, many people like him opt instead for the contraband route, taking advantage of the fact that the border is less than 200 kilometres away and the police force's meagre salaries mean officers can easily be bought.

When he first started out, Xiang recalls, he used to travel in person on board the lorry to China. He used to pay between 20,000 and 30,000 yuan at every control point, the equivalent of between 2,000 and 3,000 euros, and he knew exactly which soldiers would be on guard at any particular moment. However, his highly organized system still was not always enough to protect him from nasty shocks, such as one occasion when he found himself surrounded by soldiers pointing their guns in his face. In the Wild West, Xiang knew he was risking his money, his freedom or even his life with every contraband operation he carried out. Nowadays, after having invested an unrevealed amount of money over the years, he has what he calls a 'secure channel'; in other words, contacts on his payroll throughout the route who, whether they are police officers, soldiers or customs officials, allow him to get the jade stones out of the country without any trouble or questions. Many of the best quality gems from Hpakant enter directly into the illegal business, the traders assure us.

Although in theory jadeite should leave the country via the auction houses in Naypyidaw,[21] in fact a high proportion enters China along contraband routes such as the one that Xiang has managed to forge over the years.[22] At the auctions in the Burmese capital – just as at others in Hong Kong, Shanghai and Beijing – the traders are not in the least bit interested in the suffering of the people living in jade extraction areas. Once the raw material leaves the mine and arrives in China, it rises steadily in value until it is finally transformed into a luxury Asian product sold on Nathan Road, the most prestigious shopping street in Kowloon, Hong Kong. There, luxury jade jewellery is proudly displayed in the shop windows of one of the fifteen jewellery stores belonging to Chow Tai Fook – the most important retail player in the sector – which are scattered over just a handful of blocks. On seeing a necklace containing thirty-seven pieces of jade in a shop window with a price tag of HK$13.7 million, or over 1.2 million euros, it is impossible not to think of the suffering, poverty, drugs and death witnessed on a daily basis in Hpakant. With all that money, how many families could be given a decent life?

With such high prices for the end products, rather than focusing on the processing aspect the traders and middlemen concentrate their efforts on coming up with the jadeite stones that will make them rich – if they don't ruin them, that is. 'The jade industry is very risky. It's like going to the casino,' warns Catherine Chan Sin Hung, president of the Jade Manufacturers Association of Hong Kong. This is not only due to the scarcity of jadeite and the naturally speculative character of Chinese investments. It is also a consequence of the lack of investment options in China and the great amount of money in circulation there, driving prices through the roof. This situation is not helped by the fact that the whole business is based on chance. In the auctions, for example, buyers make their bids after making a cut in the rocks so that they can use their experience to get some idea of the quality of the raw material inside. However, they will not know the true value of what they have bought until they can open the rock completely. 'If you're lucky enough, you can earn a lot of money. The price can easily jump up to a hundred times,' Chan assures us. However, the failures are also well known. It is not for nothing that jade is known in China as the 'risk stone'.[23]

It is therefore not surprising that the market is inundated with low quality jade sold as imperial jade, a type of fraud that can only be detected using technology. 'If the jadeite turns out to be regular jade treated chemically with resins, the price can fall to less than half its original value, even down to just 10 per cent of that value,' explains a gem expert who is analysing a jade and diamond bracelet valued at 1 million euros that has just been sold at the International Festival of Jewellery in Hong Kong. If the imperial jade piece is also antique, the price can skyrocket. A jade piece of this kind, 80 centimetres wide and 80 kilos in weight, which dated back to the time of Emperor

Qianlong in the 1700s and included an engraving of a classical thirteenth-century painting that took over twenty years to carve, gave the staff of Christie's quite a few headaches when it came to valuation. Based on the fact that the item was sold in 1945 for 80,000 pieces of silver, they settled on a pre-sale price of between 500,000 and 800,000 euros. The piece was finally sold to a Chinese collector for 5.14 million euros.

Following the trail of the jade across the world, from Hpakant to the jewellery stores of Nathan Road in Hong Kong, Wangfujing in Beijing and Nanjing Road in Shanghai, helps to uncover the decisive role played by China in Kachin State. It demonstrates that China plays a part in the excesses and injustices taking place in the region; in the violation of human rights and the miserable working conditions; in the unequal distribution of wealth and the severe impact on the environment. But that is not all. It also illustrates the nature of the marriage of convenience between the two countries.[24] Faced with the difficulties caused by international sanctions, fully in place until mid-2012, when the Obama administration eased some of the restrictions,[25] Burma has offered itself up to its hungry neighbour, using the lure of its abundant natural resources and a legal environment that is typical of dictatorships. China has not let this opportunity pass it by, as can also be seen from its significant geopolitical and energy interests in the area.[26] In exchange for privileged access to Burma's extractive industry, hydroelectric contracts and the Indian Ocean, Beijing has offered Rangoon diplomatic security, investments and arms at a time when the West tried to isolate the regime. Although Burma has other options available to it, such as partnerships with India, Thailand or Singapore, the alliance with China has provided a valuable lifeline to help the regime maintain power and, consequently, to continue with decades of abuse. Although this partnership is undoubtedly motivated more by self-interest than friendship, it effectively manages to fuel and perpetuate the status quo under the pretext of 'no interference' and 'peaceful coexistence', two of the guiding principles of Chinese foreign policy.

In fact, this economic penetration has spread throughout the region. 'South of the clouds'[27] China is deploying all its commercial power to make South-East Asia the spearhead for its economic expansion. It is developing infrastructure, investing here, there and everywhere and stocking up on raw materials in the region. However, this situation is not restricted to South-East Asia. Thousands of kilometres away, China is enthusiastically unfolding its tentacles in an iron-rich desert on the Pacific coast of Peru. Unfortunately for the local people, the consequences there are just as devastating.

MARCONA, THE HIJACKED MINING CONCESSION

After a ten-hour, 500-kilometre journey from Lima, the car reaches the crest of a hill and the mining community of San Juan de Marcona finally comes into view. We drive down towards the town along a deserted black asphalt road. A gusty wind is blowing and we can taste the desert dryness in our mouths as we look out at a sandy, ochre, almost lunar landscape that ends at a distant cliff signalling the edge of the Pacific Ocean. In the distance we can see a dust cloud created by heavy vehicles driving in and out of the mining facilities. There is also a dirt runway for the occasional use of aeroplanes chartered by the Chinese company Shougang Hierro Peru. One by one, the signs lining the road make it clear who is in charge in this unwelcoming place: 'Private concession. Shougang Hierro Peru.' Here, the Chinese state-owned mining company is literally lord and master of all.

San Juan de Marcona is one of those places where it seems a miracle that anybody can live at all. Everything is silent and there are hardly any vehicles moving along the town's central avenue with its handful of cheap restaurants and shops selling only the most basic necessities. Rows of low houses made of grey concrete – some of them painted in garish colours – are scattered along the main streets, providing modest dwellings for the miners and their families. Cracked paintwork and broken staircases are commonplace, as are wires stretching from building to building and clothes hanging in doorways. The streets are full of rubbish, which is gathered in piles on sandy street corners. There are no parks, trees or any green areas at all.

As well as harbouring Peru's only active iron mine, the small town of San Juan de Marcona is also notorious for the often violent conflicts which regularly break out between its inhabitants and the Chinese state-owned company Shougang. The company is China's sixth biggest iron and steel producer and the current owner of the concession, after having bought the state-owned Peruvian company which previously mined the area in 1992.[28] Despite the rich dividends yielded by its investment,[29] two decades later Shougang has still not resolved its differences with the small population of people whose welfare and future depends entirely on the company. 'In 1992 we thought that the Chinese were going to make things better,' comments Agustín Purizaca, a technical consultant and adviser to Marcona's mayor. However, those hopes were soon dashed, and then the trouble began. 'They've tried to put up a Chinese arch in the town three times, and every time the people have knocked it down,' he recalls. 'The only thing they understand is violence,' he concludes, summarizing the unsustainable nature of the situation.

The problems are caused by the very nature of the mining concession, which includes the entire town within the boundaries of its 670 square kilometres. Therefore, while on paper Shougang only owns the minerals contained in the area's subsoil, it also acts as the owner, agent and administrator of the land and, by extension, of municipal services such as electricity, water and the drainage system. This legally dubious privilege, which is effectively an act of extraterritoriality, has been fraying tempers within the local community for the last two decades. The locals complain that the behaviour of the company has had a serious impact on their daily lives; it is Shougang that decides how many hours of water or electricity are available to the community each day,[30] while the company's refusal to release land to allow the town to expand has stifled urban development. 'Shougang objects to every single project that the town suggests. They want to take charge of everything under the pretext that they own the place,' Purizaca insists.

The residents of San Juan de Marcona have to live with the unpleasant sensation of being unwanted guests in their own homes. They feel like strangers in their own birthplace and marginalized in the mine where they have sacrificed their health, blood and souls. 'It's like our lives have been hijacked. We feel like we're living in a Chinese colony,' Purizaca argues. The issue of accommodation is a prime example. As the town has mining camp status, Shougang provides its employees with basic accommodation in the lodgings built by the former American concessionary company in the 1960s and 1970s. However, if employees are fired or reach retirement age, they are immediately evicted from their homes. There is no reward for service to the company. Any type of construction is frowned on by the company. For instance, the residents even have to ask Shougang's permission to build new niches in the small cemetery on the outskirts of the town in order to bury their dead. That is how Shougang repays a life's worth of sacrifice.

Many of these former workers end up migrating to Nazca, Arequipa or Lima. The side effect of this forced migration is population decline: the population of San Juan de Marcona has dropped from 25,000 to 14,000 inhabitants in less than two decades. Those who do decide to stay despite all the difficulties have nowhere to go. Shougang refuses to sell, hand over or release land, despite the fact that they technically *only* own the minerals contained in the soil and not the land itself. As a result, the only alternative for workers excluded from the company is the *Ruta del Sol*, the Route of Sun, a shantytown on the concession's land that has grown from strength to strength on the basis of collective desperation and battles with the police. Dozens of families struggle to make ends meet on this rocky wasteland next to the cemetery under the watchful eye of police officers on Shougang's payroll. With their own hands they manage to build themselves something more or less like a home, with just enough space for a bed, a small stove and their belongings. Oblivious to the poverty all around them, children play with toy cars made of bits of wood and wire in the doorways of their houses, which are really little more than hovels with cement walls covered in pages from sports magazines and roofs made of asbestos and corrugated iron; miserable rat holes without floors, electricity or running water.

It is a quite different picture in the town's only residential area, which is home to the fifty or so Chinese employees who manage the local workers at Shougang Hierro Peru. They live in the original houses built back in the days of the Marcona Mining Company – houses with gardens, sea views and the general air of a middle-class American suburb. Although they have grown slightly shabby after all this time, the houses still bear the marks of the era when San Juan was in fact an oasis in the middle of a desert. Back then, the American mining company paid for the education of the miners' children and ran a hospital with American doctors which the older members of the community remember as 'one of the best in Latin America'. These were days when the Marcona Mining Company was considered – in stark contrast with its present Chinese owners – to be a model mining company. Now, nothing is left but the memory of better days.

Things have got so bad that the Chinese managers rarely leave their homes. 'You only see them every now and then. It's a small town and we all know each other here. They could easily end up getting into trouble,' Purizaca explains. We have to ring the bell several times before anybody opens the door of the house belonging to Fan Fu Li, one of Shougang's senior managers. The door is opened by a sleepy-looking Chinese employee in a white vest. Like an animal sensing danger, he immediately puts his guard up and defends himself against our questions with a foolproof barrier: he is polite but distant, infinitely patient and ready to roll with the punches if necessary. But most of all, his lips are sealed. 'The boss isn't here and I don't know when he'll be back. I don't know anything about what happens here,' he repeats, time and time again. Protecting himself by stonewalling, this junior Shougang official is not about to give anything away. The exact same story would later be repeated in Beijing, when Shougang rejected all our requests for an interview.[31]

This is a familiar situation for any journalist working in China and one which we came up against many times throughout our investigation into the 'Chinese world'. Whether out of distrust or self-defence, the Chinese tend to make it clear that a foreigner is not 'one of us'. However, all this suspicion vanishes into thin air if the foreigner happens to be guaranteed by a respected compatriot. Especially in Chinese communities far from the motherland, the art of *guanxi* makes all the difference. In Africa, for example, the mere fact of being accompanied by an adventure-loving young Chinese friend opened the doors to all the major Chinese infrastructure projects. Our intrepid friend was not with us in Marcona, but that was not the only problem. With emotions running high in the community as a result of the highly troubled workplace situation, the Chinese officials have opted for a policy of silence. They do not say a word, for example, about the 2007 riots that ended with Shougang's head office going up in flames. Javier Muñante, director of one of the community's two trade unions, provides us with a revealing piece of information: 'We've been on strike every year for the last five years.' The signs of this conflict are clearly visible around town, with buildings dotted with graffiti denouncing the company.

It is time for the change of shift at Shougang Hierro Peru and lines of buses can be seen carrying miners home. Through the windows of the buses, the miners' faces are dark with iron ore and they are still wearing their red or green helmets. They look weary and the expression in their eyes is proud yet sad. They have been fighting for twenty years against a company which marked the beginning of its operations in the country by firing 1,500 workers. Nowadays, over half of the company's 3,938 workers – most of whom were previously employed as full-time staff – are either on temporary agency contracts or are sub-contracted, allowing Shougang to save around 40 per cent on labour costs with every new worker they hire. The only miners with decent salaries are those who were already on the payroll when Shougang bought the mine.

This discrimination in pay, which can lead to two employees with the same amount of experience and skills earning dramatically different salaries, involves offering an average daily wage of $14, while the Peruvian mining sector pays almost double that amount.[32] On top of this, the workers also complain of arbitrary dismissals, poor working conditions and hostility towards union members. In the union headquarters, several miners volunteer to air their grievances on the condition that they remain anonymous; the company's reprisal against two fellow workers who vented their anger in the New York Times is still fresh in their memories.[33] Pedro is one of these volunteers. He has been working in the mine for thirty-three years, in charge of calculating how many explosives are needed for each blast. He works up to ten hours a day, six days a week, in exchange for a monthly wage of just 2,200 nuevos soles, which is around $792.[34] 'It's barely enough to live on. Isn't this exploitation?' he asks, faced with the difficulty of sustaining a wife and four children on these meagre wages.

As might be expected, these precarious working conditions also extend into the area of safety. The use of insufficient and out-of-date equipment leads to ten accidents in the mine every month. Furthermore, 30 per cent of Shougang's miners suffer from lung diseases associated with exposure to mineral dust – or pneumoconiosis – while many more experience varying degrees of deafness.[35] 'By the time we retire, we have less than five years left to live,' one of the miners at the union headquarters assured us. 'The number of accidents is an outrage. The company is only interested in producing iron ore,' one of his colleagues added. Meanwhile, Shougang's production level and income is growing year on year. This model of pushing for maximum production with a complete disregard for any kind of knock-on effects has formed the basis of the 'Chinese miracle' over recent decades and has led to the creation of one of the most unequal societies in the world.[36] This same model is now being faithfully reproduced in San Juan de Marcona. A similar situation can be seen in China's other mining investments in Peru, where it is a key player: just eight Chinese companies control 295 mining concessions in Peru.[34]

To complete the image of the perfect disaster, Shougang's activities in Peru are also having a toxic effect on the environment. Although the dumping of unprocessed residues into the sea and other harmful practices were inherited from the previous North American concession company and therefore cannot be attributed to Shougang alone, the fact is that the Chinese company has shown very little interest in protecting the environment. Shougang is considered one of the nineteen most polluting companies in China,[37] while in Peru the company's outrageous treatment of the environment has been penalized several times. However, this has not prevented the marine life in the water close to the mine installation from being pushed to the edge of extinction. 'There are hardly any shoals of fish left in the area,' says Santiago Rubio, president of the fishing community of San Juan de Marcona.

The traditional local fishing industry provides a livelihood for 600 families, the only group in the area that is not dependent on the mine. When we meet him in his home, Rubio explains that in order to catch the kind of white fish used in *ceviche*, the fishermen have to sail further and further away from the bay and 'spend eight hours each day diving under water to catch 14 kilos of fish'. For this work they manage to earn just 40 nuevos soles, or $14 per day. On San Nicolás beach, Rubio slips on a battered-looking wetsuit, dives into the water without any breathing apparatus and emerges from the bottom of the sea with his hands full of sparkling black sand flecked with shining gold particles. 'Heavy metals,' he explains. The waves break against the shore, dragging a reddish residue with them. The smell of poison fills a beach that has been stained ochre in colour by iron ore deposits. A few hundred metres from the beach, a pipe drains away the toxic residues of the mining process into an enormous ditch.

Shougang Hierro Peru supplies the group's other companies with the raw materials needed to make steel, which are extracted from this forgotten corner of the Ica desert.[39] Furthermore, the area's privileged geography provides the company with a natural deep-water port where the raw materials can be loaded – just two hours after being extracted from the ground – onto boats heading to China, thereby carrying away the benefits of an added value industry for the motherland. The message is perfectly clear: the ends justify the means. The victims and the damage are left in the gutter, thanks to the silent complicity of the Lima government, which is quick to defend this new Chinese 'Messiah' who is always ready to pour money into Peru's extractive industries.

Against this background, the 'great lady of steel', as Shougang is known in China, has plenty of leeway to deal with the long-term costs of an on-going conflict situation. In fact, despite the events described here, the company has no scruples when it comes to bragging about their contribution to development in Peru.[40] However, none of this changes the fact that the mining community is filled with a constant climate of confrontation. 'The majority of people here feel a lot of anger towards the Chinese,' warns one of the dispossessed workers living in the *Ruta del Sol* slum. He says it with the desperation of a man who knows he cannot win, but without any sign of the anti-Chinese sentiment common in many other places. The feeling shared by Marcona's inhabitants is not xenophobia, but rather a profound sense of disappointment towards the supposed Chinese 'friend' who promised so much and has only let them down.

After two decades of fighting against a company that tramples on their rights on a daily basis, the battle seems to have been lost. The fact is that Shougang is not just any normal company: it is a Chinese state-owned company. This may not seem overly important to anyone unfamiliar with the inner workings of the Chinese political-economic system, whether in Marcona or elsewhere in the world. However, what we are really seeing here is the long shadow of the all-powerful Chinese state. The fact that China's strategic national objectives and the needs of these companies are generally interchangeable and complementary gives state-owned companies – in this case Shougang – a clear sense of immunity that allows them to commit all kinds of excesses. This is particularly true when, as in the case of San Juan de Marcona, the authorities in the host country make no attempt to put an end to the abuse, contributing greatly to the vulnerability of the affected communities. What is more, China's lack of any kind of civil society, independent media or opposition parties provides the regime's companies with a considerable degree of security. Under these circumstances, who is going to stand in Shougang's head offices in Beijing and hold the company to account? Even more importantly, who is going to rein in China's reckless behaviour outside its own borders?

THE PITFALLS OF THE 'CONTRACT OF THE CENTURY' BETWEEN CONGO AND CHINA

If Marcona seemed like a remote place, crossing the border between Angola and the Democratic Republic of Congo (DRC) through the Angolan province of Cabinda is in another league altogether. This is a hostile place, isolated and wild, a classic no-go zone where Africa can easily show its darker side. The aeroplane landed at about seven in the morning at the airport in Cabinda, a city that shares its name with the oil-rich province where it is located. After a short taxi ride, we reach the military-controlled border crossing. 'It's Sunday. It's closed,' two soldiers on the Angolan side bark at us, leaning on their regulation Kalashnikovs. Things were getting complicated at one of Africa's most troubled borders of recent years.[41]

After several hours of stubbornly waiting, we finally get our hands on the Angolan exit stamp and step across the border towards a run-down hut flying the blue, red and yellow national flag of the DRC.

Suddenly, three Congolese soldiers dressed in sandals and civilian shorts snap out of their Sunday lethargy and, dodging the mess of empty beer bottles they have just finished drinking, promise to help us 'even though the post is closed on Sundays'. The border's extreme isolation clearly makes them feel untouchable and they quickly make us the targets of their somewhat dubious intentions. One of them is chewing *khat*, the so-called 'African drug', and bombards us with questions about the beauty and voluptuousness of our wives. Another of them makes a note of our visas and defiantly makes us recite every last word written in them: a strange mixture of interrogation and simple curiosity.

Suddenly, things take a turn for the worse: they want to know whether we're carrying 'espionage material'. They say they have to inspect the contents of our bags, which happen to be full of cameras, hard disks and laptops – not very easy to explain away considering that we are there on tourist visas and are supposedly 'celebrating' – in a place where nobody would dare to celebrate anything – Spain's World Cup victory in South Africa. Fortunately, luck is on our side. A less than thorough inspection allows us to dodge the bullet and face up to the soldiers' final whim: the payment of a 'crossing fee'. Three hours later, after a lot of explaining, false smiles, pleading and footballing talk – as well as parting with $100 – they let us go. With our nerves decidedly on edge at the thought of what might have happened but didn't, we enter the DRC, a country ten times the size of the United Kingdom and the scene of the most savage Western colonial barbarity on the continent.

A rickety fifteen-year-old Toyota 4x4 drives us at full speed towards Muanda through a fierce-looking landscape and along 27 kilometres of sandy roads with very little traffic and hardly any signs of life. Only a battered-looking abandoned tank breaks the monotony, as well as a couple of drivers repairing the punctured tyres on their ancient vehicles. The wild, intense, majestic landscape brings to mind the descriptions written by the Polish journalist Ryszard Kapuscinski in *The Shadow of the Sun*, his unparalleled chronicle of decolonization in Africa. We are eventually stopped at a makeshift security control in a village in the middle of nowhere, where an angry-looking soldier collects what is clearly an illegal toll fee. Soon after this we arrive in Muanda, a small town with unpaved streets littered with rubbish and a total disregard for the law. It is one of those places where the police are much more dangerous than the bad guys, as we had the chance to find out for ourselves. One particularly aggressive plain-clothes policeman literally kidnapped us without showing us any kind of identification, and held us illegally for several hours before the Spanish consulate rescued us from his money-grabbing grasp.

It does not take us long to realize that there are no laws, state, certainty or security of any kind in this remote corner of the DRC. It takes us around twelve hours to travel the 400 kilometres to Kinshasa along the N1 road, which runs parallel to the railway built by the British explorer Henry Morton Stanley in order to open up trade towards the sea, as this stretch of the River Congo is impossible to navigate. Every encounter with another vehicle puts our lives at risk, as we can tell from the lines of wrecked cars sleeping the sleep of the just in the ditches at the side of the road. Ancient lorries come out of nowhere, dazzling drivers with their beaming headlights and forcing them to perform a skilled balancing act on the narrow road to avoid either falling into a hole or ending up under the lorry. Whenever we pass through a town or village, where the chaotic traffic forces us to slow down, hordes of children, vendors and thieves swarm around the vehicle to beg, sell fruit or simply rob the passengers. That is the DRC: a constant movement along a knife edge, a continuous risk that at any moment things could go off the rails or explode in your hands. It is a place where tragedy lurks around every corner.

China has arrived triumphantly into this chaotic scene in recent years. Beijing has chosen one of the poorest, most underdeveloped and corrupt countries in the world as a partner in the biggest and most ambitious contract of all the many agreements it has signed in Africa to date.[42] On the basis of the contract signed in 2008, China will take on responsibility for building the infrastructure essential for the DRC's development in exchange for permission to exploit the country's immense reserves of copper and cobalt for the next three decades.[43] As part of the deal, the Chinese state will contribute millions of dollars in funding[44] as well as the experience and technology provided by two of its biggest state-owned companies and, no doubt, a good part of the workforce[45] needed to build and repair thousands

97

of kilometres of roads, streets, bridges, railways, airports and dams, as well as constructing dozens of hospitals, universities and low-cost housing.[46] Beijing will also provide money and expertise to modernize the mining infrastructure required to exploit the fabulous reserves of copper and cobalt in the Katanga province on the border with Zambia, in the heart of Africa's so-called 'Copperbelt'.

At first glance, there is no doubt that the 'contract of the century' represents a unique opportunity for the ex-Belgian colony to build up the all-important infrastructure that the usual benefactors have all systematically denied it for one reason or another. The DRC is currently financially unviable, as can be seen from the fact that even Chinese companies, who are famous throughout the business world for their ability to overcome every type of obstacle, usually end up abandoning the opportunities here for logistical reasons.[47] We were able to see this for ourselves over the course of our hair-raising journey between Muanda and Kinshasa, on the country's only overland route to the Atlantic Ocean. It was also evident when we had to fly from the capital to Lubumbashi, the mining epicentre of the country, because there are no roads joining the Congo's two most important cities and the only alternative is to travel by boat, a journey that would take several weeks.

Kinshasa's main thoroughfare, the Boulevard du 30 Juin – a name which commemorates the date in 1960 when the former Congo achieved its independence – represents one of the first impacts that the Chinese contract has had on the country. With its four lanes of traffic in both directions, this spacious, spotless asphalt road lined with ministries, shops, hotels and embassies looks like a copy of the Avenue of Heavenly Peace in Beijing which, in 1989, the tanks travelled down on their way to violently crush the student uprising in the area around Tiananmen Square. As well as roads, the African country will also develop its healthcare industry to combat its heart-breaking infant mortality rates and improve its energy network to alleviate the country's regular power cuts. As such, at a first glance the exchange of 'minerals for infrastructure' could not be more tempting for the Congolese government, as China is literally serving up an entire development plan on a silver platter: a remarkable opportunity for a 'great leap forward'.

Under these circumstances, Beijing is happy to present the contract as a model co-operation agreement to all and sundry, a shining example of the 'win-win policy' that it is currently employing throughout the developing world.[48] Of course, no other country apart from China would give the green light to such a gigantic pay-out with such significant long-term risks at a time of political and economic turbulence in the African country. However, a closer reading of the contract, its appendices and amendments – which fell into our hands despite not being available in the public domain – suggests that the intentions behind the document might be quite different from those put forward by Beijing. The main question raised by the deal is one of fairness. For a start, the value of the resources that China will obtain by exploiting the Congolese mines overwhelmingly exceeds its investment. While the state-owned Chinese companies will bring $6 billion to the table via the Chinese Exim Bank, the amount of profit that the cobalt and copper could yield for Sicomines[49] – the joint enterprise charged with managing the investment, implementing the construction of the new infrastructure, operating the mine and distributing the profits gained from exploiting the resources – will potentially reach between $40 and $120 billion – in other words, between six and twenty times the value of the investment.[50]

A mere glance at these figures makes it crystal clear that in the long term China is set to gain much more from the contract than the DRC, even after deducting the cost of modernizing and maintaining the mining operation, a process which will stretch to several billion dollars. Secondly, the contract establishes that during the credit repayment period – part of which must be returned at a market interest rate of 6.1 per cent – the Chinese businesses involved will be exempt from any kind of tax payments, including royalty payments.[51] Some sources, such as the activist Jean-Pierre Okenda, argue that this arrangement is illegal. Furthermore, once the credit has been paid off, the 'commercial exploitation' of the mine will generate a flow of taxes that will revert to the joint enterprise Sicomines rather than to the Congolese state. The contract sets out that these taxes will go towards the cost of constructing a second wave of infrastructure, but does not go into any detail about what this might involve. As a result, the DRC, which relies on mining as its main source of economic resources, will lose out on earnings of around $20 billion.[52] Moreover, if the mining continues at the expected rate, the country's copper and cobalt reserves will be completely exhausted in less than three decades.

Finally, the contract does not stipulate who is going to acquire the minerals, or how much they will be sold for. This means that the Chinese state will have de facto control over the entire commercial process, thanks to its majority stake in Sicomines. As the Chinese credit will be repaid with minerals, it is in Beijing's interest to fix the price as low as possible, so that the infrastructure that it builds in the country will yield the highest possible return in copper and cobalt. This represents a dangerous situation, to say the least, in which lender, seller and client are all the same legal entity: the Chinese state. Faced with the inherent weakness of the Congolese state and its institutions, how will it be possible to stop China from doing whatever takes its fancy in order to carry away the maximum amount of resources in return for the smallest possible investment? When the Congolese government is incapable even of ensuring peace throughout its own territory, how will it ensure that the Chinese companies spend as much as they promised to spend on cement, lorries and roads?

'China was aware that the contract violated current legislation in the country and so it demanded that the national assembly should approve a new law' in order to validate the contract, to 'legalize the illegal' as Okenda explains, referring to article 15.1 of the contract.[53] In order to defend its own interests and minimize the risk involved, Beijing used a contractual clause to force through what was quite clearly a violation of its policy of 'no interference in domestic affairs', another favourite motto of Chinese diplomacy. It was not the only violation of this kind. The contract also awarded Beijing the right to be a preferential creditor and required that the Congolese state should back up this simple commercial contract with sovereign guarantees[54] – a clause that was later amended after the intervention of international financial organizations, which argued that it would lead the African country into a high-risk debt situation.

'I don't think the contract will have any lasting effect on the country. The idea of building roads was conceived not for the development of the nation, but in order to win more votes,' said the Congolese MP Jerome Kamate when we interviewed him in Kinshasa. Kamate interprets the use and effects of the contract in electoral terms: the re-election of President Joseph Kabila.[55] The head of state promised voters a revolution in terms of infrastructure known as 'the Five Works' and is reliant on China to achieve this. This explains why the construction of infrastructure was divided into two phases, the first of which was due to finish just before the elections in November 2011, won by Kabila. 'It is thought that building new infrastructure will help create small businesses which in turn will help develop a new middle class, as has happened in China. However, 90 per cent of my voters are illiterate. Where is this middle class supposed to come from if there isn't even a basic level of education in this country?' Kamate asks. His analysis of the situation leaves no room for doubt: 'China will take away all the resources and the infrastructure will not be used.'

The first indications of this can already been seen in the country, particularly in the case of newly built hospitals and universities which remain unused because the DRC is unable to supply them with electricity, doctors or lecturers.[56] Meanwhile, China is meeting all its objectives. It is guaranteeing its long-term supply of copper in order to fuel its production of electric cables, fibre-optic materials and armaments, and its supply of cobalt, a highly valued raw material that is used predominantly in the production of batteries for mobile phones, laptops and cars.[57] However hard Beijing and Kinshasa try to label the contract as a 'co-operation agreement', its doubtful degree of fairness and far from favourable conditions clearly indicate that this is in fact a mining contract, pure and simple, without any trace of the benevolence described in China's official rhetoric. In other words, not only does the 'contract of the century' seem to be tailor-made for Chinese interests, it also highlights the very real gap that exists between China's official discourse and its real-life activity in the developing world.[58]

4

China's 'Black Gold' Offensive

'If the water is too clear, you will never catch a fish.'
Answer given by Li Ruogu, president of the Chinese
Exim Bank, in response to a question regarding
accusations of corruption by Chinese businesses.[1]

Mehri is nudging her husband silently with her knees. She is doing it as subtly as she can, but even so the tablecloth rises slightly with every onslaught. Her husband, Artem, does his best to ignore her and to carry on with his story as if nothing is happening, although he does begin to look a little confused. After a while she starts hitting him harder. At that point he breaks off in mid-sentence and for a moment everything is silent. Then we all exchange conspiratorial glances and smiles: between them and between us. Mehri, who is clearly nervous and upset, offers us more water. On her way to the kitchen she instinctively looks out of the window for the umpteenth time to make sure nobody is listening. Artem, good-natured and stocky, turns around to check on her. 'I'm sorry,' he explains. 'My wife doesn't like it when I talk about politics.'

We are in the outskirts of Ashgabat, the capital of Turkmenistan. In this country the size of Spain, nestled between Afghanistan, Iran and the Caspian Sea, the desert takes up 90 per cent of the territory and the sale of gas pays for the delusions of grandeur held by the only two presidents who have ruled the country as yet in its short history. Our voyage through the 'Chinese world' and China's demand for hydrocarbons have brought us to this most surreal of all the former Soviet republics, a state which might well be classified as the most extravagant, paranoid and brutal dictatorship on the planet if there was not such a long list of competitors.

The Jepbarovs (not their real name) live in a modest apartment with a spacious living room dominated by a striking carpet, a fine example of Turkmen craftsmanship.[2] Artem lovingly shows us a treasure trove of antiques and books from the Soviet era which are hidden away in one of the bedrooms: cigarette cases decorated with Lenin's face, glass statuettes of Stalin and drawings illustrating the roles and traditions of the former Soviet Union, which Artem refers to with a certain degree of nostalgia. 'Our lives have got worse since independence. We used to have better lives before. Now we're living in a dictatorship,' he argues, temporarily freed from the censorship imposed on him by the violent nudges of his wife.

While the life of the Jepbarovs is not exactly squalid, it is certainly not easy whichever way you look at it. Artem can barely keep his family going on his earnings from the market, where he sells souvenirs based on the Soviet era and the mandate of the country's first head of state, the narcissistic Saparmurat Niyazov, also known as Turkmenbashi, or 'father of the Turkmen people'. Meanwhile, Mehri's name is just one more on the country's long list of the unemployed which, according to unofficial sources (the official ones are either unreliable or non-existent), includes around 60 per cent of the population.[3] If the paternalistic state did not massively subsidize electricity, water and gas prices, rents and a monthly allowance of 120 litres of petrol, existence would be simply impossible for this family – as it would be for the rest of the country's 5 million inhabitants. 'I barely make 300 dollars a month,' Artem complains. 'How am I supposed to feed four people on that?' This is how 'new communism' works in Turkmenistan: the state supplies the basic needs of the people and the people do what they're told. Anyone who doesn't conform suffers the consequences.

However, visitors to Ashgabat are unlikely to get any sense of this hardship at a first glance. Based in a valley surrounded on all sides by a sandy and mountainous landscape, the city has the look of an oasis in the middle of a desert. It is full of imposing official buildings made of white marble, imported especially from Italy on the president's orders, and spacious boulevards with up to twelve lanes, such as the one leading to the residence of the head of state. The city is also dotted with splashes of gold: domes, gates, fountains and, above all, murals, busts and statues of Turkmenbashi. Everywhere you look there is evidence of abundance, majesty and an enormous cult of personality. However, the splendour of the city, which is lit up by thousands of spotlights every evening, is nothing but a façade hiding the country's sad reality. The Turkmen people live in clusters of houses built in the style of the Soviet era and spend their time in indoor courtyards where children play football on miserable pitches, men repair their battered old Lada cars, and women gather in groups to discuss the hardships of daily life. This city may look like a museum but it has no glamour at all for Ashgabat's 650,000 inhabitants.

Instead, the long shadow of the regime stretches into every aspect of life, from microphones hidden in hotels – a practice inherited from the Soviet era that we were warned about by certain diplomats – to censorship and control of the media. Barely 10 per cent of the population has internet access, making it very difficult to get information from the outside world. Repression is a visible, everyday occurrence: with batons in hands and whistles at their lips, policemen can be seen everywhere on the streets of Ashgabat. They jealously watch over every inch of the city, fully alert despite the blistering 50 degrees heat of the summer. Everything is forbidden here, from taking photographs to ballet shows. As for foreigners, the openly xenophobic regime has gone so far as to ban the hundred or so Westerners living in the capital from falling in love with any of the locals.

'After 1992, they threw me out of the university. I was a lecturer there. I love the Humanities. But they fired me, along with many of my colleagues, because we're not from the *tekke* tribe. That's the tribe that the president comes from, as well as most of the authorities', Artem explains, bitterly, referring to the blatant discrimination that the government actively promotes. 'Everything here functions on the basis of corruption. A place to study at the public university, which is supposedly free, actually costs between 20,000 and 80,000 US dollars in bribes. And as if that weren't enough, the lecturers are terrible. You have to pay to do any kind of job. Everything is completely corrupt. How am I supposed to get enough money to send my children to university if I only earn 300 dollars a month?'[4]

The country's real beneficiaries are the bureaucrats and the government elites, who run the state as if it were their own feudal kingdom.

They control 85 per cent of the economy through state-owned companies and, with the president at the helm, refuse to lift a finger unless
there is some kind of bribe or commission involved. 'In order to make
an appointment with the president – who approves and controls
everything in this country – you have to pay out a minimum of
20,000 dollars,' explains one expert in the country. This amount
apparently increased by between '10 and 15 per cent' after Gurbanguly Berdymukhammedov succeeded Turkmenbashi as the head of
state following a farcical election in 2007.[5] It is therefore hardly surprising that Turkmenistan is ranked 177 out of 183 in the 2011 Corruption
Perceptions Index produced each year by Transparency International.

CHINA LANDS IN TURKMENISTAN

We are busy haggling over the price of a bottle of local cognac with a
photo of Turkmenbashi on the label, when all of a sudden a horde of
television cameras and bodyguards comes bursting into Ashgabat's
Russian Bazaar. The cameramen and photographers – both Chinese
and locals – are all looking expectantly at He Guoqiang, at that time
one of the nine members of the Politburo Standing Committee of the
Communist Party of China,[6] who has kindly volunteered to take part
in this performance. 'What enormous watermelons! They are fabulous!' he exclaims to an overwhelmed fruit seller, who laughs nervously,
clearly not sure what to say. His translator and assistant quickly set
up another shot in which He, considered one of the most important
men in China because of his position on the body that effectively pulls
the strings in the country, puts on a traditional Turkmen hat while a
trader hands him a basket of fruit. Everyone is smiling, hugging and
nodding happily, all of which is captured in minute detail by the
cameras.

By pure coincidence, we happen to have arrived in this country
with its golden statues and ridiculous personality cult at the same
time as a high-ranking Chinese official. His presence in Ashgabat,
however, is certainly no accident. This chemical engineer has not come
to Turkmenistan in order to learn a local recipe for fertilizer, or even
to give advice on how to combat corruption, a role that he has had in

China ever since he was made head of the Central Commission for Discipline Inspection in 2007. Instead, his visit has everything to do with the great wealth hidden in the very heart of Turkmenistan: hydrocarbons.[7] This is a treasure of such strategic importance for China that Beijing has jumped with both feet into this quagmire of bribery and hereditary succession, this backyard of Russia where at times it is impossible to tell the difference between reality and fiction.[8] The proof of China's commitment to this project can be seen in the form of a pipeline over 7,000 kilometres long, built and financed by China in order to connect Turkmenistan's gas deposits with the kitchens of Canton and Shanghai.

However, in order to follow the lead of this giant pipeline there is one more step we need to take. It is a step that will carry us as far as the edge of the Karakum desert, forbidden territory that is off the official radar. This means breaking the strict Turkmenistan laws by escaping from our persistent guide and flying to the north-east of the country, on the border with Uzbekistan.[9]

'CHINA IS HERE TO STAY'

The Turkmenistan Airlines aeroplane rises over Ashgabat just as the sun is beginning to set. The white buildings of the capital city are bathed in orange light, as is the sandy expanse of the Karakum desert which we fly over for most of the fifty-minute journey. The cabin, complete with a photograph of President Berdymukhammedov, is brimming with passengers carrying boxes and suitcases. The price of plane tickets to Turkmenabat, the country's second city and the garden of the nation, is fairly bizarre; in accordance with the regime's policy of subsidizing public services, the journey costs just $13 each way.

When we arrive at Turkmenabat airport, Lei Li is waiting for us at the exit as planned. We have never met each other before, but he recognizes us straightaway, and greets us with an outstretched hand and a smile.[10] Our visit to the basecamp of the state-owned hydrocarbons company China National Petroleum Corporation (CNPC) is clearly a joyful occasion for this Chinese employee. After all, for just a few hours it will break the routine that has dominated his life for the whole three years he has spent in this remote and lonely corner of Central Asia. One by one, we climb into the shiny new Toyota Land Cruiser V8 with its diplomatic licence plates. The Turkmen driver sets the GPS to take us straight along the M37 towards Farab, the closest town to the CNPC basecamp, a facility made up of four settlements which is aimed at exploiting the gas reserves stored in the country's subsoil.

Lei is joined by a Chinese colleague who actually works in Turkmenabat but who has to return to the company's headquarters at the end of each day, along with the rest of his colleagues: Turkmen authorities have banned Chinese men from spending the night in the town to stop them from having sexual relations with local women. According to one local resident we spoke to, this rule was enforced after some local women ended up getting pregnant by Chinese workers. 'There's a nine o'clock curfew now. Nobody is allowed to leave the camp after that time,' the local explained. It seems that the regime's blatant racism and hostility towards foreigners stretches to the Chinese too, despite their privileged access to the country's natural gas sector.[11]

After crossing the Amu Daria river, we eventually come to a military control post that is co-ordinating the flow of vehicles and people and which cannot be crossed without a special permit. There is no way that we can cross this internal border with our tourist visas – in fact, our very presence in the area is technically illegal. However, Lei does not seem particularly bothered by this fact. 'They're friends. They're coming with us,' he blurts in Russian at the young soldier who is examining our passports with suspicion. After an uncomfortable silence, the soldier lets us through. After travelling for around 50 kilometres along a desert road dotted with herds of sheep and propaganda posters, we finally arrive at the CNPC's biggest settlement in Central Asia.

The precinct is made up of four camps – two of them close to the gas treatment plant and another two based around 20 kilometres away – which are home to roughly a thousand people, most of them Chinese. 'There were around 4,500 Chinese people here when we first built the complex and the gas pipeline,' Lei comments, after kindly putting us up in one of the rooms in the precinct. A stroll along the road that unites the different camps makes it clear that there are two specific risks to human life here: the heat (almost 60 degrees during the day, over 40 degrees at night) and the desert snakes and scorpions. Wide fluorescent lines are painted on the sand on either side of the road. 'Snake poison,' Lei explains. 'Four or five people were bitten over the last year. There are two doctors in the camp who are experts in these cases.'

Despite being in the middle of nowhere, the living conditions are exceptional: six buildings with just one floor each contain rooms with air conditioning, a satellite internet connection, plasma TVs, private bathrooms with hot water and big, comfortable beds. Elsewhere in the precinct, basketball courts and ping-pong tables give the engineers, geologists and administrators a chance to keep fit and kill time, which can seem never-ending, while Sichuanese chefs prepare typical dishes from the region in the precinct's kitchens. 'We've built a greenhouse so we can grow all kinds of Chinese vegetables ... even Sichuanese chillies!' Lei tells us, proudly.

These home comforts are somewhat surprising. They are far and away the best conditions that we would see throughout the course of our journey, and they seem to create a sense of well-being and camaraderie among the workers. At sundown, Turkmen and Chinese colleagues get together to compete in ping-pong tournaments or go walking or jogging along the roads that unite the various camps. The majority of local workers, who arrive at 6.30 in the morning on Chinese King Long buses and wear orange overalls bearing the CNPC logo, seem to be happy. When we ask them about it, they give us the thumbs up and say they are pleased with how things are. They hide their smiles behind the desert scarfs that cover their faces in the style of Palestinian guerrillas, protecting them from the salt that has been left hanging for ever in the air as a result of the slow death of the Aral Sea, causing asthma and bronchitis.

However, apparently things have not always gone so smoothly. One Chinese worker tells us about an incident in September 2009 when local employees helping to build the camp's facilities alongside Chinese workers rose up in arms against the company as a result of deductions made to their salaries and certain contractual conditions. The locals attacked the Chinese employees, injuring thirty-six of them, and vandalized cars, computers, tables and other furniture until the police intervened to calm things down. The precinct even had to be closed for two days. Nowadays the rules are stricter: employees are forbidden to drink alcohol, bring women into the camp or even to wear clothes other than the company's uniform during working hours. Keeping the peace is essential in a place of such strategic importance to China's interests in the region.

Anatoly, a young local geologist, does however seem satisfied with the conditions offered by the company. 'I earn more than my father and mother put together,' he declares proudly, before telling us that he is currently applying for a similar job with a German company operating in the Caspian Sea. 'I don't want to spend thirty years of my life here,' he argues, in reference to the timeframe for Turkmenistan's supply of gas to China, according to the contract between the two countries. However, many people, Anatoly among them, believe that 'China is here to stay'. There is no shortage of strategic reasons why this might be true: it is estimated that Turkmenistan possesses the fourth largest natural gas reserves in the world, and China's gas consumption is likely to triple over the next two decades.[12]

Night falls heavily over the precinct, swallowing everything in its path. All that is left alive in the darkness are the flames which rise over the gas treatment plant. 'We're measuring how much gas we can extract per day to send to China,' Anatoly explains. The aim is to reach 65 billion cubic metres each year – a little less than half of China's current gas consumption – for the next five years.[13] In order to make this happen, China has had to bring two loans to the table with a total value of $8.1 billion via the China Development Bank (CDB).[14] These loans were lent under favourable conditions and were given directly to the local state-owned company Turkmengaz.

It is no small matter that the CDB is acting as the lender here. Along with the Exim Bank, the CDB is one of the two Chinese banks that act in response to China's geostrategic interests abroad rather than for strictly commercial reasons. These designated 'policy banks' carry out the financial side of China's diplomatic strategy, granting billion-dollar loans with the sole aim of securing the country's supply of natural resources, giving support to Chinese SOEs in their ventures abroad, and tightening political relations with countries of strategic interest to

China.[15] These agreements, carried out using the formula 'your resources for my loans and/or infrastructure', are common between China and its partner countries, who are always rich in natural resources. Few nations in the so-called 'developing world' can resist being seduced by China's vast supplies of quick and easy money. The temptation to secure millions of dollars in loans – often at preferential rates – in return for providing China with long-term acquiescence to exploit their natural resources is generally far too strong. Beijing has successfully understood the needs of its foreign business partners and therefore offers them an irresistible menu.

This process highlights one of the peculiarities – and strengths – of China's international offensive for natural resources: the power of 'China Inc.' In other words, China's effective use of all the cogs in the state's machinery in order to secure juicy contracts and strategic investments in countries that are in dire need of funding. The financial (banks), economic (state-owned companies) and political institutions, the last of which has the final say, work together as one body to achieve the country's national objectives. The leitmotif is always the same: obtaining or guaranteeing China's long-term supply of natural resources, ousting the competition, and gaining in terms of political influence and power.

The financial viability and environmental effects of the projects financed by Chinese policy banks and carried out, in the vast majority of cases, by Chinese state-owned companies are often pushed to the side-lines. That does not mean, however, that Chinese banks and the companies involved in these projects do not try to make their overseas investments commercially viable, particularly when these are not state priorities. Even if they do require the state's approval, Chinese corporations are trying to become more independent from the political powers in terms of the day- to-day running of their business, but when push comes to shove it is the Communist Party that provides the score for the orchestra (banks, corporations, diplomats) in order to play out their symphony.[16]

Of course, resorting to the use of a triumvirate – made up in the case of Turkmenistan by the CNPC, the CDB and the diplomatic community – in order to achieve strategic objectives is not something unique to China. Other countries also use their development banks in order to further their diplomatic objectives or to benefit their companies; for example, by granting a loan on the condition that the receiving country must buy a specific quantity of local equipment or contract services from the lending country. However, this can hardly be compared to China's proposals or methods. In terms of scale, for example, China currently possesses the largest currency reserves in the world,[17] providing the country with a devastating amount of financial muscle. It is also important not to underestimate the amount of leeway provided by the lack of any real counterbalance (from the press, civil society or opposition parties) in the Chinese single-party system, which means that China is free to carry out its projects exactly as it pleases.

THE OBLIGATORY PATH OF CORRUPTION

'The governments of Central Asian countries such as Turkmenistan and Kazakhstan see Chinese people and businesses as a source of money that is willing to pay bribes and participate in systems of corruption. That's what you have to go through if you want to do business in this country. The bribes are usually small amounts, a little bigger from time to time. For Chinese people, this is nothing unusual because of our tradition. We consider it easier to deal with things in that way rather than causing bigger problems. You just pay up and then the problem goes away.' The words of a high-ranking Chinese businessman in Turkmenistan, whose name, role and other details are omitted here for obvious reasons, perfectly summarize the 'flexibility' demonstrated by Chinese corporations when it comes to walking the line of the law. When we ask him how CNPC manages to square these bribes within its budgets and balance sheets, our contact answers with complete honesty: 'We plan these payments into our budgets. We know about it here in Ashgabat and they know about it in Beijing. They know that's how things work here, and so we include the bribes in our balance sheets. We don't have any other choice.'

Suddenly one of his colleagues walks into the office, interrupting our conversation. Our source politely makes his apologies, leaves the room and returns around five minutes later. 'An example of what I was talking about has just happened at the airport. We have a problem with the Turkmen immigration department. They don't want to allow some of our employees into the country. Fortunately I have a lot of friends there, thanks to *guanxi* and the network of relationships I've built up here. It's essential to build solid personal relationships in order to do business here.' Of course, China is not the only country prepared to follow the codes of corruption and bribery in order to further their interests in Turkmenistan. Allegedly Russian, German and Turkish businesses operating in the hydrocarbon, automotive and construction industries act in a similar way and consequently have to increase their project budgets by between 20 and 30 per cent to include the payment of 'commissions'. Investors also have to do a ridiculous amount of grovelling to the nation's leader, for example by commissioning foreign translations of the *Ruhnama*, a work written by President Niyazov which, like Mao's 'Little Red Book', aims to provide guidance on how to behave as well as an official history of the nation.[18]

A prime example is seen in the case of the French company Bouygues, the world's second biggest construction company and a key player in Turkmenistan's property industry. Between 1994 and 2010, the company managed to secure over fifty construction projects to the value of 2 billion euros thanks to its close ties with the country's authorities. Among other things, these ties were built by translating the *Ruhnama* into French and by the relationship developed over the years between Niyazov and the chairman and CEO of the French company, Martin Bouygues.[19] When we tried to arrange a meeting with the staff of the French embassy in Ashgabat, they rejected our proposal in order to steer clear of any compromising questions about the activities of the business group whose leader is a close friend of former President Nicolas Sarkozy.

Like the rest of the corporations operating in the country, CNPC is not prepared to 'pass up the many opportunities offered by Turkmenistan', despite the country's widespread corruption and systematic violation of human rights, as our contact in the Chinese company explained. CNPC has therefore become extremely involved in what the company calls the 'silk road of the energy industry', getting hold of as many gas assets as possible in the Central Asian country. This carefully calculated strategy, which China has also undertaken elsewhere in the region, has seriously jeopardized Russia's dominance in the area, a position of influence inherited from the Soviet era.

Beijing made its strategic entrance into the country of golden statues at a time when sales of gas from Turkmenistan to Russia had dropped by 90 per cent, significantly affecting the Turkmen economy. Russia's official reason for drastically reducing its acquisition of Turkmen gas was an explosion in a pipeline in April 2009. However, in reality Russia's actions were most probably motivated by the fall in the price of gas after the 2008 financial crisis. As Russia channels and resells gas from Turkmenistan to the West through its own infrastructure, it appears likely that the country deliberately caused a reduction in its gas supply by orchestrating the incident. This behaviour highlights Moscow's former role as the caretaker of Turkmen gas, as Russia's pipelines were the only route for Turkmen gas to reach other markets before China's arrival in the country.[20] The Russian–Turkmen crisis lasted until Russia resumed exporting Turkmen gas in 2010, by which time Ashgabat had lost $1 billion in income every month.[21]

However, this will not happen again now that China has offered the country an alternative. The pipeline built by CNPC means that Turkmenistan is no longer dependent on Russia. It has also significantly boosted Beijing's influence not only on the Turkmen regime, but also in Uzbekistan and Kazakhstan, countries on the route of the pipeline which are also planning to supply gas to China in the future. This is just one more step in China's strategy to become lord and master of the entire region, as we saw in Chapter 2. Thanks to its sales of gas to China, Turkmenistan – whose gas exports make up 80 per cent of its total exports – has found a new source of income to allow the Turkish company Polimeks to continue building gold statues to the glory of the president. Meanwhile, corruption and tyranny continue to mar the daily lives of the Turkmen people.

A HELPING HAND FOR THE
ISLAMIC REPUBLICS

While China's dramatic entrance into Central Asia's energy sector does represent a serious setback for Russia's hegemony in the region, it is not the scene of the world's biggest geopolitical changes resulting from the country's urgent energy needs. The greatest impact has in fact taken place in the epicentre of the world's oil supplies, the Middle East, and its offshoot in north-east Africa. Despite the risks this may cause to its relationship with the West, China has found two oil-rich allies in the region who are both well-known enemies of Washington and Brussels: the Islamic republics of Sudan and Iran.

On a trip down Khartoum's Nile Avenue, the city's main thoroughfare and home to a significant part of Sudan's economic and political institutions, it is easy to see the Chinese presence in what was the biggest country in Africa until July 2011, when it was divided into two nations.[22] The street is full of buildings constructed using Chinese and local labour, giving a new look to the northern capital. Meanwhile, the surrounding areas are bursting with Chinese-run shops selling consumer goods and groceries, travel agencies aimed at the growing Chinese market, and clinics offering acupuncture and traditional Chinese medicine with doctors hailing from the provinces of Hubei and Henan. One particular corporation has changed the country's economic map: CNPC.[23] 'It's the most powerful company in Sudan', we were told time and time again by the local civil servants, experts, activists and journalists who we met for cups of tea and conversation. This is a reference to the million-dollar investments that have greatly boosted the local economy in return for oil, thereby filling the coffers of the state controlled by the dictator Omar al-Bashir.

China made its move into Sudan's oil sector in the 1990s, after Washington accused al-Bashir's regime of promoting and financing international terrorism. Before becoming the number one enemy of the West, Osama bin Laden had free rein in Sudan, a country that became radicalized in political and religious terms (including introducing Islamic *Sharia* law across the whole territory) after the coup d'état supported by Brigadier al-Bashir in 1989. That was when

American companies such as Chevron chose to pull out of Sudan, just before the United Nations and the United States imposed parallel sanctions on the country. The regime was forced into a corner and started desperately looking for investments for its oil industry, which is now the main source of state financing. As has happened in so many other places, China came to the rescue. 'Sudan's main problem in the 1990s was capital investment. China and other partners such as Malaysia came here with their investments and today they are considered partners,' explains Salah Elding Ali Mohammed, a government adviser on energy affairs, when we meet him in his office near the Ministry of Oil. 'We couldn't have investments from Western companies because of the embargo.'

Chinese investments arrived in the country just when the West was attempting to isolate Sudan, strangling the economy by withdrawing investment as it did with the apartheid South Africa of the 1980s. While Europe and the United States were pulling out of Sudan to put pressure on a regime which, like neighbouring Libya, was encouraging Islamic fundamentalism and jihad, China was busy taking advantage of the opportunities emerging from this vacuum. For Beijing, which became a net importer of crude oil in 1993, Sudan represented an ideal opportunity to boost its energy security by entering decisively into the Sudanese oil sector under exceptional conditions: CNPC, Sinopec and other Chinese oil companies managed to obtain shares in around 40 per cent of the country's oil assets, despite their obsolete technology and limited experience in the international crude oil industry.[24] According to Ali Mohammed, China was not the best option; it was the only one. 'China is the only choice for Sudan. The Western companies didn't want to co-operate with us for political reasons,' he explains.

Since then, China has become 'the only player or the dominant player' in Sudanese oil wells, according to a Western diplomat who we interviewed in Khartoum. Furthermore, China also played an exceptional role in the construction of two new infrastructure projects of undeniable political and economic importance: an oil refinery close to the capital and the only oil pipeline that transports crude oil from the south of the country as far as Port Sudan at the edge of the Red Sea.

Beijing has played the part of loyal squire to al-Bashir's regime for many years as a result of its interests in the Sudanese desert. In fact, this is even true in issues that go beyond the energy sector. Firstly, China's investment and technology have provided highly significant economic support to the regime, which took advantage of the 'wind from the east' to start exporting crude oil for the first time at the end of the 1990s.[25] Since the end of the last century, the vast income provided by oil sales has provided a huge boost to the Sudanese economy, which was previously reliant on agriculture.[26] However, Chinese capital did not just help Sudan to escape the bankruptcy that the Western embargo threatened to cause. It also propped up al-Bashir's regime in other ways, helping the country to rearm itself thanks to the arsenal of weapons supplied largely by the state-owned China North Industries Corporation (NORINCO). These weapons helped the dictator to successfully carry out several incursions into the south of the country during the civil war that ravaged Sudan until 2005. Most significantly of all, the weapons allowed the regime's followers to commit the first act of genocide of the twenty-first century, in Darfur.[27] Chinese money indirectly stained Sudanese oil red with the blood of the people killed in this unequal war in the west of the country. China's vote at the Security Council of the United Nations in favour of imposing an embargo on arms sales to the Islamic country didn't count for much. This double game, in which Beijing acts as a supposedly responsible power on the one hand and as a loyal ally of al-Bashir on the other, has allowed Chinese military trucks, fighter aircraft and semi-automatic weapons to fall into the hands of China's Sudanese associates. According to several reports by the United Nations, these weapons have contributed to the deaths of at least 300,000 people.[28]

As if that were not enough, those same weapons were used by groups sympathetic to the Sudanese regime when fighting against the peacekeeping troops of the African Union and the United Nations, which paradoxically included soldiers sent by Beijing.[29] 'China is very much implicated in the human suffering in Darfur. China is one of the biggest powers now emerging in the international arena and a member of the UN Security Council, which means they have responsibilities towards peace and the security of individuals,' argued the Darfur-born human rights lawyer Salih Mahmoud Osman, winner of the 2007 Sakharov prize for his activism during the conflict, when we met him in his modest office in Khartoum.

Against this background, it makes perfect sense that Chinese diplomats should have felt some misgivings about the independence of South Sudan, the world's newest state. China has been a staunch ally of President al-Bashir and the northern Arab government and, with its eyes fixed on its objectives, Beijing wanted anything but a change in the status quo. China feared that the secession would lead to millions of dollars of investment going down the drain, as 80 per cent of the oil reserves are in the South, on a border that is still in dispute and in a territory threatened by the possibility of future conflicts.

However, as 90 per cent of South Sudan's budget depends on sales of crude oil, the country is not in any position to put the brakes on production. What is more, it depends on the North to export its oil produce, as the oil has to travel through northern territory to get to the sea. 'There's a feeling on both sides that the oil must be exploited and they have to co-operate,' explains Harry Verhoeven, an expert in Sudan at Oxford University. China has already set its chameleon-like diplomacy in motion to start building relationships with the government of Juba, the capital of South Sudan, in order to get the biggest possible return on its investment. Sudan still contains fifteen years' worth of oil, and China – whose responsibility as an international power has been thrown into serious doubt over Sudan – does not plan to leave the party until the music stops playing.

CHINA COURTS THE OIL OF THE AYATOLLAHS

Despite the sweltering heat and the dense cloud of pollution, Tehran's exasperating traffic jams do at least offer an interesting visual spectacle. It's dusk and there is no room to breathe on the so-called Ashrafi Esfahani 'high speed road' that links the north and south of the Iranian capital. Cars are charging across each other on every side, making life very difficult for our imperturbable taxi driver in his clapped-out Peykan car. Propaganda posters are dotted along the side of the road, along with hand-painted murals immortalizing the heroes of the 1979 Islamic Revolution, with the Republic's founder Ruhollah Khomeini as the main protagonist. There are also plenty of witticisms and ingenious drawings, similar to those seen all over the Malecon Boulevard in Havana, alluding to the imperialist United States and its Israeli 'henchman'. 'Down with the USA', blurts one classic. Another more evocative image shows the American flag hanging upside down, with the original stars and red stripes replaced by bombs and spurts of blood.

These words and images offer a picturesque summary of the state of mutual antagonism that has existed between the Islamic Republic and the United States throughout three long decades, after diplomatic ties went up in smoke as a result of the 'Embassy Hostage Crisis'. China has benefited from the fact that this official enmity has not only spread to other Western countries but has also intensified since President Mahmoud Ahmadinejad rose to power in 2005, embarking on a nuclear adventure that has led to direct confrontations with the international community. Under these circumstances, there is no doubt that China's role is fundamental. In the context of an embargo that has left Iran severely isolated, the constant flirting between China's diplomats and the ayatollahs has allowed Beijing to become a key economic player in a country that boasts the world's fourth largest proven oil reserves (after Saudi Arabia, Venezuela and Canada) and the second largest reserves of natural gas (after Russia).[30]

'Five years ago there were no Chinese people here,' explained an executive at one of the biggest Western oil companies in Iran, demonstrating how quickly Chinese influence has progressed in the country. The figures speak for themselves: while the flow of trade between the two countries was insignificant just a decade ago, China is now Iran's biggest trade partner, generating an annual trade volume of around $36 billion – including both the official trade and that which enters the country via Dubai. The tightening of sanctions against Tehran has led to a lack of investment in the natural resources sector which, as in the case of Sudan, has left the door wide open for China. Under pressure from the United States, the oil companies ENI, Total, Repsol, Shell, BP and others have had to put the brakes on their business in Iran to avoid jeopardizing their position in the American market. 'The Americans say: it's either the Iranians or us. And so we're all either on stand-by here or we've left the country[31] out of fear of compromising our commercial interests in the United States,' our source explains.[32]

An example of the dilemma faced by the Western oil companies is seen in the case of the Spanish company Repsol, which reacted to United States pressure by gradually pulling out of Iran in order to safeguard its interests in the Gulf of Mexico. According to what we heard on the Tehran grapevine, exiting the country must have cost the company no less than 300 million euros. Under these circumstances, it is not surprising that Chinese state-owned oil companies have been able to make a triumphant entry into the sector, despite the fact that their technology is far from a match for its Western competitors.[33] 'Yes, the Chinese have become a major player in Iran, but only because they arrived in an empty playing field,' the executive points out. 'The sanctions represent a *sine qua non* condition for China's presence in Iran. If there were no sanctions, Western technology would have taken over the sector,' adds a French expert in Iranian affairs, Clément Therme. As such, China makes up for what it lacks in technology with two valuable wild cards: political connections and financial clout.

'The alternative would be Russia as they have the technology, but they don't have the capital,' concludes John Garver, a professor of international relations at the Georgia Institute of Technology and adviser to the United States government. Mehdi Fakheri, vice-president of the Iran Chamber of Commerce, Industry and Mines, argued along the same lines when we met him in Tehran: 'There aren't many options in terms of gaining access to technology and ready money. The Chinese cannot easily be replaced.' Protected by the state and the unlimited resources of the Chinese public banks, the oil companies CNPC, Sinopec and China National Offshore Oil Corporation (CNOOC) have partially filled the void left by Western companies with investments that could amount to $40 billion, according to official Iranian sources.[34] In addition, China became the world's largest buyer of Iranian oil in mid-2012, when the exports of Iranian crude oil collapsed as a consequence of the new wave of sanctions passed by the United States and the EU – separate from the UN's sanctions and rejected by Beijing – to block the international trade of Iranian hydrocarbons.[35] This is a great relief for the ayatollahs' regime which – given that hydrocarbon exports make up 27 per cent of Iran's GDP – has no choice but to pin its hopes on China. The total investment has allowed Iran to keep up its production of crude oil and to continue as one of

China's biggest oil suppliers.[36] This is all despite the fact that – as China itself has recognized – Tehran's income from sales of natural resources could be 'potentially linked' to Iran's nuclear programme.[37]

As China is conquering Iran as quickly as Western companies are abandoning the country, the situation raises an infuriating question for the European oil companies: with the international embargo in full swing, how have Chinese oil companies managed to get hold of the safe-conducts that give them preferential entry into the energy sector of a top oil producer in the world? In other words, why do Sinopec, PetroChina and CNOOC have free and easy access to Iranian oil fields while Shell, Total, ENI and Repsol are forced to pack their bags? The answer, of course, lies in the influence of the all-powerful Chinese state, even when it comes to facing up to Washington. The Chinese regime has not hesitated to use its political power to protect its businesses from American initiatives to isolate Iran, demonstrating the extent of its growing international influence. Proof can be seen in a revealing diplomatic cable sent by the United States embassy in Beijing on 26 March 2008. The cable refers to a warning made by a high-ranking Chinese government employee to an American diplomat in reference to any attempt Washington might make to impose sanctions on Sinopec for its operations in Iran: 'It is a very serious issue and I can't imagine' the consequences that it could have for bilateral relations, he said.[38]

This cable confirms that Beijing has marked out the boundaries very clearly for Washington: under no circumstances may the sanctions affect China's large oil companies. In the light of these events, Washington seems to have given in to pressure to avoid these 'unimaginable' reprisals, allowing China privileges that would lead to sanctions for any Western company. The fact that the Chinese government has put its foot down on this subject is, of course, closely linked to the great importance that Beijing gives to its energy security. However, in practice these events have paradoxically led Sinopec and the CNPC to replace Western corporations in supplying Iran with 30 per cent of its petrol consumption, which technically isn't related to Beijing's energy security. The Islamic Republic's capacity to refine oil has been reduced by the United States' sanctions and so the country needs to buy petrol from foreign suppliers.[39] Therefore, China is ready for business.

'The number of Chinese companies sanctioned by the United States has fallen since 2002. At the beginning of the century, fifteen or sixteen Chinese companies were sanctioned each year. Now it's barely three or four per year, and none of the big Chinese oil companies are included in that number,' John Garver tells us, explaining Beijing's influence in the sector. 'China has a greater capacity to resist the pressure of the United States than any other country,' Clément Therme concludes. All this no doubt has something to do with the fact that, as Secretary of State Hillary Clinton herself admitted, it is difficult to stand up to the world's banker.[40] What will be the consequences of all this? An executive of a European oil company in Tehran ventured a guess at what the future might hold if the current situation continues: 'In five years' time, the whole energy sector will be in the hands of the Chinese.'

TWO-HEADED CHINA TAKES ON ANGOLA

With an unmistakable touch of alchemy, a gentle breeze mixes with the smell of lobster, spiced chicken and sautéed broccoli on the terrace of the Shanghai Baia restaurant, complete with fabulous views over Luanda and the Atlantic Ocean. It is summer 2010. A noisy group of Chinese businessmen are wolfing down their food like there's no tomorrow, while the glimmer of lights reflected from skyscrapers plays across their faces – skyscrapers whose apartments are squabbled over by expat oil-sector employees for rents of no less than $10,000 per month. The businessmen keep coming out with expressions such as *'duo shao qian?'* ('how much?'), including one man in particular who asks the question with his mouth full, sending little bits of food flying out across the table. Just a few metres away, luxury yachts are moored outside the *Ilha de Luanda* Nautical Club, allowing business magnates based in the second most expensive city in the world to set sail for the open sea and escape the chaos of the Angolan capital.[41]

It is impossible to walk through Luanda's city centre without wondering how things got like this so quickly. Back in 2002, Angola was just coming to the end of Africa's longest civil war: twenty-seven years of conflict which not only caused irreparable social and economic damage to this country of 18 million inhabitants, but also swept away a significant part of the infrastructure built by the Portuguese before the country's independence in 1975. For example, an estimated 300 bridges were destroyed throughout the country as a result of the conflict. Less than a decade later, hordes of cement lorries have brought the city's main roads to a complete standstill, unable to cope with the demand for the several hundred road works which are being carried out all over the country. Over fifty Chinese state-owned companies and 400 private Chinese companies are frantically carrying out construction projects, building stadiums, repairing roads, constructing new housing and sprucing up ministries. The money needed to finance all this comes from the country's subsoil: sales of crude oil from Africa's second largest oil producer generate $52 billion each year.[42] A large chunk of these earnings comes from the sale of crude oil to China, as Angola is now its second biggest oil supplier after Saudi Arabia.

The World Bank has come up with the term 'the Angola model' to describe this revolution, which aims at giving structure to the country with a brand new network of roads, railways and universities. This is part of a direct exchange of oil for infrastructure that has been taking place since the 1980s and which is used by several other countries as well as China. It is a model which Angola's autocratic government led by President Jose Eduardo dos Santos[43] has been strongly promoting since 2004, coinciding with China's arrival in the country. The inter-governmental agreements between Luanda and Beijing function on the basis of a simple pact: Chinese construction companies carry out projects across the country and receive payment directly from the Chinese Exim Bank (representing a transaction between Chinese entities), while Angola uses its state-owned energy company Sonangol and its subsidiaries to supply China with the stipulated quantity of oil needed to pay off the Chinese loan.

In this way, countries such as Angola which urgently need to rebuild their basic infrastructure but do not have access to a qualified workforce, let alone the necessary funding, can obtain quick results and, in the case of working with China, highly favourable financing. This model also stops corrupt authorities from gobbling up the loan money, preventing millions of dollars destined for public projects ending up in bank accounts in Switzerland or the Cayman Islands. This is achieved by the fact that the government never actually receives the money, which is transferred directly from the bank to the service provider.[44]

Despite the apparent benefits of this model, China's arrival in Angola is the result of Beijing's opportunism, as we have seen in the other cases described in this chapter. After the civil war, dos Santos's administration (which came to power in 1979) needed financing in order to move forward with its government plan. However, the traditional lenders – the so-called Paris Club – and international institutions such as the International Monetary Fund required Luanda to carry out reforms to its financial, political and economic sectors. With the aim of enabling one of the world's most corrupt countries to become economically solvent, these organizations also insisted that Angola should pay off some of its previous loans before they would provide it with debt relief for its accumulated unpaid debts.

This tug of war continued until March 2004, when China arrived on the scene to wreck the plans of the wealthy countries. The Exim Bank simply lent Luanda a fresh $2 billion and the African country managed to escape its debts scot-free.[45] China offered some fabulous lending conditions to a country that was trying unsuccessfully to restructure its debt at the time: an interest rate of the Libor bank lending rate plus an extra 1.5 per cent and a repayment period of twelve years (with a four-year grace period).[46] Using the full power of its cheque book, Beijing was making a move that would allow it to enter the heart of Africa's oil resources; in July 2004, Sinopec defied all the odds by taking over Shell's shares in the deep-water oil asset Angola Block 18, supposedly as a reward for the credit given by China.[17] That was just the beginning of a relationship which has seen the Chinese state lend Angola over $14.5 billion via its state-owned banks in return for payments in oil and long-term permission for its companies to access Angola's natural resources.[48] Despite the sheer size of this investment, it still does not provide a full picture of China's success in the country: on top of the loans offered by the state-owned Exim Bank, CDB and the Industrial and Commercial Bank of China

(ICBC), Angola has also received contributions from China's supposedly private sector.

With its twenty-five floors and gold-tinted glass structure, one building in particular dominates Luanda's architectural panorama. It is located next to the National Assembly, and when night falls over the dangerous Angolan capital the building is lit up by coloured lights that can be seen all over the city. At the top of the skyscraper are the initials CIF, which stand for a legendary name in the history of China's expansion across the planet: China International Fund. The inside of the building houses the well-guarded offices of one of the most opaque and mysterious Chinese companies that we have come across over the course of our journey through the Chinese world. It is also one of the most powerful in Angola thanks to its loans of between $2.9 and $9 billion to the Angolan government, as well as its contacts amongst the elite members of the state.[49]

CIF is officially a private company that was created in Hong Kong in November 2003. It forms part of a labyrinthine network of Chinese companies (all of them based at the same Hong Kong address: 10/F Two Pacific Place, 88 Queensway) which has been set up to negotiate with Luanda's government within four specific sectors: oil, diamonds, construction and financing.[50] CIF represents the financial arm of the group, although it is also involved in the diamond industry through its involvement with the Angolan state-owned company Endiama. The other two most important companies in the conglomerate, China Sonangol International Holdings (CSIH) and Sonangol Sinopec International Ltd (SSI), represent the only two Sino-Angolan joint enterprises in Angola's oil sector. These companies play a significant role in this area, although the American company ExxonMobil is still the biggest foreign player in the sector.[51]

With such an impressive portfolio, anyone would expect CIF and the other companies in the group to be backed up by solid credentials and internationally recognized experience. Nothing could be further from the truth: the company has never worked in the construction industry before, despite the fact that it has won tenders to build Luanda's new international airport and to repair the colonial-era Benguela railway. Its website contains various vague references to other projects carried out by the company, which also operates – strangely enough – in other countries that are characterized by a lack of transparency and abundant natural resources. As such, the conglomerate is present, either through CIF or CSIH, in places such as Guinea, Congo-Brazzaville, Zimbabwe, Madagascar and Nigeria.[52]

It is not even as if the controllers of the company are well-known personalities within the industry: the people behind the business structure are a string of directors and presidents who have little or no savoir-faire when it comes to working in the crude oil or diamond sectors, with the exception of Manuel Vicente, president of the Angolan state-owned oil company Sonangol. Even more surprisingly, despite the concerns that CIF's activities raise as a result of its million-dollar contracts, even the all-powerful Chinese state has either not been able or not wanted to throw light on the conglomerate's origin. At least, that is what the Chinese ambassadors in Guinea, Nigeria and Angola have declared time and time again, along with representatives of China's Ministry of Foreign Affairs.[53]

Under these circumstances, we decided to try to find out more ourselves about the conglomerate. We opted for the most direct form of research possible: knocking on the company's door. We went personally to CIF's offices in Luanda, Hong Kong and Singapore, but the company refused to answer our questions or to grant us an interview. We wondered why this was. Was it because of the company's lack of transparency, its habitual opaqueness, or its connections with figures such as Pierre Falcone?[54] 'The explanation is very simple; the deals through China [i.e. CIF] have become the easiest and most effective way of plundering the country.' The voice of Rafael Márquez de Morais, a journalist and activist against the excesses of the Angolan government, trembles with anger when we meet him at his home in Luanda.

De Morais has followed China's actions in Angola for many years and compares China's role with that of the West, which also does not escape his criticism. 'There is no difference between West and East in terms of obscure deals. Whether it is the US, China, Spain, Portugal ... the purpose is the same: to really get access to the decision makers in the Angolan government and to get as much as they can in the easiest way possible.' The only difference, he clarifies, is a 'difference in scale' when it comes to China, a country which he sees as carrying out a 'new imperialism'. 'CIF has established several major construction projects in Angola. None of them have been delivered. None. And that leads us to another question: do they really give loans? Does the money really come in and does it get stolen or what?' During our stay in the Angolan capital, we manage to get as far as the doorway to CIF's star project in the African country. This is nothing less than the construction of an international airport which, at a cost of over $2 billion, was due to be ready by the end of 2010. However, there is no trace of what should be Africa's biggest airport. Around 30 kilometres along the Viana–Catete motorway, the amount of activity around the airport's grounds is small to say the least. Hardly any vehicles can be seen on the dirt track leading to the supposed jewel in CIF's crown. Under a punishing sun, the armed soldiers from the Presidential Guard who are protecting the entrance look as if they are really quite bored. After twenty minutes of verbal jousting, we still haven't managed to break the resolve of the 'chief', a stoutly built high-ranking military officer wearing a beret and a handgun at his belt. 'This airport is a maximum security zone and the Angolan army has been entrusted to guard it by direct orders from the president of the nation. It is forbidden to enter this area,' he concludes. Close to the site, a Chinese family who opened a Chinese restaurant two years ago in the hope of attracting workers from the project feel like they have shot themselves in the foot. They barely make enough to get by. 'Business has been very slow since the very beginning. There are no customers,' they tell us.

We later spoke to a Spanish construction worker living in Luanda who pointed out that if the two nearby concrete factories were not producing cement – which was the case – then that would confirm the lack of activity at the airport. 'If those factories aren't active then there is no work going on, because concrete is essential in every phase of constructing an airport. If there was an airport being built there, there would be a constant queue of lorries going in and out.' What we saw on the motorway between Luanda and Viana therefore powerfully reinforces the hypothesis put forward by Rafael Márquez de Morais. He maintains that the loans announced by the CIF either never arrive or only partially arrive in the country. The loans therefore serve as a pretext, justifying the 'repayment' made by the Angolan government for services that are never fully carried out. In other words, they lay the groundwork needed to allow government officials to rob the country's natural resources on a massive scale. It is an enormous case of looting, pure and simple.

'They say: "OK, here's a loan for the airport." Five or six years later, there is no new airport and there is no money to account for. So a new loan is issued for the same airport. And that money disappears too. So, what happens is the state gets indebted, which justifies 200,000 barrels being sent per day to China, for instance,' de Morais argues. He says that this structure allows the state to plunder the country without causing any irregularities in the accounts. 'In what other way could you steal, for instance, 200,000 barrels of oil a day? It is not very feasible for a government official to say "take this oil for me", because of the international scrutiny and because you can check the cargo against what has been sold. But if you say that you are shipping 200,000 barrels of oil to China per day to pay back loans, that is just fine. You owe, so you pay.'

De Morais has coined the term 'transparent looting' to describe the process known by other organizations as 'trade mispricing'. This is a particularly urgent problem in Angola, as is shown in a recent report that puts forward some hair-raising figures to describe the extent of the pillaging: $6 billion in 2009 alone.[55] This figure – the equivalent of one-sixth of the total national budget – describes the amount that the country's political elites, with President dos Santos at the helm, supposedly diverted away from the country illegally that year by inflating bills and payments for projects that were never undertaken.

CIF and its associate company CSIH play a key role in this process of systematic and well-disguised looting based on the artificial inflation of state costs: the two companies issue invoices for the loans and claim quotas of crude oil for their repayment, thereby justifying the transportation of thousands of barrels of black gold to China. This way, 'in terms of international scrutiny, everything is transparent. You need a company [CIF] to launder what you are stealing from Angola. CIF provides the evidence needed [to justify what is supposedly being spent by the state],' de Morais explains. On the Angolan side, another ad hoc organization is just as indispensable in allowing this looting to continue: the (now defunct) National Reconstruction Cabinet (GRN).

The cabinet was created in 2005 by the president and, under his direct orders, was supposedly in charge of administering the funding provided by CIF to rebuild the country. The GRN, which was not required to submit to any type of control or provide statements of accounts, was led by General Manuel Hélder Vieira, aka 'Kopelipa', chief of the president's Military Bureau. 'Since taking control of the relationship with China, General Kopelipa has basically surpassed everyone in terms of his personal business empire: aviation, banking, telecoms ... Everything! Out of nothing, he has become one of the richest men in Africa. That has to do with the Chinese loans and the money he has managed as head of the reconstruction office [GRN]. The Chinese have become the most effective [vehicle] for corruption and for siphoning billions of dollars out of the country,' de Morais argues.

What is the role of the Chinese state in all this? Research carried out by a group of experts at the US-China Economic and Security Review Commission shows that various Chinese shareholders in the CIF conglomerate have either current or former ties with Chinese state-owned companies. However, perhaps the most uncomfortable revelation for Beijing was the fact that one of the group's shareholders, CIF's director Wu Yang, lists his place of residence as the same address as the headquarters of the Chinese secret services (28/F 14 Dong Chang'an, Beijing).[56] All the same, there is no irrefutable evidence that Beijing is behind CIF and its network, as there is in the case of the Angolan elites.[57] However, it is still difficult to believe that the Chinese government does not know who is who, especially when several of its state-owned companies – such as railway specialists CSR, the state-owned construction company CITIC and the oil company Sinopec – are either subcontracted by or associates of CIF and CSIH.[58]

How and why do these state-owned companies embark on million-dollar contracts with CIF when the Chinese state officially disowns the conglomerate? This question raises many others: how can a technically private company be capable of drawing on a volume of finance that would normally only be available to a state? How is it that a private Chinese company is, to all intents and purposes, competing with the Chinese state itself? And why hasn't the Chinese government intervened to neutralize a company that is seriously compromising

China's reputation as a result of its shady business dealings in oil-rich African dictatorships?

'If China hasn't taken action against CIF it's because it doesn't want to risk its business interests in the Angolan oil sector,' explains Alex Vines, head of the Africa Programme at the think-tank Chatham House in London. 'Some Western companies have decided not to play along with the Angolan political elites [referring to the widespread corruption], because they have access to the necessary technology and that has protected them. However, China doesn't have that and so it has had to play the game,' he continues. 'China has had to adapt somehow to the situation laid out for them by the Angolan government.' In other words, nobody can do business in the country without hands dipping into the till. Perhaps this explains why CIF seems to be nothing more than a structure designed to fulfil the demands of the Angolan elites without dirtying the hands of China's state-owned companies. That way, China still manages to get a slice of the pie in the Angolan oil sector.

THE CHINESE DREAMS OF CHÁVEZ THE TELEVANGELIST

'You have to be really careful. Sometimes they stand on the bridges over the motorway and dangle a string from there with a spark plug on the end that makes the vehicle's windscreen explode when it hits the car. When the driver stops the car, they attack him. Or sometimes motorcyclists tackle you at traffic lights, or in the middle of the road, and they point a gun in your face. You have to hand over everything you've got, there and then. That's just the way things are here.' These are the somewhat worrying words of Eduardo, our driver in Caracas, the moment we arrive at the Simón Bolívar national airport and set out in his 4x4 towards the Venezuelan capital. While Eduardo continues with his long list of the life-threatening dangers that are a part of Venezuela's violent reality, we make our way over hills covered in poverty-stricken houses which are home to the main body of voters for the president Hugo Chávez. Here they are called *ranchos*, run-down hovels piled one on top of the other without any degree of living space or privacy for their inhabitants: miserable holes where people struggle to get by any way they can.

One thing that is not lacking here are the layers of red, blue and yellow paint which people use to cover their homes with: the colours of the national flag. These buildings form a striking mosaic that presents a clear picture of the situation in this Latin American nation from the moment you set foot in the country. This has been Venezuela's new landscape ever since Commander Chávez rose to power in the country with the biggest oil reserves on the planet.[59] Venezuela is now a gigantic stage where ultra-nationalism and the encouragement of patriotic ideals – with those of Simón Bolívar prominent among them – has infected every aspect of society, dividing the country to such an extent that there are now only two options open to Venezuela's 30 million inhabitants: you're either a *Chavista* or you're not. 'You can't go around openly saying you're against Chávez. That would make lots of problems for you,' Eduardo tells us, always happy to offer a lesson in social norms during a long wait in one of Caracas's infernal traffic jams.

It is no easy task to describe this 'televangelist', as the Mexican historian Enrique Krauze calls Chávez in his great biography.[60] Chávez is certainly an egomaniac, obsessed with power and with the omnipresence of the media. In Krauze's words, 'Chávez sees absolutely everything that happens to him as an integral part of Venezuelan History.'[61] He is at once a populist figure, a conjurer who adores the drama of television (if you're not convinced, take a look at his rigorously live television programme, *Alo, presidente*, which starts at a specific time but has no rules about when it is going to end) and an ideologist whose foundations lie, as Krauze puts it, half way between Fascism and Communism. He is the only person capable of appearing on live television to call the president of the United States a 'donkey', or to nationalize private companies – with a shout of 'expropriate it!' – despite the fact that they had been operating in the country for decades. He is an 'imitator' of both Fidel Castro, his present-day mentor, and the leader of Latin American Independence, Simón Bolívar, Chávez's idol from beyond the grave. For better or for worse, this is the man who, with the support of the voters, decides the future of Venezuela and aims to build what he himself has nicknamed 'twenty-first-century socialism' – much to the delight of China. In August 2012 Chávez was leading the polls to be re-elected as Venezuela's president, despite the rumours about his bad health.

Since Chávez came to power in 1999, and particularly since a failed coup in 2002 which attempted to overthrow him – an event which some sources attribute to the United States – China has found itself almost unintentionally becoming Venezuela's number one ally. The failed coup radicalized Chávez, who went from aiming to diversify Venezuela's trade and diplomatic policies to openly championing the creation of a strategic alliance against Washington and – to a lesser degree – Europe. Since then, he has seen China as a counterweight to the United States and as providing the perfect pretext for breaking away from the 'imperialist' North Americans. The fact that Beijing is not in the least bit interested in this anti-Western crusade, since it would never compromise its relationship with Washington for a cause of this kind, has not stopped Chávez from showering his 'Chinese comrade' with tributes, in the broadest sense of the word. In return, Beijing is shrewdly keeping quiet and graciously receiving everything that Venezuela has to offer.

While Beijing attempts to keep a certain distance to avoid becoming part of Chávez's circus, the Chinese are also rubbing their hands together with glee at the thought of all the opportunities that he is handing to them on a silver platter. The figures speak for themselves in demonstrating the power that the Asian giant has gained in the Venezuelan economy. China has sold two satellites and a considerable number of weapons to the regime and, once again, has dug deep into its bottomless pockets to grant the country torrents of loans in exchange for natural resources: in 2010 the China Development Bank granted Venezuela $20 billion in credit, along with another $4 billion agreed with the Industrial and Commercial Bank of China,[62] as well as a combined investment fund worth $12 billion. All of this is down to the power of the most precious of Venezuelan resources: the gigantic reserves of 'black gold' in the Orinoco Belt.[63]

At a rate of 640,000 barrels per day, China has not yet overtaken the United States as the biggest buyer of Venezuelan crude oil.[64] However, this figure is expected to reach a million barrels per day by 2014, according to the agreement signed between the two countries. In terms of Chinese investments, the most important development in the hydrocarbons sector was a result of Chávez's decision to handpick China and Russia for the right to exploit the so-called Junín Block in January 2010.[65] According to the Venezuelan authorities, the plan is that Chinese corporations will pour $40 billion into the rundown Venezuelan oil sector by 2017.[66] These dramatic figures are allowing China to make a decisive entrance into Venezuela's oil sector while simultaneously supporting its own policy to diversify energy supplies, thereby reducing its dependency on the unstable Middle East.[67]

José Toro Hardy, the renowned Venezuelan economist and former adviser to the Venezuelan oil company Petróleos de Venezuela S. A. (PDVSA), recalls that 'in 1994, 1995 and 1996, when the oil sector opened up to foreign investment, things went very badly for China. It was an era of total transparency: the tenders were all made public and broadcast on television so that the offers made by all the different companies could be seen at once. It was completely different to how it is today.' Venezuela's Bolívarian experiment is now happening in inverse proportion to the rise in China's interests in the country. 'Caracas isn't interested in a commercial relationship with China. It wants to create political and diplomatic ties in order to stand up to the United States. I have no doubt that China is taking advantage of the fact that Venezuela wants to trade its oil for ideological reasons,' Hardy insists.

To carry out this 'great leap forward' in bilateral relations, Chávez decided to use the Venezuelan economy's pride and joy and its biggest source of support: PDVSA, the flagship company of the regime. As well as being one of the world's largest oil companies, the state-owned PDVSA is in charge of managing Venezuela's oil resources, contributing vast sums of money to the Republic.[68] Chávez also uses this corporation, which has been transformed into a multi-purpose fund during his presidency, to carry out his social justice projects such as nationalizing companies and distributing Chinese electrical appliances throughout the country. Furthermore, it is through PDVSA that Chávez has managed to secure the supposed preferential treatment which, he assures the world, Venezuela receives from China. However, perhaps things are not entirely as they seem. 'China sees Venezuela as a fool with lots of money and lots of resources. It sees a country where it is easy to take things. This is more a case of Venezuelan stupidity than Chinese colonialism.'

The above diagnosis of Brigadier-General Guaicaipuro Lameda, Chávez's right-hand man and president of PDVSA between 2000 and 2002, leaves no room for doubt. During a two-hour interview at his home in an upmarket area of Caracas, this stern man, who held what is considered to be the second most important public role in the country after the Presidency, told us that he believes China is taking advantage of Venezuela's *Chavista* hysteria to gain access to its natural resources. Among other things, he recalls that during his leadership of what was then the biggest company in Latin America he was forced to give special treatment to the Chinese company CNPC against the interests of PDVSA. 'In the year 2000 the idea of negotiating with China over a contract to develop Orimulsion [a type of fuel] was put forward. We didn't support the plan at PDVSA because it wasn't in the company's interests. However, Chávez personally pushed for the contract and asked me to ensure that it would be signed before the changes to the hydrocarbons law came into place, because once the law was approved it wouldn't be possible to endorse the benefits he planned to give to China. Chávez wanted to give Beijing special treatment, which explained his urgency to sign the contract. I had to choose somebody with personal ties to the government to carry out the negotiations with the Chinese, because nobody at PDVSA was in favour of the agreement. It wasn't economically beneficial for us,' he recalls.[69]

'There were two levels of negotiation in our conversations with the Chinese company: one between PDVSA and CNPC and another between the Chinese ambassador and Chávez. As the talks progressed between the two companies, CNPC's representative would call the ambassador whenever things were getting tough. Then the ambassador would call Chávez, and Chávez would call me. Everything we had agreed the previous day would end up taking a step backwards, and things always went in favour of the Chinese.' One of the things that China managed to squeeze out of Venezuela in this way was the removal of a clause limiting the final uses of the Orimulsion. As a general rule, PDVSA always endorsed agreements tying the use of this type of technology to the sole purpose of generating electricity. This is because this type of crude oil is sold at a price equivalent to the price of coal, which has similar uses, and is therefore much cheaper than conventional oil. 'This clause was removed on the insistence of the Chinese delegation. In other words, they can technically do whatever they like with the heavy oil, as it can also be used to make asphalt. But, of course, they only pay the price of coal.' According to Lameda, Chávez justified this unfavourable agreement for PDVSA by arguing that it was carried out within the framework of the country's overall relationship with China. Chávez argued that the fact that Venezuela would lose money with the Orimulsion contract was acceptable under those circumstances because Beijing would undertake many future projects in the country.

It wouldn't be the only time that China would gain privileged access to Venezuela's oil reserves under occasionally unbelievable conditions: a cable from a PDVSA official published by WikiLeaks revealed that China had been buying Venezuelan oil at prices as cheap as $5 per barrel, when the market price for a barrel was $78. Far from being grateful for the Venezuelan leader's generosity, mercantilist China had resold the crude oil to the United States, Africa and Asia, thereby obtaining significant capital gains – much to the chagrin of the Venezuelan government which saw Beijing as a loyal ally.

This type of 'offering' given to countries with ideological ties to Venezuela, such as Ecuador, Argentina, Iran, Bolivia, Belarus and Cuba, is typical of Chávez's regime.[70] As such, the guarantees in oil which Venezuela has brought to the table have allowed China to provide the $6 billion in financing needed to remodel the Cienfuegos oil refinery in Cuba. A similar project within the same framework – Venezuelan guarantees, Chinese loans and Cuban benefits – is also planned for Cuba's other refinery in Matanzas.[71] Therefore, while Beijing extends its tentacles across the length and breadth of Venezuela's oil sector, it is also indirectly getting caught up – almost by accident – in Chávez's schemes and crusade against the 'American empire', on this occasion with another 'old friend' of the United States – Cuba. For Beijing, however, this is nothing personal: it's just business, pure and simple.

'There's a world of difference between what China says it is doing out of solidarity with our country and its real actions. In actual fact,

China just robs you and takes away everything it can.' These are the words of Hector Ciavaldini, another former president of PDVSA who was once one of Chávez's most staunch supporters. Ciavaldini, who visited Chávez in prison to convince him to stand in the 1998 elections, looks back at the naivety shown by the Venezuelan president on his visit to China in 2000: 'He studied Mao's teaching very closely before going out there, but in Beijing at that time all the paintings of Mao had already been hidden away in the attic.' In this way, Ciavaldini strongly condemns China's ambiguous relationship with Venezuela. 'You tell the Chinese that you're a Fascist-Leninist and they buy into it for their own gain.' Ideology doesn't exist when it comes to business interests. Chávez does not escape Ciavaldini's criticism either: 'Nobody in Venezuela knows the conditions under which we are selling crude oil to China. It's shocking because you start believing that these are disadvantageous conditions and, if that's true, it represents a betrayal of our country. And he'll have to pay for it, because crimes like that can't just be written off.'[72]

5

The Foundations of the Chinese World

'The Americans come here to drop bombs. We are in Sudan to construct roads, buildings and hospitals. We are here to bring happiness to the Sudanese people.'

Fan Hui Fang, Chinese businessman and owner of
an arable farm on the outskirts of Khartoum

Dawn is breaking when we pull up alongside a row of adobe houses at the edge of the road for a breakfast of tea and sugared buns on the outskirts of Omdurman, a vibrant commercial hub to the north of Khartoum. It is six o'clock in the morning and many of the locals are stretching themselves sleepily. The light of the new day reveals a savage, lonely landscape torn apart by poverty and extreme weather conditions – and yet, at the same time, it is immensely beautiful. The black asphalt road gleams brightly as it stretches out across a horizon of golden sand dotted here and there with camels, herds of cattle and odd donkeys tied to shrubs.

Soon after leaving Omdurman, our two Toyota 4x4s begin to slow down as they reach the first military control post of the day, impossible to pass without the necessary permit. The soldiers on guard duty recognize the vehicles and stand to one side, saluting. Without stopping, we continue on towards the north of the country and the border with Egypt, travelling along a road that runs parallel to the River Nile. This would never have been possible if we had not arrived hand in hand with the Dam Implementation Unit (DIU),[1] an all-powerful organization operating under the direct supervision of Sudan's president, Omar al-Bashir. Its task is to co-ordinate the construction of dams so that the country will have access to the foundations necessary to introduce a new economic model less dependent on crude oil once rates of oil production begin to drop in 2013. It is a strategy in which China is set to play a crucial role.

Out of all of the dams built along the banks of Sudanese rivers, the most important and controversial is on the Nile at Merowe, 350 kilometres north of the capital. Inaugurated in 2009, President al-Bashir's favourite structure is the clearest indication of the recent co-operation between Beijing and Khartoum. This explains why we were heading to Merowe, although in order to do this we had to pass ourselves off as university professors, submit to various interrogations and demonstrate endless reserves of dogged determination.[2] It is impossible to get to Merowe without an official permit because of the area's completely restricted access and a string of military controls. Therefore, our only option that summer of 2010 was to be escorted and 'guided' by a delegation from the DIU as we headed towards one of the most contentious infrastructure projects carried out by China outside its own borders.

Khartoum publicizes the dam and its accompanying infrastructure work as the beginning of a new era for the country's economy. According to its promoters, the importance of the dam stems from the 1,250 megawatts of power generated by its ten turbines, as well as the possibilities offered by the water canal system in terms of the large-scale development of agriculture which will revive Sudan's old dreams of becoming the breadbasket of Africa.[3] 'Merowe is the biggest ever work of hydroelectric engineering to take place in Sudan, and probably in the whole of Africa,' boasts Awad, the master of ceremonies provided by the Sudanese authorities to chaperone us throughout our visit to the dam. Encouraged by the sense of status provided by wearing a tie in the middle of a desert, our friendly guide tells us about the project's many benefits, but neglects to mention the fact that this shining example of Sudanese infrastructure is also one of the most controversial in the country, both because of its exaggerated costs and the complete lack of transparency in terms of the project's social and environmental impact.

Still 150 kilometres from Merowe, we head along a new road built by the Chinese which forms part of the infrastructure package accompanying the project. In the heart of the Nubian desert there is barely any traffic or any sign of life apart from a few random settlements where humans and animals defy death in one of the hottest places on the planet. In fact, the terrible heat is precisely one of the arguments put forward by the dam's critics, who question its location because of the high rates of evaporation in the area: in this place where temperatures can easily reach 50 degrees, over 8 per cent of the water brought into Sudan by the Nile is lost when the river becomes stagnant. Experts point out that if the dam had been built in another location, such as on the Ethiopian side of the Nile, water loss would have been seven times smaller. Another source of criticism is the fact that studies measuring the environmental and social impact of the installation were carried out after the building work had already begun. 'The research on this subject was also superficial and incomplete. We are repeating the same mistakes made in Egypt on the Aswan Dam, which was an ecological disaster,' says Asim al-Moghrabi, Sudan's leading environmental expert on the River Nile, who has been studying this essential life source for over forty years.

On the outskirts of Merowe, we turn off the road towards 'New Amri 3', one of the new settlements that the authorities have built in the heart of the desert to house the people displaced by the dam's construction. The village is home to hundreds of families who live in simple adobe houses surrounded by walls which protect them from sandstorms. There are hardly any signs of life: a handful of children in school uniforms are chatting at the side of the road; a pair of women in white headscarves walk across a dirt track; and a policeman on guard duty sits on a plastic chair with an assault rifle resting on his lap. As our 4x4s make their way along the village's dirt tracks, we pass two mosques, a health centre, a school, two mobile phone masts and a stretch of sand with two iron goalposts which passes for a football pitch. The village may be new, but it is clearly dead: an impossible place with no hope of a future.

Awad strictly refuses to let us get out of the cars at New Amri 3, probably to avoid a repeat performance of what happened the first time we stopped, when a local inhabitant approached us to protest against the damage done by the dam. Looking visibly tense, Awad responded with a forced smile before his assistants made the aggrieved local go away. This sense of deep dissatisfaction among the local population is all too evident in a hostile climate caused by the forced relocation of tens of thousands of people. This is on top of years of violence and repression, inadequate compensation and the unannounced flooding of dozens of villages which were home to 4,700 families, who lost everything.[4] The region's indigenous Manasir, Amri and Hamdab tribes claim that the dam has completely swept away their traditional agricultural way of life. The fertile land along the banks of the Nile, where generation after generation of their families sowed dates and other crops, celebrated weddings and prayed for their ancestors, is now entirely submerged. Nowadays they live in a sterile environment where farming is impossible, putting an end to the communities' only source of livelihood. After losing their homes, the communities are barely managing to survive by fishing and the money sent by relatives.[5]

At the top of a steep slope looking down on the village, at a safe distance from the protests of the people, Awad acknowledges that the relocation process is the biggest problem they have had to face over the course of the project. 'Twelve thousand families have been affected; that's ninety-six thousand people.[6] It's not easy to turn people away from the place where their ancestors lived off the land,' he admits. However, he quickly reverts to describing the many advantages of the dam for the local population. 'Before the dam, some of the villagers had to go out in the morning in search of water and wouldn't get back until the evening. Now they just turn on a tap and they have water. The children go to school, they have healthcare and mobile phones and they can get to Khartoum in just over three hours.' Among all these benefits, he plays down the fact that these people have been left without a way of life. 'They can do other kinds of jobs. They can work in transport, hospitals, public services or jobs connected to Khartoum ... The dam will develop the whole region and bring new opportunities for everyone,' he insists.

China's influence can be seen everywhere in this remote desert. As we travel through the area, we begin to understand the extent of this development project, based on a Chinese model and Chinese funding.[7] As we cross an empty, perfectly asphalted road built by Chinese companies which stretches as far as the border at Wadi Halfa, we pass an irrigation canal which has allowed wheat to be grown in the area for the last four years. Next we cross the Nile over the imposing Friendship Bridge, courtesy of the Chinese state-owned company China National Petroleum Corporation (CNPC), before entering the Merowe Medical City, a hospital complex in its final phase of construction. Furthermore, the monotonous ochre-coloured landscape is interrupted by an infinite column of high voltage towers, also installed by the Chinese consortium. These towers are used to carry the electricity generated by the dam as far as Khartoum and Port Sudan – the end of the 1,500-kilometre Chinese oil pipeline used to transport Sudanese crude oil bought by China. Some sources argue that this crude oil acts as a guarantee for the loan granted by the Chinese Exim Bank to finance the Merowe Dam.

A little further on we reach the new airport, a fabulous 18-square-kilometre structure with a VIP terminal, a mosque and a 4-kilometre-long runway with landing space for planes as big as the Airbus 380. More modern than the airport at Khartoum, its facilities oversaw the arrival of eighteen planes the day when the dam first opened. However, it is now completely empty apart from the guards patrolling the lodge at the entrance to the precinct. The fact that there is little demand to fly to this forgotten corner of the earth does not really come as much of a surprise. Standing inside this enormous airport without any movement of planes or bustle of employees, passengers or vehicles definitely gives an eerie sensation, almost a sense of nuclear panic. However, from the runway which we have driven out to in our Toyotas, Awad calmly assures us that the future is just around the corner. 'This airport will grow enormously over the next few years. Aeroplanes will come here from all over the world and it will be used to export wheat and other agricultural products. Thanks to the dam, agriculture will develop, immigrants will arrive from the south and we will have access to hospitals, public services and tourism,' he predicts. Awad's words sound like a means of justification, a way of making sense of this enormous waste of infrastructure in the middle of nowhere with no current sign of any benefits.

There is no doubt that the Merowe Dam is the centrepiece of this network of future infrastructure that fuels the country's elite's dreams of wealth for this remote region which few people could even pinpoint on a map. As we drive closer to the dam, we are reminded of the

words of President al-Bashir: 'Merowe is the project that will eliminate poverty in Sudan.' The full grandeur of the project becomes clear
as soon as we cross the military-controlled entrance, where a sign
welcomes us in Mandarin: 'Congratulations to the Merowe Dam!'
After a brief technical description of the project, Mahjub Ali, the chief
engineer who has come to meet us, explains that 'the Chinese consortium which led the construction of the dam required 25 million cubic
metres of rocks and another million and half cubic metres of concrete', as well as the titanic efforts of between 3,000 and 5,000 Chinese
workers over the course of six years. Although the structure officially
opened in 2009, a contingent of Chinese workers are still finishing off
minor building works during our visit to the dam, living in a simple
camp presided over by the Chinese flag. As we go by, they stop working for a moment to exchange a few polite words of greeting and even
let us take their photographs before industriously turning back to
their work under the blazing sun.[8]

The view from the top of the 67-metre-high structure clearly demonstrates the magnitude of the second biggest hydraulic project on the
waters of the Nile after the Aswan Dam: upriver, an enormous 176-
kilometre reservoir has irreversibly flooded fertile land, entire villages
and a unique archaeological legacy dating back to the prehistoric era;
downriver, the dam is spitting out a spectacular stream of pressurized
water, creating violent waves and splashing everything in its path until
the river eventually returns to its natural course and rhythm. Mahjub
Ali uses highly technical rhetoric to describe the benefits of the new
installation: 'In 2008, Sudan's entire energy consumption was just
750 megawatts, the same amount required by New York City, and
only 15 per cent of the population had access to electricity. Thanks to
Merowe, that figure has now risen to 30 per cent. That is why more
dams are either being built or already being upgraded in Sudan,' the
engineer concludes.

In fact, Merowe is the first – and most important – of a series of ten
dams which are already in operation, or under construction, or have
been approved by the Sudanese government. In many cases, China is
playing a decisive role either in the building or financing of the
projects – if not both.[9] As our vehicles set off at full speed back along
the road to Khartoum, we can see China's unmistakable hallmark on

Merowe's superstructure and the entire development project. The image of another no less controversial project cannot help but spring to mind – the gigantic Three Gorges Dam in the middle reach of the Yangtze river. Despite being separated by thousands of kilometres, Merowe and the Three Gorges Dam share some surprising similarities both in terms of their conception and their form.

THE CHINESE FRIEND NEVER SAYS 'NO'

In 1999, a delegation sent by the Sudanese government set off across the world in search of capital to finance the Merowe Dam, which back then was only in the planning stage. However, the project had a weakness that frightened off potential investors: it did not comply with international standards on environmental and social issues. Therefore, after knocking on the doors of various financial bodies in various countries, the delegation returned to Khartoum empty-handed. At that time, China had already been working for five years on the Three Gorges Dam, the biggest of its kind in the world, which it had had to finance entirely with its own funds for the same reason that led to the failure of the Sudanese delegation: the refusal of the World Bank and other institutions to get involved in projects with such clearly bad environmental and social consequences. As if that were not enough, the United States had accused Sudan of promoting terrorism, further marginalizing the country on an international level. Under these circumstances, while the rest of the world refused to finance the Merowe Dam because of their legitimate suspicions about the project, China came to the rescue.

Coinciding with Sudan's oil boom at the start of the century, the Chinese Exim Bank granted Khartoum a loan of $608 million to finance its star project, which had an initial budget of $1.8 billion but which eventually ran to costs of around $3.5 billion, although the opaqueness typical of contracts with China makes it difficult to be precise about this figure.[10] The loan was not, however, merely a financial operation. It was contingent on awarding the dam construction contract to Sinohydro, the company that had been selected for the

Three Gorges project and which is currently building 107 dams across the world, according to the NGO International Rivers.[11] Another Chinese consortium was chosen to install the high voltage towers. 'The Chinese are fast and cheap, and to top it all they give you loans. How were we supposed to say no?' argues Asim al-Moghrabi, the Nile expert. The complete offer was, of course, irresistibly tempting: a 'turnkey' project that not only involved granting loans that were supposedly guaranteed with oil, but also the construction of the dam at the most competitive price on the market. The timeframe for carrying out the project was also quick and reliable thanks – mainly – to the Chinese companies' outstanding experience and their enormous supply of cheap labour. And all this could take place without any awkward questions about the impact on the environment or the local population.

As is shown by China's success across the planet, where it is building dams, roads, railways and football stadiums, this formula is so attractive that the two Chinese policy banks – China Development Bank and the Exim Bank – have managed to overtake the World Bank as the biggest lenders to the developing world.[12] In this sense, China's contribution to the progress of the receiving countries is undeniable – as is demonstrated by the energy capacity provided by the Merowe Dam and the whole parallel development project – even when there is some debate over the cost-benefit analysis of the project. However, it is not China's investments which are causing distrust, but rather its lack of attention to their side effects. Or, to put it more directly, China's utter contempt for any environmental consequences, the destruction of a unique archaeological legacy or the violation of the rights of thousands of people who have been forcibly relocated and pushed into extreme poverty. This is a carbon copy of the situation at the Three Gorges Dam.[13]

For all the reasons above, China should be held accountable, according to Ali Askouri, an activist who championed the cause of Merowe's victims and played a decisive role in gathering international opposition to the dam. 'The World Bank chose not to finance the dam as a result of pressure from various international organizations. There is no Western money behind the project and therefore it could never have gone ahead without Chinese funding or the technical expertise of companies such as [the German] Lahmeyer,' Askouri told us in Khartoum. He also describes the sense of immunity enjoyed by Chinese companies, particularly in comparison with the potential consequences faced by their Western competitors, as is shown in the case of Merowe itself.[14] 'Western companies can be brought to justice, but it is impossible to submit the Chinese to any real scrutiny. It is difficult to put pressure on Chinese corporations.'[15]

China takes refuge in one of the stalwart principles behind its foreign policy – that of 'no interference' – in order to give the green light to projects which, like Merowe, have such harmful consequences that the World Bank and other organizations flatly refuse to get involved. Furthermore, China's influence is not inconsiderable given that it is the world's leading lender in projects of this kind.

According to International Rivers, up to May 2012 China had been involved in 300 dam projects in 66 countries worldwide. Many of these were backed by unconditional loans from Chinese financial bodies, with the Exim Bank leading the way, despite controversy and criticism due to their potential damage to local societies and the environment. Would Chinese construction companies have won tenders for these projects if they had not come bearing unconditional funds backed by Chinese banks? Would they have been able to send their Western competitors packing if they had adopted international standards? Would many of these structures even exist without China's help? In the context of the current economic crisis, China's financial capacity plays a key role in getting these infrastructure projects off the ground. This is why Peter Bosshard, one of the directors of International Rivers, believes that it is essential to be able to influence the lenders in order to curb the excesses. 'Dam construction companies don't generally show a lot of respect for their social and environmental responsibilities. Financial bodies tend to be more sensitive to the risks; the people who provide the financing are the ones who can decide whether to pull out of certain projects, particularly if they are using public money.'

However, a project's social and ecological costs do not as yet carry much weight in the decisions made by Chinese financial bodies about whether or not to invest in a project. Out of all the Chinese lenders, the Exim Bank is the only one which has published its best practice guidelines on environmental and social issues (first published in 2004 and updated in 2007) However, these guidelines are demonstrably vague and, even worse, are difficult to use to screen projects in practice. The Exim Bank has only once agreed to suspend its funding for a project as a result of ethical reasons: this took place in 2010, after an NGO proved that the construction of a dam in a national park in Gabon violated the bank's own best practice guidelines. Despite the undeniable merit of such a decision, the general rule is still unfortunately the opposite outcome: in 2012 the Exim Bank and other Chinese financial bodies continued financing projects throughout the world when other international institutions wisely kept their distance.[16]

Furthermore, given the nature of China's political system, there is not much hope that the people with the power to change things – generally those in charge of the country's political system, banks or state-owned companies – will begin to feel pressure from civil society. In China, academics, journalists and NGOs do not have the same degree of influence as in democratic systems. 'There are over 3,000 NGOs in China, but certain matters are effectively off-limits. For example, there is practically no public debate on China's involvement in international affairs. That, of course, makes all the difference [in terms of the influence of the civil society in other countries],' Peter Bosshard argues. As always in China, change needs to come from within the power structure itself.

Under these circumstances, the opinion piece published in the official newspaper *Global Times* in January 2011 by Li Fusheng, deputy director of assessment studies at the Exim Bank, came as both a surprise and a relief. In reference to his recent visit to Laos and Cambodia (organized by an American institution) to evaluate the environmental and social impact of Chinese investments, Li did not hold back:

> We take it for granted that we go [to these countries] to help the local population with our investments, but that is not all the people living in those countries see. They probably think that the investments are being carried out for economic and diplomatic gain, or they believe that the companies need to do better than they are currently doing. The dominant voices in the receiving countries (which normally come from within

the local government) express their gratitude, but there are some marginal voices (which come from the inhabitants, the NGOs and some media sectors) who express their dissatisfaction and criticism for our work.

Li Fusheng recognized the damaging effects that Chinese investments may have on the local people, and thereby went much further than the usual 'win-win' rhetoric and mentions of the close political ties between the countries:

> In order to do something well, it has to be done carefully. Everybody in the receiving countries recognizes that China's aid and investments have contributed to the rapid development of their infrastructure, to their energy generation and their agricultural capacity. However, at the same time they are concerned about their forests and vegetation, their migratory fish, the safety of the environment and the relocation of the local people ... Therefore, whenever a study is carried out into the viability of a particular project, it is very important to also carry out an evaluation into the environmental and social impact of that project.[17]

It could be said a little louder but it couldn't be said any clearer. In a country that obsessively controls the flow of information, this opinion could not be more direct or to the point. Perhaps, at last, we are seeing the first step in encouraging the Chinese corporations which are rebuilding Africa and Asia to take greater responsibility for their actions.

BEIJING: PRECOCIOUS STUDENT OF THE IMF?

'Why do you ask whether a study has been carried out into the environmental impact? That information is not relevant to you,' Liu Yang replies dryly, when we interview the director of Sinohydro in Ecuador in his Quito-based office. Months earlier, the Chinese company had begun preparatory work on the construction of a new dam on the River Coca, the most important infrastructure project currently taking place in the Latin American country. The government in Quito had therefore intervened to ask Liu to meet us. However, after spending just two minutes with this grave, monosyllabic, middle-aged man, we realize that Liu is not interested in helping us and that this is going to be a short meeting. He speaks perfect English and can just about get by in Spanish after spending two years in Ecuador, but he clings to the strategy of speaking only in Mandarin in order to put an intermediary – the translator – between us and him.

As the Exim Bank granted nearly $1.7 billion to finance 85 per cent of the hydroelectric project – its biggest investment in Latin America to date – we are interested in finding out the technical details of the project in order to understand why a dam which requires such a small dyke (as we would later see) costs such a lot of money. 'I think it is better not to answer on financial matters,' Liu continues along the same lines, as the tension in the room begins to build. Next we decide to try to make friends by using a very straightforward question, and so we ask him about the strategic reasons behind Sinohydro's recent arrival in Latin America. Again, we come up against a brick wall: 'That information is not relevant for your book,' he concludes, refusing to budge. And, with that, the interview is over.

Early the next morning we decide to head off to El Chaco in the Napo province, around 160 kilometres north-east of Quito, to see for ourselves how Sinohydro is leading the project. The route into the heart of the Ecuadorian Amazon along a lonely road skimming the edge of bottomless ravines, with stunning views of turbulent rivers and no less spectacular waterfalls, does not disappoint us. After four hours of travelling along winding roads through lashing rain and thick fog on the route of the Trans-Ecuadorian oil pipelines which cut through the Amazon jungle, we arrive at the natural paradise where the future dam belonging to the state-owned Coca Codo Sinclair will provide the national power supply with 1,500 megawatts of electricity, or a third of the country's total energy requirements. Standing on a suspension bridge over the River Coca, just above where the dam will be built, a group of the company's employees explain that, rather than just a dam, what they are building is a 25-kilometre channel that will take advantage of the uneven water levels to carry water to a particular point down river, where it will speed up to create a waterfall.

'The water collection zone will only require a very small dam. It is just a question of accumulating enough water to channel it through the new route, a 9-metre-wide tunnel that will cross 25 kilometres of bare rock,' one of the technicians explains. Several kilometres away, three diggers are opening up a new path that will stretch for 34 kilometres through the heart of the jungle, providing access to the installation. One of the machines is sweeping away vegetation and knocking down trees, pulling them up at the roots and leaving a trail of overturned earth, rocks and craters behind it. The other two diggers are attempting to flatten and level out the path, making it possible to move through the quagmire so that other machines can arrive to asphalt the road. Luo Chun Hua, an engineer at Sinohydro, is one of the three Chinese employees working in the middle of the jungle, alongside a handful of Ecuadorians. He is carrying a machete in one hand, which he uses to cut a path through the vegetation, and a distance measuring tool in the other. As he gives out instructions, he complains about the mosquitoes and the constant rain, and warns us to watch our step: 'There are snakes everywhere.'

Luciano Cepeda, Coca Codo Sinclair's technical manager, looks back anxiously over the six months spent negotiating the specialist technical details of the project with Sinohydro. From the quality of the cement to the excavation technique and the process of manufacturing the materials, the Chinese refused to be controlled by their client, Cepeda tells us. 'They said: "You sign the contract and after sixty-six months [the agreed period for undertaking the work] I'll hand you the key to the project." In terms of quality and the effect on the environment, it's an outrage. No other country in the world would put up with this,' explains the man responsible for evaluating and supervising the whole construction project. Cepeda recognizes Sinohydro's track record as the world's biggest dam construction company. However, he argues that 'undoubtedly' the deciding factor in the selection of the Chinese company for this contract was the fact that 'it could provide the funding' – 85 per cent of the $1.982 billion needed for the project, to be precise.

The financial negotiation was also a tortuous process. A year after negotiations began it all came crashing down as a result of what the Ecuadorian president, Rafael Correa, considered the 'ill-treatment' of the Ecuadorian negotiators at the hands of the Chinese delegation.

This effectively put an end to negotiations. 'Suddenly negotiating with China is worse than negotiating with the International Monetary Fund. They're asking us for ridiculous guarantees,' Correa declared, angrily, referring to Beijing's demand that Ecuador's Central Bank should 'use its national assets as a guarantee'. Correa described this as an 'outrage' and threatened to amend his policy towards China, which was acting like a precocious student of the IMF during the negotiation process. These strong words struck a painful blow to a Chinese regime which greatly values discretion and which was not best pleased by this public outburst of squabbling. However, Correa's diatribe was effective: not long afterwards the Chinese delegation signed the agreement, giving the green light to the loan and, therefore, to the Coca Codo Sinclair dam.[18]

What was not mentioned in the press, according to our contacts in Quito, was the fact that the Ecuadorian president played a wildcard which threatened to hit a very raw nerve for China: none other than Taiwan. 'The key point was that Correa said: "If China forces those conditions on us, we'll go to Taiwan, as they're prepared to treat us better." The following day the Chinese ambassador in Ecuador reacted to this news and two days later negotiations started up again,' said Diego Vega, director of international relations at the National Planning and Development Office, when we met him at his office in the Ecuadorian capital. Vega formed part of the first delegation involved in negotiating the Chinese loan. Thanks to the president's warning, China not only agreed to fund Ecuador's biggest single infrastructure project, but has since then become practically the only viable option for other ambitious infrastructure projects which Quito hopes to set in motion in order to boost its development: a plan that will play a key role in the country's future.[19]

For Ecuador, China's 'complete package' – or, in other words, its low costs and financial muscle – is as attractive as it is unavoidable in the midst of Correa's current confrontation with the 'United States empire' and its 'like-minded' financial institutions,[20] as well as the legal risk that Ecuador poses in terms of foreign investment. However, while China represents Ecuador's only way of securing funding, Beijing's bottomless pockets allow its state-owned companies not only to make money but also to consolidate the country's strategic priorities.

'China's strategy of undertaking infrastructure projects in return for preferential access to natural resources, a strategy it has employed effectively in other regions, notably Africa, is on the increase in Latin America; namely in Ecuador, Venezuela and Argentina', according to a recent report.[21]

As well as oil, China's main interest in the small Latin American country is its mining sector, where enormous reserves of copper, gold and silver remain relatively intact. Alongside its construction work, China granted another $2 billion to the Ecuadorian state in June 2011,[22] thereby confirming that, despite the bumpy start in relations between the two countries, things are now cruising along nicely.

STADIUM DIPLOMACY, OR TROJAN HORSES?

The cases of Sudan and Ecuador – two radically different countries many thousands of kilometres apart – show just how well China's financial package fits the needs of developing countries, particularly in this era of empty coffers and dwindling cash flows. From the point of view of the receiving countries, the new 'world's banker' offers an irresistible short-term alternative to help them build new infrastructure. It is a highly tempting cash offer: soft loans, low costs and high speed. Furthermore, if the country in question is not keen to submit to the requirements of international social or environmental standards or best practices, or if for some reason they find themselves at loggerheads with the West, China is willing to come to the rescue under the pretext of 'no interference' in the affairs of other countries. This is in stark contrast to the behaviour of other international actors, who consider it unacceptable not to observe these standards.

Thanks to the enduring ties emerging from these relations, China has gained a much greater economic and diplomatic influence than it had probably ever expected to achieve in so short a time. However, while the crisis has clearly only accelerated a phenomenon – the emergence of China – that was bound to take place sooner or later, the fact is that its form and events have fitted perfectly with the official strategy masterminded by the Communist leaders. On the one hand, China is now able to guarantee its future supply of raw materials, and, on the other hand, their state-owned companies are able to 'go out',[23] become more international and take on new markets. While decades ago China's foreign infrastructure projects all had an undeniable ideological component, as we will see in the case of the famous TAZARA railway in Africa, the motivation behind its present-day projects is clearly strategic.

Paving the way for the new China's future also contributes to the development of other countries, as we were able to see for ourselves over the course of our journey. Examples can be seen throughout the three continents: from rebuilding a war-torn country in the case of Angola, where Beijing is constructing thousands of homes and building a transport network practically from scratch, to constructing new roads in the Democratic Republic of Congo or developing oil pipelines in Sudan, Turkmenistan and Burma. The same can be seen in the ambitious railway projects planned for Venezuela and Argentina, or the impossible roads being built in Iran and Mozambique, or the construction of a strategic route connecting Xinjiang with the Indian Ocean via Pakistan-administered Kashmir; not to mention the quantum leap achieved by installing and launching satellites in Nigeria and Venezuela. There is no doubt that infrastructure construction plays a highly strategic role in China's silent world conquest, mainly because of the sheer scale and visibility of these projects. Their role is so important that Beijing even uses them as instruments for exercising its soft power, regularly including them in its hotchpotch of foreign aid and intergovernmental co-operation.

The first and only report on Chinese foreign aid, published by the Chinese State Council in April 2011, states that China had built and financed a total of 2,025 projects in foreign countries by the end of 2009.[24] While infrastructure projects are used as a means of furthering China's own interests – for all the reasons explained above – they are also undoubtedly used in order to reward loyalty and to seduce the less enthusiastic countries of strategic interest to China. However, many believe that this strategic method of persuasion also has a darker side, which involves placing a Trojan horse in a country as a means to facilitate China's expansion into that market.

In order to see one of these 'gifts' for ourselves, we decided to fly to

San José in Costa Rica, where we arrived one rainy, tropical afternoon in October 2010. As we will see in more detail in Chapter 8, the most important country in Central America was also the second to last to move over to Communist China's camp after a lifetime of loyalty to Taiwan. Costa Rica therefore clearly deserved a prize.

Seen from close quarters, China's gift to Costa Rica certainly looks spectacular. The delightful National Stadium, a present from Beijing at the very reasonable price of $89 million, is located at the heart of the country's capital. When we visit, the building work is almost finished. Outside the premises, groups of Costa Rican workers and Honduran immigrants are paving the last of the walkways, carrying heavy sacks and breaking up stones. However, the real action is happening inside the building. Rosi, one of the few Chinese women working on the project, welcomes us in as soon as she is satisfied that we are not locals. 'The design and the construction work are all completely Chinese. The stadium has a capacity for 35,000 spectators,' she explains. Meanwhile, we watch a handful of machines laying asphalt on the athletics track while several employees of Anhui Wai Jing, the Chinese state-owned company in charge of constructing the stadium, fit seats into the stands. 'There were 800 Chinese people working here at one point, but now there are just 134 of us left,' Rosi explains, confirming that China's donations come with their own Chinese workforce and construction materials, which can enter the country tax-free.

The gift is clearly motivated by politics, as is the case with the dozens of similar stadiums that China's 'stadium diplomacy' has established in Africa. Many of these stadiums are presented as gifts, while others are tied to some form of co-operation between the two countries.[25] However, in Costa Rica the Chinese company took advantage of the construction of the 'stadium of friendship' to create a subsidiary company which was able to compete in tenders for public and even private projects from a distinct advantage because of its on-site workforce and ability to bring its materials into the country tax-free.[26] Antonio Burgués, a former minister in the ex-president Óscar Arias's government, Costa Rica's first ambassador to Beijing and a great conversationalist, has no doubt that the stadium is really a Trojan horse aimed at entering, penetrating and conquering the Costa Rican market.[27]

'A gift?' he says, when we meet him in a fashionable café in San José. 'China doesn't hand out gifts. If China gives you a stadium, it's taking away a hospital from their people, because China is still a developing country. So, how is it supposed to give you a present?' he argues about China's various donations. The case of the Chinese subsidiary company caused quite an uproar in the midst of a honeymoon period between the two countries. It was not only that San José refused the visa applications of a hundred Chinese workers who were supposed to be building a housing complex. The argument really took off when it emerged that the commercial attaché to the Chinese embassy in San José and executives of the Chinese state-owned company were working together to pressure and bribe Costa Rican embassy staff in Beijing into giving the green light to the work permits. The outcry among politicians and the media, the complaints about unfair competition on behalf of the local construction companies and the refusal to grant the visas caused the Chinese company to abandon the private project altogether.[28] However, the scandal did not stop China from honouring its promise and completing work on the National Stadium as planned.

Burgués knows all about these pressures. He tells us that the Chinese authorities refuse to let the subject drop when it comes to the question of 'flexibility' in Costa Rica's immigration policy towards China: 'It's an issue that comes up again and again. Whenever they agree to grant you an interview they spend 30 per cent of the time talking about this issue,' explains the man who put the brakes on a plan to allow huge numbers of Chinese immigrants into Costa Rica during his time as ambassador in the Chinese capital. 'The Chinese have a strategy and they do whatever they have to do in order to get what they want, either with the left hand or with the right,' he says, referring to legal and illegal practices. 'The [Chinese] ambassador is responsible for keeping up appearances and never gets involved in shady business dealings. However, there's always somebody inside the embassy, the commercial attaché or someone like that, who is prepared to give it a try,' he continues. This is why he thinks that 'it's important to set the boundaries with China, because they're not a democracy. We need strong institutions; we can't just let the big bad wolf come here and blow our house down as if it's made of straw,' he argues. 'China wants to Africanize Latin America. They see us as poverty-stricken and corrupt.'

FEEDING 1.3 BILLION PEOPLE

Another example of China's strategic investment in infrastructure can be seen in the $1.4 billion project currently being undertaken in Argentina by the Chinese state-owned company Beidahuang State Farms Business Trade Group. Originally from the northern province of Heilongjiang, Beidahuang is China's leading soya producer. In 2011, the corporation signed an agreement with the local government of the Rio Negro province (close to Argentinian Patagonia) to develop 320,000 hectares of land that are currently unusable. Over the next five years, Beidahuang will invest $850 million in bringing water and energy to the area in order to irrigate the land and make it suitable for cultivation. At the same time, the company will bring an additional $500 million to the table to improve infrastructure in the province. A significant part of this money will go towards redeveloping the port at San Antonio-Este, which China will have the right to use for the next fifty years.

The dock capacity will be improved to allow the entrance of Chinese vessels weighing up to 40,000 tons – four times the size of the ships that can currently access the area. These will be used to transport Argentinian soya, corn and fruit to China. 'You have the market and the money. We have the climate, the land and the environment. We're perfect business partners: put what you have where we can use it and we will both benefit. That's what we told the Chinese,' explains Óscar Gerardo Gómez, the representative of the Rio Negro province in Buenos Aires, when we meet him in the Argentinian capital. 'Without this investment we couldn't have carried on planting anything at all. In exchange, we assured China that we will give them all the crops produced over the next twenty years. It will all [referring to the sales of food] be carried out transparently and at the market price,' he assured us.

China has thereby guaranteed its supply of the harvest yielded by these 320,000 hectares of land for the next two decades. The most interesting feature of the agreement is the fact that most of the land, which is currently unproductive and unsuitable for farming because of a lack of water, will still belong to its original owners. China will take 30 per cent of the land – around 100,000 hectares – to guarantee its investment, but the landowners will be able to recover their land after twenty years by paying 'the market price at that time'. Giving away 30 per cent of the land does not seem excessive considering that a hectare of unproductive land in the region currently costs $200 and the price is likely to rise to between $5,000 and $10,000 per hectare as a result of China's investment, according to the Argentinian government. 'Lots of people are going to get rich,' Gómez predicts, referring to the small and medium-sized landowners who currently own the stretches of land.

The owners' only obligation is to farm their land. 'The Argentinian owner farms the land with the help of the Chinese company, which will facilitate loans to allow the owner to buy machinery and seeds. Beidahuang will decide what needs to be planted, as it has committed to buying the produce. The role of the producer, who will benefit enormously from the Chinese investment, is to grow crops. If they don't want to do it themselves, the owners have two options: rent or sell their lands. But whoever is in charge of the land has to produce crops, come what may, because if they don't [the land will] be expropriated,' says Gómez, one of the architects of the agreement.

China currently has access to 3,000 hectares of land on which to carry out experiments into which types of crops adapt best to the climatic and environmental conditions of the Rio Negro area. 'Beidahuang plans to establish research centres to develop their technology on Argentinian soil. They also want to see which products acclimatize most easily to local conditions. It might be soya, corn, fruit, vines or olives,' Gómez explains. The Rio Negro authorities, which enjoy a considerable amount of autonomy from the national government along with the other Argentinian provinces, are confident that the Chinese deal is 'the biggest development project ever carried out in Argentina'. They fully expect that 'other regions in the country will emulate this project to benefit their own economies'. The most optimistic forecasts suggest that 100,000 local jobs will be created thanks to Chinese capital. Some of these will be directly linked to the creation of a new workforce to farm the land, while other workers will be responsible for developing the various services linked to agricultural production, such as transport, storage and refrigeration.

'This agreement is excellent for the province. Nobody else is producing crops on this land and, what's more, the agreement is not dependent on the national government. It's the kind of deal that everybody dreams about. It's a matter of expanding the frontiers of crop production,' argues Mariano Turzi, professor of international relations at Torcuato Di Tella University. He believes that the nature of this investment is different from those carried out by the multi-national food companies operating in Argentina, such as Cargill or Dreyfus. 'It's not the same. In this case the Chinese state is behind the investment,' he argues, referring to Beidahuang's capacity as China's most important food production company to carry out a multi-million-dollar investment in a country overshadowed by legal insecurity.[29]

'The other investors don't do this because they have no faith in Argentina's investment framework,' the representative of Rio Negro had already told us in his office in Buenos Aires. In fact, an expenditure of this size in a country with few legal guarantees, legendary logistic bottlenecks and a politicized and troubled agricultural sector entails a significant amount of risk for China. If the investment comes to fruition as planned, it will represent a powerful example of what Beijing calls 'win-win co-operation'; if soya is to Argentina what oil is to Saudi Arabia, a multi-million-dollar investment in such an unstable market can only be justified in strategic terms. The fact that the long shadow of the Chinese state lies behind Beidahuang is, of course, no coincidence. The risks become justified when the nation's number one priority is to feed the most highly populated country on the planet.

This explains why China's investments in Argentina and Brazil, the most powerful agri-food sectors in Latin America, go far beyond a simple commercial transaction.[30] 'China has invested a lot of money in Africa in order to extract and transport natural resources. In terms of food security, the strategy is the same: we have to invest in order to guarantee our supplies,' says Zheng Fengtian, a professor at the University of Beijing and a leading expert in China's agricultural production, when we meet him in the Chinese capital. 'China wants to remain self-sufficient in terms of food such as rice, which is a fundamental part of the Chinese diet and therefore highly strategic. However, this is not possible with other products, such as soya or corn, which are used to feed animals. We need to import these products, but how should we do this? There are three strategies, which are very similar to China's means of securing its oil supply: firstly, buying from the global market; secondly, acquiring shares in international food companies in order to control them; and, finally, buying land in other countries. The least desirable of the three options is buying in the global market, for security reasons. What would happen if the large food producers such as the United States or Brazil decided to put a ban on exporting their products?' he asks.

The investment in Rio Negro therefore allows China to enter Argentina's agri-food sector in order to contribute to its national security without being at the mercy of the market. Most importantly, this guarantees China's food supplies even in times of shortage, such as during the financial crisis or the dramatic drought in 2012 in parts of the United States, which have caused a relentless and apparently lasting rise in food prices. This situation has already had political consequences in the Arab world.[31] 'Although we can supply ourselves with basic food products, Argentina is very important for China, a country with a population of over 1.3 billion people. Its importance is shown by the fact that Argentina is now China's third biggest food supplier. China therefore sees Argentina's agricultural sector as both a commercial opportunity and a strategic requirement. Both things are very important for China,' explains Yang Shidi, commercial adviser to the Chinese Embassy in Buenos Aires.[32]

The $1.4 billion investment in Rio Negro therefore makes perfect sense for Beijing, particularly when the future is worrying to say the least for countries such as China and India which have enormous upwardly mobile populations and limited natural resources and which are experiencing a rapid rate of urbanization.[33] 'The pork consumption per inhabitant is increasing by half a kilo each year. We also need to take into account the impact of the exodus of rural workers to the city: each year 1 per cent of China's population, or around 13 million people, stops working in rural areas and goes to live in the towns,' Yang explains.[34] The national diet is becoming more sophisticated, which has led China's average annual meat consumption per person to rise from 25 kilos to 54 kilos in just two decades. This means that extensive additional resources are required in a country which has only a meagre production capacity of its own: China has to feed a fifth of the earth's population with just 7 per cent of the world's arable land.[35]

'Nowadays, the majority of people in China have no problem getting access to food. However, when their lifestyles become more sophisticated, they change their diet and instead of rice their meat consumption will increase. The resources needed to produce a kilo of meat are the same as those needed to produce several kilos of grain,' says Cai Fang of the Chinese Academy of Social Sciences, as he explains that a change in diet also means a drastic increase in grain production. This is on top of a shortage of other types of resources such as water, of which China has one of the lowest indexes per capita in the world.[36] Furthermore, climatic changes have also caused a fall in crop harvests. This extremely complicated situation is further exacerbated by the fact that the biofuels industry has recently begun to compete with crops for human food supplies.

Consequently, companies in countries such as South Korea, Japan, the Persian Gulf nations and China are now considering the possibility of buying fertile land in Asia, Africa and Latin America in order to guarantee a future food supply for their populations. This phenomenon has captured the attention of the international media and institutions such as the World Bank and the Food and Agricultural Organization of the United Nations (FAO). Activists and NGOs warn that this 'land grab' process represents a new form of colonialism, causing the displacement of indigenous populations who see their land as their connection with their ancestors. A further area of concern is the potential creation of countries with single-crop policies that will essentially grow crops in order to satisfy the demands of others, without taking care of their own food security.

Information published by the media suggests that China is one of the main forces behind this global trend of buying land, after acquiring hundreds of thousands of hectares in places such as the Philippines, Madagascar and Brazil in order to gain complete control over the production of soya, among other types of crop.[37] This has sparked a reaction among several governments, such as the Brazilian and

Argentinian authorities, who have been quick to approve legislation to limit or restrict arable land purchases on the part of foreign investors. 'China's process of leasing land in foreign countries is still in its early stages. In our country, when we want to make a significant investment in something, we always test it out first to get an idea of the local environment. There is a lot of land in Africa, but there is also a lot of conflict there. That's why Latin American countries such as Brazil and Argentina are better,' Professor Zheng concludes. 'It is very likely that we will see more land being bought in the future,' he predicts. This plan inevitably brings to mind the suggestion of Mark Twain in the nineteenth century: 'Buy land. They're not making it any more!'

JACKPOT IN THE SPECIAL ECONOMIC ZONE!

The modern motorway offers a pleasant drive south from Yunnan and passes through Mengla before finally tackling the last few kilometres up to the border with Laos. The activity there is minimal, which explains why most of the shops selling souvenirs, pieces of jade and fake *Pu-er* tea have already closed for the day, and there are no customers to be seen at the restaurants serving Yunnanese cuisine. Although we cross the border into Laos at the regulation border post, many Chinese residents prefer to leave the country via a 2-kilometre motorbike ride through the jungle. This is the illegal route to Boten, where a private Chinese enterprise called Golden Boten City Company has set up one of the enterprises that has caused the most embarrassment for Beijing's authorities since the start of China's expansion across the world. Just a few metres from the border, the Laotian government recently declared Boten a Chinese Special Economic Zone, an area measuring 6 square kilometres that was supposed to attract Chinese investment to build factories and workshops thanks to the area's favourable fiscal conditions and tempting land prices. The low wages of the Laotian people were expected to provide the final piece of the puzzle needed to turn the area into a successful industrial zone. However, Boten has instead become a Chinese sanctuary for unadulterated pleasure: a paradise of gambling, prostitution and drugs.

Before the Chinese company and the Laotian government sealed their alliance, Boten was a small town whose inhabitants made a living from agriculture or selling live monkeys, bears and other wild animals at markets. As has happened in many other towns along the Burmese and Laotian sides of the border, all the economic activity in this enclave of 5,000 Chinese inhabitants now revolves around the casino inside the Royal Hotel. The stamp on our passport confirms that we are in Laos, but nothing has actually changed since we crossed the border: the only language spoken in Boten is Mandarin, the common currency is the yuan and China Mobile provides the mobile phone signal. It's Friday afternoon and the street is getting livelier by the minute, which shows that many more people must surely be arriving through the jungle than via the official border crossing. A sign at the entrance of the Royal Hotel, a tall building that looms over the town, welcomes us with a somewhat paradoxical message: 'Gambling is illegal for citizens of Laos and China'.

As we walk further into the depths of this pale yellow building with 380 rooms – all of them fully booked – we find an enormous shrine to the cult of gambling, full of state-of-the art slot machines and electronic roulettes imported from the United Kingdom. However, these are just the prelude to the real centre of the betting culture: a game of baccarat. As people look at us inquisitively, we realize that the setting could not be more surreal: amid a cloud of cigarette smoke and the shrill cries of women holding baskets full of gaming chips, dozens of Chinese punters crowd onto the green carpets while croupiers hand out shares of good luck and the little balls spin around the roulette tables. There are few signs of enjoyment in the room, which is filled instead with a mixture of anxiety and wild jubilation. Betting is serious here, with piles of chips for up to 1,000 renminbi placed on just one number in each game of roulette. There are also several signs of superstition, with altars covered in floral offerings to the god of fortune.

This gigantic centre of debauchery, which would be illegal in China, is divided up into rooms with suggestive names, such as 'the chamber of total happiness' (*bai fu ting*) or 'the room of riches' (*fui gui ting*).

1. Khartoum – A Chinese agricultural worker and his Sudanese counterpart in a Chinese farm on the outskirts of the Sudanese capital. One of the main problems faced by China is how to feed 1.3 billion people with limited resources. For this purpose, the Asian giant has started looking for food abroad.

2. Xai-Xai, Mozambique – Chinese and Mozambican workers on a road that unites Maputo with the centre of the country. Hundreds of thousands of Chinese people are working in developing countries, building infrastructures that are usually funded by Beijing.

3. Khartoum – A Chinese entrepreneur and his client pose alongside the building which they are constructing in the Sudanese capital. China has become the main business partner of the Islamic Republic of Sudan, where it invests billions of dollars in oil and provides support to Sudan's dictator, Omar al-Bashir, despite the accusations of genocide in relation to his activities in the Darfur region.

4. Luanda – A Chinese worker shows his bedroom, which he shares with other Chinese workers who arrived in Angola to rebuild the former Portuguese colony after twenty-seven years of civil war. With these simple and sometimes miserable living quarters, the Chinese companies are simply reproducing the labour standards of their own country throughout the world.

5. Maputo – Employees of the Chinese state-owned company Anhui Wai Jing inside the national stadium which it has built in the Mozambican capital. 'The friendship between China and Mozambique will prevail like Heaven and Earth', says the slogan at the stadium's entrance. However, disputes over the company's working conditions have created an atmosphere inside the building site which is anything but friendly.

6. Luanda – A Chinese foreman poses along with his workers at the site of one of the biggest construction projects that China has undertaken in Angola. With scaffolding made out of bamboo, the Chinese state-owned company CITIC is building a 'new Luanda' on the outskirts of the capital, which will provide thousands of new homes.

7. Merowe, Sudan – Tireless Chinese workers are photographed during the construction of the controversial Merowe dam. This gigantic engineering project, which was aimed at taking advantage of the River Nile's currents in order to produce electricity, has caused irreparable social and environmental damage to this poor area of northern Sudan. It is the most important Chinese hydraulic infrastructure in Africa.

8. **Cairo** – A group of *shanta sini*, as the Egyptians call these Chinese street vendors, display their products before setting off to sell them door-to-door, as they do on a daily basis. Without speaking a word of Arabic and with barely any knowledge of Africa, the thousands of *shanta sini* who travel throughout Egypt demonstrate the courage, perseverance, humility and will to succeed of the Chinese people.

9. **Beira, Mozambique** – A Chinese entrepreneur at his timber warehouse in the port city of Beira. Along with corruption and a lack of scruples about the environment, the enormous demand for wood has led China to become one of the biggest threats to the world's forests, as seen in Siberia, Mozambique and Burma.

10. **Dalnerechensk, the Russian Far East –** Anatoly Lebedev is one of the people who is fighting the hardest for the survival of the Siberian forests. This highly intelligent and courageous man has shown how the indiscriminate logging of rare wood species has endangered local biodiversity. 'The Siberian tigers have no food so they go into the villages to eat dogs,' said one of his collaborators. This is something that had not been seen before.

11. **Karakum Desert, Turkmenistan –** A Turkmen worker at the base camp of the Chinese oil company CNPC in Turkmenistan, near Uzbekistan. China has built a 7,000-kilometre-long pipeline to transport gas from Central Asia to the kitchens of Shanghai.

12. **Tehran –** A Chinese engineer in charge of constructing a road which will connect Tehran with the Caspian Sea. China is one of Iran's strongest economic and political allies, despite the international isolation of the Islamic Republic as a result of its plans for nuclear development.

13. **Marcona, Peru** – The lack of any social or environmental sensibility on the part of the Chinese mining company, Shougang Hierro Peru, has forced the local people in this town on the Pacific coast to rise up in arms. 'There are strikes every year,' the leaders of the mining trade unions said. Marcona's miners feel exploited and badly treated by the company.

14. **Havana, Cuba** – Every morning, some Cubans practise the art of *tai chi* in Havana's Chinese district. This tradition is inherited from the time of the arrival of the first Chinese immigrants on the island in the mid-nineteenth century.

15. Myitkyina, Burma – A Burmese man poses in front of Chinese-owned gold mines. Chinese companies have a very strong presence in the Burmese jade mining sector. They control every aspect of this profitable business, from extracting the jade to selling the stones at the markets of Shanghai and Hong Kong. On a local level, the activities carried out by these companies have caused an environmental and social disaster. 'Almost all the miners are addicted to heroine,' sources say.

16. Vladivostok, Russia – Tens of thousands of Chinese people have emigrated to every corner of the planet in search of new opportunities. This Chinese woman works in a Chinese hairdressing salon in Liu Desheng's market in Vladivostok.

Everything is watched over closely by dozens of security cameras which, as well as guarding every corner of each room, also allow the business to expand into the motherland. Thanks to the cameras and the internet, the casino can cross the border virtually, allowing Chinese customers to bet in real time from the safety of their own homes without worrying about being hunted down by the police. This vice on the other side of the border has created a new job opportunity for the many chancers wandering the streets of Boten: the role of middle-man or agent.

Sitting at the casino's most select tables or betting on several tables at once, it is easy to recognize these opportunists by the mobile phone wires dangling from their ears. These devices allow them to communicate with the casino's real customers, who are able to follow the developments on each table through their computer screens. 'What table do you want to bet on? How much do you want to bet? What number do you want to bet on? Do you want to leave the game?' we hear them ask their clients, discreetly but unashamedly, as we wander through this theme park for gamblers. The only time they take a break from following their clients' orders is when they stop to change their phone batteries. As night falls, the activity around the casino reaches its peak. Pawn shops hypnotize customers with neon lights, tempting them to sell their watches, jewellery and computers in order to carry on with the betting binge. Meanwhile, restaurants draw them in with the delicious aromas of chilli and ginger. The darkness also gives the town a chance to break away from any sense of discretion imposed by the light of day: at seven o'clock in the evening a horde of prostitutes descends upon the casino's customers, offering two hours of love in exchange for 300 yuan (35 euros).

There are dozens of these girls from all over China, perhaps a hundred or so. Dressed in short skirts and extravagantly made up, they hand out business cards containing just the telephone number of their pimp and a number between 1 and 9 to identify them. In this enclave in northern Laos where the Laotian state simply doesn't exist, even prostitution is controlled by the Golden Boten City Company, or simply 'the Company' as it is known here. It is the lord and master of everything in Boten. The company collects taxes, approves regulations, and fixes the price of rent. It even enforces justice through a group of gangsters with access to an illegal prison, where they harass, torture, kidnap and – according to local hearsay – even kill defaulting customers who borrow money from the casino and fail to repay it. 'If you have contacts or money on the other side of the border, you may live. If not, you'll be tortured or even killed. Some people say they've seen bodies floating in the river,' a young woman working in a hairdresser's told us.

In this scene from 1920s Chicago in Laotian territory, a group of mercenaries wearing imitation Chinese police uniforms are in charge of security. Although they drive cars bearing the word 'police', they do not follow any type of moral code, let alone the law. Here it is debts that decide who will live and who will die. The Company has turned Boten into the Wild West. 'If something happens, we take care of it ourselves. If you contact the Laotian police, they come to us to ask us to resolve the situation,' explains Mr Huang, a director and partner of the Golden Boten City Company, when we meet him for a brief interview in his office. The walls are hung with photos of the company's executives posing with Laotian politicians, including the prime minister. However, a video of the company's thugs torturing and mistreating Chinese debtors which was filmed on a mobile phone and broadcast by a television station in Hong Kong has forced a reaction from the Chinese authorities, who have been trying to close down the casino ever since.

According to Huang, future plans for Boten include four new hotels, a golf course and various types of tourist attractions, despite the plans announced by the Laotian government in March 2012 to close down the casino and hand the SEZ to another Chinese investor. In any case, on our journey through South-East Asia we were able to confirm that Boten is not an isolated case. Equally well-camouflaged casinos in Special Economic Zones are a daily reality in the middle of the Laotian or Burmese jungles, where Chinese companies set up enormous tourist complexes which are funded by the money that flows into the casinos. We spent the night in one of them: the Golden Triangle Special Economic Zone. Five hours and 250 kilometres away from Boten, this SEZ is based on the banks of the Mekong river, in the heart of the world's most famous opium cultivation and trafficking area.[38] There is no trace of industrialization or manufacturing

complexes which would give work to the local population and contribute to the area's economic development. Just enough infrastructure
is built to get the area up and running, including access roads cutting
through the jungle and jetties on the river. In reality, the SEZs are no
more than simple 'exception zones' controlled by a form of Chinese
investment which brings to mind the terrible colonialist abuse suffered by China a century and a half ago. This time, however, the order
is reversed: now it is Chinese capital that has found its 'concessions'.
China's current treatment of Boten or the Golden Triangle can readily
be compared with the debauchery prevalent in a China that was over-
run by opium and prostitution at the beginning of the twentieth
century.

6

The New Victims of the 'Factory of the World'

'The friendship between China and Mozambique will prevail like Heaven and Earth.'

Chinese motto at the entrance to the
National Stadium in Maputo

On the outskirts of Maputo, the splendid National Stadium shines with a light of its own amid the gloomy squalor of one of the poorest countries in Africa. To get to the stadium, we have to make our way through the dense traffic of crowded minibuses and pick-up trucks which bring the suburbs of the Mozambican capital to a standstill. This lack of movement extends all the way to the dusty gutters at the side of the road. Lined with buildings on either side, the N1 motor-way reveals the essence of Africa: a parade of women with babies on their backs and sacks of rice or corn on their heads, children in uni-form on their way to or from school and street vendors selling all kinds of produce, from coal, tyres and firewood to mobile phone cards, fruit and petrol. The air is filled with the stench of rubbish and plastic being burnt somewhere nearby.

In the open area beside the stadium, dozens of people with poverty radiating from every pore are laying out basic products on blankets on the ground. They are selling cheap clothes, sickly looking meat and fish and lukewarm drinks, as well as nail varnish and bars of soap, vegetables and dried fruit, tomatoes, oranges and various tools. They manage to survive somehow despite the sun beating down, their mea-gre sales and the incessant cries of their babies. Just a few metres away, a walled precinct with a firmly locked entrance and a Chinese-style roof hung with red Chinese lanterns is home to the building site of a magnificent new football stadium with a capacity for 42,000 spectators. Built by the Chinese state-owned company Anhui Wai Jing,[1] the stadium was once hailed as the pride and joy of the entire nation. That was until strikes, quarrels and violence transformed the most symbolic Chinese project in Mozambique into a veritable minefield.

On the wall beside the great metal door that separates these two worlds, a poetically written official motto describes the blood ties that supposedly unite the two countries: 'The friendship between China and Mozambique will prevail like Heaven and Earth', it solemnly declares in Portuguese and Mandarin. Another motto refers to the 'perfection' of a project that will bring 'glory to China'. We walk through the entrance and once again find ourselves in the middle of one of those enigmatic and winning Chinese infrastructure projects that Beijing offers at a discount price in exchange for conquering the world, as we saw in the last chapter. We wondered what life must be like behind these walls as the distorted sound of 1980s Chinese pop music from the precinct's loudspeakers assaulted our ears. This time we were not following the quality roads to find out the effects of a dam or the nature of 'turnkey' infrastructure projects. This time we were interested in the working conditions of the thousands of anonymous people who build these edifices. Is being a link between Heaven and Earth really a divine experience?

Deng, the project manager, welcomes us with a friendly smile. The only thing needed to change his initial distrust into a warm welcome is a short conversation with our Chinese guide, who soon manages to win him over. Once again we are able to confirm that 'a compatriot's word' can work wonders at a great distance from the motherland. Deng authorizes our entry into the site and designates his chief engineer, Jiang Ning, as a host to guide us around the precinct. Dressed in fuchsia coloured corporate overalls, Jiang tells us that he came to Mozambique from his native province of Anhui in eastern China when work on the stadium was just beginning.[2] That was almost two years ago, and he has not been back since. In return for a significant pay rise, the promise of a guaranteed future career and his son's wellbeing, the company demands the highest possible level of commitment. In other words, two full years of hard labour without seeing his family and a harsh daily routine starting at half past seven in the morning, six or seven days a week. More rewards await him at the end of his time in Mozambique: new opportunities in new countries. This suits Jiang nicely. Aged thirty-five, his only priority in life is to secure his future – even if that means he will not get to see his son grow up.

With so many obligations, the 260 Chinese employees – all of them from Anhui – have hardly left the building site during the twenty-four months they have spent in Mozambique. 'We hardly ever leave the camp. We don't speak Portuguese. We don't know the area. And if we go out we end up spending money, when what we really want to do is save it all,' Jiang explains. What is more, the camp is calm and ordered compared to the lively chaos outside, and the employees' working and living conditions would be the envy of the millions of rural workers in China who help fuel the 'factory of the world' in return for miserable wages. It is not just that the stadium's workers make three times what they would earn in a similar role in their own country. They also live in decent cabins flanked by small gardens, sleep four to a room in beds with mosquito nets, watch Chinese television, have access to an internet connection and enjoy regional Anhui cuisine three times a day, just to make them feel at home.

'Life is good here. I have my own bedroom and I spend my spare time watching films and playing mah-jong. I can talk to my son over the internet. I have no complaints,' Jiang explains. As we wander through the precinct, we see many striking splashes of fuchsia against the grey ground: small groups of Chinese and Mozambican employees working together to lay asphalt on the athletics track, finish off the paths into the stadium and put the finishing touches to the electrical installations. Everything seems perfectly normal, but appearances can be deceptive. The relationship between the Chinese and local workers is not good at all, and has deteriorated through a lack of communication, the discrimination suffered by the African workers and previous quarrels between the two groups. Jiang does not mince his words when it comes to discussing his local colleagues. 'We want to finish this project as soon as we can so that we can go home. They don't want to work overtime, they work very slowly and they're always complaining.' However, Jiang himself justifies these complaints – almost unintentionally – when he tells us that an unqualified Chinese worker earns $850 a month and has excellent access to accommodation, food and medical insurance, while Mozambicans barely make over $150 per month, without any additional benefits.[3] Speaking in Portuguese so that their Chinese bosses will not understand them, some of the local workers take this opportunity to show their dissatisfaction with the unfair treatment. 'We're treated very badly. Some of the bosses are very harsh,' one of them explains. 'They pay us very little,' another one says. 'They pretend to pay us, so we pretend to work,' he concludes, ironically.

Celso, a twenty-four year old labourer and welder, is particularly keen to strike up a conversation with the *branquinhos*, or 'white men', but we are accompanied by his Chinese bosses. Sweating generously under his blue helmet, he is wearing sunglasses, a face mask and a white overall whose original colour can only be seen at shoulder level, as it is covered in grease from his chest to his toes. A white crucifix hangs around his neck, standing out strikingly against his black skin. We shake hands amicably and he smiles at us, until one of our questions instantly wipes the grin from his face.

'What's it like working here? How do the Chinese treat you?'

'Very badly ... There are lots of problems here ...'

'Would you like to tell us what's happening? Shall we meet when you finish work?'

'Yes. I get out in an hour, at five thirty.'

'We'll be waiting for you in a white car at the main entrance.'

'I'll be there ...'

Celso arrives punctually for our meeting. He climbs into the car with a serious expression and gets straight to the point. As his story unfolds, we realize that Jiang Ning, the site's helpful number two, failed to give us the whole picture when he described and justified the working conditions of his African colleagues. With his clear gaze and direct way of speaking, Celso describes working conditions that border on exploitation, and which are so untenable they would be illegal anywhere else. He explains that he works nine-hour days without a break, not including overtime, and that he works for entire months without a single day off so that he can earn extra money. The company does not provide contracts, medical insurance or any kind of benefits, let alone accommodation or transport. To make things worse, there is a new surprise with every payslip. 'Each month the company takes away part of my salary, and I have no idea why,' he complains. These insufficiently explained deductions, which vary from month to month and from person to person, have led the workers to feel that the company is 'stealing' from them. Celso also complains that they are not given anything to eat during the working day, despite the fact that the Chinese employees eat lunch punctually in the 'Chinese only' canteen every day. The Mozambican employees are only given some stale bread when they work overtime. 'Did you see the bread rolls they brought us in plastic bags?' Celso asks us. 'Well, they don't put anything inside them. Nothing at all.'

Just as in China's production lines, red capitalism in Africa imposes a merciless code on its workers: earning a miserable salary requires first a big sacrifice. Celso's reward for the abuse he suffers is frankly grotesque: a monthly wage of between 3,500 and 4,000 meticais, or between 75 and 87 euros.[4] This is a pittance even in Mozambique, where the minimum sum needed for a family to survive is 5,000 meticais per month, or around 110 euros.[5] 'They treat us in the worst possible way. I wish I could work for a non-Chinese company, as the conditions would be much better. But I don't have a choice, because there's no work in Mozambique. It's either this or nothing,' Celso explains with a mixture of repressed anger and resignation. When it comes to choosing between a miserable but stable wage inside the stadium and a life of street vending, uncertainty and total poverty in the outside world, Celso and his colleagues opt for survival.

In the context of these unstable working conditions, humiliating treatment and barely justifiable discrimination,[6] with Chinese workers earning almost six times more than their colleagues with similar responsibilities, the rising tension has led to tragedy at the precinct in Maputo, as it has done in many other places around the world where the Chinese have imposed their own work-related logic. It was on 30 April 2010 – the day before Labour Day – that a strike broke out, which led to outbreaks of violence before the predictable intervention of the police, who took the side of the stronger party. The result: one man died, several people were wounded by flying bullets and many more were dismissed. Weeks after our visit to the National Stadium, representatives of Anhui Wai Jing denied by telephone that there were any problems with their projects in Mozambique, assuring us that they were operating 'in accordance with the country's rules and regulations'.[7] Soon after finishing and delivering the stadium, the Chinese company was officially recognized as one of ten Chinese corporations which, in 2010, had made the greatest 'contribution to the economic and social development of the African countries ... and helped to improve the living standards of the people in Africa'.[8]

While we enjoy some refreshments at the legendary Café Continental on Maputo's Avenida 25 de Setembre, the Portuguese sociologist João Feijó confirms that what we have seen at the National Stadium and other Chinese projects in Mozambique is the rule, rather than the exception.[9] Feijó is one of the most knowledgeable authorities on labour conditions in the former Portuguese colony and has carried out a study into the working conditions that Chinese companies offer in Mozambique:[10] 'With the exception of Huawei, labour conditions in the Chinese companies are terrible. They are clearly the worst,' he argues.

Feijó's analysis draws a perfect comparison with what has been – and still is – the general outlook in factories and building sites in Canton, Shanghai and Chengdu. 'The Chinese system is all about production, capitalism and profit. They treat local workers as simple anonymous beings. The workers are not learning much as there's no knowledge transfer and they don't have any promotion opportunities.' They work much longer hours than they are paid for, he continues, which explains why employees rarely last longer than six months. 'As soon as they find a better alternative, they just go.'

While we were gathering evidence about the reality of labour conditions in Mozambique, we couldn't help wondering whether China is really the winning option for the developing world that it usually believes itself to be. We found ourselves thinking back to the sugary-sweet atmosphere at the Egyptian convention centre in Sharm el-Sheikh, where the African and Chinese leaders – led by Wen Jiabao and his anti-colonialist speeches – staged their own private honeymoon at the Forum on China–Africa Co-operation. In this loved-up atmosphere, nobody dared to spoil the *mise-en-scène* by reproaching China for its careless attitude towards labour conditions in Mozambique and other countries. And so during one of the breaks we had approached Zambia's Minister of Commerce at that time, Félix Mutati, with a double-edged question: 'Minister, is China really an opportunity for Africa?' Mutati responded perfectly amicably, arguing that in terms of delivery, speed and costs, China was the best possible option to help Africa face up to the challenges of development. 'The bottom line is impact. Politicians are judged by what we create, not by commitments that arise from our conversations. They won't re-elect me if I don't build a road. If I build one, I'm a hero,' he explained.

However, he recognized that accepting China's offer meant making some 'sacrifices' and that it was important to 'minimize the ugliness' of the situation. Mutati apparently subscribes to the theory commonly held by the African and Chinese political elites that it is necessary to suffer now so that the next generations will be able to reap the benefits. This sacrifice, of course, falls upon the shoulders of the long-suffering workers – the weakest links – as in the end they are the ones paying the bill for this future success. The minister not only gave the impression of wanting to play down the importance of collateral damage in the workplace, but even came to the rescue of Chinese companies operating in his country. 'There have been accusations about who pays higher wages and provides the best working conditions, the Chinese or the Western investors. However, we have around 200 Chinese companies in Zambia now, each of them offering different conditions. We therefore have to use practical examples; don't come here with a generalized view,' he challenged us. This conversation convinced us that we would have to go to Zambia to see for ourselves what is happening on the ground.

The symbolism of the historic ties between China and Zambia provided an added incentive for our choice of the ex-British colony as our next destination: the two countries forged a close relationship after the former Northern Rhodesia gained its independence in 1964. This relationship came to fruition in the TAZARA project, a still active but dilapidated railway which covers the 1,860 kilometres between Dar es Salaam, the capital of Tanzania, and the heart of the 'Copperbelt', Zambia's mining province.[11] The railway represented a gigantic project for the then poverty-stricken Chinese state: a $500-million investment and the deployment of over 25,000 Chinese citizens, including labourers, foremen and engineers.[12] The words of the minister certainly seemed reassuring. Did this mean that labour conditions offered by Chinese companies to employees from China's 'old friend' in Africa were different – and better – than those in Mozambique?

IN SEARCH OF THE MINISTER'S REALITY

Eight months after our conversation with Félix Mutati, we finally made our way into western Zambia through Lubumbashi, the capital of the Congolese province of Katanga, after progressing at a snail's pace over the last few kilometres in the midst of an endless string of lorries crammed with copper and cobalt. In this distant corner of the world, crowds of people loaded with bundles swarm around the fence separating the two countries or launch themselves at the crowded immigration desk where the paperwork is dealt with by hand on carbon paper, without any sign of computers. The constant traffic has turned this border post into a madhouse: 5,000 tons of minerals travel through here each day on their journey from the mineral deposits of the Democratic Republic of Congo to Zambia's processing factories, and then on towards the ports of Dar es Salaam and Durban in Tanzania and South Africa. From there, the cargo sets sail for destinations across the world, but most of all to China. Hundreds of lorries, brimming with minerals, wait for days at a time in the queue to cross the border, which has encouraged the creation of a frenzied commercial atmosphere full of prostitutes offering cheap and unsafe sex, brokers arranging transport to the nearest town, and chancers on the hunt for new opportunities amid the chaos.

Entering Zambia from the DRC, a country where the simple act of turning on a tap or getting water out of your shower is a luxury in its own right, feels like a kind of blessing. Life instantly seems more pleasant in Zambia which, along with its Congolese neighbour, is home to the so-called 'Copperbelt', an area that harbours 10 per cent of the world's copper and a third of its cobalt reserves. The sun is just beginning to set as we arrive in Kitwe, Zambia's second city and the scene of labour unrest dating back to the colonial era, when the country's first big mining strikes broke out in 1935 and 1940 and some fifty-six people died.

Soon the streets around the city centre are cloaked in darkness, bereft of any public streetlights. It's the weekend, and alcohol is flowing freely. Groups of young people are moving here and there, in cars or by foot, in search of a good time. Meanwhile, we're in search of Chinese residents. 'Try the casino, that's the best place to find them,' the locals tell us. After entering the Edinburgh Hotel, which has its own betting centre, two Zambian tourists confirm that we have hit the jackpot. 'This is Chinatown. The atmosphere is really strange. Nobody even smiles,' they tell us, nervously. Kitwe's casino is small, with just six gaming tables, two for roulette and four for blackjack. All of them are full. Hardly anyone is drinking, even though the drinks are free. Four prostitutes are standing at the bar looking bored; their charms have failed to have the slightest effect on their potential clients. We count a total of thirty-six Chinese men, two Russians, a Pakistani and an African. The Russians noisily celebrate every win, while the Chinese gamblers smoke non stop, with reserved yet anxious expressions. Other Chinese men are sitting around on sofas, dozing off or fiddling with their mobile phones while they wait for their bosses, the mining employers, to break the bank. We approach several of the Chinese customers, but nobody wants to talk. The atmosphere couldn't be more strange; it is almost like being in a mafia den. This place is ruled by codes that are tailor-made for unscrupulous tough guys with plenty of spare cash – in other words, the codes of mining territory.

In the morning, these codes are also observed at the sites of the region's mineral deposits for which they were created, such as the mine in Chambishi, for example, 30 kilometres away from Kitwe. It is Sunday and there is hardly any movement in the dusty town, apart from several young men playing pool in two bars with music pumping out at full volume and a reverend and his faithful congregation singing their hearts out at the Sunday mass. Chambishi is not only known as the home of the first Special Economic Zone that China has financed and built in Africa.[13] Sadly, it is also infamous for the violence that has been unleashed against the Chinese employers as a result of the working conditions imposed on their African workers. 'The situation hasn't got any better since the last riots. Everybody is unhappy with the Chinese,' says Chiseni, a plumber at Fifteen

Metallurgical Construction Company, the Chinese state-owned enterprise responsible for building mining infrastructure. Chiseni is referring to the violence that broke out in 2007, resulting in one death, a significant uproar among politicians and the media, and the cancellation of a planned visit to the area by the Chinese president, Hu Jintao. It was the first time a Chinese leader has had to suspend his plans in Africa as a result of social unrest. However, the situation in the region was nothing new: unsafe working conditions had already caused an accident in 2005 which killed fifty-one workers at the explosives plant run by Beijing General Research Institute of Mining and Metallurgy (BGRIMM).[14]

It is lunchtime, and Chiseni and his colleagues Lubinda, Chalebaila and Bright – all of them around thirty years old – are more than happy to have a Coca-Cola with us and talk about the hardships they say they suffer on a daily basis. Like Celso at the National Stadium in Maputo, their initial warm welcome is replaced by serious, almost anxious looks when they find out what has brought us here. However, they rarely get the opportunity to air their grievances, and so now they jump in with both feet. They tell us that their monthly salary for working eight-hour days, six days a week as carpenters, plumbers and painters ranges between 500,000 and 600,000 kwachas, or 70 to 85 euros.[15] This represents just a fifth of the monthly income needed to sustain a Zambian family of six, according to local unions. They also have no access to insurance or accommodation, and we guess from their simple and shabby work clothes that their equipment is probably unsafe as well as insufficient. 'The supervisors ask too much from us and the treatment is very aggressive, even physically aggressive. There's a lot of tension on the site,' one of them adds. Boyd Chibale, director of research at the National Union of Miners and Allied Workers (NUMAW), one of the country's two most important mining unions with 11,250 members, explains that working conditions in Chinese mines are comparatively the worst in the country.[16] 'The Indian, Canadian and Australian investors pay much more: at least 1.5 million kwachas per month [215 euros],' he assures us.

Even in the 1960s, 1970s and 1980s, the British giant Anglo American – which left the country in 2002 amid fierce controversy and accusations of various misdemeanours – offered 'much better' conditions than those provided by the Chinese companies today, Chibale tell us. 'The Chinese have increased productivity because of the machinery and technology they have brought in. However, there is now stagnation in terms of the workers' living standards, labour conditions and salaries. In the past, strikes, protests and riots were at a minimum, but now they're quite common. And we've only ever seen workers being shot at during the era of the Chinese investors.'

The latest episode of violence in Chinese mines took place in August 2012, when workers striking at the Chinese-owned Collum Coal Mine staged a protest that turned violent; a Chinese supervisor was killed after being hit with a coal trolley. Employees were demanding that their pay be raised to match Zambia's new minimum wage, which was approved earlier in the year and increases minimum salaries in the sector to $230 a month. It was not the first time that the Collum Coal Mine hit the headlines. At the end of 2010, two Chinese foremen fired indiscriminately at a crowd of miners at this mine in the south of the country who were taking part in a demonstration demanding better working conditions. The miners had to climb down a 1,000-rung ladder deep into the earth to risk their lives in extremely dangerous conditions in exchange for just four dollars a day. In a highly contentious decision, while eleven miners were still lying in hospital with bullet wounds, the courts dismissed a case that was initially going to be tried as attempted murder.[17]

Chiseni, Lubinda, Chalebaila and Bright give a human face to a form of twenty-first-century exploitation that seems to transport us back in time to the British Industrial Revolution. We saw the same look of powerlessness and desperation on their faces that we had seen elsewhere on our journey, faces that express the unbearable feeling of being held hostage by their Chinese bosses. Just before we said goodbye, we asked the men the same question we had put to Félix Mutati at the Forum on China–Africa Cooperation in Sharm el-Sheikh: 'Is China an opportunity for the poor people of Africa? What would you think if I told you that China is here to help Zambia?' Their answer is instinctive and fierce: 'Lies! . . . Nothing but lies!' they shout angrily, almost in unison. 'Chinese propaganda!' one of them hisses, as they walk slowly away along the dusty streets of Chambishi.

KING COBRA: AN ANTI-CHINESE HERO

In terms of China's role in the heart of Zambia's mining industry, the difference in perception between the government minister and the workers who struggle against their Chinese employers on a daily basis – between the political and financial elites and the common people – perfectly summarizes the situation in the country. The Zambian government has placed its bets on a strategic alliance with Beijing, as it considers China the perfect travelling companion along the road of long-term development for its fabulous mining sector. Zambia hopes that the investments in its mining industry will propel Zambia towards an 'African Industrial Revolution', which is seen in Lusaka as an essential factor in helping the country to rise out of poverty. All this is no doubt caused not only by the enthusiastic reforms carried out over the last few decades, but also by Zambia's attractive current investment framework, which has been strongly criticized for its staunchly neo-liberal leanings and which has clearly had a decisive impact on the country's growing job insecurity. Hungry for raw materials, China has taken advantage of this situation, becoming the only foreign investor to continue investing in the Copperbelt since the financial crisis, despite the fall in the international price of copper.[18]

The fact that Zambia has pinned all its hopes for the future on its mining industry, and therefore on Chinese investments, has led to a situation in which Chinese investors are essentially given free rein to do whatever they like in the country's Copperbelt. While this is demonstrated by Lusaka's offer of tax holidays and the removal of customs duties for foreign investors, it is also particularly evident in the Zambian government's lax attitude towards the continuous flaunting of the most basic labour standards in Chinese mines, including the dismissal of the case against the two Chinese foremen who shot and wounded their employees. 'Foreign investors are very comfortable in Zambia. The unions are very active, but the government prefers to protect investors over the people,' the union leader Boyd Chibale told us during our meeting in Kitwe. While Lusaka's dreams of wealth become a reality, 80 per cent of the Copperbelt's population live on less than two dollars a day, with Beijing's complicity. Is this the 'sacrifice' which Félix Mutati talked about that day on the shores of the Red Sea?

Chinese mining companies should not technically benefit from highly favourable treatment, but the working conditions they offer their employees – many of them on temporary contracts – are comparatively the worst in the country. This precarious employment situation, which causes suffering among some of Zambia's poorest inhabitants, has made the companies the target of hostility. Michael Sata, the populist leader of the opposition Patriotic Front party at the time of our visit to Zambia, had pinned his presidential hopes on the use of markedly anti-Chinese discourse directed at the former government's weakest flank. 'King Cobra', as he is known, argued that the suffering of Zambia's miners stems from the fact that they are treated as unwelcome guests in their own country. 'The Chinese enjoy corrupt [investment] conditions. When I become president, we are going to implement labour laws . . . If the Chinese don't want to obey the law, they can just pack their bags and go back to China,' he told us firmly in an interview just a couple of months before the presidential elections. Sata's diatribes against Chinese companies have made him a hero in the Copperbelt, where he counted on widespread support, and in September 2011 he won the presidential elections, becoming Zambia's new leader.[19]

Is China really an opportunity for the developing world, we asked ourselves throughout the course of our travels. For better or for worse, there is no doubt that the country's expansion has left deep marks on the countries it has affected. However, it would be unfair to play down the positive impact that this expansion has had – either directly or indirectly – on millions of people around the planet. We must not forget the thousands of jobs created, the flow of capital generated by its long-term commitments to purchase natural resources, or the new infrastructure it has built in the developing world. Equally, it would be wrong to dismiss the cheap products made in the 'factory of the world' which are affordable for low-income populations, China's multi-million-dollar investments or its aid and co-operation projects. However, as well as the other negative factors which go hand in hand with China's expansion – such as corruption, the total disregard for human rights, and its actions' impact on the environment – all China's good work is undoubtedly eclipsed by its approach to labour conditions. This factor has arguably caused the most harm to China's image abroad, particularly because of the visibility and sensitivity of a subject that affects the poorest of the poor, as we saw for ourselves in the mines of Peru and Burma,[20] the building sites of Sudan and Angola, the big infrastructure projects in Mozambique and the mining sites of Zambia's mineral deposits.[21]

The Chinese companies' casual treatment of their employees, contempt towards unions and complete lack of concern about alleviating conflict – a consequence of their stubborn, almost despotic approach to their position of power – inevitably brings to mind past colonialism in Africa, but this time with Chinese characteristics. 'Common trends at Chinese businesses in Africa [included] hostile attitudes towards trade unions, various violations of workers' rights, poor working conditions and several instances of discrimination and unfair labour practices', a recent study into the workplace situation in Chinese companies in ten African countries concluded.[22]

We were therefore not surprised by the blunt conclusion of Boyd Chibale, the Kitwe union leader, when he told us that 'the Chinese are ripping off lots of money and are giving back very little'. Back in Maputo, the sociologist João Feijó also struck at the foundations of the 'mutually beneficial co-operation' on which Sino-African relations are based. 'The Chinese companies are not doing anything for Mozambique; they're doing it for themselves. But I don't think the Chinese really care,' he concluded.

The description of what is really happening on the ground grates horribly against the background of Chinese official rhetoric. While the sign over the entrance to the Maputo National Stadium, in one of Africa's poorest countries, boasts that 'friendship between China and Mozambique will prevail like Heaven and Earth', Chinese companies are not even paying their local employees enough to meet their basic needs. What is more, the salaries they pay them are six times less than those of their Chinese employees.

This troubled workplace situation, which has severely damaged China's image in many of the affected areas, does not seem like a particularly difficult problem to solve. What is preventing these companies from handing out employment contracts, paying their employees an extra $50 per month or offering them basic medical insurance? What is stopping them from providing their workers with regulation gloves or helmets, or putting some meat or cheese inside those bread rolls? What is preventing them from treating their workers with dignity and using dialogue to improve the situation? At a first glance, it seems like an enormous miscalculation on the part of the Chinese government not to intervene more to tackle this issue, even if they do not have the capacity to reach every Chinese company operating around the world. However, perhaps the answer to these questions lies not so much in bad faith as in the labour conditions in China itself, where the millions of workers who have carried out the 'Chinese miracle' are still being exploited.

Liu Guijin, the Chinese government's special representative for Africa, admits that these problems exist and explains that Beijing – after refusing to share responsibility for supervising these companies with its media or civil society – is in over its head. 'Our government is making efforts to educate the Chinese companies to properly carry out their corporate social responsibilities, to follow fixed rules or regulations and to observe local laws . . . But there are so many companies scattered everywhere in Africa, and we cannot guarantee that 100 per cent of them are performing perfectly well.' A glance at China's domestic situation is enough to see that, in general, these Chinese companies are simply reproducing abroad the same labour pattern that has been in force in China for the last thirty years, ever since Deng Xiaoping outlined China's journey to wealth along the path of 'socialism with Chinese characteristics'. One of the driving forces behind the growth of this new model was to put the endless human resources of the planet's most populated country to the service of the 'factory of the world', a tactic that included paying meagre salaries to the workforce. It was a winning formula: low labour costs made Chinese products very competitive, contributing significantly to the fabulous increase in China's GDP over the last three decades, an invaluable factor in the country's development. As China became rich, pure economic logic dictates that the salaries of the workers who generated a significant part of that wealth should also have risen in proportion to their productivity. However, this explosion of wealth hasn't filtered down through an increase in salaries.[23]

Here, then, is the source of the abuse; here lies the evidence that a significant part of the Chinese model's success rests on the shoulders and tireless work of the Chinese people. Now that China is at the height of its expansion across the world, the hardships of red capitalism have become visible in Africa and other places; however, they have already been around in China for some time. Three decades later, the unscrupulous exploitation of China's working classes is continuing and even spilling out beyond the country's own borders.

CHINESE NEO-SLAVERY IN THE HEART OF AFRICA

Liu Jianxin and Liu Senlin are all too familiar with this state of affairs. That was why these two men decided to set off on a new adventure abroad, without a word of French between them. Their destination was Gabon on the West Africa coast, their task was to build a road through the centre of the country, and their reward was a salary three times greater than they could earn in China. However, the dream soon turned into a nightmare, and their African adventure almost ended in suicide. Liu Jianxin was not new to Africa: he had previously worked as a steamroller driver for a Chinese state-owned company in Nigeria and Zambia. His friend, Liu Senlin, was something of a road-building veteran himself and felt he had nothing to fear from a journey to Africa. He had already faced up to the reality of a shattered Iraq in 1991 after the first Gulf War, when he had travelled to the Arab country to pave roads. However, this time both of them found themselves unprepared for what awaited them. They arrived in Gabon to work for a Chinese construction company and just a few months later they were forced to desert the camp to escape from the slavery to which they and their workmates were being subjected. That was just the beginning of an odyssey that would see them having to flee from the thugs that their boss had sent after them and beg to survive in the heart of Africa.

Our first contact with the men was by telephone in 2010. They were in Gabon, and we were in Beijing. That was when they told us their story. It had all started in 2009. Liu Jianxin arrived in Gabon in

July and his colleague arrived in December. 'Straightaway I saw that the conditions were going to be difficult, even inhuman. We had to share a 90-centimetre single bed with another colleague, we weren't paid for working overtime and we were only given two days off each year,' the younger of the two Lius explained. There were roughly forty workers at the camp, all of them Chinese. Half of them had family ties to the head of the company, Lei Youbin, while the rest of them mostly came from the Chinese province of Hubei, where an advert in the local paper, *Chutian Dushibao*, had offered a monthly salary of 1,000 euros – a fortune in rural China – in return for helping to build a road. However, in reality they had to work like dogs for endless hours under a punishing sun. Some local men also took part in the work, although only as temporary extra workers. On the other end of the telephone line, the men sounded pleasant and polite. They were even glad to have had the chance to appreciate the beauty of the sea for the first time in their lives.

Two months later, back in China, we met them at our Beijing office along with two of their workmates – Ru Liyin and Li Gao[24] – who had suffered the same ill treatment at the hands of Aolong, the private Chinese company in question. The company had been subcontracted by the state-owned China Communication Construction Company (CCCC) to build a stretch of the 112-kilometre motorway between the towns of Fougamou and Mouila in central Gabon. The bleakness of the workers' description of events, as well as their desperate appearance of men who had lost everything, brought a lump to our throats. 'They fed us rotten rice. We were working for fourteen hours or more each day. They didn't pay us the salary stipulated in our contracts. We were slaves. That's what our boss told us and that's how we felt.' The words of Liu Senlin sounded devastating in the mouth of a Chinese man, accustomed as they are to suffering unspeakable hardships without a word of complaint. Sitting around a large wooden table, his colleagues nodded silently, hanging their heads, clearly angry and hurt by the injustice they had suffered.

After the first month of work, the promised salary never arrived.[25] The company paid part of their wages, but most of the money was held back under the pretext of delays in the company's billing system. The situation got worse in the second and third months, when the workers still did not receive the income they had been promised in their contract. 'After the fourth month, we decided to pack it in. Three colleagues and I decided to resign.' Convinced that it was time to put an end to their African adventure, the men all handed in their notice. 'We were called one by one into the boss's office. The first to go in was Wang, one of our workmates. Half an hour later, he came staggering out after taking a beating. I was next. Several men hit me while the boss watched. It lasted for about ten minutes,' Liu Senlin explains, as he shows us the marks left on his body by the attack. The two Lius decided to make a run for it. It was on 18 April 2010.

They left the camp by foot, with no other plan except to run away as far as their strength would carry them. None of their workmates joined in the escape out of fear of reprisals, but they helped them out with a bit of money. 'We managed to get as far as a nearby police station, but we couldn't ask for help because we don't speak a word of French. The policeman got an idea of what had happened from the gestures we were making and he found us a driver to take us to the nearest village,' they tell us. By that time the camp boss had realized that the two had gone missing, and so the company sent four Chinese thugs to hunt them down. The runaways began to fear for their lives and so, in the hope of getting some help and to recover their salaries, they made their way to the offices of CCCC, the company which subcontracts Aolong, to meet with a representative of the state-owned company. The company's reaction could not have been more brutal: first they refused to see the men, and then they told them to go back to work and stop causing trouble.

Desperate, and without any help or money in a foreign country with a language they did not speak, the two men set off on a very different African adventure to the one they had imagined. Over two days of travelling 400 kilometres along Gabonese roads – hidden in plastic bags on regional buses – the two Lius fled from the gangsters sent by Lei Youbin, the head of Aolong, who was ruling the camp with an iron fist in order to subdue the rest of the workers and prevent other desertions. 'It took us over two days to get to Libreville, the capital of Gabon. We got help from some Chinese people there who gave us food, but most of all a local taxi driver helped us by giving us money and shelter for five days.' Unfortunately, the Chinese Embassy in Libreville was not so helpful, choosing to wash their hands of the affair and to blindly follow the usual guidelines. 'We can't do anything. Go back to work and don't talk to the foreign press,' one embassy representative told them, refusing to give them his name.

When we checked these facts with the embassy in Libreville, we received the same treatment as the two fugitives: a 'diplomat', who refused to give us his name despite demanding our full personal information and the names of the media companies we worked for, assured us that the embassy 'had done everything possible to reconcile the two parties'. In other words, they pressured the workers into submitting to exploitation and mistreatment without even the guarantee of receiving a salary in return. The all-powerful Chinese state, capable of investing in projects across the planet and exerting its draconian control over a population of 1.3 billion people, was incapable of bringing a modest Chinese company into line after it exposed Chinese citizens to cruel and illegal abuse. Liu Senlin explains that the embassy's rejection left them with no alternative but to turn to the local and international press. 'After we were interviewed by the local television station, the Gabonese people started stopping us in the street to give us money. But the Chinese people who had helped us when we first arrived turned their backs on us, saying the Chinese community in Gabon had lost face when we uncovered the scandal,' he remembers bitterly.

The impact of the media uproar was a mixed blessing. Handled properly, a scandal of this kind could have caused the African Development Bank, the institution which is financing the construction of the road and which, in theory, has rigorous requirements for companies involved in the project, to withhold its payments and begin investigating these events. However, the defenceless Chinese workers, with no knowledge of the law or even the local language or customs, and with no money or support from their embassy in Gabon, were unable to achieve their aim of using the media to end the abuse taking place at the camp, hundreds of kilometres away from the capital. Instead, the media reports reached the ears of Lei Youbin, their Machiavellian boss, who picked up the telephone and sent several thugs on a courtesy visit to the fugitives' families in China, threatening them with reprisals if their relatives did not stop causing trouble.[26]

A month later, the two Lius received an encouraging phone call. 'Come to my office. They're going to give you the money,' said the director of the state-owned company that had wanted nothing to do with them just weeks before. They were met by three men dressed in police uniforms, who handcuffed them and shut them in a room where they were left for two days. 'Lei Youbin bribed them to arrest us,' the two workers insisted. Forty-eight hours later the police and their boss's henchmen took them to the airport, where – without passing through any immigration controls – they were put on a plane to Beijing. Their boss had decided to get rid of them once and for all by packing them off back to China. The nightmare had come to an end, but the legal battle in the Chinese courts was just beginning.

THE LAWYER OF LOST CAUSES

At our office in Beijing, Liu Jianxin, Liu Senlin, Ru Liyin and Li Gao demonstrate the typical characteristics of millions of these emigrants who serve as cannon fodder to fuel the longings of collective wealth in a new China. These workers are prepared to suffer terrible hardships in return for a salary, and therefore they rarely complain about having to do a hard job, however arduous it might be. However, they will go to any lengths to air their grievances when they become the victims of injustice, such as when salaries go unpaid. Like two pieces of the same puzzle, the proliferation of this type of abuse against emigrant workers has also created a generation of lawyers who will fight tooth and nail to protect their rights, despite the restrictions imposed on them by the government. Lawyer and client, both of them on the side of China's poorest people, are two faces of the same injustice, a phenomenon that has tainted China all too often. Now that China's investments and infrastructure projects have spread across the world, the shockwaves of this abuse are being felt beyond China's own borders.

Zhang Zhiqiang is one of these heroic figures. Short and stocky with stray bits of hair falling into his eyes, this lawyer and activist is one of the followers of the imprisoned 2010 Nobel Peace Prize winner, Liu Xiaobo. He is an expert in fighting against the abuses suffered by Chinese rural workers who leave their homes with all their belongings in a bundle on their backs, in search of a better future in the towns of eastern China. He has represented over 500 clients since 2007, when he too left his life as a *mingong* to become the Robin Hood of the Chinese courtrooms. 'I began studying law in 1997, while I was working in the sewing workshop at a multi-national sportswear company. My foreign boss encouraged me to continue with my studies after my shift,' he recalls. Today, this brave and tireless man, who travels all over China wearing a t-shirt with an image of the five mascots of the Beijing Olympic Games behind bars, is the defender of a caste of people who have 'no rights': people who have been trampled on and left in the gutter of life in Communist China, a country that aspires to become the leading world power of the twenty-first century.

Since 2009, Zhang has been carrying out his work almost free of charge, in exchange for barely 5 or 10 per cent of the reparation won by the aggrieved worker, which tends to be just a few thousand euros at best. 'I used to do it for free. Now I need to charge something in order to support my family, because the number of these cases has multiplied. But I give free legal advice over the phone. I receive an average of three calls a day,' he explains. Thanks to our intervention, Zhang represented the two Lius in an open court case against Aolong at the People's Court of Wuhan district in Hubei. Paradoxically, after the two Lius returned to China the company filed a case against them, demanding compensation for breach of contract. It was the first time that Zhang had taken on a case that had occurred outside China's borders, although he predicts that it will not be the last. 'The government's policy to encourage companies to go abroad will lead to an increase in this type of case,' he argues, proudly telling us that he has lost 'just five cases' in his whole career.

On 10 December 2010, the Chinese justice system only partially made amends for the suffering of the two Lius. The court ordered a payment of 19,180 yuan (around 2,000 euros) in unpaid wages to Liu Senlin, the veteran labourer who had worked in Saddam Hussein's Iraq. In the first instance, the judge also ordered the payment of 25,000 yuan (around 2,600 euros) to Liu Jianxin, his companion on the African adventure. The two remaining workers, Ru Liyin and Li Gao, lost their case in the first instance, having signed a document after their return to China exempting the company from the payment of any compensation or unpaid salaries. Strikingly, Aolong's abuse went completely unpunished and the company's illegal practices cost them nothing in legal terms and very little in labour terms. As at the end of August 2012, the company was still offering work in Africa to labourers from Hubei through tempting adverts in *Chutian Dushibao* and other major newspapers and websites. The company's headquarters in the African country were still a minefield of abuse.[27] Nothing had changed in the country of dizzying changes.

LABOUR EXPORT AGENCIES

The two Lius and their workmates fell into the grasp of Lei Youbin after being seduced by an attractive advertisement in the local press. However, many other emigrants like them are recruited in a surprising variety of ways. As he makes his way along the country roads of China's Chongqing Province, Liu Ning has no idea that he is on a mission with deep historical roots. His role is one that dates back a hundred years: the role of 'immigrant hunter'. Every day he sets off in his small car in search of the workers who will build the next dam in Ecuador, a road in Sri Lanka or a football stadium in Guinea. In the country's most remote villages, where the unemployment rate reaches double figures, Liu Ning uses his excellent people skills to convince labourers, machine operators, farmers and the unemployed to move to the dangerous Democratic Republic of Congo or the mysterious Karakum desert in Turkmenistan. 'I'm looking for machine operators, technical directors and rural workers. We promise them a salary of between 5,000 and 9,000 yuan and a two- or three-year contract,' he explains.

Wang Yinqiong, a carpenter from Chongqing, is one of these potential workers. He is short, lean and friendly. He has a thin moustache and dresses in a military jacket and trousers, and has lived through much hardship. At the age of twelve, when China was at the height of its economic opening-up process, he set off towards Hubei to work as a painter and decorator on a building site. It was his first job. He earned a single yuan (10 euro cents) for each day he spent decorating the walls of what was to become the new China. Since then, he and his country have taken different paths in life. The country has been transformed beyond all recognition, although the bare bones of its structure have remained the same. For Wang, on the other hand, nothing much has changed. He is married now and has two children, but economic uncertainty still plagues him like a curse. He has travelled tirelessly, exploring many of China's provinces in search of a better job that would pay just a few extra cents per hour or for an opportunity that would change his life and that of his family. He has travelled for thousands of kilometres in crowded trains or on foot, bearing the cold and exhaustion with his tools on his back. He has travelled on buses in a China that was yet to be built, driving deep into the valleys surrounding the Yangtze river basin and along the endless Chinese coastline with its millions of factories and workshops. He took a plane just once, when a wealthy client paid for his ticket.

Wang's life can be summarized as a continuous struggle just to be able to live from hand to mouth. Aged forty-four, this life journey has now brought him to live in a shack with two colleagues on the building site of a skyscraper in Chongqing. In this frustrating and noisy city of over 32 million inhabitants, with endless traffic jams and horrific pollution, the three men share everything: three beds with wooden boards and no mattresses, a small electric stove, a cooking pot, a feeble light bulb hanging from the ceiling and asbestos to keep the rain out. With the walls lined with plastic to fight off the damp and left-over food scattered all over the shack, they live in a state just above abject poverty. Wang pays a high price for a monthly salary of around 200 euros, as he gets to spend time with his family just once a year. 'For the last five years I've only seen my wife and two children at Chinese New Year,' he tells us. China's growing presence abroad therefore seems like a fantastic opportunity to leave this life of hardship behind him. And, so, Wang has decided to try his luck in Angola.

He has been assured that he will multiply his salary several times over by playing his part in the reconstruction of this country, along with the other 300,000 of his compatriots estimated to be working there.[28] He made the decision several months earlier when his brother-in-law, who had emigrated to Algeria, told him about the high salaries on offer. Word of mouth is unbeatable in China. The certainty of being able to quadruple his income was enough to convince Wang: he went straight to an agency to get the ball rolling so that he would be contracted by a Chinese company in Angola. 'I want to go to Angola because they'll pay me a good salary there. Any country is OK with me if they pay me well,' he assures us. Despite never having set foot in Africa, he already has a plan: to work his heart out in exchange for 100,000 yuan, or 13,000 euros. He is confident that this amount will pay for the education of his youngest son, who is currently ten years old, thereby laying the groundwork for his children to have a better life than he has had. 'I don't want them to be migrant workers like me. I want them to be able to live a decent life,' he concludes. If there is any money left over, he tells us, he would like to open a shoe shop in his hometown, Zhong Xiau.

Wang has already paid his 14,000 yuan to the agency run by Miss Lei Lin in Chongqing, so that it can start making the necessary arrangements to set his dreams of the 'new world' in motion. The director of the Meilian agency is in her thirties and speaks basic English. She set up the company in 2002 and has been sending Chinese emigrants abroad for the last six years. The agency has sent out a thousand workers, almost all of them to Africa, and has established around a dozen offices in various districts and counties in Chongqing. The agency only accepts male workers aged between thirty and forty-five, and prefers them to be actively in work but with aspirations to earn more. The majority of candidates are low-waged, experienced manual labourers, but university students also apply to go to Japan or Singapore to work in the service, packing or hotel industries. Cooks, for example, have the opportunity to travel all over the world thanks to the current appeal of Chinese gastronomy. Family support and a strong personality are essential attributes. 'Many workers get excited about the idea of going to work abroad. But they have to be capable of doing a very hard job,' Lei Lin warns us.

The 982 labour export agencies currently registered in China – as well as the many thousands more that operate on an unofficial basis[29] – are the natural successors of China's nineteenth-century 'recruiters'. Today these agencies use adverts in newspapers and local television channels to carry out the same work once undertaken by the people who filled the ports of Hong Kong, Shantou (Canton) and Amoy

(Fujian) with emigrants prepared to take on a lifetime of debt for the chance to try their luck on the other side of the Yellow Sea or even distant Cuba. Recruitment is carried out by word of mouth, flyers and adverts or by sending agents such as Liu Ning all over China to summon potential emigrants by loudspeaker to a meeting in the village square, with the full approval of local village and party leaders. 'Our employees go from house to house trying to convince the locals,' Lei tells us. 'There are two types of emigrants. Men with no work experience who want to go abroad; we offer them training. Then there are skilled workers who are not yet convinced; in those cases we try to convince them, even though it takes time.'

The reason for this reluctance is the payment system for emigrant workers. The fact that wages are paid in various stages to ensure that the employee will stay at the worksite until the end of the contract raises understandable suspicions. 'Many workers don't want to go to Africa because they are scared they won't get paid,' Lei admits, as we remember the desolation on the faces of the four emigrants from Hubei when we met them after their return from their Gabonese adventure. We also think of the dreams of men like Wang Yinqiong the carpenter, who have worked and suffered all their lives and now hope to get on board the last train of progress. Not getting paid is just one of a string of abusive and often illegal practices suffered by workers at the hands of employers and agencies, who achieve their respective goals of minimizing labour costs and earning commissions by offering potential workers employment contracts that protect the employer over the worker. 'Model' employment contracts such as the one used by the Meilian agency to convince their workers to commit to a project are clearly an invitation to abuse and injustice.[30]

'A lot of the contracts don't look OK,' Geoffrey Crothall of China Labour Bulletin[31] explains in reference to the fact that these documents offer the workers anything but a decent level of legal protection. 'It's difficult to see how the overseas labour [agencies] have done anything really to help workers' rights. All they're interested in is their commission.' The dire economic needs of emigrants like Wang Yinqiong or the two Lius, along with the greed of the agencies and the indifference of the provincial Chinese governments, who encourage the exportation of Chinese labour simply to reduce local unemployment rates,[32] all clearly stack the odds against the emigrants. Although the agencies exist purely for commercial reasons, they receive the enthusiastic support of the provincial leaders in charge of administering regions with high unemployment rates. It is no accident that agencies have started sprouting up like mushrooms in Chongqing: the region contains 1.5 million workers in the construction industry alone.[33] The question is, what are the Chinese authorities doing to mitigate possible cases of abuse?

Sitting in his leather chair, Xiong Yaozhi fidgets awkwardly each time we ask him a question. He is the head of the Emigrant Workers Abroad section of a governmental organization, the Foreign Economic and Trade Commission of Chongqing district, whose task is to promote, facilitate and supervise relations between recruitment agencies, employers and employees. In other words, it tries to impose order on a process that fuels the abuse that is paid for – as always – by the weakest members of society. Xiong is polite but sparing in his words, and he begins the interview with an attack: 'Foreign journalists always misunderstand China.' Without taking his eyes off the reports laid out on top of his desk, he also bluntly tells us that 'many Africans are quite undisciplined, not to mention lazy'. When we ask him why China has to take its own workers all over the planet, he refers to the speed of the projects. 'Big infrastructure projects need to be done quickly and Chinese workers are more capable of working quickly.'

This type of thinking extends as far as the highest echelons of the Chinese government. 'It's a way of making sure that projects are completed on time,' said the evasive then-spokesman of the Chinese Ministry of Foreign Affairs, Qin Gang, when we met him at the University of Oxford in the spring of 2011. In fact, a predominant form of discourse exists among Chinese government employees, diplomats, entrepreneurs and academics to justify sending Chinese workers abroad by suggesting that there are no qualified workers in the recipient country of origin or, if they do exist, that they will not be as efficient as their Chinese counterparts. This means of justification, which occasionally verges upon xenophobia, may be valid in the case of some countries such as Angola or the Democratic Republic of Congo, where war has led to a massive deficit of human capital. However, this argument is not sustainable in countries such as Iran,

Mozambique or Costa Rica, where we found that it is used equally often despite the surplus of workers in these countries. In Cuba, for example, Chinese government officials use the argument that 'Cubans are not motivated by the low wages imposed on them by the socialist system' to defend the fact that Chinese investments on the island are always accompanied by a Chinese workforce. This series of excuses leads to what must be a unique phenomenon – the massive export-ation of workers – which in itself says a lot about China's perception of non-Chinese.

After half an hour of conversation, Xiong seems more relaxed. He lights a cigarette and begins to talk more confidently. He assures us that his department is trying to supervise employment contracts to ensure that they will not exploit the weakness or ignorance of the workers by offering them unrealistically high wages for their ser-vices – sometimes as high as 8,000 euros – or unfair working conditions.[34] He then tackles the question of the rights of emigrant workers. He starts by following the official party line, but little by little this begins to fall apart. 'China's policy is to prioritize people. Emigrants are people and we have to take care of them,' he says in a fatherly manner. He does, however, recognize that 'some companies try to take advan-tage and don't consider certain issues such as security or the payment of salaries. The workers who are in a good position are happy, but some companies don't even offer basic working conditions. That is when workers go on strike,' he admits. It does seem strange, however, that Chinese employees in the heart of Africa can exercise the right to go on strike, while they would not be able to do so in China. 'Some emigrants have worked in several countries. They understand the workplace situation perfectly and they can get very sensitive. They start going on strike over the smallest issues,' he concludes.

Finally, we question him about the role of the authorities in terms of guaranteeing workplace rights. 'When there is a conflict, we work with the local governments to resolve it. For example, when there is inadequate accommodation or if there is an issue with the quality of the food. Most of all we intervene when workers are paid late or not paid at all.' In the case of a problem with the contract, guarantees or labour rights, Xiong argues that the workers' rights depend on the capacity of the countries in question to uphold the law. 'Technically, they should follow the legal process in force in that country. However, some African countries have a very weak and basic legal system and do not uphold the law. Nothing can be done in those cases,' he admits. In these situations, the only option left to the dispossessed workers is to resort to seeking the protection of the Chinese courts, and even then this is not always possible. As for the courts themselves, we have already seen what their sense of justice entails when it comes to choosing between the powerful and the weak.

7

The Chinese Miracle
Defies the Planet

'Fighting against Nature is an infinite pleasure.'
Mao Zedong, 1917

From the dirt track leading into the woods, we watch as the forest unfurls its explosive natural beauty in what seems to be an infinite wilderness. This is hostile, impenetrable territory for staunch urbanites like ourselves and, in general, for any strangers to the remote district of Krasnoarmeysky in the forestry heart of the Russian Far East. A brief incursion into this natural tangle with Anatoly Lebedev, a leading environmental expert in the region, is enough to give us a sense of the sheer exuberance of this unique universe tucked away between the Pacific Ocean and inhospitable Siberia. Barely 100 metres into the bushy undergrowth, the chirping of birds and the sounds of the forest's diverse fauna ring deafeningly in our ears. The humidity is so high that we can almost touch the air, leaving the forest's native species and occasional human visitors competing for oxygen.

In this uniquely diverse ecosystem, the sun struggles to break through the tops of the lush Korean pines, oaks and fir trees. Occasionally a clearing opens up in the forest and a halo of light beams vertically down to the ground, revealing an army of ants, beetles and slugs resting on the base of a felled tree. These small oases of light and warmth – a shock to the human sensory system – are simply warning signs pointing to one of the greatest environmental tragedies striking the sparsely populated Primorsky region: deforestation on a massive scale.

With the sleeves of his old shirt rolled up to his elbows, Lebedev stops in his tracks every now and again to lean against a tree trunk measuring a metre or so in diameter, warning us to check that none of the deadly ticks that transmit fatal encephalitis have become stuck to our skin or clothes. Whenever he does this, a swarm of bloodthirsty mosquitoes descends on him, swirling about his head of grey hair. However, this is no problem at all for this exceptional man in his seventies whose mission is to save the forests and their inhabitants from the greed and negligence of Russian entrepreneurs and officials and their Chinese associates.

The plundering of Russian forests was initially caused by the economic depression that has plagued Siberia and the Russian Far East since the fall of the Soviet Union, Lebedev explains with an air of melancholy. 'Before the end of the USSR there were state-owned industries for exploiting forestry resources. They took on the entire production chain, from felling the trees to processing the wood. All the added value remained in the area; they even produced wood pulp to make paper. Tens of thousands of people worked for those companies, which sold timber to the domestic and foreign markets. But after the capitalist revolution, as I call the collapse of the Soviet Union, these companies went bankrupt and a painful period of privatization began.'

Born in Vladivostok in 1941, Lebedev is the founder of the NGO the Bureau for Regional Outreach Campaigns (BROC). This intelligent and well-spoken man began to take an interest in the environment when he set foot for the first time in the immensity of the Arctic. 'My father was an icebreaker captain. As an engineer, I was involved in two missions to the Arctic. I came into contact with many writers, geologists and other members of the intellectual elite. That was when I began to understand the importance of the spiritual relationship between humans, industry and the environment. This was why I created BROC in 1997,' says the man who became a representative of the regional assembly in 1989 after 'the first and last democratic elections in Russia'. During that time Lebedev was at the forefront of various legislative initiatives to protect indigenous territories and populations. 'It was the first time that anything like that had been done in this country.' Before this he had done almost every type of job imaginable: naval engineering and military service, followed by work as a journalist and later as an environmental activist. Not to mention his stint as a KGB agent.

'As a result of my skills as a paratrooper and submariner, as well as my education in philosophy and the arts, the authorities involved me in the surveillance of people who were considered to be "mentally unreliable". I was supposed to inform the KGB about their "erroneous" behaviour,' he recalls. 'What I really did was warn people to be more cautious in their conversations and then I told my superiors that the person in question supported the Communist regime and that everything was fine.' Nobody was safe in those days: after being 'betrayed by a friend', Lebedev barely escaped being imprisoned in a labour camp. He forms part of a generation of Russians trapped between the Communist repression of that era and the oligarch-run system that has been introduced into the new Russia. Angered most of all by the new generation's loss of culture and integrity, Lebedev speaks bluntly about the looting process that followed the fall of the Soviet empire, when a small group of people – many of them ex-Communist officials – fought a merciless and violent battle for the country's wealth.

The collapse of the Soviet system swept away the livelihoods of thousands of families in the region who not only lived off the income generated by the timber industry, but also off the exploitation of other forest products such as honey, ginseng, wild fruit, wild boar meat and bear fat. Contrary to what many people expected, the dismantling of the state-owned industries did not lead to a more efficient use of these resources. Instead, it resulted in a looting process carried out by what were effectively mafia organizations. 'The state-owned companies had to be destroyed and privatized. The private investors, many of them ex-Soviet officials, literally killed each other in a fratricidal war over who would buy the privatized companies.' This was no surprise: the biggest country on the planet also harbours the world's largest reserves of coniferous forests, with 57 per cent of the world's total temperate forest surface area. They represent an endless source of resources with enormous potential which, as has also occurred in the country's energy and mining sectors, the post-Soviet elites have been quick to get their teeth into.[1] After the collapse of the USSR the forests went from being under the control of the government to being subjected to a process of violent pillaging, as the only thing that mattered was – and still is – the ability to get rich quickly.

First, the entrepreneurs began to savagely and unsustainably loot the area's tree species, felling them without thought to maximize profits. At the same time, the victims of the closure of the state-owned enterprises – the former employees who found themselves destitute – headed to the forests in search of a means of supporting themselves. Forced into a state of desperation by a lack of job opportunities, they carried out random raids into the forest with nothing but vans and a few chainsaws to get hold of the odd bit of rare wood that could later be resold. The scale of this attack was much smaller, but the constant and disorganized string of raids had disastrous long-term consequences. 'They started to compete for the forest's resources. Lots of unemployed people entered the industry illegally, without access to a concession, selling to the Chinese as soon as the border with China opened,' explains Lebedev. It was 1991 when China entered on to the scene. 'The Chinese bought everything, whether it was legal or not. Lots of people in the rural areas of Siberia are very grateful to China, because in those days it was the only option left to them. Some forest villages still exist today thanks to Chinese demand. If that hadn't happened, they would not have been able to survive.'

Since then, the corporations responsible for most of the modern-day drama have been logging indiscriminately using unsustainable practices with concessions obtained in a variety of ways. 'The problem is caused by the companies who carry out intensive logging, destroying everything in their path. These companies can count on the support of corrupt civil servants because they pay a lot of tax. State-owned companies are also awarded concessions in the hope that they will protect those areas, but what they actually do is fell trees for commercial aims, even in vetoed areas.' This whole system is fuelled by *opshack*, a system of corruption which infects every level of Russian society, from the figures at the top of the power pyramid to the minor officials at its base. It is similar in some ways to the 'revolutionary tax' levied by guerrillas and mafia gangs, but in this case the 'tax' is extorted by state bodies: the police, forestry agents, guards, customs officers and officials. Businessmen, thugs and oligarchs also demand their share. The briefcases full of money even get as far as the Kremlin itself. 'If you don't pay your bribe you're out of the business,' Lebedev assures us.

Corruption and bribery help to 'legalize' the criminal behaviour which is now threatening to wipe out a unique ecosystem within the next two or three decades. Although wood is obtained illegally, under-the-counter payments make it possible to get hold of the documents needed for this wood to enter the legal circuit: certificates of origin, species and quantity, as well as felling and export licences. Everything, in fact; nothing is impossible if you name the right price, Lebedev tells us. 'In a completely corrupt country, there is no control whatsoever; control is just impossible. Any agent is potentially corruptible. Corruption is part of the system. When the inspector on duty catches somebody trafficking or felling wood illegally, that person simply offers him 100 dollars and everything is resolved. The forestry guards earn barely 10,000 roubles per month, or around 300 dollars. They earn so little that if you bribe them just once they earn more than they would in a whole month. How are they not going to be corrupt?' As he describes this drama, which goes far beyond environmental issues, Anatoly Lebedev's voice begins to crack. He opens his eyes wide and talks bluntly about the current situation. He seems to feel a certain amount of nostalgia for the past. Sometimes he mixes his own personal story with that of deforestation, as if to show that the environmental degradation in the region is a direct consequence of the moral impoverishment of Russian society.

1998: THE CHINA FACTOR, YEAR ZERO

While the anarchic privatization of the assets of the former Soviet Union has clearly played an important role in the drama of the Siberian forests, one specific year stands out for the particularly damaging effect it had on the forests and their native species: 1998. 'Several things happened at once that year. On the one hand, the Russian economy collapsed and the financial system went into crisis, dragged down by the Asian crash of 1997 which led to the devaluation of the rouble. At the same time, fast-growing China banned logging across much of its own territory as a result of flooding. All this had a great impact on events,' Lebedev recalls.

After banning national logging,[2] China faced the challenge of sub-stituting its enormous domestic wood supplies with imported resources. It was Russia that took up the challenge. The neighbouring country, which exported just half a million cubic metres of wood to China in 1996, had increased its rate of supply several times over by 2004. China is now Russia's biggest customer, importing almost 18 million cubic metres of wood each year, with a particular demand for rare hardwoods such as oak or various varieties of Siberian pine.[3] The same Russian forests that had previously taken on the reconstruction of post-war Japan and the industrialization of South Korea now faced the challenge of supplying China's enormous demand. But the recon-struction of Japanese cities destroyed by Allied bombs in the Second World War – several decades before China's arrival in Siberia – pales in comparison to the challenge posed by the Asian giant, a country of 1.3 billion people which has transformed itself into a mass exporter of goods and is currently undergoing a fierce process of urbanization.

The effects of this drama can be clearly seen in Dalnerechensk, the capital of eastern Siberia's timber industry. This small rural town is dotted with houses which are home to 30,000 tough and wary-looking inhabitants. These resilient people live through terrible winters where vodka is the habitual means of survival, while dancing to 1980s music in clubs that seem frozen in. The town's dynamic railway sta-tion stands out powerfully against this background of decay. This station is the point of departure for Siberian forestry resources on their way to China. Several bulging forty-wagon trains are lined up on the tracks, waiting for the green light to set off towards Suifenhe, the vibrant Chinese city on the other side of the border.

Each day, a dozen locomotives with up to sixty wagons loaded with 3,000 cubic metres of wood pass into the neighbouring country at this border post alone, the major gateway of Russian wood into China. This represents an annual supply of 10 million cubic metres of precious wood, covering a surface area roughly equivalent to the size of Iceland or Portugal.[4] The train station at Dalnerechensk smells of freshly cut wood: the trains transport unprocessed trunks of pine and oak, many of them with the remains of fresh resin still on the bark. At the base of each trunk, an inscription in chalk indicates the wood's origin, quality and, most importantly, the telephone number of the relevant middleman or merchant. These are dominated by Chinese characters because, as Lebedev explains, 'the Chinese have taken everything. Unlike the Japanese, who used to buy their wood supplies in the market, the Chinese have come to Russia to buy the wood directly. They are present in every village in the region.'

The Chinese enter the business as soon as the tree has been felled, but they do not participate in the logging process itself. 'All the logging is carried out by the Russians. The Russian companies obtain a concession and they exploit it, especially in the winter when the snow is solid and the roads are accessible. The Chinese take part in the wholesale selling and the wood processing. They're shareholders, employers and workers. They take on the whole range of activities. They also act as intermediaries: they buy and resell wood.' In other words, they control the entire process from top to bottom. An example can be seen at the processing plant run by Shi Wei Hua – or 'Natasha' as she calls herself locally – on the outskirts of Dalnerechensk. This was the only plant which welcomed us into its premises, which consist of two wooden huts and a small processing facility. As we travelled along the road which runs parallel to the railway line, we approached several of the many sawmills and timber warehouses in the area, some of them veritable fortresses with their own security systems and bad-tempered Siberian dogs. One by one, each of them refused us access to their site, as they are clearly conscious that deforestation in Russian Siberia is a delicate issue.

A handful of Chinese workers and just one Russian, Sasha, are working hard to keep up a brisk pace in the sawing and processing of the wood, under the watchful eye of Natasha, who rules the company with an iron fist. The large trunks of Korean pine are being chopped up to separate the bark from the wood. They are then quickly transformed into lumber and piled up ready to be sold. The workshop conditions are basic; the equipment mostly consists of manual tools and old-fashioned machinery and the noise is deafening. Health and safety measures are kept to a minimum: there are no helmets, dust masks or barriers protecting the employees from the gigantic saw. A stumble, error or simple bad luck could easily lead a worker to find himself an arm down in a matter of seconds. The small wooden cabin with three rooms harbours a modest kitchen, a dining room with a table and benches and an office where Natasha carries out her administrative tasks: buying and selling wood, producing logistical diagrams and paying the weekly salaries. The employees sleep in another hut: six men live in just one room with enough space for four built-in beds and a television, while another room is home to three women. These are simple dwellings without any luxuries where the employees spend most of their free time either sleeping or watching the small television resting on a stool, especially during the savage winters which hit this part of the world.

Sasha, the young Russian, is of medium stature and is dressed in a military uniform. He is twenty-five years old with a blond crew-cut. We approach him in the middle of his lunch hour, when he is sitting at the only table along with his Chinese colleagues, but at a little distance apart. All the workers are eating Chinese food, but he is the only one using a fork. 'They pay me 250 roubles [6 euros] for a day's work. It's a very small amount,' he tells us. Natasha admits that on average the Russian employees are paid 20 per cent less than the Chinese. 'This company would not be viable if it only had Russian employees. The Russians drink a lot and are very undisciplined. The Chinese are better workers and they don't cause trouble,' she explains to justify this difference in salaries. 'We don't force anybody to stay here. If somebody isn't happy, they can leave,' she continues, using a type of discriminatory language which we found ourselves hearing fairly often throughout the course of our journey through the 'Chinese world'. For the Chinese, it is others who have to adapt to their standards – in terms of employment, salaries or the environment – and not the other way round.

This system allows Natasha to make an honest living in return for a long string of sacrifices: dealing with the inhuman winters, the absence of her loved ones and the hard life of an illegal migrant. However, all this will soon become even more difficult as a result of the shortage of raw materials. With her piercing gaze, Natasha does not try to hide her thoughts about the current state of the forests. 'We used to work mostly with hardwoods, but production levels have fallen dramatically. There are no reserves left,' she admits, leading us to believe that the chainsaws have devastated the region's oak forests. 'Now we only work with softwoods.'

THE SIBERIAN TIGER BECOMES
A CANNIBAL

Although the corrupt tendencies of the Russian bureaucrats cannot only be attributed to the Chinese buyers, the latter do play a key role in the looting of the Siberian forests. The Chinese arrive in Siberia with ready money, offering astronomical prices to families or businesses in exchange for the most valuable wood, without showing any interest whatsoever in its origin or legality. Furthermore, a network of hundreds of buyers spread across various strategic geographical points have allowed the new emperors to take control of every aspect of the buying and selling process.[5] 'Chinese demand is encouraging this situation. At least half the timber trade comes from illegal logging. This is doing irreparable harm to the forests,' Anatoly Lebedev tells us. 'The problem is not just the illegal logging, but also the plundering of everything that comes out of the forest. The Chinese aren't interested in where the forestry products come from; they don't care about the origin of the wood. It's available on the market and so they think it's not their responsibility. They therefore feel very comfortable with the bribery system. Those are the rules of the game and they are more than happy to take part. They don't have any problems with it whatsoever.' The only thing that matters to the new business leaders is the profit that can be made by operating at the ground in the sector: on Russian soil they pay $350 for a cubic metre of top-quality oak, while this price doubles to over $700 once they have crossed the border.[6]

Vladimir Bojarnichov, an environmental expert at the Pacific Institute of Geography at the Russian Academy of Sciences in Vladivostok, distributes the blame in equal parts for what is happening in Siberia's natural treasure-trove. 'The Chinese and the Russians share responsibility on a fifty-fifty basis for what is happening in our forests. The Chinese government is supporting its local economy and giving people incentives to exploit the forest. It has said to its people: "Our neighbour is now poor. If you want to get rich, now is the time",' he tells us at his lecture theatre on the outskirts of Vladivostok. Most of all, Bojarnichov denounces the policies adopted by Beijing and China's local provincial governments to create wood processing industrial zones on the other side of the border to enable China to absorb all the added value from Russia's raw materials.

Within this framework, the provincial banks have granted concessional loans and the authorities have improved the infrastructure networks close to the border, as well as developing land and lowering taxes. All this has been done in order to lay the foundations for industrial areas such as the one that has transformed Suifenhe into such an important and enterprising provincial hub.[7] At the same time, Beijing has refused to approve laws which would impose a greater level of control on the wood's origin. The result is a city like Suifenhe, which barely three decades ago had a population of just 10,000 impoverished inhabitants and now boasts 30,000 residents, some of them as rich as Jiou Peng, who – as we saw in Chapter 1 – picked us up at the station in his shiny new Porsche Cayenne. On top of this, the city has a floating population of up to 100,000 people who have been attracted by the job opportunities which Suifenhe offers as one of the timber capitals of China.

It is therefore hardly surprising that the buyers of the wood in this border town with its shiny new buildings and shopping centres welcome the merchandise like manna from heaven. The Siberian trees have become a source of employment and exceptional wealth: over 300 businesses are currently operating in the four wood-processing zones set up by the authorities. It is estimated that a minimum of 12,000 jobs have been generated in the area thanks to the resources obtained from the heart of Russia's forests. In the rest of the country, over 200,000 workers[8] are making a living in the timber industry based on importing untreated Russian timber.[9]

With such strong economic ties, nobody is surprised that the authorities reject any initiative aimed at controlling and tracking the origin of the wood, as is required by law in the United States and the European Union.[10] It would not be a complicated process in the case of Russian wood, as a mere sixty or so companies based in northern China monopolize around 80 per cent of trade in Russian timber.[11] It would not take much to throw down the gauntlet and demand that these companies should take responsibility for their actions. However, millions of jobs and enormous profits in markets across the world – including those of the Swedish giant IKEA – are at stake, which explains China's complete lack of interest in making such a move.[12] 'China is not going to stop illegal wood entering the country, because that would have a serious effect on its economy. It's not feasible to expect China to do anything that would put the brakes on its economy,' said Xiangjun Yang of the Forest Stewardship Council (FSC), an NGO aimed at ensuring the legal origin of wood, when we met her in Beijing. For the Chinese, economic development is the end that justifies the means.

The effect of these developments is being keenly felt in the Russian Far East, and not only in terms of the decline in the area's tree reserves. Deforestation has severely disrupted an ecosystem which is struggling to adapt and survive in the face of so much destruction. The most obvious example is the case of the emblematic Siberian tiger, Vladimir Bojarnichov explains. The indiscriminate logging has swept away key forest species such as the oak, and this has violently shaken the base of the sustainability pyramid, irreversibly affecting the food chain of the native fauna. In order to better understand this phenomenon, we went to visit Nikolai Salyuk, a geologist at the Moscow Institute and an activist in Primorsky's forests since 1975. This experienced hunter and nature lover could tell us why the Siberian tiger, the king of the region's native fauna, has found itself pushed to the edge of extinction. 'The acorn, a key food source for the wild boars, is disappearing as a result of the logging process. As the oak population decreases, the quantity of acorns also decreases and the wild boars emigrate in search of a more suitable habitat for their survival. The tiger, which feeds on wild pigs and other prey, also leaves its traditional environment and therefore its feeding habits have changed.'

The explanation is simple: the indiscriminate logging has left the forest in a highly fragmented state, destroying its biodiversity. 'In twenty-five years I have seen many changes in the tiger's behaviour. The tiger is an animal which naturally hunts alone, but sometimes it now hunts in groups. It has also started approaching human settlements, where it attacks dogs at sunrise because they're an easy prey,' Salyuk points out, as he plays with a puppy at his home on the edge of the forest. 'They're so hungry that sometimes they even eat each other. I've witnessed instances of cannibalism,' he assures us. With his unrivalled knowledge of the local environment, he has no doubts about who is responsible. 'The timber industry has endangered the tiger's survival. It is the timber industry which has forced the animal into this extreme situation.'

Three months and tens of thousands of kilometres later, we were able to confirm that this was far from an isolated case. Instead, what is happening in Siberia – one of the largest ecological reserves on the planet – is just the tip of the iceberg in terms of China's looting of rare hardwoods on a worldwide scale. Africa was the next stop on our journey.

MOZAMBIQUE: OTHER SPECIES, THE SAME CHINESE PATTERN

Completely oblivious to the danger that he is causing to our health and his four-wheel drive, our driver Li roars with laughter each time the Mitsubishi plunges at 100 kilometres per hour into one of the potholes plaguing the EN 1 highway between Maputo and the port of Beira. On the stretches of road where the asphalt – which has been partly repaired by Chinese companies, whose workers toil under a burning sun – offers a welcome respite from the otherwise tortuous journey, we find ourselves mesmerized by the stunning landscape around us. During the day the magnificent blue of the sky eclipses the green and brown tones of the tropical land. The turquoise sea makes sporadic appearances along the route. When night falls, the thick darkness does not quite manage to swallow everything around us. From the heights of the Tropic of Capricorn, the stars emit a stunning halo of light.

After passing Vilankulos, the midpoint in the 1,000-kilometre journey between Maputo and Mozambique's second city, two unconnected yet parallel phenomena perfectly sum up the situation here. The first appears suddenly, in the middle of the road, after we have just reached the brow of a hill: a group of policemen pounce on us, 'armed' with somewhat dubious old-fashioned handheld speed cameras in the shape of hairdryers. The 'fine' ($20 or $30 for the *brancos*) must be paid immediately although we never see the bill, demonstrating that corruption is the typical modus operandi used by the people who should theoretically be upholding the law. The next phenomenon is less abrupt but equally worrying: columns of smoke are rising up on either side of the road, filling the air with the smell of burning vegetation. These are fires started by the local people, who destroy hectares of forests in order to win territory so that they can practise itinerant agriculture. The ashes of *tanga tanga* and ebony are used as a sad fertilizer for the crops sown by the region's tribes and minority groups, demonstrating that the forest here is under constant threat.

However, the precious species which fill the forests and national parks of central and northern Mozambique, near the fertile banks of the River Zambezi, often do manage to avoid going up in flames. This is not because they are resistant to fire – like the fireproof *chacate*, for example – but because they are simply no longer there: before the flames can reach their gigantic trunks (some of them 30 metres high) they have already set sail in a cargo ship to China. Just before we arrive in Inchope, a town approximately 50 kilometres away from Beira, we run into a group of illicit local woodcutters. There are six of them, none of them older than twenty-five, resting on a pile of logs. They examine us defiantly, grasping their axes for the first few minutes of the conversation. After the obligatory small talk about football and women, they gradually begin to relax. One of them, João, speaks for the whole group.

'We work for ten hours a day. We come into the forest and we cut wood which people later buy from us. Sometimes the Chinese come directly to buy from us. We work in a group because the trees are very big. They give us ten dollars each to take them what we've felled.' In China, the price of a cubic metre of rare hardwoods (mahogany, ironwood, ebony, rosewood and *wenge*, the most expensive of all) range from between 600 and 1,700 euros. João is unable to say exactly how much they fell each day: 'Sometimes five, sometime ten trunks.' Without a chainsaw this is backbreaking work. Some of them are barefoot, while the more fortunate among them get by with flip-flops and woollen gloves. They all wear caps or hats to hold the cloths which hang down the back of their necks as far as their shoulders. 'That's to protect us from the cobras and other poisonous snakes. They often fall out of trees while we're working and land on our backs,' João explains.

Ana Alonso is no stranger to these forest raids. This Spanish businesswoman owns a concession (Euromoz) of some 60,000 hectares – the equivalent of the metropolitan area of Madrid – made up of undergrowth, savannah and grassland. We meet her in Beira, the timber capital of the country and the departure point for many of the ships that transport the raw material which will end up as luxury parquet flooring or the type of sturdy wooden tables that decorate China's most exclusive urban offices and homes. She is fifty-seven-years old and dresses in khaki camouflage clothing. She drives an old Toyota jeep and we can recognize her from a distance because of her long hair. After seventeen years spent living in the country, she does not mince her words. She gets straight to the point: 'The sector here is dirty and corrupt. Chinese corruption has filled the pockets of Mozambique's middle and lower level officials. The provincial forestry services have got rich very quickly.'

Alonso's outspoken attitude means that she has to be accompanied at all times by a bodyguard armed with a rifle: corrupt officials, businessmen, mafia agents and even government ministers have threatened to have her killed because of her campaigning work against deforestation and illegal logging practices. 'When I receive a death threat from someone important in the country I publish a full page advert in all of Mozambique's major newspapers, reporting who is trying to intimidate me and why. Publicly exposing the threat is a way of protecting myself,' she explains bravely as she shows us a few examples at her home. As we begin to learn more about the inner workings of Mozambique's timber industry, the similarities with what we have seen in Russia become more and more evident.

In fact, the pattern would be exactly the same if it wasn't for the fact that the participation of Chinese state-owned companies in Mozambique is far greater than in Russia:[13] while Chinese companies do not dirty their hands by participating in the actual logging process, they do lend money to Mozambicans to get them to act as 'straw men' by giving the companies access to concessions that are technically only open to Mozambican nationals. By granting loans to Mozambicans so that they can buy the necessary materials (chainsaws, lorries, etc.) and pay the cash deposits required by the authorities to exploit the concessions, the Chinese companies pile the locals with debt, forcing them to sell the resources gained from the forest to the Chinese under highly favourable conditions.[14] As it is illegal to export unprocessed first- and second-quality wood species, bribes are used to ensure that the wood nonetheless leaves the country. 'The whole system is completely corrupt because this helps to increase profit margins. If the companies exploit the concessions legally and follow the laws and rules governing exports, they can make a maximum 10 per cent profit. However, if they bribe the officials so that they can export unprocessed wood, avoid paying taxes and fail to commit to reforestation plans, the profit margin will exceed 50 per cent,' Alonso assures us in reference to the Chinese middlemen. The Chinese apparently take to this chaotic system like ducks to water. 'Other foreign companies are also corrupt in some ways, but the Chinese have a whole system of corruption in place so that the industry will work for them. If there are different levels of illegality, the Chinese are the most illegal,' she argues.

The roads on the outskirts of Beira are lined with warehouses run by Chinese people. After several failed attempts, we manage to convince Zheng (not his real name) to let us take a peek inside his facilities, which are about the size of a football pitch. At one end of the warehouse, various types of tree trunks are waiting in piles for lorries to arrive so that they can be immediately stamped and sent on their way without any great level of scrutiny. 'I buy the wood from some Chinese people who live to the north of the country. There are lots of Chinese people there. I don't know where the wood comes from or whether it has been felled legally or illegally,' he admits. At the other end of the warehouse, a hazardous machine consisting of a saw and a power generator serves as a sawmill. 'All the technology comes from China. There is nothing local here,' he tells us. Originally from Henan province, Zheng arrived in Beira four years ago, attracted by 'the opportunities offered by the country'.

He lives alone, having left his family behind in China. He plans to return to his own country once he has made his fortune, which does not seem like a very distant prospect. 'I've made several hundred thousand dollars,' he tells us frankly. The Mozambican forests foot the bill for this newfound wealth: each month Zheng exports between thirty and forty 18-ton containers to China, or 7,500 tons of timber each year.[15] 'Because of the Chinese, 25 per cent of the forests have disappeared in the provinces of Sofala, Zambezia and Nampula, to name just a few. In four or five years there will be nothing left,' Ana Alonso concludes. If the logging continues at its current rate, Mozambique's entire reserves of hardwood will be wiped out in less than a decade.[16]

THE INHERENT DANGERS OF CHINA'S NATIONAL INTEREST

The list of countries, like Russia and Mozambique, whose forests are suffering as a result of Chinese demand and the corruption and negligence of the local elites is extensive: Papua New Guinea, Indonesia, Burma, the Democratic Republic of Congo, Madagascar, Gabon, Equatorial Guinea . . . the list goes on. The effects of all this would no doubt be much less severe if the client was not the most populated country in the world and the biggest producer of wooden products on the planet.[17] China's dependence on other countries to satisfy the needs of its market is growing constantly in the face of enormous rates of consumption, which will require new suppliers at some point in the immediate future.[18] This explains why the country is exploring every corner of the world in search of the precious – and lucrative – raw material.

The same factors which we saw in Russia and Mozambique are evident in all the abovementioned developing countries which China has turned to for its wood supplies. The first of these is the generalized use of corruption, which fuels both the timber industry and environmental abuse. This is perhaps the most critical common denominator in this process, as it allows Chinese businessmen to gain easy access to large quantities of precious specimens without having to concern themselves with the origin of the wood, its legality or the methods used to obtain it. Secondly, resources are exported in their natural state without creating any kind of processing industry that might generate wealth on a local level in terms of employment or investments. The Chinese authorities' complete lack of interest in monitoring the origin of the wood – a process routinely carried out by more responsible countries – completes the modus operandi of this perfect crime.

What is the social and environmental impact of this drama on the rest of the world? To begin with, it is causing a silent but rapid looting of hardwood forest species in the developing world, with a steady decline in reserves in places such as Africa and Latin America.[19] In terms of socioeconomic factors, the participation in the payment of bribes helps to perpetuate systems of corruption. Furthermore, exporting the raw material in its original form prevents the development of any economic impact in terms of employment, added value or the transfer of technology or knowledge. While the Chinese government and businessmen are, of course, not the only ones to blame, there is no doubt that they hold some responsibility, particularly in terms of the Chinese state's indifference to ending or substantially reducing the country's consumption of illegal wood. China could do much more to prevent this, but the destruction of the forests and its socioeconomic impact are seen as a necessary evil, or rather as the side effects of a more important necessity: the country's own development and well-being.

On the contrary, in the interests of its own economic prosperity the government contributes to ensuring that China – a country which controls a third of the world's furniture trade, exporting furniture to the value of over $16 billion in 2010[20] – continues to launder illegal timber on a massive scale:[21] illegal baobabs, ebony and mahogany enter its territory and are transformed into parquet flooring, tables, cupboards and sofas which are then exported to the lucrative markets of the United States and Europe. Alternatively, they are sold in Shanghai or Canton, where a rosewood bed with a Ming dynasty design can be sold for $800,000.[22]

CHINA'S HEGEMONY OVER THE MEKONG RIVER

One example of these lucrative business dealings can be seen in the Chinese town of Jinghong in the south of Yunnan province, a few kilometres from the border with Thailand and Burma. Jinghong is a peaceful town full of tropical vegetation and Buddhist temples where the local people, many of them from the Dai ethnic minority, bet on cockfights in their spare time. The main streets are lined with luxury shops selling jade, and furniture made of Burmese wood, attracting customers who are oblivious to the drama taking place in Burmese mines we saw in Chapter 3. However, it was not the impact on the Burmese forests that had brought us on our second journey to the region. Instead we had come in search of the mythical water serpent which runs through Jinghong – the 'city of dawn' – and stretches for 4,880 kilometres through the heart of Asia until it finally comes to rest on the coast of Vietnam: the Mekong river.

Although we have booked our tickets in advance, Bai Haiping still asks us to confirm one day before the journey in case the water levels have dropped and our trip needs to be cancelled. 'Yes, there's enough water. The boat leaves tomorrow at eight thirty,' our tourist guide confirms over the telephone. The amount of traffic through the area has dropped off significantly lately as a result of the low water levels on this stretch of the river. Now, just two small speedboats head off each month towards Thailand along the Lancang – the 'Turbulent River' – as the Chinese part of the Mekong is known. The authorities blame climate change and the recent drought – an event which is remembered for the disastrous effects it had in 2010[23] – for the current situation on the river. However, from the Xishuangbanna Bridge over the Mekong we can glimpse another contributing factor: the hydroelectric projects built along the river.

The only way we can approach the enormous cement wall blocking the murky waters of the Mekong is by taking a short journey in one of the small canoes belonging to the local fishermen. 'The foreigner can't come in here,' a policeman manning a checkpoint on the road to the Jinghong Dam had told us. Tensions are running high in the area. While it is not one of the biggest Chinese dams, it has had one of the biggest effects on the local population. 'The dam has affected the ethnic minorities who live on the river banks, as well as having a direct impact on the Xishuangbanna nature reserve,' explained Yu Xiaogang, director of the Chinese NGO Green Watershed, whose organization estimates that several thousand people have been evicted from the area. When we compare this with the social and environmental impact of the Three Gorges Dam, the Jinghong Dam is clearly a smaller project. However, its peculiarity resides in the fact that it is the last in a series of four dams which have already been built on the Chinese side of the Mekong, while another four are currently under construction or in the planning stage.[24] This sequence of hydroelectric barriers is aimed at supplying energy to China's eastern regions, the country's industrial heartland, as well as facilitating business with Thailand and Laos, countries which buy electricity from China.[25] All this work is being undertaken unilaterally by China: from the approval of the first dam (the Manwan Dam) in 1986 to the present day, Beijing has never consulted any of the countries (Thailand, Laos, Cambodia, Vietnam and Burma) which lie on the path of a river with the second greatest levels of biodiversity on the planet after the Amazon.[26]

A dozen soldiers from the People's Liberation Army make an appearance at a military post on Jinghong's port, slightly dampening the spirits of the fifty or so tourists waiting for an exit stamp on their passports so that they can set off along the river towards Thailand. Once we have climbed into our small, rickety boat, the motor roars into action and we finally set off downriver along the Mekong. The urban scenery immediately disappears and the thick vegetation of South-East Asia dominates both riverbanks, while at times the fog makes it impossible to see the rocks projecting out of the sandy current. Whenever the boat runs across another vessel, as constantly happens with the modest rafts of the Burmese fishermen – easily recognizable by the satellite dishes installed on their wooden roofs – it slows down. The same thing happens whenever we see a Chinese cargo ship travelling upstream after transporting 'Made in China' products throughout South-East Asia.

Ploughing its way stealthily through the water into Burmese territory, our boat soon stops so that two soldiers can collect the toll fee from our captain: a wad of red notes which may or may not be required by law. Further on, the river begins to widen and comes to life with women washing clothes on the riverbanks and men breaking their backs farming the fertile lands alongside the 'mother of waters', as the Mekong is known in the Thai language. However, most of all it is the hustle and bustle of pointed fishing boats that lends a mystical air to a river which begins its journey in the Himalayas and whose resources provide a means of survival for over 60 million people. Som Wang's boat is almost 20 metres long and is equipped with blue leather seats recovered from a wrecked bus. Despite the flimsiness of the boat it is a fabulous vessel, with its bow covered in colourful posters and a music system playing the popular Thai hits of the day. The tanned skins of this Thai fisherman and his crew are covered in tattoos, including one on Som Wang's back showing a fish about to swallow a hook: a symbol of the passion of these men who have spent most of their lives fishing around Chiang Khong, a small fishing town in northern Thailand. 'My father taught me all my fishing skills. I started when I was nine years old, following his instructions about how, when and where to fish,' he says, smiling, as he tells us how his family have lived off the Mekong for generations.

This way of life is now in danger. 'Ten years ago there were hundreds of active fishing boats in the area. By 2008 there were only sixty left. Today there are no more than thirty.' This decline has been caused by the 'great changes suffered by the river', which have led to a dramatic fall in the diversity of the river species as well as the quantity and weight of the fish. 'We used to know exactly when the river seasons were going to change. There were two of them: the rainy season and the dry season. We used to understand the natural cycle of the Mekong and we knew that there would always be fish in certain places. All that has changed now,' explains thirty-eight-year-old Som Wang, who refuses to let his son follow in his professional footsteps. 'There's no future in it,' he tells us.

It is difficult to blame one single agent for the changes that have taken place in such a rich and complex ecosystem as the Mekong. However, in Chiang Khong everybody points the finger at China. On the one hand, the local people blame Beijing for building the dams which have forced the river to such extremes: the water levels are now not only affected by rainfall, but also by the opening and closing of the sluice gates used to generate electricity. On the other hand, the people accuse China of being interested only in the river's commercial uses, which have led Beijing to demolish the rapids and rocks along the main stretch of the river in order to make it more accessible by boat, thereby eroding the riverbed. Despite the irrepressible smiles on the faces of the Thai people, there is much resentment in Chiang

Khong against their neighbour. This is particularly true among the local fishermen, who now have to find alternative ways of making a living. Most of them transport merchandise or passengers to Laos, on the other side of the river. 'We used to be able to make a lot of money if we worked hard during the fishing season, but now I can barely make 500 bahts [around 12 euros] working from four o'clock in the morning until seven o'clock at night. As well as the decline in the fish population, the size of the fish has fallen: species that used to weigh seven or eight kilos now hardly even reach two kilos,' Wang complains. One of these species is the legendary giant catfish. This fabulous migratory creature is one of the biggest freshwater fish on the planet, measuring up to 3 metres in length and 300 kilos in weight. This marvel is now in danger of extinction as a result of the impenetrable walls which block its path as it travels upstream.

Niwat Roykaew, founder of the local NGO Chiang Khong Conservation Group, has been following the changes in the river as it travels through seven Thai provinces since 1996. He has come to exactly the same conclusion as the fishermen who took part in a demonstration outside the Chinese embassy in Bangkok in April 2011 in protest against the planned Chinese hydroelectric projects along the Mekong river. 'The problems started in 2003, when building work began on the Daochashan Dam. The water levels began to fluctuate dramatically outside the seasonal period. The fishermen could no longer understand the river's natural cycle,' says Roykaew, a man with the appearance of a classic 1970s hippy. These incredible oscillations, which can see water levels fluctuating by up to 3 metres in just 24 hours without any rainfall being recorded upstream, have led to terrible and unprecedented situations. 'The fishermen now find themselves "fishing" birds,' he explains. 'It's a common practice among the indigenous population to leave their fishing rods buried in the earth for hours at a time while they go away. When they come back, the fishermen find that the hooks are out in the open, as the river's water levels have dropped so dramatically. As a result, they end up catching birds instead of fish.'

The local communities which do not make a living from fishing have been equally badly affected. 'The increase in the river's water level has also flooded and devastated the crops of the many local people who plant tobacco or corn along the river banks. It has also destroyed the livelihood of the many women who used to collect and dry algae. When the algae is exposed as a result of the fall in water levels, the sun burns it and makes it unusable. As a result, many families have left Chiang Khong in search of work in other places,' Roykaew explains.

NATIONAL SOVEREIGNTY AND THE IMPORTANCE OF 'NO INTERVENTION'

As the Mekong represents such an important resource for neighbouring countries such as Vietnam and Cambodia, it is somewhat surprising that Beijing continues to make decisions about the river unilaterally, particularly considering the harm that this behaviour does to the country's image.[27] China's level of collaboration with these countries has increased very slightly in recent years, particularly since 2010 when Beijing was criticized for not sharing information about the country's water resources during a period of historic droughts. Partly as a result of pressure from the international press, Beijing now shares some of the information gathered by its meteorological stations in Yunnan. However, the level of co-operation is still far from ideal. While China actively insists on being given a role in keeping with its international status at organizations such as the United Nations, the WTO or the World Bank, it flatly refuses to enter into multilateral talks with the downstream countries, which are already engaging in dialogue aimed at guaranteeing the sustainability of projects along the main course of the Mekong river.

The organization responsible for bringing together the countries which share the river's resources is the Mekong River Commission (MRC), an international institution created in 1995. China, the only country so far to have built dams along the Mekong, joined the institution in 2002, although – like Burma – it is not a full member.[28] Unfortunately for the other nations involved, China has only joined as a dialogue partner, which in practice means that it participates in meetings but does not share any information or submit its river activities to the institution for review. This way of saving face in the diplomatic arena without having to take on any undesirable commitments is simply not good enough, according to Yu Xiaogang, the director of Green Watershed. 'It would be good for the health of the river if China could join the MRC as soon as possible.' Sadly, although the Mekong's sustainability has reached a critical point, the situation does not seem likely to change any time soon. 'China is still a long way from becoming a full member of the MRC,' admits Tiffany Hacker, spokesperson for the Commission, when we meet her at the institute's headquarters in the Laotian capital, Vientiane.

As a way of subliminally justifying its absence from the river commission, China argues that it was not invited to form part of the commission when it was first established, which was largely a result of its conflict with Vietnam. Beijing's decision has also doubtlessly been influenced by its belief that joining the institution would prevent it from being able to develop the river in its own territory exactly as it pleases. However, He Deming, probably China's leading expert on transboundary river-related issues, offered an additional argument when we met him some days earlier: 'The MRC is not an independent institution because it receives funds from countries outside the Commission. Furthermore, it does not have enough power to resolve these problems,' he argued during a particularly tense interview at his office at the University of Kunming. 'I never talk to foreign journalists,' he had previously told us.

As Hacker explains, the MRC does indeed receive funds from countries such as France, the United States and Australia. However, this money is provided for specific scientific research projects, making it difficult to accuse the organization of being politicized. The truth is that China objects to having to give up its current ability to make unilateral decisions about the river. 'If China was a member of the MRC, it would have to notify the Commission about any projects on the Mekong six months in advance, so that these projects can be debated and studied by the rest of the countries. The decisions made by the MRC are not binding, but they do act as a counterweight, as the rest of the countries examine the environmental studies and plans for each project,' Hacker points out. For China, a country obsessed with preventing other countries from dictating its international agenda, this is an act of interference in its domestic affairs. 'Co-ordinating projects between six countries would be very complicated. In our system everything is done according to a pyramid approach: the order is given from the top and carried out at the base. We believe that other countries should follow this model, because if you let everybody give their opinion it is difficult to make decisions,' says Jiangwen Qu, a professor at Kunming's Centre for Asian Studies, in justification for China's stance on this issue.

An analysis of China's treatment of the other countries with which it shares transboundary rivers clearly demonstrates that the situation on the Mekong is not unique.[29] With the exception of North Korea, the other counties which share important water resources with China (India, Russia and Kazakhstan) condemn Beijing's unilateral approach. In the case of New Delhi, some sources even warn of the possibility of a future war over water supplies; however, these disputes seem to be more closely linked to the general climate of tension which characterizes relations between the two countries.[30] While the issue of the Mekong river is no doubt the most important and controversial of these water-related disputes, the place where Beijing most forcefully imposes its own will on others is on the border with Central Asia. Here China has diverted water from the rivers Irtysh and Ili for its own agricultural use in Xinjiang province, and particularly in order to benefit the region's oil industry.[31] Although relations between China and Kazakhstan have grown stronger in recent years, this has not led to a greater degree of co-operation on an issue as important as water resources. Astana has warned its Chinese associates that by diverting the course of the rivers they are threatening the survival of Lake Blakhash, an area which is currently endangered despite being one of the most important freshwater sources in the region and home to one of the most diverse ecosystems on the planet. However, these warnings have fallen on deaf ears as China continues to dodge the issue.

Water – an issue of national security for Beijing – is non-negotiable. Apart from the needs of a country of over 1.3 billion inhabitants, the main reason for this is found in China's orography, as the Himalayan mountain range plays a key geographical role in terms of water resources. China is what is known as an 'upstream' country; in other words, it is a nation where rivers begin. This means that the country has access to an independent freshwater supply, and also that it is able to control other countries' resources (with all the power and potential for conflict that this entails).[32] This situation has led Beijing – officially a staunch champion of 'win-win co-operation' in terms of its diplomatic relations with other countries – to show 'very little interest' in its neighbours' priorities.[33] In fact, China was one of only three countries, along with Turkey and Burundi, to vote against the United Nations Convention on the Law of the Non-Navigational Uses of International Watercourses, a text which took twenty-seven years to produce in order to reach a majority consensus.[34] What would happen if China had to battle with a powerful neighbour who was damaging a river which flowed through Chinese territory and represented an essential life source for millions of Chinese people? What would happen if, for instance, the Yangtze river began in Siberia and Moscow turned its back on the environmental and socioeconomic disaster taking place in Chinese territory? How would the Chinese government react then?

THE ENVIRONMENT: A CONSTANT CAUSE FOR CONCERN

Following the trail of the Russian and Mozambican hardwood which provides fuel for China's industries, or learning about the Asian giant's plans on the Mekong and other transboundary rivers, serves to show that protecting the environment is not one of China's current priorities. As a result, environmental damage caused by China's bad practices, demand and investments is a constant cause for concern in most – if not all – of the twenty-five countries visited as part of this investigation. We have witnessed the outrages committed by Chinese companies – many of them state owned – along with the complicity or negligence of the countries in question, in places as different and distant as Burma and Ecuador, Peru and Sudan, or the heart of Africa's Copperbelt. In all these settings, the urgent need to fuel the factory of the world and a country that is home to one-fifth of the Earth's population is combined with a lack of sensibility or respect for the environment on behalf of China's small, medium and large investors.

The general rule is: don't let environmental damage interfere with good business.

The fierce competition, the desire to maximize profits, the demands of Beijing's political strategies and China's longing for economic prosperity are all contributing factors which lead corporations such as Shougang or Zijin in Peru, Sinohydro in Burma or CNPC in Sudan to pay very little attention to their impact on the environment. The behaviour of these and other Chinese companies abroad can once again be understood within the framework of domestic affairs: China is following a pattern of behaviour outside its own borders which has been the common denominator inside the country for the last three decades.[35] We have seen examples of this at the Irrawady river basin in Burma, where businessmen are savagely exploiting the region's gold mines, and in Vietnam's Central Highlands, where bauxite mines threaten the survival of ethnic minorities who have lived off coffee and tea plantations in the region for hundreds of years.

Likewise, this same pattern – which lacks any sense of environmental ethics – governs the behaviour of tiger poachers in Russia and Burma, who illegally sell bones, skins and organs to the lucrative and increasingly demanding traditional Chinese medicine industry. The same pattern is followed by Ethiopian hunters and their Chinese associates who, along with other international buyers, endanger the survival of the African elephant in order to make a fortune by ripping off their ivory tusks, a valuable material in China where it is made into signature stamps. 'The skin of a rare feline costs 150 dollars in Addis Ababa and can be sold for 15,000 dollars on the black market in Wenzhou, the home of Chinese entrepreneurs,' said a Chinese resident in Africa who once trafficked in this type of merchandise without following any code other than the code of fat profits.

This lack of scruples whenever juicy dividends are involved reveals one of the 'strengths' of Chinese investments over their Western and local competitors: the lack of a Chinese civil society which could put the brakes on the supremacy of profit over the environment. Without NGOs that can act independently and condemn these actions without fear; without a free press; without a civil society in the wider sense of the phrase which could painstakingly examine the conduct of China's economic and political actors (which today are tied more strongly than ever to the Chinese version of 'state capitalism'), China runs the risk of continuously producing the same mistakes abroad which have endangered the environment in its own country, thanks to this sense of impunity.[36] The pyramid system used by the current Communist regime – in which a few people give orders while the others obey and execute them – is clearly far more effective than public consultation and collective participation, as Professor Jiangwen Qu explained in justification of China's stance on the Mekong issue. However, the long-term benefits of this system are questionable, to say the least.

It is precisely this lack of any real counterweight which has led Chinese companies to take on projects that have been abandoned by other corporations which, while their own environmental records may not be exactly spotless, do at least consider some investments to be unviable because of their high social and ecological cost. Many cases of this can be seen in Peru,[37] where the quintessential example is the behaviour of the Chinese mining company Zijin in the so-called Rio Blanco project. In 2007 the company took over a fabulous copper concession which had previously been held by the London-based mining company Monterrico Metals in the northern region of Piura, on the border with Ecuador. The British company had abandoned the project after years of violence and death caused by clashes with organized opposition from around 2,200 local families. These rural families live in an area spanning 6,500 hectares where the purity of the water and the area's unique microclimate enable them to make a living by exporting certified ecological products like coffee, bananas, mango and other fruits to the attractive American and European markets. Water pollution as a result of mining activity would be the downfall and death of this community. However, when the British company pulled out, Zijin – whose environmental record in China leaves much to be desired[38] – stepped into the breach. The community has been in uproar ever since. In his office in Lima, Javier Jahncke, the head of the Ecumenical Foundation for Development and Peace (Fedepaz), an organization which has been following the case, hit the nail on the head with just one phrase: 'They have no problem with getting involved in such a conflictive situation, even though this was why the British company ended up leaving.' This case is very similar to that of the Chinese state-owned company Erdos Hongjun Investment Corp., which took over a project in the Cambodian province of Mondulkiri in 2010, shortly after it had been rejected by the Australian group BHP because of its impact on the local environment.[39]

There is no shortage of examples like these. As can be deduced from China's involvement in the controversial Merowe Dam project (see Chapter 5), Chinese investors will move mountains whenever there is profit involved. Of course, this attitude is not unique to Chinese companies: the West has a long and sad history of using harmful practices across the world. However, the irresponsible behaviour of Western companies comes under much greater scrutiny and the price of its excesses, both in terms of economic costs and public image, leads them to be much more cautious – at least in theory. As things stand, the problem posed by China's sheer size and its huge number of inhabitants is perhaps one of the greatest challenges facing the planet today.

8

The *Pax Sinica* of the Middle Kingdom

'There is only room for one tiger on a mountain.'
                                                    Chinese proverb

The sun is just breaking through the peaks of the Himalayas as the eagles begin their distinctive daily dance. It always happens at dawn, when the light is just starting to flood into the Indian village of McLeod Ganj close to the town of Dharamsala. They spread their wings and glide in circles as if following some kind of ritual, silhouetted against a clear sky of the purest blue, like something out of a child's drawing. From time to time, one of them turns to face the ground and suddenly drops before taking flight again, fast and playful, to cleave once more through the skies of this place at the foot of the roof of the world. With the first light of dawn the streets begin to burst colourfully into life. Monks' saffron robes fill the main streets, which are also invaded by noisy motor-taxis that sound their horns as they make their way through the crowd. The aim is apparently to honk as much as possible even when it isn't necessary – the unspoken law of Indian roads.

The cafés and souvenir shops begin to open their doors, all of them presided over by an image of His Holiness, as the Dalai Lama is known in the area. Meanwhile tourists and faithful followers drawn here from every corner of the world by the charisma of the Buddhist leader swarm into an enclave which was seen purely as a holiday destination during the British colonial era. This status changed dramatically in 1959, when Tenzin Gyatso, the current Dalai Lama, escaped from Tibet and settled here with New Delhi's blessing, establishing the headquarters of the Tibetan government in exile.[1] Since then, Dharamsala's political significance has made it the biggest thorn in the side of the always difficult Sino-Indian relations. The tragic destiny of the Tibetan people is very evident in this remote area of the Himalayas, which is home to 12,000 Tibetan refugees.[2]

Migmar Tsering knows that anybody watching him climb the stairs leading up to the highest part of the village is going to suffer. That is why he makes sure to keep a smile on his face, as if trying to calm his companions by reassuring them that his artificial legs are not going to break and that there is no need to worry: other times of his life have been much harder. Once he reaches the top of the hill which rises up behind the main monastery, where there is a large pagoda and a tangle of coloured flags flying in the wind, he goes straight to the Tibetan prayer wheels and spins them, one by one. After a while, this forty-nine-year-old monk who is the embodiment of Buddhist faith and the fight against Chinese repression in Tibet says a brief prayer and begins to tell us his story.

'In 1993 the Chinese police came looking for me to make me sign a declaration against His Holiness. I refused. They arrested and tortured me. I decided to escape.' This marked the beginning of an odyssey to reach the other side of the Himalayas, a sad journey of exile along one of the most dangerous routes on the planet. 'I left Lhasa with two other Tibetans. We took nothing with us apart from blankets and some food. When we were halfway there we found ourselves in the middle of a great snowstorm. We couldn't see anything. We got lost and my legs became frozen,' he recalls. Close to death with gangrene setting into his limbs, Tsering was finally rescued by a group of nomads who took him over the border. He was transported to New Delhi. 'Both my legs were amputated there, as well as four fingers from one hand.' When he had barely recovered, he was hit by the full force of Indian law because of his lack of documentation: six months in prison. 'That wasn't the worst of it. After prison they took me back to the border with China.' His dramatic journey had all been for nothing.

However, like many of the other Buddhists who set out on impossible journeys of escape, his faith was stronger than his suffering and the prospect of his own death. Dragging himself along on his stumps, suffering even more hardships and risking his life, Tsering finally managed to arrive in Dharamsala, where the Tibetan government takes in all the refugees. 'When I was in hospital recovering from the amputations, I kept asking myself why I had to run away, why I did it. But when I arrived in Dharamsala and met His Holiness the Dalai Lama and was able to study Buddhism, I was happy. I had finally achieved what I had dreamed about for so long,' he tells us, full of emotion. As in so many other cases, Migmar Tsering's determination faithfully reflects the unshakeable loyalty that the Tibetan people feel towards their leader and their religion.

It takes approximately one month to cross the Himalayas by foot to Nepal, an obligatory journey for any Tibetan who wants to gain access to India. The journey is fraught with dangers, from extreme weather conditions and hunger to wild dogs, altitude sickness and, worst of all, Chinese soldiers. The Tibetans insist that the soldiers shoot to kill if they find refugees and they disobey the warnings. Despite the dangers, each year many people like Migmar Tsering flee from repression in Tibet for the sake of freedom and the ability to practise their own beliefs in India. Only a small proportion of those who leave ever return to Tibet. Faced by the prospect of life under the iron rule of the Chinese government, the rest choose to leave behind their family, property and the land where they were born.[3]

Tempa Tsering knows this suffering only too well. He meets us at the headquarters of the Tibetan government in exile in New Delhi, where he has been the senior representative since 2005. Under a Tibetan flag and a portrait of the spiritual leader which are hanging in his office, he serves us tea and tells us that he too crossed the mountain range on foot in the middle of winter. 'It was the end of 1959, months after the Dalai Lama left Tibet. We went by foot. I was around twelve years old. Having to leave your country and your dear ones is not easy; there was a lot of trauma. To that you have to add physical exhaustion: we're talking about walking at 17,000 to 19,000 feet above sea level, in the middle of winter. When we arrived in India we were a family of five, but in a few months only two of us were left,' says this man with perfect manners who is married to the sister of the current Dalai Lama. Half a century later, Tibet's 5 million people – most of them living in poverty – are still an obsession for China.

An outbreak of bloody and often fatal violence against China's presence in the region inevitably takes place every ten or fifteen years in Tibet, calling into question China's legitimacy in the region and showing that Beijing's policies are not having the desired effect. The sense of not having complete control over the territory and of being unable to assimilate all of the Tibetan people, as well as the conflict's international dimension, are making China feel very vulnerable, according to various Indian academics who we spoke to in New Delhi. In order to strengthen its authority, Beijing is therefore taking action both inside and outside its own borders – with relative success – to stem the flow of refugees, in the belief that this dissidence represents a potential militant danger to stability in Tibet.

Before the 2008 uprising in Lhasa[4] between 2,500 and 3,500 people annually escaped from repression by travelling over the Himalayan mountain range, according to Tempa Tsering. However, since then barely 700 refugees make the same journey each year. 'The Tibetan side of the border has become very tightly controlled. On the Nepalese side, [China is] training and equipping border guards. When the guards arrest Tibetans and repatriate them back to Tibet, they receive incentives,' says the representative of His Holiness in the Indian capital. At the same time, Kathmandu's policy towards Tibetan refugees has become much stricter, including repatriation, a closer surveillance of the border, the closure of the Dalai Lama's office and the police's outrageously severe behaviour of the police towards new arrivals in the Tibetan community. All this started happening just when China was becoming Nepal's biggest investor. India's traditional ally is now under Beijing's control, and that places it firmly in the Chinese camp in the battle against the Tibetan movement in exile.

The recent democratic election of the Tibetan prime minister, Lobsang Sangay,[5] who now leads the exiled government in secular matters, as well as the Dalai Lama's seventy-seven years of age, is a source of concern both in Beijing and in the region itself, as it is possible that the Tibetan movement will become radicalized after the death of the Buddhist leader. Tempa Tsering is confident that the principle of nonviolence will prevail, but he also recognizes that nobody knows what will happen if the destruction of Tibetan culture and identity continues in this way.

'Now people say that Tibet is on the verge of death. They say it would be better to do something for Tibet and die, than to do nothing and die anyway,' he points out. The future is viewed with trepidation, particularly in New Delhi, as the combination of a new generation of less moderate Tibetan leaders and the absence of a Dalai Lama who has spent decades uniting the various different factions with his balanced form of government could potentially see relations flaring up once more between the two Asian countries.[6]

'I see a hot scenario in the years to come [between China and India]. If the Tibetan movement gets radical, the Chinese will have to react, and that is going to be seen badly in the rest of the world. At the same time, the Chinese will increasingly accuse India of harbouring terrorists in our home ground, which will add more fuel to the fire in Pakistan.[7] Therefore, the best scenario for the Chinese would be to deal directly with the Dalai Lama, and not with the new generation. Not dealing with the Dalai Lama would be a historic missed opportunity for them,' argues Madhu Bhalla, director of the East Asian Studies Department at the University of Delhi.

The deterioration in relations dates back to the invasion of Tibet in 1950. This climate of mutual distrust between the two Asian powers led to the border war between them in 1962, a hugely humiliating ordeal for Prime Minister Jawaharlal Nehru's government. The wound left by the war is still raw today. With his markedly left-wing ideology, the first leader of India after the country's independence sympathized in principle with Mao Zedong's 'liberation' of Tibet. Nehru believed that the out-dated feudal system in place in the region at that time needed to be demolished and replaced with a new system along socialist lines. Furthermore, as an alternative to the two blocs of the Cold War, Nehru hoped to form an Asian axis between the two countries which had just shaken off their colonial past. As proof of his friendship, Nehru not only recognized Beijing's authority in Tibet but also decisively helped China to consolidate its power in the region by providing Beijing with invaluable diplomatic support at the UN. New Delhi provided this clear show of support in the hope that Beijing would grant a certain degree of autonomy to the conquered territory, because of India's centuries of 'sentimental and cultural interest' in Tibet. For India, this was a way of guaranteeing a lesser Chinese political and military presence on the new border.

However, Nehru's hopes of mutual friendship soon fell by the wayside. Not only did Mao distrust the Indian prime minister's good intentions, but relations also deteriorated significantly throughout the 1950s, and particularly after the Lhasa uprising in 1959 which sent the Dalai Lama into exile.[8] That year, India had 'fulfilled' its part of the agreement by recognizing China's sovereignty in Tibet. However, China had not honoured its side of the bargain, as Tibetan autonomy was abolished once and for all after the 1959 revolt. In fact, at that time Mao was already convinced that there was an Indian conspiracy behind the uprising, with the aim of undermining Chinese rule in Tibet and of eventually annexing the territory to the 'Great Indian Empire'. Beijing also misinterpreted the exile of the Dalai Lama, seeing it as proof of the Indian government's supposed support for exiled Tibetans and therefore an unacceptable act of interference in China's domestic affairs. It was then that India became China's enemy.

It is also important to take into account the undercover operations of the CIA which came to the attention of Chinese intelligence services, as well as India's policy of advancing on and militarizing the border in 1961, a policy aimed at strengthening the undefined border in the naïve belief that Beijing would not react.[9] However, the recently founded People's Republic – which had just managed to rise above its century of 'imperialist humiliation' – interpreted India's attitude in hostile terms, seeing it as a lack of respect towards the power of the new Communist China. In October 1962, Mao made a decisive move. After an erroneous historical reading of India's actions over the course of those years,[10] he decided to teach his neighbour an important lesson. He launched a lightning offensive on two sectors of the border with India, separated by a thousand kilometres. In a question of weeks, China inflicted a painful military defeat on the Indian troops.[11]

Beijing achieved both of its objectives: to stabilize the Tibetan border and to win the respect of the Indian leaders. However, in New Delhi the Chinese aggression was seen – and continues to be seen – as a 'great betrayal' which left a profound scar on the country's collective national memory and which has poisoned relations between the two nations ever since.[12]

'IF YOU GIVE US THE DALAI LAMA, WE CAN BE FRIENDS'

The official visit of the Chinese prime minister Wen Jiabao to Bangalore in 2005 left behind one phrase for posterity. In the Mecca of technology, Wen compared co-operation between India and China as like 'two pagodas, one hardware and one software. Combined, we can take the leadership position in the world. When the particular day comes, it will signify the coming of the Asian century of the IT industry.' The words of the Chinese government's number two inevitably sounded like an echo – in economic terms – of the old alliance aspired to by Nehru half a century before. The data on bilateral trade soon backed up what seemed to be a clear thawing in relations: while trade between the two countries barely exceeded $260 million in 1999, this shot up to $74 billion in 2011. One year earlier, Wen Jiabao and his Indian counterpart, Manmohan Singh, had set an even more ambitious target: $100 billion by 2015. Did this mean that the two giants had finally put their differences behind them?[13]

'The wound of 1962 is not closed. It has not healed because the territorial issue remains.[14] The border has not been settled, and India is still anxious. On other [land-based] borders, China has been able to settle its disputes efficiently and rapidly – except for the ones with India and Bhutan. So the question that comes up is: what is China waiting for?' The words of Professor Madhu Bhalla sum up the general opinion held on both sides of the Himalayas: that the territorial disputes and, by extension, the Tibet issue are still the main obstacles to restoring normality to relations between the two countries. 'We have held fourteen rounds of meetings between the representatives of the two prime ministers. So far, we have been unable to make any progress at all on the resolution of the territorial dispute,' says Gurmeet Kanwal, a retired brigadier-general and director of the Centre for Land Warfare Studies (CLAWS), the think-tank of India's armed forces. In order to break the deadlock in the border dispute, the Indian government knows that the price demanded by Beijing is both unspoken and clear: the dismantling of the Tibetan government in exile in Dharamsala. The loyalty commanded by the Dalai Lama and, by extension, the headquarters of the Tibetan government raises hackles in China as these powers are seen as an alternative to Beijing's authority in Tibet.

During our meeting, Gurmeet Kanwal shared an episode which perfectly sums up the general feeling within Beijing's circles of power. 'While at a conference in Singapore, one Chinese general told me, "Brigadier, if you give us the Dalai Lama in custody, we can be friends".' However, in democratic, religious and multi-cultural India, the option of 'giving up' the Tibetan cause – whether literally or figuratively – seems impossible.[15] And if the Tibet issue is not resolved, the territorial dispute will remain deadlocked.

A far cry from the impression created by the ever growing commercial ties, relations between the two countries are therefore still greatly conditioned by what academics describe as 'the bone in the throat of Indo-Chinese relations'. On the ground, this means that an area measuring 138,000 square kilometres, or more than Greece's total surface area, is still under dispute and represents a site of potential future hostility. Although a relative calm has reigned over the region in recent decades, mutual distrust has led to the fierce militarization of the 4,056-kilometre shared border: New Delhi has deployed six divisions or 90,000 men on the Indian side, while Beijing has four divisions or 60,000 troops positioned on the Chinese side.[16] 'We are defensively well positioned now. China would not make any major gains. We learned the lesson of 1962,' Gurmeet Kanwal assures us.

BLEEDING INDIA WITH 10,000 CUTS

It was around seven o'clock in the morning when we heard the beeping sound of a text message arriving. The first rays of sunlight were coming in through the window, and from this backstreet close to old Delhi we could already hear the noise of crowds and vehicles as the new day began to dawn. The message was sent by Huawei's PR officer in the Indian capital. 'Good morning. I'm sorry to inform you that the executives who had planned to meet you today in Delhi are out of town on an urgent business matter which has just come up in Mumbai. The interview is cancelled. Please accept my apologies.'[17] Less than three hours before our meeting, Huawei had cancelled the planned interview with the Chinese executives at its Indian office. This tactic of avoidance was strikingly similar to the one we had experienced just months before in Latin America. For a corporation which insists that it is entirely a private company and that it has no connection whatsoever to the Chinese state, Huawei had behaved exactly as a state-owned Chinese company acts when one of its executives finds himself having to deal with the insolent foreign press.

We had flown for six hours and 3,700 kilometres from Hong Kong to follow in the footsteps of Huawei – a leading Chinese company – in one of the most important technology markets in the world. More than any other corporation, Huawei represents both the strengths of the new China and the fears caused by its emergence. Founded out of nowhere in 1988, Huawei now has a presence in 140 countries, employs 140,000 members of staff and has become a powerful competitor for the major players in the telecommunications industry, such as Alcatel-Lucent, Nokia, Siemens, Ericsson and Cisco Systems. Amid accusations of piracy and of favouritism on the part of the Chinese government, the company has erupted into the sector like a whirlwind. Its winning formula has not only allowed the company to take the market by storm but has also forced the other players to drastically reduce their margins in order to compete. Meanwhile, Huawei continues to raise suspicions, not only as a result of the alleged connection between its founder, Ren Zhengfei – a former engineer with the People's Liberation Army – and the Chinese secret services, but also because of the company's refusal to be listed on the stock exchange, which fuels constant criticism because of the lack of transparency surrounding it. In 2011, Huawei's turnover exceeded $32 billion.[18]

After failing in Delhi, we landed in Bangalore in the hope of learning more about the challenges facing the jewel in China's technological crown in India's Silicon Valley. Huawei sent a top-of-the-range Mercedes to pick us up, which crawled through the traffic that has transformed the cradle of Indian talent into a logistical nightmare. At the luxurious Leela Palace hotel, the company has filled the length and breadth of seven floors with 1,200 of the 2,200 engineers working for the company in Bangalore. Most of them are young Indian nationals who crowd in groups around computers, brainstorm ideas in fifteen-minute meetings or work on new applications for Google Android. The R&D Centre in Bangalore is Huawei's biggest centre outside China, offering proof of the company's hopes for a market where it plans to invest $2 billion over the next five years. In 2013 the company will move to a modern campus on the outskirts of the city with room for 3,500 brainboxes, a nerve centre aimed at world domination.

However, in 2010 the Indian government came very close to putting an abrupt end to Huawei's ambitious plans. For almost nine months, a government circular banned telephone operators from supplying themselves with Chinese equipment under the undisputable pretext of national security concerns.[19] Amid the atmosphere of distrust and potential conflict which dominates relations between the two countries, the suspicion that equipment made by Huawei or ZTE – China's other major technology provider – could be carrying viruses or could have been manipulated set alarm bells ringing in New Delhi. Access to tenders for Chinese companies was therefore put on hold, causing a serious dent in Huawei's turnover: this dropped from $2.4 billion in 2009 to $1.6 billion in 2010, according to J. Gilbert, head of corporate affairs at Huawei India. 'Huawei was already number two in the market, and that was when it began to face a lot of opposition and lobbying from competitors. Some people started raising the question of the security threat and other issues,' he argues during our lunch at the Leela Palace hotel, clearly convinced that the controversy was orchestrated by their competitors who used their influence against them. 'It is a suspicion that has never been proved. If it was proved, we would have been banned. Even if Huawei did everything possible to become transparent, there would still be some issues brought up by our competitors. This is because Huawei is from China.'

However, beyond the commercial battle, the fact is that India has legitimate cause for concern. From its complete lack of transparency – as we saw for ourselves in Delhi – to the ties which connect Huawei's founder to the Chinese military, it is only fair to recognize that the company is one of a kind, to put it mildly.[20] This is not only problematic in a setting overshadowed by the possibility of a military confrontation, as the border conflicts between China and India are still unresolved, but also in relation to the powerful alliance which Beijing has forged with Pakistan, a nuclear power and India's bitter enemy. The possible links between Huawei and the Chinese military, and between the Chinese military and the Pakistani intelligence services, therefore raise all kinds of suspicions and fears in some Indian sectors, particularly – as we will see later in the chapter – as a result of the hostility shown by the Pakistani intelligence services towards India. This suspicion has been fed by the Chinese president Hu Jintao himself, who describes the nature of the Beijing–Islamabad axis in a highly enigmatic way: 'The China–Pakistan friendship is higher than the mountains and deeper than oceans,' said the leader of a Communist regime which meticulously calculates all of its public announcements. What was President Hu trying to say?

His statement probably was nothing more than the verbal expression of a reality: that Pakistan is a fundamental ally for Beijing at this moment in time. China offers the country its unconditional support on all fronts, and not only in the economic or diplomatic arenas. China is the largest supplier of armaments to Pakistan, and has 11,000 men currently deployed in Pakistan-administered Kashmir, which India claims as its own.[21] China also plans to link its Xinjiang region with Pakistan's naval base at Gwadar and is supplying Islamabad with nuclear reactors, a technically civilian act of assistance which the Islamic Republic may be using inappropriately.[22] Ever since India and the United States signed their military alliance in 2005, which infuriated Beijing, not least because India had not signed the Nuclear Non-Proliferation Treaty (NPT), China's tactical aggression has led it to openly recognize Pakistan's sovereignty in Pakistan-administered Kashmir, while it considers the part of Kashmir under Indian control to be disputed territory. By keeping the Kashmir dispute ablaze and strengthening Pakistan, China is aiming to trouble India on one of its weakest flanks. In other words, this tactic allows China to 'bleed India with 10,000 cuts'.[23]

In domestic terms, these bonds between the two countries also allow the Chinese government to neutralize the potential impact of Pakistan's Islamization and 'Talibanization' on the Uighur insurgency, both inside and outside Xinjiang province. 'Beijing is very worried that Pakistan could become a failing state, because Pakistan has the huge role of being a facilitator for China in the region. It facilitated the US–China relations with [the American president Richard] Nixon, as well as China's relationship with the Middle East and Saudi Arabia, and certainly with Afghanistan and the Taliban. It's all about China's broader regional interests. Pakistan is the doorkeeper to the whole region,' argues Madhu Bhalla. 'Pakistan's market is extremely important, but most of all the country is fundamental to China's security on its western border,' confirms Ma Jiali, research fellow at the China Institute of Contemporary International Relations, and one of the most respected Chinese experts on Sino-Indian relations. Both China and India believe that if Pakistan does become a failed state it will become a nuclear time bomb in the hands of whatever faction takes power, each one more radical than the last. The general feeling is: if Pakistan falls, we all go up in flames.

Under these circumstances, this 'friendship higher than the mountains and deeper than oceans' has disastrous consequences for India.

WHAT IF THE ELEPHANT DECIDES TO USE ITS FULL WEIGHT?

On 26 November 2008, a brutal Islamic terrorist attack in Mumbai left 164 people dead and over 300 injured on the streets of India's economic capital. Months later, confirmation was given of what was already an open secret in the dramatic hours following the event: Pakistan's secret services had helped finance the attack, which was carried out by Lashkar-e-Taiba, a terrorist group with known ties to the Pakistani military. It was one of the bloodiest attacks ever to have taken place in India, but it was not the first time that the Pakistani military had been accused of playing an active role. 'Pakistan has been sponsoring terrorism [against India] for two decades now,' argues Brigadier Gurmeet Kanwal, voicing an opinion which is deeply rooted in Indian society.

In view of Beijing's close ties to the Pakistani military, we were keen to find out more about China's possible responsibility in this terrorist activity. If China's associates are the same ideologues who are supposedly behind the terrorism against India, China could exert its influence to prevent new attacks, we argue. 'Does China have any responsibility?' asks Uday Bhaskar, director of the National Maritime Foundation and one of the subcontinent's leading military analysts. 'Absolutely. It is not that China doesn't know that the establishment and the army of Pakistan are supporting terrorism [against India]. They know, but China chooses to follow a policy of "don't ask, don't tell". They say, "I don't want to know about it. You can do what you want but don't tell me." China could do much more, there's no doubt about that,' he continues. Why don't they do it, then? 'When I talk to my Chinese colleagues about this, they have no answer,' he reiterates.[24]

While Beijing argues that India's suspicions are highly exaggerated or even completely unjustified, India's circles of power in the fields of academia, diplomacy, the military or journalism consider China's complicity and responsibility for Pakistan's undercover war against India as a proven and indisputable fact. 'It wouldn't be possible without China's active support. This is about keeping India in a state of constant disequilibrium. This is what it means to wound and bleed India with 10,000 cuts,' the Indian experts say. There is, of course, the underlying question of China and India's rivalry over regional supremacy, but, according to Uday Bhaskar, what we are seeing here is also a case of two countries which are in some ways philosophically incompatible. China's regime governs the country like a private corporation, while India is a completely different type of animal. 'The very existence of India, with its secular democracy, its diversity and the fact that India is succeeding despite its shortcomings, poses a challenge to China. The form in which India interprets itself, including its constitution with its principles and values, and the way that India manages diversity are causing the greatest sort of anxiety for China, because it repudiates the Chinese system. That is burning the Chinese up inside,' he argues.

How, then, will the two most populated countries on the planet face up to the future? Will they be able to live alongside each other? Is there room for two tigers on the same mountain? Like other analysts we consulted, Uday Bhaskar foresees a turbulent future. He explains that the potential risk is rooted in the way in which China interprets its place in the world: 'China's objective at a global level is to seek multipolarity; but in Asia [it] wants unipolarity. This is the challenge facing India. Tension with China is inevitable.' And how will India react? we ask him. In his answer, he draws on his knowledge of the strategic culture of the subcontinent. 'In India today the most amount of interest is generated by political controversies, and maybe cricket; not national security issues. India will respond slowly, it won't do anything in a hurry ... But if we do have to respond, it will not be insignificant. When we react, it takes time, but we react strongly,' he warns. In this way, the comparison drawn between India and the elephant is not incorrect: 'It takes time to turn around. But once it turns, and if it decides to sit down, then it brings a lot of weight [to the issue].'

CHINA DISPLAYS ITS FIRST AIRCRAFT CARRIER

We have already seen evidence of China's strategy of building relations of trust and friendship in southern Asia based especially on economic clout, as is seen indisputably in the cases of Nepal and Pakistan. However, this tactic is not limited to these two countries alone. Beijing is spreading its tentacles throughout the region and especially into India's neighbouring countries, which it manages to win over using million-dollar investments, military co-operation and diplomatic seductive power. This 'strategic siege', as it is known in India, has led China to dip its toes into the Indian Ocean, which has historically been included within India's sphere of influence. Beijing has invested in the Pakistani deep-water port in Gwadar[25] – at the entrance to the strategic Strait of Hormuz and just 70 kilometres from Iran – as well as container ports in Bangladesh, the Maldives and Sri Lanka. China also upgraded the facilities and infrastructure in the militarily significant Coco Islands in Burmese waters, just 18 kilometres away from the border with India.[26]

What is China hoping to achieve? Is it aiming to geopolitically isolate its regional rival? Or is it simply trying to increase its naval power in order to protect its maritime routes and, therefore, its economic interests? Whatever the answer might be, China's eruption into its periphery waters has led to an immediate counter-offensive from New Delhi, who has decided to play China at its own game. India has extended its military co-operation with a cast of countries from the Persian Gulf to the Pacific, creating especially important – albeit somehow symbolic – links with Japan and Vietnam, the two countries which are most concerned about the 'peaceful rise' of China. Furthermore, India plans to increase the number of naval vessels to 145 over the next decade, complementing three aircraft carriers which are meant to be in operation by 2017. This can be interpreted as a clear statement of intent, particularly considering that this is a country where a large part of the population remain below the poverty line.[27]

This glimpse of future tension in the Indian Ocean provides a good example of what the Indian military analyst Uday Bhaskar warned us about during our meeting: 'When China becomes more powerful, it will act in a more assertive way.' China is already demonstrating signs of authoritarianism in other waters with a much greater geopolitical importance for Beijing at this time: the South China Sea. These waters carry 25 per cent of world trade and around 80 per cent of China's oil imports from the Middle East and Africa. It is here that Beijing has several territorial disputes on the go with five regional countries over the sovereignty of the Spratly Islands,[28] as well as a dispute with Vietnam over the Paracel Islands.[29] 'The *peaceful rise* of China? Do you see how they're behaving in the South China Sea? They [the other countries in the region] are really petrified, like a rabbit when you shine a torch in its eyes,' Bhaskar argues.

The analyst highlights China's current display of bravado in these waters, as well as its unilateral ban on fishing and the pressure that it is putting on foreign oil companies to suspend any exploration activities on behalf of other countries. Confrontations between Chinese warships and Vietnamese or Filipino fishing boats have consequently been a regular occurrence for decades, leaving frequent diplomatic clashes and a trail of dead bodies in their wake.[30]

As well as these sea-based activities, it is also important to take into account Beijing's coercive diplomatic tactics. These tactics begin with China's hopes of dealing with the disputes in the South China Sea bilaterally – drawing on the usual Chinese strategy of divide and conquer – and end with an increase in China's naval military capacity in the region, where it is using Hainan Island and its nuclear submarines as strategic battering rams. In its diplomatic dealings and conversations surrounding this issue, Beijing defaults to using a map dating from 1947 and a 1935 variant, both of which were drawn up before the foundation of the People's Republic. The map is used by China to ambiguously claim almost everything, although it is unclear whether they are 'merely' claiming all the atolls within the nine-dashed line or everything within that line – waters, island, resources and all.

China has never explained the scope or significance of this map, according to Ian Storey, from the Institute of Southeast Asian Studies (ISEAS) in Singapore. 'The short answer is, we don't know [what it is based on], because China has never explained what this map means. I go to conferences and I talk to the Chinese all the time, and I say: What does this mean? I never get an answer. I think it's because they haven't decided what it means.' The official statement that China uses today is: 'China has indisputable sovereignty over the South China Sea islands and adjacent Waters'. However, we discovered the real reason for China's official silence on the matter in an attic in the heart of Ho Chi Minh City, the economic capital of Vietnam.

In order to find out what the other countries involved have to say on the matter, we had arranged to meet with several Vietnamese historians and experts based in the country. One of them is Dang Dinh Dau, who has spent decades carrying out an enormous document study, exploring every resource from the United States Library of Congress to archives containing maps of Asia drawn up by Portuguese and Spanish missionaries in the sixteenth century. Dang has spread out copies of these fabulous maps in his attic, all of which confirm his theory: Imperial China never considered the territories to the south or west of Hainan Island in the South China Sea as its own. 'China's territorial claims over the Paracel Islands began in 1910, when it became aware of the territory's strategic importance. However, in the earlier maps made by Western missionaries, and even in the maps drawn up by the Chinese empire itself, China's territory ended at southern Hainan,' he concludes.

As Beijing is therefore unable to bring any forceful historical or legal precedent to the negotiating table, it has instead opted for a display of its present and future military power. In South-East Asia, this is causing genuine concern, according to a high-ranking source that we met in Taiwan. 'Publicly, we all in the region talk about engaging with China, but when the doors are shut we ask the US Navy not to go too far away.' Ian Storey sums up this feeling in similar terms: 'There's a growing sense of anxiety in the region about China's growing military power and where it is going.' These fears have not been calmed by the public presentation of the *Liaoning* (formerly known as the *Varyag*), China's first aircraft carrier, which is operational from September of 2012.

There is no doubt that access to an aircraft carrier makes all the difference. A navy without an aircraft carrier is a defensive navy; a navy which includes one is a combat unit ready for action. If we also take into account the pace at which China's military budget has grown over the last decade,[31] part of which has gone towards increasing its naval capacity, as well as speculations that China could be constructing one or more additional 'made in China' aircraft carriers, it is easy to imagine the 'rabbit' paralysed by the glare of China's warships. This is not so much because of the military significance of the *Liaoning*: at the end of the day, it is still just a piece of updated Ukrainian junk from the 1980s, which came very close to ending up as a floating casino at the port of Macau. Its real importance is entirely political. What is really worrying here is the clear message being sent by Beijing.

'An aircraft carrier is used to project power across the world . . . China will use [the aircraft carriers] to show their presence in the South China Sea, to show that China is the dominant player there, and it has the aircraft carriers to prove it. No country in South-East Asia has ships any way near that level and never will: it's too expensive,' Storey explains. With the launch of its first aircraft carrier, China is announcing its intention 'to be a strong military power with aircraft carriers. It's a symbol.'

Military experts explain that the new Chinese ship has not awakened excessive concern in Washington, particularly as the United States has up to eleven aircraft carriers at its disposal. America is much more concerned about the Dong-Feng 21-D, a Chinese missile capable of sinking an aircraft carrier. Although it has not yet been tested, the missile represents a dangerous threat both because of its long range and because it is difficult to detect and block. With the creation of a naval arsenal which will eventually include one or more aircraft carriers, a long-range anti-aircraft-carrier missile and nuclear submarines, the overarching question is obvious. Why does the 'peaceful rise' of China require such a large arsenal? Is a war between China and the United States in the Pacific inevitable?

China is more interested in regional stability than anyone, but it is also quick to defend its 'core interests' in its maritime periphery, from Taiwan to the Spratly Islands via its maritime routes and the Straits of Malacca, a bottleneck situated between Malaysia, Indonesia and Singapore which is key to the energy route stretching from the Middle East to Asia and America.

China and the United States share many interests in the South China Sea and, by extension, the Pacific Ocean, where they both champion stability, peace and the free passage of commercial ships. However, their geopolitical aspirations and strategic aims, with Washington determined to stay in an area where it has been made welcome and Beijing set to play a dominant role in the region, could threaten these declarations of good will. It is therefore precisely in these waters where the interests of the two powers could potentially come into conflict. Three areas of risk begin to appear: from north to south, they are North Korea, Taiwan and the islands of the South China Sea. According to the experts, there is no doubt about it: there is tension on the horizon. After all, the hegemony of the western Pacific is at stake.

MISSION: RECOVER TAIWAN

In the context of the escalation of tension in the South China Sea, South-East Asian countries opt for the dual strategy of co-operating with China on economic issues, while also sheltering with the United States on military matters. In this game of chess, Taiwan plays a vital role in the geopolitics of the region. The 'rebel province', as Beijing still sees the island, benefits from an exceptional geographical location at just 100 nautical miles from continental China, right in the path of the maritime route which carries oil from the Middle East to north-east Asia and the United States. From the point of view of the United States military, Taiwan's proximity to China's coastline makes it an 'unsinkable aircraft carrier'. In Beijing, the current status quo is seen as the Achilles heel of its national security, as it is blocking China's strategic development in the western Pacific.

Obsessed with reverting to the territorial integrity which existed before 1949, the Chinese government has been fighting a relentless crusade to move towards the permanent integration and absorption of Taiwan. Even after the six decades of de facto independence which Taiwan has enjoyed, ever since nationalists led by Chiang Kai-shek fled to Taiwan after losing the war against the Communists and formed the Republic of China, Beijing's historic mission has been to recover Taiwan. Reclaiming Taiwan for the mother country is clearly one of Beijing's most important objectives in terms of foreign policy. Achieving it would represent a decisive step towards rebalancing power with the United States and thereby securing hegemony of the region.

To win over its rebel province, China is showing Taiwan the economic benefits of becoming integrated with the world's fastest-growing market while simultaneously displaying the military force it would be prepared to unleash on Taiwan should the island dare to make a false move that would bring its future sovereignty into question. Since the 2005 approval of a law authorizing the use of force against Taiwan should it declare its independence, China has been steadily increasing the number and sophistication of the missiles distributed along its south-east coast, all of which point directly at the island. The latest figures provided by the Taiwanese secret services estimate that there are between 1,600 and 1,800 missiles currently pointing at Taiwan, ready to open fire the day that Taiwan crosses the line.[32]

'Taiwan would like to promote peace and stability in the Asia-Pacific region. That is why we feel that [relations] on the two sides of the Taiwan Strait have implications not only for Taiwan and mainland China, but also for the whole region in terms of regional and strategic balance, regional development, and regional peace and security,' said the Taiwanese deputy minister for Foreign Affairs, David Lin, when we met him in Taipei, acknowledging the fact that relations between Taipei and Beijing transcend domestic issues. Until now the island – and, by extension, its American ally – has contributed to a balance of power in regional waters which is equally beneficial to other allies of the United States such as Australia and Singapore, and China's territorial rivals, such as Vietnam and the Philippines. The presence of the United States in the region compensates for China's superior military power in South-East Asia where, as we have seen, it has various on-going territorial disputes.

'In this region, who is mainland China's real enemy? Japan is not a military power, and neither is South Korea. There is no serious threat, and yet mainland China has been continuing its expansion of military operations for decades. It is difficult to understand this mentality. Mainland China wants to become a regional power, but in what sense? Will it become more aggressive or is it still sincere about keeping its commitment to peaceful development? That is why China is still a potential threat to regional peace and stability. Many [South-East Asian] countries don't want to say it out loud because they have very strong economic relations with China, but in their hearts and minds they still consider mainland China's military expansion as a threat . . . I hope mainland China can receive this message from the region, so that it can fulfil its commitments [to security in the region]. But I am not quite sure . . . whether mainland China can fulfil its commitment,' Lin argues.

For obvious reasons, Taiwan is the country which is most attentive to Beijing's every gesture, trying to decipher its message down to the last comma. 'Beijing wants the world to think that it will use force. Its strategy is to be ready, to act as a deterrent, but preferably not to use force,' explained the former deputy minister of defence and former professor at Georgetown University, Chong-Ping Lin. 'However, China has developed a major new strategy which goes beyond military issues. The best option is to absorb Taiwan without using force.' The other possible way of integrating the island into Chinese territory is via the economic route. In fact, bilateral trade reached $75 billion in the first half of 2012, while it is estimated that Taiwan has invested over $200 billion in mainland China, most of which will go towards building electrical component factories, a sector in which the island is a leading player.

On top of this, the two countries adopted an Economic Co-operation Framework Agreement (ECFA) at the end of 2010 to relax restrictions on bilateral trade. The aim was to boost commercial exchange and investments by reducing or eliminating customs duties on over 700 products. This highly significant legal tool brings Beijing and Taipei closer together than ever before, just when Taiwan has become more reliant on China's economic power as a result of the global crisis. In practice, there is little doubt about the importance of the ECFA: it is a point of no return on the path towards economic integration between Taiwan and China. It may also, perhaps, be a step towards the island's definitive assimilation.

To understand the effect of all this on bilateral relations, we travelled to the Taiwanese capital at the end of 2009, when the agreement was being negotiated behind closed doors and the critical press was throwing their hands up in horror. These were some of the 'sweetest' moments experienced in six decades of tumultuous relations. The Taiwanese president Ma Ying-jeou, the leader of the nationalist Kuomintang Party (KMT), who replaced the pro-independence leader Chen Shui-bian of the Democratic Progressive Party (DPP) in May 2008, came to power with the determination to make a 180-degree U-turn and reverse the atmosphere of extreme tension and confrontation which had dominated the Taiwan Strait over the previous two government terms. Barely a year after taking up the presidency, Ma established direct daily flights between China and Taiwan, while simultaneously reinstating naval and postal links. The Kuomintang and the Communist Party of China – which had fought against each other in the civil war that raged on and off between 1927 and 1949 – reinforced their relations with visits, meetings between high-ranking officers and smiles on the front pages of newspapers. There was even a rumour of an imminent meeting between the two presidents, Ma and Hu Jintao. The historic enemies were apparently becoming bosom friends.

The ECFA was at the core of President Ma's economic policy, as he hoped to rebuild relations with Beijing based on three negatives: no to confrontation, no to independence, and no to reunification. As well as the impact of the economic crisis, Taiwan had found itself excluded from the Free Trade Agreement (FTA) agreed between China and the countries in the Association of South-East Asian Nations (ASEAN) because of the island's international diplomatic isolation. The treaty came into force in January 2010 and the resulting loss of competitiveness immediately led to a fall in Taiwanese exports. Under these circumstances, President Ma's Kuomintang presented the ECFA to the island's 23 million inhabitants as an essential step in bringing

Taiwan out of the crisis and reducing unemployment. In other words, it was seen as the perfect recipe to avoid economic strangulation.

'Taiwan cannot be excluded from the FTA because of its relations with China,' explained Chun-Fang Hsu, deputy director of the Bureau of Foreign Trade, when we met her in Taipei. Chung-Fang was in charge of negotiating the agreement with the Chinese authorities, which came into force in September 2010. 'We don't want to be marginalized economically while trade becomes global. And to avoid that we first need a pact with China,' she told us, suggesting that the ECFA also to some extent represents Taiwan's pass of safe-conduct to help diffuse its international isolation. The Taiwanese government insisted that the nations which subscribe to the 'one-China' policy – and therefore refuse to recognize Taiwan as a sovereign nation – would refuse to sign an FTA with the island without a previous agreement with China.[33] Once the ECFA was approved, it would leave the door wide open for bilateral agreements between Taiwan and other countries, something which to this date has not yet taken place.[34]

The agreement has further divided a Taiwanese society which has historically always been extremely polarized on the issue. While the Taiwanese people are pleased with the strengthened commercial links with China because of the opportunities they offer, they are also wary of the potential adverse effects of these relations. On the one hand, people are afraid that by opening 250 Taiwanese sectors to Chinese investment, including some as sensitive as the microelectronics sector, Taiwan may be vulnerable to theft of its national 'know how', which is arguably the greatest asset of an economy whose vitality and success led it to be seen as one of the 'Asian Tigers' which dazzled the world. On the other hand, there is some concern that the arrival of Chinese products without customs duty will cause the collapse of some of Taiwan's national industries. However, the greatest reservations about the agreement relate to the potential effect that it may have on Taiwan's eventual independence, whether real or de facto. How will Taiwan ensure that economic integration will not increase Beijing's influence over the island which may lead, in the medium or long term, to definitive assimilation? Or, to put it another way, will Taiwan pay a political price in terms of reunification?

'We think our government is very naïve,' said Bi-Khim Hsiao, spokesperson of the main opposition group, the pro-independence DPP. The danger of the ECFA is that Taiwan 'runs the risk of really becoming a subsidiary of China, because we will be much more vulnerable to pressure'. In the eyes of the opposition party and some sectors of Taiwanese society, as well as in the opinion of outside observers such as the former prime minister of Singapore, Lee Kuan Yew, the agreement is seen as an irreparable step towards reunification.[35] 'For Taiwan's leader, Ma Ying-jeou, the ECFA is useful in the short term to help him become re-elected [something he achieved in January 2012]. For Beijing, it serves their own purpose of unification,' argues Professor Chong-Pin Lin.

'In 2004, after I left the role of Taiwan's deputy defence minister, I gave a keynote speech at a conference on the defence industry in the United States. My main point was that Beijing has developed a new grand strategy which is predicated on using instruments that transcend pure military force. I said that Beijing would stress the use of economy and culture. People laughed at me . . . China has understood that it is easier to buy and absorb Taiwan than to attack it. The ECFA is the typical example of this. It is a very important step in that direction.'

THE FALL OF BEIJING'S *BÊTE NOIRE*

On 20 May 2008, just an hour after leaving the presidential office of the Republic of China, Chen Shui-bian, who had governed the island since his historic victory in 2000 as the opposition DPP candidate, was notified that he was forbidden from leaving Taiwan and that an investigation was being opened into allegations of corruption against him during his term of office. That was how Chen, who had just lost his presidential immunity after President Ma's first election, began his dramatic descent into hell as a result of charges of corruption, money laundering and accepting bribes which also implicated his wife, Wu Shu-chen, and his son-in-law. Months later he was formally accused by the public prosecutor's office, and on 11 September 2009 he became the first president in Taiwan's history to be sent to prison. He was originally given a life sentence, but this was reduced on appeal to eighteen years in prison, which he is currently serving. The *bête noire* of Taiwan's Kuomintang and the Communist Party of China – the politician who had dared to oust one and defy the other – had been taken out of circulation for good.

The electoral victory in 2000 of this lawyer and defender of political dissidents during the era of martial law on the island represented a milestone for the young Taiwanese democracy, which had only celebrated its first multi-party elections in 1996. Born into a humble family, this self-made man who had been sentenced to a year in prison for libel during martial law was Taiwan's first non-Kuomintang president, thereby breaking fifty years of the nationalists' hegemony over power. He was also one of the island's most controversial leaders, not only because of his staunch opposition to the 'one-China principle', but also as a result of the accusations of corruption that marred his second presidential term from 2004.

Chen became a passionate champion of Taiwan's independence, advocating a referendum to legally declare independence for the island, which caused tensions to escalate between Taipei and Beijing. 'Beijing was very unhappy, but it said nothing to Taipei. Beijing went to Washington and gave the Americans a warning: "If you don't rein in Chen Shui-bian, then we will have to take matters into our own hands." . . . The result was twelve warnings [against the declaration of independence] sent from Washington to Taipei between June 2007 and February 2008,' explains Professor Chong-Pin, who served in Chen's government.[36]

In Taipei we went to see Tao Liu, Chen's right-hand man and former speechwriter. In his offices at the Ketagalan Foundation, Tao explained that he – along with a section of Taiwanese society – believes that, while the legal charges of corruption against Chen have 'some basis in irregularities committed', they were really part of a political plot to get Chen out of the picture.[37] 'What happened to Chen was an act of political revenge which was specifically aimed against him. He beat the Kuomintang and, after eight years away from power, the Kuomintang came back and they wanted revenge. I personally think that if the same standards that have been applied to Chen were applied to any other political party, none of them would survive that level of scrutiny,' Tao assured us, referring to the laws limiting expenditure on political campaigns and to the use of the special state fund that allows presidents to use certain amounts at their discretion without being called to account.

'Corruption is a very convenient accusation if you want to destroy somebody. For the last twenty or thirty years the Kuomintang had accused pro-independence politicians of being radical or irresponsible. Then they started to use the term "corrupt". In China, corruption is regularly used to attack enemies. President Chen has no doubt whatsoever that China was involved in his case, but he has no proof.' It was crystal clear what Tao Liu was suggesting: independently of whether or not Chen had his hand in the till, the former president was the victim of a political witch hunt.

Although Chen has been in prison since he was found guilty, despite rumours in 2012 about his bad health, we asked Tao if he could put us in contact with the former president so that we could hear his version of events. 'Give me the questions and I'll see what I can do,' Tao replied. 'He's very closely guarded.' Months later, Tao emailed us a handwritten (and stamped) document and another typed document with Chen's answers in Mandarin, which are partially reproduced here:

> On 11 November 2008 I went to the inquiry office and made the following speech: 'Today I am going to Taiwan's Bastille ... because I am the greatest obstacle to the process of a union between Taiwan and continental China with the co-operation of the Kuomintang (KMT) and the Communist Party of China ... I have been sacrificed to calm the rage of Zhongnanhai [the headquarters of the Chinese government].' Over the course of the investigation it has become evident that the Chinese government is behind all this, with the aim of punishing me for rejecting the 'one-China principle' and to strike a blow to pro-independence politicians by using me as an example. None of this is a secret; these are all real facts ...
>
> In July 2008, the Taiwan Affairs Office of the Communist Party of China (CPC) made a plan to approve a political strategy to resolve the Taiwan issue. The plan aimed to attack Chen and his closest collaborators, because they believed that an attack against Chen and his allies would spread throughout the ideological division of the Democratic Progressive Party and keep the DPP embroiled in ideological chaos for

a long time, preventing them from progressing towards independence and thereby reducing the pressure on the Kuomintang . . . with the aim of resolving the Taiwan issue by 2012 [the date of the Taiwanese presidential elections won by Kuomintang] . . .

I do not plead guilty to the charges the investigators have brought against me, or to the verdict of the court. If I am guilty of anything, it is of being 'the president of Taiwan', of being against the 'one-China principle' and of championing 'Taiwan and China, two countries on either side of the Strait', which violates the Anti-Secession Law approved on 14 March 2005 by the Communist Party of China . . .

I have been sacrificed in a collaboration between the CPC and the KMT to put an end to the pro-independence party (DPP). There are only two people in the world who could take power away from the KMT: one of them is Mao Zedong and the other is Chen Shui-bian. However, now that the KMT and CPC have moved from war, struggles and arguments to conciliation and co-operation, I am the greatest obstacle to the process of union, so I am the one who must be eliminated as soon as possible. For the KMT, my sin is having 'stolen power' [a reference to his electoral victory in 2000], which in Chinese tradition is a crime worthy of death. For the CPC, I am the greatest traitor of the Chinese nation . . .

To defend the sovereignty of the state, Taiwan must not degrade itself by becoming part of the People's Republic of China as a special administrative region . . . The enemy of the DPP is not inside Taiwan; the KMT is only a competitor. The CPC is the real enemy.

Chen Shui-bian, 23 January 2011

In July 2011, another former Taiwanese president was charged with embezzling public funds to the value of $7.8 million. The public prosecutor's office began an investigation into eighty-eight-year-old Lee Teng-hui, an emblematic political figure in Taiwan's democratic history, for having allegedly diverted state funds during his time in office (1988–2000). Strangely, the accusation of corruption coincided with Lee's clashes with President Ma, whom he had criticized in recent years over his growing relationship with Beijing. All this provided more fuel to speculations about a Taiwanese plot against the figures who oppose President Ma's policies to promote the Taipei–Beijing axis.

TAIWAN'S INTERNATIONAL ISOLATION

While the growing relationship between Taipei and Beijing and the increase in China's military capacity have opened the door to a new geopolitical scenario in the Asia-Pacific region, the Taiwan issue has also provided Beijing with some important diplomatic victories. Up until the beginning of the 1970s, Taiwan was represented at institutions such as the United Nations – where it occupied the place now held by China – and was recognized by a large number of countries, including the United States. However, now that there is no Cold War and China is becoming increasingly integrated into the international scene, only the Vatican and twenty-two countries with little international weight support Taipei in its pro-independence cause, mostly as a result of the economic gains yielded by their loyalty rather than any ideological motivation. Malawi was the last country to turn its coat in January 2008, but the most important recent victory for the Communist authorities was definitely Costa Rica's decision to break ties with Taipei in 2007.

The importance of this Latin American country is two-fold. First, by guaranteeing Costa Rica's loyalty, Beijing made its first break into Central America, which until then was a Taiwanese stronghold. Secondly, the decision to establish ties with Communist China was endorsed by Óscar Arias, the president of the country and winner of the 1987 Nobel Peace Prize, which lent added prestige to the event. Beijing therefore managed to obtain diplomatic recognition in Central America's most democratic country, laying the groundwork for the creation of a domino effect in the region which would deal the final blow to Taiwan's already fragile international support.

A symbol of this new friendship between San José and Beijing is seen in the recent construction of Costa Rica's 35,000-capacity National Stadium, built on the ruins of a former airport. Its construction was undertaken – not without conflict, as we saw in Chapter 5 – by the Chinese state-owned company Anhui Wai Jing, after Beijing agreed to provide the $90 million needed to build the stadium as part of the aid package offered to Costa Rica in return for breaking ties with Taiwan.

We travelled to Costa Rica at the end of 2010 to see for ourselves how things had evolved between San Jose and Beijing since the relationship was established. In Taipei the ambassadors of Honduras and the Dominican Republic had assured us, not very convincingly, that their countries maintained their relations with Taiwan for noble causes, such as the defence of human rights. 'We share democratic values and we believe in them. That is why we support them, not because of dollar diplomacy, and not because of the help that Taiwan gives us. We haven't gone with the highest bidder,' the Honduran ambassador, Marlene Villela, assured us from the building on the outskirts of Taipei which is home to all of the diplomatic legations. If that was true, why would a Nobel Prize winner decide to break ties with democratic Taiwan in order to join ranks with the Communist Chinese dictatorship? Who took the first step? What was the reaction of the rest of the countries in the region? What moves did China make behind the scenes in order to secure the diplomatic backing of San José?

To find the answers we arranged to meet with Óscar Arias. His assistant opened the door of his house which, strangely enough, is located just opposite the recently opened Chinese embassy. Inside his opulent home, decorated with designer furniture, terracotta soldiers and shelves full of books, numerous photographs make it clear who Arias's colleagues have been over the course of his long and respected political career: Bill Clinton, Lula de Silva, Nelson Mandela. On the table in a living room, which looks out onto a tranquil garden, lies a copy of Tony Blair's memoirs. Fifteen minutes later, Arias appears looking serious and polite as he takes a seat on the sofa.

'A country as small as ours is condemned to be commercial, to be a natural merchant,' he begins, when we ask him why he decided to establish ties with China. He goes on to paraphrase John Maynard Keynes: 'When the facts change, one has to change,' he explains to justify Costa Rica's about-turn in diplomatic policy. 'In my first term of office [1986–1990] I already wanted to break off relations with Taiwan and establish links with China, but I was fighting too many battles and one more would have been excessive.' Before making the decision he therefore had to wait for his second term of office (2006–2010), which required a constitutional reform in the country, because up until then only one presidential term was allowed per candidate. 'China is Costa Rica's second biggest trade partner. That says everything that needs to be said about why we had to establish relations. It's not possible to turn one's back on China. People elect you to lead, not to be pleasant.'

When justifying his political decisions, Arias does not fail to mention Taiwan, which he criticizes for its 'tight-fisted aid'. He assures us that he never went to Taiwan to ask for funding to pay for his electoral campaign, which other candidates supposedly did, not only in his country but across the entire region. Did that mean that China did not offer anything in return? 'The negotiator, Bruno Stagno, is the one who knows the details on that matter,' he told us, evasively. Arias had already defended the intellectual reasons which had led him to throw himself into China's arms, but he did not want to go into any details. As Arias is a master in the art of dodging questions, we assumed that the conversation was over. So we went to see Bruno Stagno, the former minister of foreign affairs.

'The key moment took place on 18 May 2006,' Stagno told us at his home in San José. 'Mexico invited me to a dinner at the Mexican capital which was going to be attended by every Central American country apart from El Salvador. To my surprise, the Chinese Minister of Foreign Affairs Li Zhaoxing was there. I immediately realized that all of the countries present were in conversation with China about establishing relations.' One small detail revealed that China was particularly interested in building a relationship with Costa Rica. 'At one point in the dinner, he [Li] turned to me and said in French, "Both of us love Paris and that is why I think that the French capital would be the perfect setting for negotiating the establishment of bilateral relations." I immediately understood that he knew everything about our government. He knew that I'm married to a French woman and that I studied in France. I understood that the real negotiation process was already beginning, because I doubt that any other ministers there spoke French and could understand what he had said to me.'

Soon after that a process of negotiations began which, according to Stagno, was spied on by Taiwan. 'They tried to influence the Costa Rican press by giving them printing machines as gifts and inviting journalists to travel to Taiwan. Taipei knew that if it lost the support

of Costa Rica it would be defeated in the diplomatic battle.' This
'betrayal', as it was seen by Taipei, finally took place in Beijing at two
o'clock in the morning on 31 May 2007, after three rounds of negotiations. While China was raising the red flag in Central America, the
'rebel island' saw the move as a well-aimed diplomatic blow. In order
to achieve it, China had to bring $430 million to the table: $30 million in cash, $300 million through buying bonds in the Costa Rican
Treasury, and $100 million in the form of donated Chinese goods
(including the National Stadium).[39]

Just as Taiwan had feared, Costa Rica's decision had a significant
impact on the other Central American governments. Countries such
as Panama, Nicaragua and El Salvador began to show their willingness to follow the trail blazed by San José by recognizing China.
However, by then Beijing had put the brakes on new additions to the
club of countries which had sworn eternal fidelity to China in order
to avoid jeopardizing its relationship with Taipei.[40] With Taiwan's
recent change in policy and with Chen Shui-bian safely out of the picture, the new defections would have caused a wave of discontent in
Taiwan which could have potentially derailed negotiations over the
ECFA or disturbed the honeymoon that was beginning to take place
between Beijing and Taipei. Therefore, after the first piece had fallen
it was China itself which paradoxically put an end to the domino
effect. The international and diplomatic battle had already been won:
it seems that a truce is justified if the final goal is China's reunification
with Taiwan.

Bruno Stagno makes a positive assessment of the last few years of
relations between his country and China, although he admits that
bilateral ties do have their challenges. 'Japan and South Korea take us
more seriously now,' he assures us, suggesting that the relationship
with Beijing has helped to improve Costa Rica's international position. However, he admits that 'Costa Rica has lost some freedom' in
terms of its foreign policy, in relation to issues such as Tibet or human
rights. 'The honeymoon is not going to last forever,' he concludes.
'Chinese companies are going to have to adapt to local standards. We
have always told China not to make the same mistakes as Taiwan,' he
explains, in relation to the visa scandal linked to the construction of
the National Stadium (described in Chapter 5).

ENVELOPES FOR BUYING
JOURNALISTS

Perhaps the 'mistakes' mentioned by Stagno have something to do with the episodes experienced by at least two Costa Rican journalists at the newspaper *La Nación*. The broadsheet, one of the most respected in the country, has closely followed relations between San José and Beijing and had therefore briefly covered the demonstrations carried out by the spiritual group Falun Gong – another spectre of the Chinese regime, which is banned and persecuted in China – in the Costa Rican capital ahead of the first visit of the Chinese president, Hu Jintao, to the country in November 2008.

'One day a Chinese journalist called me and said that his name was Jia Zechi. He told me that he was the chief correspondent in Mexico at the newspaper *Wenhui* and that he was in San José for a few days. From the beginning he showed an interest in finding out about the atmosphere surrounding Hu Jintao's visit, particularly in relation to potential protests by groups critical of Beijing's regime. We arranged to have dinner to chat about it,' one of the *La Nación* journalists told us in the Costa Rican capital. 'We met at the restaurant of the Grano de Oro Hotel, close to the Paseo Colón. At least six people of Chinese origin entered the restaurant in the space of ten minutes. Jia was a young man, about thirty years old, and dressed in informal clothes.

'He immediately began to ask me about the Falun Gong group and he told me the Chinese version of the conflict. Then we talked about Tibet, also following the official version, and in the end we didn't say anything at all about the diplomatic relationship between China and Costa Rica, which is what he had originally said he wanted to talk about. He only took notes once, when I told him about the appearance and number of the Falun Gong protesters. Over the course of the conversation I became very aware of several people who appeared to be Chinese who were walking around the restaurant and who changed table on at least one occasion,' remembers the source, who at that point was already beginning to suspect that Jia was not the journalist he claimed to be.

'When I was about to leave, he told me that he had a present for me. He joked about the idea that the Chinese always give tea as a gift and he took out a red packet which he said contained special green tea. When I had already stood up from the table, Jia added that he had "something else" for me, as he understood that the meeting and the information I had given him meant that I was working overtime. He immediately took out an open white envelope, which I could see contained money in cash. They looked like fifty-dollar notes and I think there were no less than fifteen [$750].

'I immediately rejected the offer, giving personal and ethical reasons based on company policy and common sense, as I didn't feel that I was working for anybody at that time. He tried to insist, using arguments such as "we Chinese are not used to people rejecting our gifts" and "don't worry, it's not a cheque, it's only cash". He tried to make me take the envelope and look at the money, and he made it clear that if I wasn't satisfied with the amount then there could be more payments in the future. Straightaway, I took my hands off the table. I had realized that outside the restaurant there were two Chinese men who were going to take my photograph as soon as I touched the envelope. When I continued to refuse, Jia got up and left.'

Epilogue: The New Master
of the World

'China is not a superpower, nor will she ever seek to be one. If one day China should change her colour and turn into a superpower, if she too should play the tyrant in the world, and everywhere subject others to her bullying, aggression and exploitation, the people of the world should identify her social-imperialism, expose it, oppose it and work together with the Chinese people to overthrow it.'
Deng Xiaoping, speech made at the UN, 10 April 1974

It was raining cats and dogs in Caracas and Dr Mei Qixian insisted on accompanying us to the Chinese restaurant on the corner, barely 100 metres from his traditional medicine clinic. 'This is a very dangerous place. I don't want to leave you alone,' he insisted, with his umbrella in hand, as we walked along the rundown streets of the Venezuelan capital. A sense of paranoia caused by insecurity had spread like wildfire among Venezuela's Chinese community, which was going through a difficult time at the end of 2010 having become the favourite target of organized crime groups. The community's traditional success in business – the fruit, among other things, of a matchless capacity for self-sacrifice – had made them juicy prey for kidnappers, murderers and crooks whose criminal activity had multiplied exponentially since Hugo Chávez came to power.[1]

Walking along behind this thin, fragile man whose Spanish is barely comprehensible despite having lived in the country for twenty years but who makes up for this with exceptional poise and exquisite manners, we saw in him all the virtues that are innate to the Chinese people. Mei had arrived in Venezuela from his native Enping in Canton province with the sole purpose of practising acupuncture and building himself a better future. He chose to try his luck in an unknown land on the other side of the world, with nothing but the basic knowledge of a type of medicine which sounded like little more than shamanism in the Latin American country at that time. However, his skill in the ancient techniques of traditional Chinese medicine and his own hard work triumphed over the prejudice and xenophobia which dog the footsteps of Chinese emigrants wherever they go. Today, Mei enjoys a comfortable life and the social status which comes from having been the personal doctor to three Venezuelan presidents.

Characterized by a constant sense of struggle and the blind determination to succeed, Dr Mei's story was something that really stuck in our minds. It mixed with the memory of the *shanta sini* pushing their heavy bundles full of cheap clothes through the dark streets of Cairo, or the image of the Chinese workers exploited in Gabon who we met at our office in Beijing. It also mixed with the tales of all the other anonymous emigrants with their enviable will to survive and their hard and honest work who we had met throughout our journey. With their admirable flesh-and-blood stories, some of which are captured in this book, they are all silently weaving the spider's web of a historic and unstoppable phenomenon. They are the living proof that China's hour has finally arrived; that the Chinese world is already here.

These courageous labourers, engineers, tailors, traders, cooks and entrepreneurs put a human face to China's conquest of the planet. It is their hands which are carrying out the biggest reconstruction of Africa since the colonial era, building the new Angola, laying asphalt on thousands of kilometres of roads throughout the continent. Meanwhile in Central Asia, their work building oil and gas pipelines has allowed gas from this remote and strategic region to flow into the kitchens of Shanghai and Beijing. This titanic effort, which has created new ports, roads, dams and football stadiums across the world, is perhaps the most visible face of China's global expansion. However, it is just the tip of the iceberg.

The long shadow of the Chinese state inevitably looms over all these infrastructure projects. It is determined to regain the superpower status in this new century which it enjoyed for hundreds of years, up to the beginning of the 1800s. 'The world talks about the emergence of China as if it were a new phenomenon, while in Beijing it is simply seen as a return to the natural state of things: a state in which China comes first in everything,' says Pankaj Ghemawat, economist and professor at Harvard University. The developing world – with its abundant natural resources and virgin markets waiting to be exploited – plays a fundamental role in this strategy aimed at situating China once more at the centre of global affairs.

In developing countries, China's re-emergence is not only looked on with approval but with outright enthusiasm in the case of many political elites. 'This twenty-first century is the century for China to lead the world. And when you are leading the world, we want to be close behind you. When you are going to the moon, we don't want to be left behind,' said the then Nigerian president Olusegun Obasanjo during Hu Jintao's visit to the African country in 2006. This speech sums up the sense of relief which is generally felt by the leaders of developing countries when faced with the prospect of a multipolar future world, with China eventually taking the role of conductor of the orchestra. Beijing's powers of seduction combine the use of a subliminally anti-colonialist discourse with a chameleon-like diplomatic strategy, while simultaneously using multi-million-dollar investments to unfold the tentacles of its influence throughout the planet.

Beijing's double standards demonstrate the first of these factors. For example, China intervened at the UN to put an end to the civil war in Sudan, and yet it also gave a ceremonial welcome to the Sudanese president, Omar al-Bashir, who is wanted by international law. An example of the second factor can be seen in the $340 billion which Chinese companies (most of them state-owned) paid out between 2005 and 2011 in places such as Sri Lanka, Zimbabwe, Brazil and other countries. All this took place within the context of a crisis which caused the West to fall into the trap of its own financial system, giving China the boost it needed to become the new 'world's banker': the perfect springboard for conquering the world.

History shows that access to financial clout is essential. Experts pinpoint the transition from European to American dominance in the early twentieth century when the United States became the world's biggest lender and – like China today – a manufacturing superpower.[2] Under Washington's lead, the United States went on to create the United Nations and to found international financial institutions such as the World Bank and the International Monetary Fund, as well as liberalizing trade. These three elements are characteristic of the world order established after the Second World War. China is currently living through a similar situation to the one experienced by the United States during the interwar period: industrial expansion and access to an almost unlimited amount of financial muscle. If this is so, does this not suggest that the Asian country is treading the same path towards overturning the current status quo and laying the foundations for a new world order?

Perhaps it is too early to give a definitive answer to this question. However, there is no doubt that the whole planet can now hear the deafening grinding of the tectonic movements caused by the rise of China, whose unique model, values and modus operandi are generally looked on with a mixture of admiration and fear. The new world order is excellent news for many countries in the developing world. China's pragmatism offers undisputable benefits to, for example, the many African countries that today have access to infrastructure which they had never even dreamed of, as well as affordable Chinese products. We are not only talking about a great variety of hardware, 'Made in China' jeans and mobile telephones, but also cars, technology and machinery which are particularly attractive in Africa, Asia and Latin America because of their competitive prices. But that is not all. As well as offering cheap goods to supply these markets, China is also a reliable long-term buyer.

In this sense, China's insatiable demand for raw materials represents a golden opportunity for countries which are rich in natural resources. Chinese companies working in the extractive sectors are more inclined to take risks than their Western competitors, and they arrive in these markets with their own financing, technology and human resources under their arms in order to maintain, increase or embark on the production of oil wells, rubber or soya plantations and mineral deposits. With the support of the Chinese state, state-owned corporations can make decisions quickly and do not turn their backs on business opportunities with meagre margins, as they know they are also entrusted with securing the nation's strategic interests: China's future supply of raw materials and, by extension, its energy security.

Chinese demand and consumption have sent the price of raw materials rocketing to record highs, resulting in lasting trade flows and significant incomes which, in theory, should serve to modernize the receiving countries and help raise millions of people out of poverty. Furthermore, the value of the resulting infrastructure is not insignificant and should not be taken lightly, even if many of the roads or railway lines were originally conceived in order to facilitate projects aimed at extracting natural resources. However, China's 'charm offensive' for natural resources fuels the heated debate surrounding the real impact of these projects. What returns are the owners of the resources getting on these projects? 'There is no denying the positive effects [of the charm offensive], which have an impact on the balance of trade and allow an outflow of income which filters down to the entire economy. However, that is not enough. That is not how development happens,' says Javier Santiso, a former senior economist at the Organization for Economic Co-operation and Development (OECD) and current professor at the Esade Business School in Madrid.

The views of this renowned academic go straight to the crux of the matter. His words refer to the strategic error being made by many countries rich in raw materials: by not insisting that China should provide added value to their economies and by positioning themselves as simple primary suppliers of resources, they are wasting the opportunities offered by China's urgent need for supplies. It would only be a simple matter of using the strategy enforced by Beijing thirty years ago[3] when it opened its doors to foreign investments in exchange for knowledge transfer and the creation of wealth and added value at a local level. An example of what might have been but wasn't can be seen in the case of lithium, a rare material of strategic importance because of its role in the production of batteries and mobile phones. Bolivia is one of the countries with the largest reserves of lithium in the world. 'The lithium export market is worth a billion US dollars; the market for exporting electric batteries is worth 25 billion dollars and the market for exporting the cars which use electric batteries made from lithium is worth 200 billion dollars,' Santiso explains.

'Being positioned, as Bolivia, at the first link in the production chain is a waste of a strategic opportunity.'

With a few rare exceptions, this is exactly what is happening with Chinese investments in Africa, Asia and Latin America, as far as we could tell. In Peru, Burma, Russia and Mozambique, to mention just a few of the countries which China has turned to for long-term supplies, all these million-dollar investments and long-term supply contracts only serve to provide access to raw materials, which are exported in their unprocessed form. In Africa, the fiasco of China's Special Economic Zones – which were originally conceived to lay the foundations of an industrial base on many different levels – show that it is not only the receiving countries which are wasting a golden opportunity; the Chinese companies also seem none too interested in contributing added value. What wealth is therefore being generated by these gigantic investments? Who is really capitalizing on the opportunities offered by China? Are the local populations profiting at all?

To answer these questions, we gave a voice to the people who should presumably be benefiting the most from China's presence in these countries: the employees working for Chinese companies and the communities where these corporations have set up camp. The conclusions are very revealing: not only do they not feel that they are benefiting but, furthermore, China is surprisingly not always welcome despite its enormous deployment of resources. This negative perception of the new employer is fed by the disastrous working conditions which are the common denominator in Chinese projects, as well as the companies' complete lack of environmental sensibility, the meagre transfer of technology and knowledge to the local populations, and the general conviction that China is there purely for its own gain.[4] This feeling is shared even by those who are not directly affected by these projects. Talking to academics, politicians, journalists, trade union representatives and NGOs, the sense of disappointment caused on occasions by China's expansion became even more evident.

In this sense, our experience in China has shown us that the overwhelming figures relating to the magnitude of Chinese projects – both inside and outside its own borders – often distort reality. Investments which seem very impressive in terms of quantity turn out to be irrelevant in terms of the quality of the benefits offered to the local populations. An example of this can be seen in the $6-billion contract between the Democratic Republic of Congo and the Chinese state-owned companies, whose enormous expenditure will all come to nothing or very little at all if it ends up being reduced to a mere exchange of minerals for infrastructure. Above all, the attitude demonstrated by Chinese corporations seriously calls into question the creation of wealth on a local level in the form of new jobs. Many of these corporations injure the sensibilities – and often the dignity – of their African, Asian and Latin American workers by importing their habitual inhuman treatment from China. The 'win-win' rhetoric described by the Chinese government has certainly been thrown into doubt.

Therefore, the question is: who is capitalizing on the opportunities offered by China if it is not the local populations? Having read this book, you probably already know the answer: the local elites, whether economic and/or political, in both democratic countries and autocratic regimes. In many cases, these elites see business opportunities with China as a short-term transaction, or even as a chance to get themselves a slice of the pie. No doubt Beijing can most easily achieve its objectives with those regimes which pay no attention whatsoever to the standards – whether social, environmental or workplace – which must be observed in other countries around the world. Both sides win – China and the elites – while the prevailing lack of transparency allows them to keep their scheming under lock and key. The fact that the Asian country is silently managing to achieve its objectives and, in some countries, ousting its competitors, is not particularly surprising. The fundamental issue is not the fact that China is conquering the world; what is really important is how it is doing it.

It is all being allowed to happen under the tired pretext of no-interference in the domestic affairs of other countries, an excuse which means nothing but suffering for millions of people as a result of Chinese projects. Is this the new world under China's leadership, we asked ourselves as we witnessed first-hand the disasters taking place in northern Burma, the Peruvian mines or along the Mekong river.

In March 2011, when we had already visited almost all of the countries covered in this investigation, we were invited to participate in a China–Africa conference at the University of Oxford. At the conference, Qin Gang, the former spokesperson for China's Ministry of Foreign

Affairs, revealed, probably without noticing, the true nature of China's global expansion in his presentation. Qin fundamentally defended two ideas: first, that 'Africa's great problem is the lack of development' and, therefore, that China's investments and infrastructure-building are playing a decisive role in that development;[5] and, secondly, that 'China's success [in Africa] is due to the fact that we never, ever take orders from foreign countries', which confirms that 'there will be no change in our foreign policy of no intervention [in the affairs of other countries]'.

Qin Gang's analysis could not be more consistent. Among his continuous references to 'economic development' he never once mentioned the values which go hand in hand with progress, such as justice or equality, as if development was something abstract and separate from those it aims to serve – human beings. This confirms what we have seen so many times both in China itself and on our journey across three continents: the fact that China has engaged with the developing world with the old model of prioritizing mostly its own economic growth above everything else, without showing any interest whatsoever in the side effects of this policy.[6] On the other hand, Qin's insistence that Beijing will not make even the slightest modification to its policy of no intervention essentially means that it not only reserves the right not to observe internationally accepted practices, but also – more importantly – that it is not prepared to submit to any kind of scrutiny.

Also in Oxford, Portuguese MEP Ana María Gomes, author of a report on China's impact on Africa,[7] hit the nail on the head in her speech. 'Development cannot be achieved without good governance, respect for human rights and the rule of law,' she rightly said. In this sense, she pointed out that 'China is largely responsible for maintaining and perpetuating the power of the rapacious local elites'. This is clearly a reference to the same elites who are capitalizing – occasionally obscenely so – on the benefits which go hand in hand with China's resurgence. 'To stop the elites from getting ever richer and the people from getting ever poorer, what is needed is civil society,' she insisted. The MEP had uttered the magic words: civil society.

Alejandra Alayza, co-ordinator of the Peruvian Network for Fair Globalization (RedGe) in Lima, put the value of civil society into perspective with a fitting comparative example. She told us that when Peru was negotiating its Free Trade Agreement (FTA) with the United

States and Europe, her NGO was in constant contact with its American and European counterparts to lobby not only in Lima but also in Washington and Brussels to achieve fairer conditions in the treaty. In other words, NGOs in various countries went beyond the 'national issue' in order to jointly influence the text for the benefit of their respective populations. 'In the negotiations of the FTA with China, however, we found that there was no civil society in the Asian country to help us in the fight over issues such as labour rights or the environment.'

Alayza's words indicate that the lack of a civil society, a free press or rule of law to keep, watch, set limits, denounce or punish the inappropriate actions of China's corporations abroad – as happens in democratic countries – means that it is left to the receiving countries to impose limits on these actions. The lesser the supervision, the greater the potential for conflicts and abuse. As a result, the counterweights that are common in other parts of the world, but are either scorned or non-existent in China, are now more important than ever in Africa, Asia and Latin America. Without this scrutiny, the companies – with their indisputable ties to the Chinese state – will have free rein to continue with their irresponsible actions. As is obvious, the lack of checks and balances makes a difference.

'A country with free speech is wonderful, because things can be exposed to society. Rule of law is fundamental to the consolidation of democracy. You cannot fight corruption where rule of law is not respected,' said Paulus Noa, director of the Anti-Corruption Commission (ACC) when we met him in Namibia. In his office in central Windhoek, Noa assured us that corruption – which is more widespread among Chinese emigrants than any other group on a local level – presents a real headache for one of the most democratic countries in Africa. 'At the ACC I haven't heard of any cases of corruption involving other foreigners, only the Chinese. I'm not saying that the others aren't doing it, but the scale of the cases is not comparable. If we allow the Chinese or anyone else to come here and corrupt every official here, I am telling you: the future and democracy of this country will become very, very weak. If we do otherwise [than fight corruption], our economy will collapse and we will be like any other African country. We have to fight anyone who wants to corrupt our society.'

Noa's words reflect the sense of fear caused by China in Namibia.

This has been particularly true ever since an employee at the Chinese state-owned Nuctech, a specialist in manufacturing airport security components such as scanners and X-ray machines, was implicated in a corruption case which also indirectly implicated Hu Haifeng, the president of Nuctech at the time and the son of the Chinese president Hu Jintao. As soon as the Chinese representative of Nuctech in Namibia was arrested, along with two Namibian nationals, China's censorship machine swung into action, escalating from the usual lack of coverage of the event on television, radio and in newspapers to a ferocious internet censorship campaign. In an atmosphere of total paranoia, this went as far as blocking every webpage which contained the word 'Namibia'.[8] This information blackout on every level, which has hindered this investigation everywhere from Iran to Sudan and from Kazakhstan to Venezuela, just as it has during our years working as reporters in China, burst on to the scene once more to defend the interests of the party-state.[9]

With all its highs and lows, there is no doubt that China's tempting and efficient formula – based on the firepower of its state capitalism – has allowed it to advance relentlessly through the developing world, which may perhaps be seen as a prelude to a future conquest of Western markets and, eventually, a new world order controlled by Beijing. The current growth of China's influence is a natural consequence of Beijing's growing confidence in its own strengths, which has been greatly affected by the Western economic crisis. In a way, the crisis has threatened the entire Western model, and in China it is seen as evidence of the decline of a system based on liberal democracies. 'Today, China is the alternative. Our model shows that there is another way. And who knows, maybe it's better than the Western way,' says Li Guofu, a diplomat who has worked in the United States and Africa and who is a Middle Eastern expert, with an unusual degree of openness.

'The West wants to impose its own system on the world, everywhere from China to the Middle East. They want to establish an agenda based on human rights and democracy . . . But, we ask ourselves why we should follow this model when it is perhaps out of date,' Li insisted, defiantly, in a café in central Beijing. This sense that the West's momentum has now passed is fully or partially shared by other developing countries, and even by some Western scholars, which now see China as a new and unquestionable paradigm of efficiency. As if that were not enough, this new world leadership is being run by an emerging country – one of their own – which is also prepared to lend money, make investments and reinforce political ties without imposing any conditions or asking any awkward questions. Therefore democracy, the albeit imperfect system which has brought more prosperity, well-being, justice, liberty and equality to human life than any other idea conceived by Man, now finds itself having to compete with the 'Beijing Consensus', as the Chinese model has been labelled.

China's 'magic formula' is well known: on the one hand, the interventionism of an omnipresent state in its economy and society; and, on the other hand, a fierce degree of political control which includes the submission of the state powers – as well as the media – to the one party which holds a monopoly on power without having to be accountable to anyone. The efficiency of this authoritarian system, which is grossly described as 'harmonious' by the propaganda machine, offers many countries a shortcut to development at a very high price, paid for by the people left behind. This Chinese pragmatism has clearly triumphed in the developing world. In emerging nations which are characterized by civil liberties and the division of power, the local political elites show signs of giving in under the pressure of the excitement caused by China's arrival. On the other hand, this formula is particularly attractive to despotic regimes in Africa, Asia and Latin America, whose shady alliances with the biggest dictatorship on the planet help them keep their heads above water. Wherever China sees an opportunity, it chooses to act as an accomplice in these excesses rather than acting as a guardian of the law.

It is not just the fact that China has become the great champion and favourite business partner of the world's most repressive regimes (Burma, North Korea, Iran, Sudan, Cuba), or that its state-owned companies often enjoy carte blanche in their dealings as a result of the dizzying effect of the all-powerful Chinese state. What is just as important is the infiltration and acceptance of Chinese standards and values – which are highly ambiguous when it comes to good business practices or labour, social or environmental issues – throughout Beijing's sphere of influence, from the countries where it is investing to international institutions such as the World Bank or the Asian Development Bank.[10] It seems that the theory put forward by the British historian and journalist Martin Jacques may be becoming a reality: the world thought that China would become more Westernized as its process of economic opening up continued. What is actually happening is the opposite of that: the world is being 'sinicized'.[11]

Will this new world under China's leadership be a better world? Will it consist of more equal and just societies? Will there be a greater respect for the human rights of the weakest members of society or a fuller awareness of preserving the environment? Will the world be safer and more participative? In the face of such questions, this book gives an account of the impact which modern-day China is capable of having in places as remote and distant from one another as Russian Siberia and the Congolese province of Katanga in the mining heart of sub-Saharan Africa. We need a greater temporal perspective in order to find definitive long-term answers to these questions and to determine whether the Chinese model and formula is administering the sickness or the cure. But following our extensive research and experience, we cannot be very optimistic.

The West has tried to explain the nature of China's supposed future domination through the use of a Manichaean argument based on evolution and the Asian country's recent past.[12] Politicians, economists, diplomats and all kinds of experts insist that China is destined to gradually become a Western-style democracy, complete with division of power, a multi-party system and the liberalization of civil society. This will all supposedly happen as an inevitable consequence of the Chinese people's gradual increase in wealth and their growing desire for liberty, participation and justice. These same sources insist – as they have been doing for decades – that if these reforms do not take place, the only future for China will be either revolution or the implosion of the State. Following this argument, they suggest that Beijing is conscious of this fact and that it has a roadmap in place to ensure that, at some point *within the next 100 years*, China will have a free, just and equal system which will not be based on economic growth at any price, repression or the wielding of power with an iron fist.

For anybody who has spent years researching and living in China, these theories and reflections sound hasty to say the least. Right in the middle of this investigation, in October 2010 the first Chinese winner of the Nobel Peace Prize, Liu Xiaobo, received the news of his prestigious award in the depths of a prison in Liaoning province, where the regime had incarcerated him for being one of the instigators of a manifesto proposing the democratization of China: Charter o8. His eleven-year sentence for a crime of opinion was not an isolated case, but rather the beginning of the greatest wave of repression against Chinese civil society since the 1989 Tiananmen Square student massacre. Coinciding with the revolutions in the Arab world, which set alarm bells ringing within Beijing's circles of power, the regime decided to crank its police system up a notch. Since then it has used both legal and illegal measures, such as kidnapping, torture or de facto house arrest, to silence hundreds or thousands of dissidents, activists, artists and lawyers.[13]

With their indestructible courage, humanity and sense of justice, these people – many of whom work on a charitable basis – had become the last beacon of hope for many citizens who have been trampled by the excesses of twenty-first-century China. The regime saw their determination as a challenge to its authority and, therefore, made them a target of its repression. 'Lawyers working on human rights cases have been moved towards positions of dissidence. They didn't want it to happen, but the system has forced them into a type of "radicalization". Activists who have been able to work in China for the last ten years can no longer work there,' explained Nicholas Bequelin of Human Rights Watch when we met him in Hong Kong. 'The Chinese authorities' fear of losing control [of power] as a result of activism has been exaggerated in order to carry out more repression.'

This backward step in terms of civil liberties has even been reflected in China's state budget, which in 2010 assigned more funds to the country's internal security ($85 billion) than to its armed forces ($82.7 billion) for the first time. This tendency is only likely to worsen over the coming years in the face of the increase in violent protests in China – around 180,000 in 2010 (double the rate of 2006) – as a result of injustices and the lack of any redress.

Bequelin's bleak analysis of the situation tallies with another event which took place on 1 July 2011: the ninetieth anniversary of the founding of the Communist Party of China. On this date, Beijing showed further signs that, despite the expectations of the West, it was in no hurry to relax the pressure exerted on a society which enjoys a certain amount of economic autonomy but which is deprived of political rights and liberties. Beijing is in even less of a rush to adopt a system based on liberal values which, according to the most recalcitrant sectors of Chinese society, will only destroy China and make it once again the object of foreign domination. All of these opinions stem from the Chinese authorities and are spread – from the top down – to every level of society. Anyone who has lived in the country and has had daily contact with Chinese academics, journalists, civil servants and activists; who has read the newspapers and watched the television; who has spoken to the Chinese man in the street; and has lived through all the ups and downs of this country knows that there is a widespread belief that the new superpower will be anything but an improved copy of the Western model. In short: the Chinese political elites – the CPC itself and the economically privileged – have no incentive at all to change the system, because they benefit from it in every sense, in particular economically. In fact, the so-called 'Chinese miracle' has to be understood in the sense that it's a miracle mainly for those elites, as the system is essentially designed and intended to serve their purposes, which are to remain in power and increase their wealth.

On that 1 July, the CPC celebrated its anniversary with a great display of pomp and ceremony, marking the end of its sixty-second year in power. The regime made use of a flood of propaganda which claimed full responsibility for the success of the country, despite the fact that it is really the 1.3 billion Chinese people who have worked so hard to make this happen. They are the ones who have suffered the hardships caused by the CPC and, from the most wretched *mingong* to the most enterprising businessman in Wenzhou, they are the ones who have rebuilt a country which was on the brink of economic and social collapse at the time of Mao's death in 1976. It is therefore up to them to make sure that 'China's century' is a historic new phase of justice and respect which will make the world a better place to live in. That is the challenge faced by the Chinese people, and it is one of such great magnitude and importance that the rest of humanity cannot just ignore it.

August 2012

Notes

INTRODUCTION

1. The Chinese authorities had chosen that particular time and date to ensure that the event would begin with as many recurrences of the number 8 as possible: the 8th day of the 8th month of 2008 at 8.08 and 8 seconds. In China the number 8 is a symbol of prosperity.
2. China Global Investment Tracker: 2012, The Heritage Foundation. These figures refer to investments and contracts of various kinds with a value exceeding US$100 million signed by Chinese companies from 2005 to June 2012. Available at: http://www.heritage.org/research/reports/2012/01/china-global-investment-tracker-2012.
3. According to the International Energy Agency, China will import 79 per cent of its oil supplies by 2030. By this date it is estimated that this will represent around 15 million barrels of oil each day.
4. Source: National Bureau of Statistics of the People's Republic of China. Available at: http://www.uschina.org/statistics/tradetable.html.
5. The quality of the 'Made in China' infrastructure is a common concern among locals due to the fact that these buildings and roads tend to fall apart after a short period of time. One of the most visible examples was witnessed by the authors in Luanda, Angola's capital. They tried to visit the Chinese-built General Hospital of Luanda, one of the country's biggest with 250 beds, but were stopped at its entrance by military police. The hospital had to be evacuated shortly after its opening because of its poor construction and risk of collapse. From the outside, the abandoned flagship hospital had a dilapidated appearance, including cracks in the main buildings. After four years of it being shut down, Beijing and Luanda agreed on a renovation plan to get the hospital open again in 2014.

I THE *MINGONGS* TAKE ON THE WORLD

1. The Chinese term *mingong* is used to refer to migrant workers, a working class made up of between 200 and 300 million people who have fuelled the so-called 'factory of the world' over the last three decades. The Chinese residency system penalizes these workers for leaving their places of birth in search of better opportunities by stripping them of rights such as the right to healthcare and education for their descendants, or by giving them only limited access to these services. As a result, for many years the children of migrants could not go to school if they travelled with their parents to other provinces in the country. The situation has improved to some extent since the introduction of schools for the children of migrant workers in China's industrial centres, although these still offer a sub-standard quality of education. In effect, the Chinese legal system has created two distinct classes of citizens with different rights and privileges, a kind of apartheid which punishes the real people behind China's economic miracle. Opposition to this state of affairs has recently begun to grow within China itself.

2. World Bank website, last accessed 7 February 2011.

3. According to Chinese academics, the privatization or dismantling of Chinese state-owned companies inherited from the Maoist era began at the end of the 1980s. It is difficult to put an exact number on the level of unemployment caused by a move from a state-controlled economy to a mixed economy. The most reliable figures estimate that between 7 and 9 million people became unemployed between 1998 and 2001, although this figure would rise to around 40 million if that time period is extended. A quarter of the total number of jobs lost as a result of the closure of businesses in the textile, military and mining sectors took place in the three provinces to the north-east of China (Liaoning, Jilin and Heilongjiang). Sources: *China Economic Weekly*, 27 October 2008. Zhang Jun Cai 中国经济周 刊》张俊才, China Labour Statistical Yearbook, 2005.

4. 'An introduction to the policy and situation of overseas labour co-operation in China', Australian International Trade Association, 24 April 2008, quoted in 'Hired on Sufferance: China's Migrant Workers in Singapore', Aris Chan, China Labour Bulletin, February 2011. In the words of a former Latin American ambassador in Beijing who the authors interviewed for this book, 'The issue of migration is one of Beijing's main priorities. No meeting with our Chinese counterpart ever passes without

him expressing his objection to policies restricting the migration of Chinese nationals.'

5. One example is seen in Ecuador, where President Rafael Correa announced the elimination of visa requirements for Chinese tourists in June 2008. This policy had to be withdrawn barely six months later after '10,638 Chinese citizens entered the country and only 3,941 left' over the course of one year, according to the newspaper *El Comercio*. It is believed that a large proportion of these illegal immigrants re-emigrated to the United States or Canada, while others are likely to have travelled to Guayaquil, where a visit to the main market in the economic capital of Ecuador demonstrates the number of Chinese migrants in the country and their capacity to set up businesses.

6. For example, official figures for 2009 indicate that 778,000 Chinese workers in 190 countries contributed currency to China worth $4 billion in that year alone.

7. English language webpage of an Egyptian newspaper: http://www.almasryalyoum.com/en/news/chinese-prostitution-ring-busted-maadi.

8. http://www.dooland.com/magazine/article_93455.html and http://news.xkb.com.cn/guoji/ 2010/0923/92395.html.

9. 'Mainland women opt to stay in Congo vice trap', *South China Morning Post*, 1 January 2011.

10. Mikhail Tersky, of the University of Vladivostok, expanded on this subject for the authors: 'In the last two years the Russian government has clamped down hard on regulating Chinese imports because the amount of contraband goods entering the country is enormous. As a result, the volume of business has reduced by over three times.'

11. According to Oleg Lipaev, representative of Russia's Ministry of Industry and Commerce in the Primorsky region, there are currently 20,000 Chinese businesses in the Russian Far East, most of which are corporations importing Chinese products. As a result, Chinese industry represents around 20 per cent of the region's GDP. 'More than 50 per cent of agricultural products here in Russia are produced by the Chinese,' Lipaev explains. When asked if he believed that prices would rise if China were to stop exporting agricultural products to Russia, he told the authors that prices would probably triple. 'The average salary in Heilongjiang province is 60 to 100 dollars. In the Primorsky region, the average salary is about 600 dollars. How can we compete? ... Ten years ago the structure of Chinese imports was mainly food and consumer goods, but now they are increasing their imports of high-tech products, like electrical equipment, machinery, cars or trucks. This is becoming a problem for

Russian industry, because we have the same position [in terms of industrial activity] in these sectors. They are completely determining our industry.' When it comes to the future, Lipaev is not optimistic. 'In the near future, it is profitable for Russia and Russian regions to trade with China, especially for the people. However, in maybe ten or fifteen years it will become a threat to the Russian economy. In five or six years the employment problem will be much worse than it is now.'

As with Africa, Latin America and Central Asia, the Chinese proposed an economic policy based on 'your natural resources for our infrastructure and products', but the Russians rejected this plan. 'Beijing says that if they have to bring the financing [of their state owned companies], there must be some intergovernmental contract [to exploit the resources] and some strong government guaranties.' However, Lipaev explains, unlike countries in Africa Russia is not interested in Chinese roads and dams in exchange for oil. 'Russia doesn't need this. We have our own money. We can build infrastructure by ourselves.' Instead, according to Lipaev, Russia suggested setting up joint ventures that would operate under Russian law, but the Chinese were not interested in this plan.

12. 'Chinese Migrants: Their Views on the Work, Education, and Living Conditions in Russia', A. G. Larin, 2007, http://www.springerlink.com/content/l57064789p2vl734/.

13. Despite the influx of Chinese emigrants and products entering the country, China is not a major player in Russia in terms of investment as it has no presence in Sakhalin, the Russian Pacific island that harbours enormous quantities of oil and receives most of the foreign investment in Russia. In terms of other industries, such as logging, Chinese companies tend to buy raw materials themselves rather than investing in Russian companies.

14. There are no reliable official figures regarding the number of Chinese emigrants in Russia. Experts and officials estimate that there are between 300,000 and 4 million Chinese living in the country, both legally and illegally. It is estimated that there are around 100,000 Chinese traders and temporary employees in the Russian Far East alone. Russia is currently cracking down hard on Chinese immigration, limiting the number of work visas to 3,000 each year in response to the complete lack of control on immigration prevalent in the 1990s. Russia actively facilitated the flow of Chinese migrants at that time by exempting them from visa requirements between 1992 and 1994. The aim was to encourage the arrival of Chinese traders to replenish Russia's severe lack of supplies caused by the collapse of the Soviet Union. As a result, thousands of

Chinese people entered the country, often illegally, from the regions bordering with Russia, fleeing from the severe unemployment that had struck the industrial regions of northern China. Source: *The Encyclopedia of the Chinese Overseas*, ed. Lynn Pan (Harvard University Press, 1999), pp. 328–31; *China Inside Out: Contemporary Chinese Nationalism and Transnationalism*, eds. P. Nyíri and Joana Breidenbach (Central European University Press, 2005), pp. 144–6; interviews with experts and civil servants in Vladivostok, Khabarovsk and Moscow.

15. *The Encyclopedia of the Chinese Overseas*, op. cit., pp. 328–31.

16. China Statistical Yearbook, 2009.

17. The Hungarian academic Pál Nyíri, who has spent the last two decades studying the phenomenon of Chinese migration, defines the expansion of these enterprising migrants across the planet as 'the emergence of a global *entrepreneuriat*, linked by a multifunctioning business network, with high mobility and dense flows of capital, goods and information, while retaining a marginal social status within the local societies'. Source: 'Chinese Entrepreneurs in Poor Countries: A Transnational "Middleman Minority" and its Futures', paper presented in Hong Kong, reproduced by permission of Pál Nyíri, VU University, Amsterdam.

18. China's most dominant ethnic group.

19. This represents around 18.3 per cent of the world's migrant population, according to the International Organization for Migration. Source: '2007年:全球政治与安全报告' ['Report on international policy and security 2007'], CASS, multiple authors, 2007.

20. *Zheng He: China and the Oceans in the Early Ming Dynasty, 1405–1433*, Edward L. Dreyer (Longman, 2007).

21. *The Encyclopedia of the Chinese Overseas*, op cit., pp. 48–50.

22. '2007年:全球政治与安全报告' ['Report on international policy and security 2007'], op. cit.

23. *The Encyclopedia of the Chinese Overseas*, op. cit., pp. 64–5.

24. Venezuela now has a population of over 28 million people, according to the World Bank. It is estimated that there are around 180,000 Chinese people living in the South American country.

25. 华工出国史料汇编/陈翰笙主编 [History of Overseas Chinese Indentured Labour], ed. Chen Hansheng, 1985.

26. When the Communists came to power in 1949, the state returned to the imperial tradition of prohibiting and punishing migration. However, Beijing was also quick to export human services and resources to third world countries for ideological reasons in the midst of the Cold War. At the beginning of the 1960s, Mao Zedong sent tens of thousands of Chinese

citizens to these countries to work as doctors, agricultural engineers and manual labourers, both in an attempt to legitimize the regime of the People's Republic and to spread the red revolution across the planet. At that time Africa began to grow familiar with the presence of Chinese workers in its territory, where they built railway lines such as the one joining Tanzania and Zambia (the Tanzam or TAZARA Railway), built with the contribution of 25,000 Chinese workers. Chinese workers also helped to increase the productivity of African rice and sugar plantations.

27. Official data suggests that there are at least 750,000 Chinese people living in Africa, after moving there to make better lives for themselves. However, there has been no reliable census – as we saw in the case of the *shanta sini* in Egypt – and it is thought that the actual figure is much higher.

28. *New Asian Emperors*, George Haley, Usha Haley and Chin Tiong Tan (John Wiley & Sons, 2009), p. 15.

29. *Charm Offensive: How China's Soft Power is Transforming the World*, Joshua Kurlantzick (Yale University Press, 2007), p. 75.

30. This expression was used by Miguel Ángel Calvete, at the time secretary general of the Chamber of Shops and Supermarkets owned by Chinese Residents (Casrech) in Argentina, which represents the owners of 7,000 supermarkets and has become a powerful lobbying group in the country. The activities of this group are explained in more depth in Chapter 2.

31. 大中华地区 or 'Great China' is the term used to refer to the commercial, cultural and linguistic interaction of Chinese overseas communities.

32. 'Chinese Entrepreneurs in Poor Countries: A Transnational "Middleman Minority" and its Futures', op. cit.

33. The first wave of Chinese emigrants to South Africa arrived at the end of the nineteenth century. This first group was made up of between 20,000 and 30,000 people, and between 6,000 and 10,000 of their direct descendants remain in the country today. The second wave took place in the 1980s, when migrants began arriving from Taiwan as a result of the good relations between Taipei and Pretoria's segregationist regime. Approximately 20,000 Chinese citizens arrived in the African country during this period, around 6,000 of whom remain today. The third and final wave, which was also the biggest, ranged from the 1990s to the present day, with migrants arriving from mainland China. Various estimates place the total number of people of Chinese origin currently living in South Africa at around 400,000.

34. Harry Sun is referring to the disastrous effects that the opium trade, started by the British East India Company in the eighteenth century, had

on the Chinese economy and Chinese society. This powerful company –
which monopolized trade until 1834 – exported the drug produced in
colonial India to China in order to make up the balance of business with
the Chinese empire, which supplied Great Britain with products such as
tea, porcelain and silk at a much greater value than the products that
they bought from Great Britain.

The introduction of opium into China caused widespread addiction
and decline among the Chinese people. At the same time, the country's
entry into bilateral trade relations with Great Britain caused a decrease
in the Qing empire's silver income. The Qing panicked and intervened,
banning the importation and trade of the drug. After various failed
attempts at negotiation, this led to the First Opium War (1839–42),
which marked the beginning of the period between 1849 and 1949 which
is known in China as the 'Century of Humiliation'. This period was characterized by a state of general chaos caused by many different factors:
the invasion by Western and Japanese forces into some parts of Chinese
territory, various unequal post-conflict treaties imposed by several foreign powers, the fall of the empire, and the bloody civil war between
Communists and Nationalists. All this to some extent explains why many
Chinese people, like Harry Sun, celebrate the Communist victory in
1949 and the subsequent dictatorship of Mao Zedong, who they see as
the man who restored dignity to China after decades of humiliation.
Source: *China: A New History*, John King Fairbank and Merle Goldman
(Harvard University Press, 2006), pp. 180–206.

35. *The Three Faces of Chinese Power: Might, Money and Minds*, David
    Lampton (University of California Press, 2008), p. 85.

36. *Overseas Chinese in Southeast Asia and China's Foreign Policy: An
    Interpretative Essay*, Leo Suryadinata, Institute of Southeast Asian Stud-
    ies, Singapore, 1978, p. 27.

37. For example, the first foreign company to invest in China after the begin-
    ning of the process of economic opening was Charoen Pokphand, the
    property of Chinese businessman Xie Yichu. For years this company,
    operating in the food and agricultural sector, was considered China's big-
    gest direct foreign investor. Source: *Charm Offensive: How China's Soft
    Power is Transforming the World*, op. cit., p. 76

38. *Mobility and Cultural Authority in Contemporary China*, Pál Nyíri (Uni-
    versity of Washington Press, 2010), p. 99.

39. Nationalism has been used 'efficiently by the regime in its Patriotic Edu-
    cation Campaign to promote the rejection of liberal democracy and the
    acceptance of an authoritarian system among the population, presenting

these ideas as indispensable for the country's development'. *China después de Tian'anmen. Nacionalismo y cambio político* [China after Tiananmen: Nationalism and Political Change], Mario Esteban Rodríguez (Ediciones Bellaterra, 2007), p. 165.

40. 'China's cosmopolitan nationalists: "heroes" and "traitors" of the 2008 Olympics', Pál Nyíri, Zhang Juand and Merridien Varral, *The China Journal*, 63, January 2010.

2 THE NEW SILK ROAD

1. *The Pattern of the Chinese Past*, Mark Elvin (Stanford University Press, 1973), p. 218.

2. Throughout the course of history Xinjiang has repeatedly fallen into the hands of foreign invaders, whether Huns, Uzbeks, Tibetans, Arabs, Mongols or Manchurians. Russia and Britain clashed over the region before the creation of the short-lived East Turkestan Republic in the 1940s. In 1949, Mao incorporated Xinjiang once and for all into the People's Republic of China.

3. The town of Kashgar, once the epicentre of the Silk Road and now Xinjiang's second most important town was – like Horgos – also listed as an SEZ. At the end of the 1970s, Deng Xiaoping, the 'architect' who led China along the path of economic opening and reform, instigated the gradual creation of SEZs aimed at attracting foreign investment and controlling the process of economic opening. These 'capitalist laboratories' operated under conditions that were an exception to the national law: they offered land at reasonable prices and highly attractive tax rates as well as a well-disciplined and cheap labour market and relaxed environmental standards. After the success of the first four zones – in Shenzhen, Shantou, Zhuhai and Xiamen – the model has been extended to other towns throughout modern China.

4. Shenzhen had a population of just 300,000 inhabitants at the end of 1970, making it a small town by Chinese standards. Excluding Hong Kong, the town now has the highest GDP per capita in China, with $14,600 annually in 2010. The average GDP per capita in China is just $2,504 for urban residents. Furthermore, along with Canton, Beijing, Hangzhou and Shanghai, Shenzhen boasts the highest consumption of luxury products in China. However, despite its wealth, Shenzhen also has the highest crime rate in the country. Sources: 'China by numbers 2011', *China Economic Review*; '中国十大最奢侈城市:上海第一北京第二(图)', *China Daily*, 29 January 2010.

5. For centuries the Silk Road was the route used by merchants who crossed Central Asia from Xian in China to Constantinople, until the rise of the maritime routes in the fifteenth century led to the Silk Road's inevitable decline.

6. Russia, Belarus and Kazakhstan agreed on the creation of a joint customs union, which set a fixed joint customs tariff in 2010. The aim was to standardize customs duties on the main products used in trade between the three countries. Although the introduction of the tariff has been fraught with difficulties, the most interesting aspect is the fact that the alliance was forged in order to stand up to Chinese competition – an attempt which has so far proved unsuccessful.

7. China currently owns two large pipelines that connect the country to Central Asia: a 3,000-kilometre oil pipeline stretching into Kazakhstan with the capacity to transport up to 30 million tons of crude oil per year, and a 7,000-kilometre gas pipeline which stretches into northern Turkmenistan via Uzbekistan, Kazakhstan and western and central China. 'Whether or not they have any economic benefits, the oil and gas pipelines mainly serve to legitimize China's presence in Central Asia. Having rights of ownership gives China a legitimate reason to defend its interest in the region,' said Murat Avezov, Kazakhstan's first ambassador in Beijing (1992–5) when the authors interviewed him in Almaty. Sources: '*El ascenso de China en Asia Central: ¿un nuevo hegemón regional en gestación?*' ['The rise of China in Central Asia: A new regional hegemony in the making?'], Nicolás de Pedro, *UNISCI magazine*, October–November 2010; *China as a Neighbor: Central Asian Perspectives and Strategies*, eds. Marlène Laruelle and Sébastien Peyrouse, Central Asia-Caucasus Institute & Silk Road Studies Program, Washington, 2009.

8. Since the implementation of its policy of economic opening at the end of the 1970s, China has been pouring money non-stop into the construction of new infrastructure. Between 1990 and 2008, China paid out 32.7 trillion yuan for this purpose. Using the conversion rate of 10 yuan = 1 euro, this represents an incredible 3.2 trillion euros. Source: '基础产业和基础设施建设取得辉煌成就', governmental document available at: http://www.gov.cn/test/2009-09/15/content_1417907_2.htm.

9. One example is seen in China's Grand Canal, a remarkable feat of engineering which was begun in the seventh century. Measuring 1,700 kilometres in length, the canal was set up to link the city of Hangzhou with Beijing via one of the largest artificial rivers in the world. The canal aimed to alleviate the drought that traditionally ravaged the country's northern provinces and to control the spread of the Yellow River, but it was also

designed to promote trade within the country and to contribute to making China's territory more compact.

10. Some of Imperial China's ruling bodies saw trade as a vulgar activity that had to be restricted, an attitude which at times led Chinese merchants to migrate to places such as Malacca where there was a much more liberal framework for buying and selling. Some experts also argue that the restrictions on trade (and therefore on contact) with the outside world were the main cause of the Ming dynasty's decision to put an end to the foreign voyages started by Admiral Zheng He at the beginning of the fifteenth century.

   For more information on the use of infrastructure for the purposes of cohesion, see 'China's roads to influence', Jonathan Holslag, *Asian Survey*, 50 (4), 2010.

11. The academic and journalist Martin Jacques offers an exquisite description of these events in *When China Rules the World* (Allen Lane, 2009), p. 70. Emperor Qianlong's quote is taken from this work.

12. The plan was approved as an outcome of the first conference in the history of the People's Republic aimed at developing Xinjiang province. Source: http://www.china. org.cn/china/2010-05/30/content_20147084. htm, last accessed 22 March 2011.

13. In the words of Wang Menshu, an engineer and adviser to China's Ministry of Railways, Beijing has begun to implement a 'high-speed rail diplomacy', referring to China's plans to extend a high speed railway throughout its territory and even beyond its own borders. According to Wang, the government plans to use Chinese high-speed rail technology to connect China with Taiwan, South Korea, Russia, Central Asia and South-East Asia. These projects, which will run to tens of billions of dollars in cost, will be carried out by two state-owned companies: the China Railway Group (REC) and the China Railway Construction Group (CRCC). The projects will be mostly financed by Beijing, in exchange for 'access to natural resources and new markets for Chinese products', according to Wang. 'The Chinese state-owned companies can negotiate their own contracts with the help of the local Chinese embassy and then wait for the subsequent approval of the Chinese State Council. The foreign governments will have to pay for the new infrastructure, but they will do so with natural resources rather than money,' Wang told the authors when they interviewed him in Beijing. China's connection with Central Asia will later serve as a gateway for bringing Chinese products into Europe. This theory has been called into question, however, after a series of scandals linked to the expansion of the railway industry in China in 2011. In February that year, railway minister Liu Zhijun was

dismissed from his post and expelled from the Communist Party over accusations of corruption.

14. Xinjiang is officially home to a total of forty-seven minority groups from fifty-five different nationalities or ethnicities, with the Uighur, Han, Kazakh and Hui/Dungan people featuring as the four dominant groups. Beijing's policies of economic and migratory development have caused a decline in the dominance of the Uighur people in the social and demographic composition of the region. In 1964, people of Uighur ethnicity made up 54.9 per cent of the population while the Han people made up just 31.9 per cent. However, the 2010 census shows that the number of Han residents in Xinjiang has now reached 40.1 per cent. This percentage would be even higher if it were possible to include the unknown number of people who make up Xinjiang's 'floating population', or de facto residents of the province who are registered as living in other areas. The Han people tend to form the majority in urban areas of the province, such as its capital, Urumqi, which boasts a significant part of the province's wealth and power. Source: Statistics elaborated by the authors based on the Xinjiang Statistics Annual 2010 (第 三篇人口与就业_3_3新疆人口普查基本情况) and the Chinese population censuses in 1964, 1990 and 2000.

15. *When China Rules the World*, op. cit., pp. 237–40.

16. The phenomenon of 'Hanification' has been underpinned by the arrival of the railway in Tibet as well as in Xinjiang. The railway from Tibet was launched in 2007 and stretches for 1,142 kilometres along the entire length of the Kun Lun mountain range at an average height of 4,000 metres. Beijing paid out an estimated 3.3 billion euros on this highly complex engineering project, over three times more than they have spent on health and education in Tibet over the last fifty years, according to pro-Tibetan groups. This has fed claims by several NGOs that the railway project's main objective was in fact demographic dilution and the transportation of natural resources.

17. In the words of Central Asian expert Sébastien Peyrouse, 'On the one hand, the customs office statistics are inaccurate because in Central Asian countries data regarding trade with China is reduced in order to limit its "psychological impact" and to keep discussions about Chinese "invasion" of the region under control. On the other hand, a significant amount of produce arrives in the country illegally.' Various experts who the authors interviewed in Almaty estimated that there is a discrepancy of roughly $5 billion between the official volume of bilateral trade and the amount of trade that is unaccounted for.

18. Interview with Kazakh expert Adil Kaukenov in Almaty; email interviews with Sébastien Peyrouse and Nicolás de Pedro.

19. Kazakhstan has a population of barely 15.6 million inhabitants, which explains the importance of trade with China in terms of its national economy.

20. Estimates suggest that China lent its neighbour at least $13 billion in 2010 alone. Under these circumstances, some observers in the Central Asian country warn that it is just a matter of time before Kazakhstan will be forced to start paying off its debts with land. 'We will start giving away our territory. We have lots of it and we have a common border [with China], so the map could be redrawn to give away a couple of thousand hectares here and there,' said a Kazakh opposition leader at a demonstration in Almaty on 28 May 2011, in reference to the impossibility of Kazakhstan paying back all of its debts to China. Sources: various, including 'Kazakh opposition calls for halt to China expansion', Reuters, 28 May 2011.

21. The volume of trade between China and the five countries of Central Asia, which together boast a potential market of 61 million inhabitants, rose to $22 billion in 2010. China holds a dominant commercial position in the region: it is the most important trade partner for Kazakhstan (if we exclude the European Union as a unitary bloc) and Kyrgyzstan, and the second most important for Tajikistan, Uzbekistan and Turkmenistan. Source: Statistics elaborated by the authors based on European Union data: http://ec.europa.eu/trade.

22. According to Adil Kaukenov, China controls 28 per cent of the country's natural resource assets (gas and oil) thanks to three recent acquisitions. First, in 2005 the Chinese state-owned petrol company CNPC bought the Canadian company PetroKazakhstan, whose assets are in the Central Asian country, for around $4.7 billion. Secondly, in 2006 the Chinese state-owned conglomerate CITIC acquired another Canadian company, Nations Energy, for $2 billion; and, thirdly, CNPC joined forces with a local company, KazMunayGas, to acquire MangistauMunaiGas for $3.3 billion. 'Bribes were the key factor in allowing the Chinese to buy PetroKazakhstan and MangistauMunaiGas,' according to a Kazakh expert who asked to remain anonymous. For more information on the total amount of resources, see BP Statistical Review of World Energy, 2012 and World Energy Outlook 2011 by the International Energy Agency (IEA).

23. Interview in Beijing with Hong Jiuyin, deputy secretary general of the SCO.

24. At the start of diplomatic relations between China and Kazakhstan, Beijing insisted that the new state should sign a separate document to the

bilateral protocol. This document not only required Kazakhstan to adhere to the 'one-China principle', but also demanded its refusal to allow 'separatist movements' on the border, according to Mara Gubaid-ullina, a professor at Kazakhstan's National University. 'The document didn't specify that it was aimed against the Uighur people, but it was clear that it was directed at them. It was the 1990s and China and Kazakh-stan were not unaware of the risk that the Uighurs might demand the creation of their own state,' Gubaidullina explained. Other experts con-sulted by the authors agreed that 'the Uighur people have now missed their moment' to become independent.

25. The Uighur diaspora is scattered across eighty countries internationally. Kazakhstan has taken in the largest group outside China, with 230,000 Uighur residents. Some experts, such as Nicolás de Pedro, Alex-ander Cooley and Sébastien Peyrouse, agree that the strengthening of political and economic ties between Beijing and Astana has caused a deterioration in civil liberties for Kazakhstan's Uighur community. This opinion was confirmed by the experience of a local Uighur representative in Astana who asked not to be named. One example of Astana's policy on this issue is seen in its treatment of Ershidin Israil, a Uighur resident in Kazakhstan, who was deported to China in May 2011. For a detailed description of the impact of the SCO on the Uighur community, see 'Counter-terrorism and Human Rights: The Impact of the Shanghai Co-operation Organization: A Human Rights in China White Paper', HRIC, 2011.

26. Source: IMF.

27. Up to the date of publication, the UN had agreed four rounds of eco-nomic sanctions, in 2006, 2007, 2008 and 2010, aimed at deterring Iran from continuing its nuclear programme. On top of these are the unilat-eral sanctions imposed by the United States, the European Union, Japan, Australia and other countries, which date back to the founding of the Islamic Republic in 1979. The sanctions target Iran's nuclear and arms industry, banks, shipping and insurance companies, as well as businesses and individuals linked to the Guardians of the Revolution. Tehran claims that the aims of its nuclear programme are strictly limited to energy pro-duction and are therefore purely peaceful, but refuses to explain inconsistencies found by UN inspectors.

28. Although all of the main Iranian banks are on the UN's 'blacklist', the factor that really bolstered financial embargos against Iran was the state-ment issued in 2007 by the international banking organization, the Financial Action Task Force (FATF). In its statement, FATF warned that

Iran was not upholding legislation in regard to money laundering and counter-terrorism. 'The statement was devastating. All of the Western banks stopped doing business with Iran. This did them a lot of harm financially,' according to an economist to whom the authors spoke on the subject.

29. Bilateral trade between China and Iran generated over $45 billion in 2011, according to data provided by Iranian officials, and the Asian country is already the major trade partner of the Islamic Republic. In addition to this figure, around $6 billion in trade between Iran and the United Arab Emirates originated in China in 2010, according to Asadollah Asgaroladi, president of the Sino-Iranian Chamber of Commerce, who the authors interviewed in Tehran.

    Iran is placed at 144 out of 183 in the Doing Business 2012 ranking produced by the World Bank, a study measuring the suitability of operating conditions in countries in terms of doing business with other nations in the world.

30. Source: Interview with Mehdi Fakheri, vice-president of the Iran Chamber of Commerce, Industry and Mines.

31. As a member of the UN Security Council, China has the right to veto the Council's resolutions. In the case of Iran it has used this right to delay and limit the scope and effectiveness of the fourth round of sanctions. Resolution 1929, in fact, could only be approved almost six months after the idea of sanctions was first proposed and following intense negotiations with China. United States experts estimate that this Chinese tactic (which has also been used by Russia) has granted Iran precious extra years in which to develop their nuclear programme.

32. At a press conference in Beijing in early 2011, Asgaroladi said that bilateral trade would reach $50 billion by 2015.

33. 'Millionaire mullahs', Paul Klebnikov, *Forbes Magazine*, July 2003. According to this article, at that time Asadollah Asgaroladi had amassed a fortune worth $400 million.

34. In May 2011, a report by the UN Panel of Experts monitoring North Korea's arms activity noted that Pyongyang was reportedly exchanging ballistic missile technology with Iran, which represents a violation of the Security Council's sanctions. The same report indicated that illegal trade was being carried out via a 'third country', which the diplomats identified as China.

35. Testimony given before the US Congress by John Garver, an expert on Iran and professor at the Sam Nunn School of International Affairs, Georgia Institute of Technology, April 2011.

36. Interview with John Garver, June 2011.

37. In practice, China's veiled defence of Iran along with the strategic importance that Beijing gives to its crude oil imports – of which Iran was their sixth largest supplier in the first quarter of 2012 – have led Chinese oil companies to continue investing in the Iranian energy sector after other foreign companies have been forced to abandon their operations to avoid being sanctioned. As such, China represents a vital escape route for this most important sector in Iran's economy. This subject will be explored in greater depth in Chapter 4.

38. According to the Stockholm International Peace Research Institute (SIPRI), in the years between 2005 and 2009 Iran was the second largest recipient of Chinese arms exports after Pakistan.

39. As well as enriched uranium for military use, a nuclear programme with military goals requires a transporting agent: ballistic missiles. Iran has produced a prototype which could be operational by 2014 at the earliest. However, the United Kingdom has claimed that the Islamic Republic tested missiles capable of carrying nuclear warheads during military exercises in June 2010. Since the 1990s, China and other countries including Russia and North Korea have supplied Iran's regime with the industrial infrastructure, teams, advice and know-how necessary for its development. Source: Interviews with experts including Michael Elleman, an expert in international security at the International Institute of Strategic Studies in Bahrain.

40. Furthermore, China has seen unquestionable returns on its decision not to support the unilateral sanctions imposed on Iran by the United States and Europe. 'China does extremely well at identifying areas that are not covered by the UNSCR [United Nations Security Council Resolutions], such as expanded military trade, banking through China and other trade. Other countries have gone beyond the UNSCR. China has not.' By doing so, China has benefited from entering areas not covered by the sanctions, thereby 'expanding trade and financial relations [with Iran],' says Aaron Dunne, an expert in arms control and non-proliferation at the Stockholm International Peace Research Institute (SIPRI).

41. On 17 May 2011, China blocked the publication of the UN report. The next day it officially denied involvement in any such trade. Word for word, the report warns that 'Prohibited ballistic missile-related items are suspected to have been transferred between the Democratic People's Republic of Korea [North Korea] and the Islamic Republic of Iran on regular scheduled flights of Air Koryo and Iran Air, with trans-shipment through a neighbouring third country.'

The diplomat told the authors that 'countries such as China and Russia have made a very important contribution to the trade between Iran and North Korea', and assured them that the report offered ample evidence of this fact.

42. Hong Kong passed the new legislation a whole nine months after the approval of the UN sanctions. Hong Kong's press raised concerns about the possibility that the legislation would be ineffective in dismantling the network of Iranian shipping companies in Hong Kong, whose ships are registered under the names of Hong Kongese companies. Source: 'Uncertain future in Hong Kong for Iranian shipping line', *South China Morning Post*, Irene Jay Liu, 30 March 2011.

The island's press has also reported on Hong Kong's apparent state of apathy when it comes to carrying out thorough controls on exports, arguing that controls are less rigorous now than they were in the past. In 1997, not long before Hong Kong's return to Chinese sovereignty, the Executive Council of Hong Kong shut down four companies suspected of supplying nuclear and military technology to Iran. Among them was the state-owned Norinco group, which re-emerged soon afterwards under a different name. In the fifteen years since the transfer to Chinese rule, Hong Kong's local government has not acted against any more companies for this reason, demonstrating what appears to be a very different political sensibility.

43. The *South China Morning Post* described the trade in American technology to Iran via Hong Kong in 'The Hong Kong connection', Irene Jay Liu, 27 February 2011.

44. However, Aaron Dunne, from the Stockholm International Peace Research Institute (SIPRI), told the authors that the difficulty in applying the sanctions should not be underestimated. 'Because of the volume of trade, the nature of the information available to enforcement actors is very limited and ... it is extremely difficult to identify consignments of concern at the border. Information is limited and the windows of opportunity to take action are also limited.' In this sense, he pointed out that 'Hong Kong and Singapore are the two most advanced countries in the region in terms of sanctions implementation and export control'. Dunne also warned that the trade in dual-use technology to Iran originates in and passes through other countries as well as China.

45. Between 2002 and 2009, forty-seven Chinese companies were sanctioned a total of seventy-four times by the United States, according to John Garver, professor at the Sam Nunn School of International Affairs, Georgia Institute of Technology.

46. Wenzhou has become one of the wealthiest and most enterprising cities in China, with a private sector that is well known for its vitality. Dozens of entrepreneurs from the area visited Dubai in search of new opportunities, taking advantage of the collapse in housing prices in late 2009. Out of the 150,000 Chinese people who are said to live in Dubai, around 20,000 of them come from Wenzhou. Source: 'Chinese hunt for bargains in Dubai', *Financial Times*, 18 January 2010.

47. The authors have found that at least Laos (San Jiang Shopping Mall), Vietnam, Saudi Arabia (China Mart and Jeddah Chinese Commodity Centre) and India (Chinese Commodity Centre in Delhi) already have markets exclusively for Chinese products. Iraq, Russia and Jordan are currently planning projects of this type. Mexico is planning to open a replica of the Dragon Mart in Cancun in the near future which – at 840,000 square metres – will be five times the size of its Dubai counterpart. Thailand has scheduled the inauguration of the China City Complex in Bangkok for 2012, with an expected surface area of between 500,000 and 700,000 square metres.

    Unlike the Dragon Mart, the property of the Emirati state-owned company Nakheel, these markets are usually controlled by Chinese entrepreneurs who, as seen in the case of Liu Desheng in Chapter 1, buy land, build the market and then hire out space to their compatriots. In this way, China conquers foreign markets not only through its capacity to produce merchandise cheaply and quickly, but also through the use of regional hubs or markets. These serve to distribute merchandise to remote places to which it would be logistically difficult or expensive to send products directly from China. One example provided by Nicolás de Pedro is Kyrgyzstan, where an estimated 75 per cent of Chinese products imported by the country are destined to be re-exported (to Uzbekistan, Turkmenistan or Afghanistan). This represents the second most important economic activity in the Central Asian country.

    Sources on Chinese markets: the authors' own research and '*Dragon Mart de Cancún estará operando en el 2012*' ['Cancun's Dragon Mart to open in 2012'], Jesús Vázquez, *El Economista* (Mexico), 22 March 2011; on Kyrgyzstan: '*El ascenso de China en Asia Central: ¿un nuevo hegemón regional en gestación?*', op. cit.

48. *The New Silk Road: How a Rising Arab World is Turning Away from the West and Re-discovering China*, Ben Simpfendorfer (Palgrave Macmillan, 2009), p. 156.

49. Created in 1961, state-owned COSCO is the second largest shipping company in the world. It owns over 800 vessels and its activities cover

1,600 ports worldwide. Considered one of China's best and most efficient state-owned companies, COSCO has played a fundamental role in the arrival of Chinese products throughout the world. On the one hand, the company's expansion has allowed 'Chinese products to be taken to every corner of the planet, and on the other hand it has secured strategic lines of communication, such as the oil route', according to Kang Ronping, an expert in Chinese multinationals and adviser to the Beijing government. The interview with Professor Kang was used as a source here in the face of COSCO's refusal to grant the authors an interview.

50. In 1963, after gaining independence from French rule, Algeria became the first country to receive a team of Chinese doctors as part of an aid package from Beijing. Since then, sending doctors abroad has become a feature of Chinese diplomacy, the country having sent more than 20,000 doctors, nurses and health professionals all over the world, most of them to Africa. It is estimated that Chinese doctors have treated around 240 million patients over the last forty-six years. Source: *Chinese Medical Cooperation in Africa*, Li Anshan (Nordic Africa Institute, 2011).

51. Between 23 September and 26 September 1991, groups of Zairian soldiers mutinied and began looting shops, factories and homes in Kinshasa and other important towns in the country. The soldiers, who were protesting after months of unpaid salaries, robbed everything that crossed their paths, dismantling factories and destroying shops. Soon afterwards the civilian population joined in with the looting. At least 117 people died as a result of these incidents, which mostly affected businesses owned by the country's expat community.

52. Zhang Qi (张琪) is a descendant of Zhang Qian (张謇, 1853–1926), a Chinese official and entrepreneur from the Jiangsu province well known for his business achievements in the textile industry. As well as obtaining the highest possible mark in the imperial exams, an achievement bringing great influence and status at the end of the Qing dynasty, Zhang set up over twenty businesses in the city of Nantong, most of them in the textile and education sectors. The best known of these businesses was Dasheng (大生), which was later expropriated by Mao's Communist government. Sources: *Encyclopedia of Contemporary Chinese Culture*, Edward L. Davis (Routledge, 2005), p. 569; 张謇——中国早期现代化的先驱, 虞和平, 吉林文史出版社 2004.

53. This figure was released by the official agency Xinhua in 2007, and it is unlikely to be a true reflection of the real number of Chinese people living and working in the continent 'for extended periods of time'. The actual figure is thought to be significantly higher.

54. 'China in Africa: after the gun and the Bible ... a West African perspective', Adama Gaye, in *China Returns to Africa: A Rising Power and a Continent Embrace*, eds. Chris Alden, Daniel Large and Ricardo Soares de Oliveira (Hurst, 2008), p. 130.

55. 'Mixed fates of a popular minority: Chinese migrants in Cape Verde', Jorgen Carling and Heidi Ostbo Haugen, in *China Returns to Africa: A Rising Power and a Continent Embrace*, eds. Chris Alden, Daniel Large and Ricardo Soares de Oliveira (Hurst, 2008), p. 320.

56. In 2010 China overtook Germany to become the world's biggest international exporter. China's entrance into the WTO was a decisive milestone in the country's expansion into foreign trade. In the words of Professor Kang Ronping, 'there is no doubt that we have gained more than other countries by entering the WTO. This is particularly true if we take into account the data regarding exports and the market share won by Chinese businesses in sectors such as the manufacturing industry.' Nevertheless, Beijing has been criticized for its protectionist methods and for not fulfilling the commitment it made in 2001 to open some sectors of its economy, such as the service industry. For more information, see *Chinese Trade Policy after (Almost) Ten Years in the* WTO: *A Post-crisis Stocktake*, Sally Razeen (European Centre for International Political Economy, 2011).

57. Evidence of this is provided by the fact that, with the exception of Canada, none of the other G7 countries (France, Germany, Italy, Japan, the United Kingdom and the United States), considered as representative of the world's greatest industrialized economies, bases its economic policy on the production and exportation of natural resources.

58. *When China Rules the World*, op. cit., pp. 73–4.

59. The reports 'The Impact of China on Sub-Saharan Africa', Raphael Kaplinsky, Dorothy McCormick and Mike Morris, Institute of Development Studies, November 2007, and 'The growing relationship between China and sub-Saharan Africa: macroeconomic, trade, investment, and aid links', Ali Zafar, *World Bank Research Observer*, 22 (1), Spring 2007, provide more information on this subject.

60. *China and Latin America: Economic Relations in the Twenty-First Century*, Rhys Jenkins and Enrique Dussel (Deutschen Institut für Entwicklungspolitik, 2009), p. 48, and 'China's Global Expansion and Latin America', Rhys Jenkins, *Latin American Studies*, 42, 2010, p. 820.

61. Several experts agree that the rapid increase in salaries in the east of the country, where the bulk of Chinese industry is found, will eventually lead China to lose competitiveness in comparison with other countries such

as Vietnam or Cambodia in industries which require a greater labour intensity. The Spanish economist and analyst Eduardo Morcillo of Interchina Consulting predicts that Chinese production costs will increase by between 300 and 400 per cent over the next decade. On top of this there will be an eventual revaluation of the Chinese currency, the yuan, which Morcillo places at around 40 per cent. However, in the short and medium term, the underdevelopment of central and western China, where the economic miracle has not taken place to the same extent as on the other side of the country, will allow China to use a surplus of cheap labour to keep some of these industries alive.

62. During the first eleven months of 2009, Chinese companies sold a total of 102,000 vehicles to Africa with a total value of $1.74 billion, transforming the continent into the biggest market for Chinese cars. Source: *Africa Magazine*, 25 March 2011. Available at http://www.focac.org/eng/ztgx/jmhz/t813155.htm.

63. In April 2011 the governments of Congo-Brazzaville and China signed a memorandum of understanding declaring that the African company Nouvelle Air Congo would acquire Chinese MA 60 aeroplanes. Source: http://fr.allafrica.com/stories/201104060804.html. China is attempting to break the worldwide duopoly held in the passenger sector of the aeronautical industry by the European Airbus and Boeing by creating Comac C919, an aeroplane with a capacity of over 190 passengers, expected to be available on the market by 2014.

64. In 2011 Huawei obtained $32 billion of revenues. In 2009, around 20 per cent of Huawei's revenues came from the African continent, where the company operates in fifty countries. Source: The authors' own calculations based on figures taken from Huawei's Annual Report of 2011 and information published by the Chinese press (http://gb.cri.cn/27824/2010/10/11/154583016588.html).

65. During his interview with the authors in Buenos Aires, Calvete refused to provide any overarching figures regarding revenue. He did however explain that each one of the shops – which stay open 24 hours a day, 365 days a year – turns over an average of 15,000 pesos (the equivalent of 2,550 euros) per day.

3 CHINESE MINES IN THE NEW WILD WEST

1. At least before the so called 'democratic transition' of 2011, there was a constant sense of being watched and of being surrounded by informers in Burma and throughout the length of the border with China. 'You can't

trust anybody. Anyone could be a government spy,' one Burmese activist told us in a café in Rangoon's Summit Park View Hotel. This paranoia is justified. There is a high price to pay for stepping out of line in Burma, as was demonstrated by the reprisals following the 'Saffron Revolution' in 2007. Before 2011, for foreigners this would mean immediate expulsion from the country; for Burmese people, it would mean prison. Therefore, the real names of our interviewees in Burma and Yunnan province have been replaced with fictitious ones for their own protection.

2. The official name of the country has been the Republic of the Union of Myanmar since October 2010, when the Burmese military regime also changed the country's flag and national anthem. The country's historical name – Burma – had already been replaced by the name Myanmar in 1989. The majority of opposition groups and several countries continue to refer to the nation as Burma as a way of denying any legitimacy to the regime.

3. 'A Choice for China', Global Witness, October 2005.

4. In an unprecedented surprise decision in 2006, the Burmese military junta moved the official capital of the country to Naypyidaw, a phantasmagorical administrative town with around 100,000 inhabitants situated 320 kilometres north of the then capital Rangoon. It is speculated that the regime's decision was made in order to reinforce its power. The majority of foreign embassies have chosen to remain in Rangoon.

5. 'A Disharmonious Trade', Global Witness, October 2009.

6. Soon after independence, a significant number of ethnic minority groups scattered throughout the country took up arms to demand a greater level of autonomy. The conflict escalated when the military junta came to power in 1962, resulting in a covert civil war which has continued with differing levels of intensity throughout the following decades and has resulted in tens or even hundreds of thousands of deaths and the displacement of 2 million people. Some guerrilla resistance groups continue their activities today, but since 1994 at least sixteen of these groups have agreed to a ceasefire and have discontinued their hostilities. The Kachins, who in 1994 accepted the truce agreement in the hope that it would lead to a political dialogue that has never happened, broke the ceasefire in June 2011 and hostilities have resumed since then.

7. In June 2011, hostilities broke out again in Kachin between the Burmese army and the Kachin Independence Army (KIA) near a Chinese-financed and -built hydropower dam in Kachin State. The fighting ended a seventeen-year ceasefire agreement and led to the displacement of an estimated 75,000 Kachins, who according to NGOs suffered human rights abuses.

The NGOs argue that, despite the KIA's ultimatum, it was the Burmese regime that in practice broke the 1994 ceasefire. According to these groups, the Burmese Army had been entering what it considered KIA's territory under the 1994 ceasefire; at the same time, the Kachin weren't allowed to set up their own political party and their military contingent was prompted to become a border-armed police. Kachin sources assert that during the conflict China allegedly allowed the Burmese Army into Chinese territory, although no evidence was ever presented. Currently, the KIA, which has between 10,000 and 30,000 effective troops, is the only big ethnic group in the country without a truce agreement in place.

8. 'Chinese takeaway kitchen', *The Economist*, 9 June 2011. Kachin people have lived in both sides of the China–Burma border for centuries. Most Kachin families in Burma have relatives in China, as both communities have intermarried for generations. According to media reports, the escalation of the conflict since June 2011 has pushed many Chinese people to flee from Northern Burma back to China.

9. Apart from Burma's large reserves, the only jadeite reserves left in the world include some small reserves in Russia and Central America. Xinjiang (China) is home to a type of white jade which, although valuable, is not of such high quality as the jadeite.

10. For more information, see http://www.kachinnews.com/news/769-russian-firm-after-uranium-not-gold-in-kachin-state.html. According to various unofficial sources, the Burmese regime is trying to develop its own nuclear programme, although it is not clear for what aims.

11. Faced with a complete lack of official figures, the estimated number of mining companies operating in Hpakant fluctuates between seventy and several hundred, according to interviews which the authors carried out with various sources. The Burmese government has shares in the mining concessions through the regional military command. This is done in alliance with the concessionary companies, who carry out the investment and take charge of exploiting the resources. Directly or otherwise, the majority of these companies are Chinese.

12. In 2010, the GDP per capita in Burma was $1,400, according to the CIA's The World Factbook 2010.

13. 'Blood Jade', 2008, published by the NGO 8-8-08 for Burma, denounced China's role in Hpakant's mines in the run up to the Beijing Olympic Games.

14. The rubble pours into the rivers, blocking their natural course and obstructing the movement of water. During the rainy season, this causes frequent floods that sweep away fragile homes made of wood and bamboo.

In November 2010, a landslide on one of the artificial mountains caused the death of over fifty *yemase*, who were buried under the earth. According to a local source, there is only one public hospital in Hpakant, which charges for its services, as well as a handful of small private practices.

15. Since hostilities broke out in Kachin in June 2011, an undetermined number of Chinese have fled the areas along the border with China. It is unclear whether the conflict has impacted on Chinese businesses in Hpakant in any way, despite the fact that occasional skirmishes have reached the area. The Kachin Independence Organization (KIO) claimed that the Burmese regime was attempting to block its main means of income – taxes – by ordering jade mining companies in Hpakant to halt production.

16. The use of opiates is extremely widespread among the jade industry workers. A source with extensive knowledge of the subject assured the authors that it is a common courtesy for jade traders to offer *Kha Pong* – boiled opium with crushed banana leaf – whenever they meet to do business.

17. 'Our fellow priests tell us that the work is so hard that the miners have to be stimulated with heroin and methamphetamines. We know miners who enter the business clean and come out hooked,' explained one of the priests who the authors spoke to. The NGO volunteer pointed out that the consumption of these drugs in Chinese mines is 'common practice'.

18. 'Authorities feed heroin epidemic in Hpakant', 2009. Founded in 2003, Kachin News Group is Kachin state's unofficial news agency. Based in Chiang Mai (Thailand), the agency is considered one of the most well-informed sources on events in Kachin.

19. The report alleges that the companies' monopoly over distributing the drug in Hpakant is guaranteed because the police are on their payroll. Although there is no hard evidence, the general perception in Kachin is that the alliance between the Burmese military forces, who act like feudal lords in the area, and the Chinese businesses also stretches into the world of narcotics. According to sources from the Kachin Independent Organization (KIO) consulted by the authors, the climate of impunity in terms of drug use forms part of the 'silent war against the new generation of the Kachin people' which the Burmese regime has launched to 'deactivate dissidence', putting an end to the region's aspirations of independence from Burma.

20. According to the *National Strategic Plan on HIV* (2009) published by Burma's National Aids Programme, 2,572,641 needles and syringes were distributed in Hpakant that year.

21. At an auction in March 2011, Burma collected $2.8 billion from the sale of 16,939 lots of jade, 206 of precious gems and 255 of pearls. Precious stones provide one of the main sources of financing for the Burmese regime, which invests just 1.31 per cent of its budget on healthcare and just 4.57 per cent on education.

22. In 2006, cross-border trade with China represented 7 per cent of Burma's total trade. The academic Winston Set Aung has calculated that this percentage would rise to 25 per cent if it included the value of illegal trade. *The Role of Informal Cross-border Trade in Myanmar* (Institute for Security and Development Policy, 2009).

23. The name for unprocessed jade is written as 赌石 in Mandarin or *du shi* in Pinyin, which literally means 'stone of risk or bets'. When a particularly large investment is required, several buyers often put money into a common fund in order to minimize the risk.

24. The close knit relations between the two countries are not enough to hide their mutual distrust. Cables released by WikiLeaks highlighted the anxiety that Beijing feels about Burma's unstable domestic situation as well as Rangoon's sense of unease about the excessive economic weight that China is employing in the country. This has coincided with growing economic and military ties between India and the Burmese regime. At the end of 2011, Burma's regime moved towards what seemed to be a kind of democratic openness, which some analysts link to the country's willingness to move away from excessive dependency on China. As a result, Washington restored full diplomatic relations with the country.

25. The 'democratic transition' undertaken by the former general and current Burmese president, Thein Sein, allowed the release from house arrest of Nobel Peace Prize-winner Aung San Suu Kyi, who had been deprived of freedom for fifteen years since 1989. The reforms made room for the easing of censorship in the country, facilitated the release from prison of hundreds of dissidents, and enabled further political reforms, among other things. Although most analysts agree that the reforms are genuine and would be very hard to reverse, some NGOs argue that they are only affecting cities – not rural areas. The new Burmese government is formally civilian, although it is controlled by the military.

26. In 2008, a total of sixty-nine Chinese state-owned companies reportedly invested in at least ninety projects in Burma involving mining, hydroelectric power, oil and gas, according to EarthRights International (ERI). In the 2010–11 tax year, Chinese investment in the South Asian country reached $13.5 billion, making China the biggest foreign investor in Burma, even ahead of Thailand.

Furthermore, in 2009 China National Petroleum Corporation (CNPC) acquired the exclusive thirty-year rights to exploit one of the biggest deposits of natural gas in South-East Asia, situated in the waters around the Bay of Bengal. The rights to exploit the deposits previously belonged to an Indian–South Korean consortium. Within the framework of the 'Shwe Gas' project, the Chinese oil company is set to complete the construction of a 2,800-kilometre gas pipeline by 2013. The pipeline will stretch all the way from the offshore deposits to Nanning in south-west China, crossing through Burma. At the same time, the oil company will also build a 1,100-kilometre oil pipeline aimed at carrying Middle Eastern crude oil from the west coast of Burma to Kunming, thereby avoiding the Malacca Strait and the maritime routes controlled by the United States. The total investment required for both pipelines is estimated at between $2.5 and $3.45 billion. In order to make the project viable, a deep water port is under construction; this will form an essential part of a Special Economic Zone on the island of Kyauk Phyu. The zone will include oil terminals, an airport and a railway network with links to China. Through sales of gas to China alone, the Burmese regime will receive almost $1 billion annually over the next thirty years.

27. This was the name given to the modern-day Yunnan province by Emperor Xian in the Tan dynasty era, recognizing the territory as being situated 'to the south of rainy Sichuan'.

28. In November 1992, Shougang Corporation bought 100 per cent of the shares in the state-owned Empresa Minera de Hierro de Peru for $120 million, creating Shougang Hierro Peru. The mine was originally the property of the United States' Marcona Mining Company before passing into Peruvian state ownership after its expropriation in 1975, up until its privatization in 1992. The reserves contain up to 1.662 billion tons of minerals. The investment includes a private deep water port located 18 kilometres from the mine.

29. According to the Mine Workers Union of Shougang Hierro Peru, the company produced 9.5 million tons of iron in 2011, despite the fall in demand caused by the global economic crisis. Income for that year reportedly reached almost 3,065 million nuevos soles, the equivalent of $1.17 billion.

30. In November 2010, Shougang provided the community with drinking water for just two and half hours each day and power cuts were extremely common, according to local sources.

31. 'Shougang does not give interviews about its overseas businesses,' said Wu Chu-Zhang from Shougang's PR department in Beijing when the

authors spoke to him by phone. This was in response to the authors' written request made several weeks before by fax.

32. *La economía china y las industrias extractivas: desafíos para el Perú* [The Chinese Economy and the Extractive Industries: Challenges for Peru], Cynthia A. Sanborn and Víctor Torres (Universidad del Pacífico, Centro de Investigación, 2009).

33. Shougang sent official letters to both employees after the publication of the article 'Tensions over Chinese mining venture in Peru' in the *New York Times* on 14 August 2010. The unions see the reaction of the Chinese company as an act of intimidation and perhaps as the prelude to an official dismissal. To find out more, visit http://www.nytimes.com/2010/08/15/world/americas/15chinaperu.html, by Simón Romero.

34. For permanent staff, the basic daily salary for workers aged over forty in the highest pay bracket is 71.6 nuevos soles, or $25.8. On top of this they receive a bonus (for working on public holidays, night shifts or open pit work) and an allowance for milk, transport and light refreshments among other things, which in total represents a wage 30 per cent higher than that of the temporary workers, according to the unions.

35. Pneumoconiosis is a type of chronic illness produced by the infiltration into the human respiratory system of dust originating from various mineral substances such as coal, silica, iron and calcium.

36. The wealth gap between rural and urban areas in China has reached a critical level, according to a survey by Central China Normal University's Institute for China Rural Studies published in August 2012. The institute's report indicated that the Gini coefficient, an index reflecting the rich–poor gap, in rural China stood at 0.3949 last year, nearing the warning level of 0.4 set by the United Nations. Source: 'Widening wealth gap in rural China nears warning level', Xinhua News Agency, 22 August 2012.

37. http://www.agubernamental.org/web/informativo.php?id=12425.

38. '*La economía china y las industrias extractivas: desafíos para el Perú*', op. cit.

39. In '*La economía china y las industrias extractivas: desafíos para el Perú*', op. cit., Víctor Torres points out that in 2007 the Shougang group, China's sixth biggest steel manufacturer, required 20 million tons of iron ore to be imported in order to supply its steel factories in the country.

40. As well as announcing that it would be investing $1 billion to increase production to 10 million tons, Shougang's president stated in 2009 that the Chinese company had contributed to the economic development of Peru by paying $333 million in taxes and spending $340 million on local

purchases, as well as generating a significant number of local jobs. Meanwhile, the company's income for 2011 alone exceeded $1.17 billion. For more information, visit: http://www.andina.com.pe/Espanol/Noticia. aspx?Id= yS/WcpdTulE=.

41. Relations between the DRC and Angola have deteriorated significantly in recent years as a result of territorial disputes, disagreements over ownership of the region's oil resources and regional geopolitical differences. Consequently, both Kinshasa and Luanda regularly carry out the mass expulsion of hundreds of thousands of nationals from their neighbouring country, which occasionally results in deaths, torture and other types of abuse. For instance, in summer 2010 over 650 women and girls were raped after being deported from Angola to the DRC, according to UNICEF. Source: http://www.un.org/apps/news/story.asp?NewsID=377 85&Cr=sexual+violence&CR1=.

42. The country suffered the most brutal colonization process in the whole of Africa at the hands of Belgium before declaring its independence in 1960. This was followed by decades of brutal dictatorship until two different wars between 1996 and 2003 left almost 4 million people dead and a country in ruins. According to the US State Department, the country's GDP per capita in 2011 barely reached $210. The DRC ranks at 168 out of 183 in the corruption perceptions index produced by Transparency International in 2011.

43. The mining concession referred to in the contract contains proven reserves containing 6,813,370 tons of copper and 426,619 tons of cobalt. In Appendix A, however, the contract states that the probable reserves could reach 10,616,070 tons of copper and 626,619 tons of cobalt.

44. The contract signed by the Congolese state and the state-owned companies China Railway Group and Sinohydro included a provision for the creation of a joint venture – Sicomines – between the Congolese state-owned mining company Gecamines and the consortium of Chinese companies. The original contract anticipated a total investment of $9 billion, $6 billion of which would go towards the construction of infrastructure while the remaining $3 billion would be spent on creating the necessary structures for exploiting the mines, where access to the mineral is complex and expensive as a result of the lack of basic services (electricity and roads). However, this investment was reduced some months later to a little over $6.2 billion to be shared in equal parts between investments in the mines and infrastructure after the intervention of the World Bank and the International Monetary Fund.

The reason behind this intervention varies depending on the source. The international organizations justify their actions by claiming that the contract threatened to ruin the already poverty-stricken DRC, since the country was offering sovereign guarantees in case the extraction of minerals was not enough to repay the credit granted by the Chinese Exim Bank. Other sources argue that it was in fact a manoeuvre to protect Western interests, as Western companies feared that Kinshasa might transfer part of its concessions to the Sino-Congolese company. On the other hand, the country's traditional creditors feared that the DRC would prioritize the repayment of the Chinese credit while its other loans would once more end up going unpaid. In this respect, it is important to point out that while the DRC was signing the contract with China, the country was also negotiating debt relief, which finally came through in July 2010 when Kinshasa was declared exempt from paying the $12.3 billion owed to its traditional creditors.

45. Article 14.2.3.1 of the contract stipulates that 'the DRC commits to facilitating the acquisition of visas and work permits for expatriate employees'. China often tries to bring its own contingent of Chinese workers to take part in its infrastructure projects across the world, as the Chinese companies consider their compatriots to be more hardworking and disciplined than the local people, as well as the fact that this allows them to communicate in their own language. However, this practice has been criticized by various sources, as it reduces the real benefit for the local population in terms of job creation.

46. One of the appendices to the original contract referred to the construction of 1,015 kilometres of railways, 3,656 kilometres of roads, 2 dams, 2 universities, 5,000 homes, 31 hospitals with 150 beds each and 145 health centres. It also mentions the restoration of 2,198 kilometres of railways, 3,652 kilometres of roads and 2 airports. In order to pay for this, the contract anticipated a total investment of $6 billion, a figure that was later reduced to half the original amount after the intervention of the IMF and the World Bank. The amount of planned infrastructure has therefore been considerably reduced.

47. A good example of this can be seen in the case of ZTE Agribusiness – a subsidiary of the Chinese telecommunications giant ZTE – which has suspended an investment of $600 million in Mbandaka in the north-west of the country. The company had planned to invest in a palm oil plantation measuring 100,000 hectares in order to produce edible oil and biofuels. In an interview at his office in Kinshasa, the head of the Chinese company in the DRC, Wang Kewen, cited the precarious transport infra-

structure as a justification for suspending the project. 'Among other factors, the main problem is logistics. If everything goes well, transporting the merchandise to Kinshasa along the Congo river takes no less than two weeks. But if something goes wrong, it's impossible to know how long it might take,' he assured the authors. Mbandaka and Kinshasa are separated by a distance of 600 kilometres. Rivers provide the main or only form of transport in much of the country.

48. Apart from the specific use of the term in this contract, Beijing frequently uses the expression 'win-win policy' to describe its initiatives in developing countries which were previously colonized by Western powers. This can be seen as Beijing's attempt to distance itself from Western strategies and, by extension, to use anti-colonialist discourse to create links with Africa and Latin America, thereby winning territory from Western countries.

49. Sicomines, the joint enterprise created on signing the contract, is in charge of managing both the $6 billion investment and the mining operation. It is made up of a consortium of five Chinese companies, led by the state-owned Sinohydro and China Railway Group, which own 68 per cent of shares, and the Congolese state-owned Gecamines, which is a minor shareholder with 32 per cent of the business.

50. This estimate is taken from 'China and Congo: Friends in Need', a 2011 report by the NGO Global Witness. The report bases its estimate on the average price of copper and cobalt over the last ten years.

51. Articles 14.2.1 to 14.3 of the contract.

52. This conservative estimate was made by Stefaan Marysse and Sara Geenen in their report 'Win-win or unequal exchange? The case of the Sino-Congolese Cooperation Agreement', *Journal of Modern African Studies*, 47 (3), 2009, pp. 371–96.

53. 'In the twelve months following the approval of the Cooperation Project [contract] by the Chinese government, the DRC commits to obtaining the adoption of a law from its parliament that will guarantee the fiscal, customs and exchange regime demanded by the Cooperation Project, as a result of its specificity. If the National Parliament of the DRC does not adopt the aforementioned law within the agreed timeframe, the Chinese business group will have the right to decide whether to continue or terminate the current agreement.' The authors' translation from the original French and Chinese.

54. 'If the Mining JV [Sicomines] has not returned the investment and interests relating to the Mining and Infrastructure Projects within twenty-five years of its creation, the DRC commits to repaying the remaining bal-

ance in other forms', according to article 13.3.4. The authors' translation from the original French and Chinese.

55. A Congolese delegation spent two months negotiating the contract in Beijing. According to rumours that the authors were unable to confirm, the signing of the contract was preceded by a 'buying spree' carried out by the African delegation in the Chinese capital, which was supposedly financed by China in order to facilitate the agreement. Joseph Kabila won a controversial presidential election held in December 2011 amid suspicions of electoral fraud.

56. Sources: Interview with Okenda and interview with the Chinese ambassador Wu Zexian, carried out by the journalist Victoire Eyobi on 10 November 2010 and published in the magazine *Entreprendre*.

57. The authors travelled to Likasi in the Congolese province of Katanga to visit the mining installations owned by the Chinese company Feza Mining, property of Wan Bao Mining, which in turn is part of the business group China North Industries Corporation (NORINCO). NORINCO is one of China's most important defence companies, and was once subject to sanctions by the United States for supplying missile technology to Iran. Central Africa's so-called 'Copperbelt' harbours 10 per cent of the world's copper reserves and 34 per cent of the world's cobalt reserves.

58. 'Win-win or unequal exchange? The case of the Sino-Congolese Cooperation Agreement', op. cit., p. 390.

4 CHINA'S 'BLACK GOLD' OFFENSIVE

1. According to the author Deborah Brautigam, Li said these words after taking part in round table discussions at the Center for Strategic and International Studies in Washington in April 2007. The phrase is a reference to an expression used by the scholar Ban Gu in his *Chronicles of the Han Dynasty*, written in the first century AD and one of the classic works of Chinese historiography. The complete expression is: 'If the water is too clear, you will never catch a fish; the man who is too strict will never have friends.'

2. The names of people and places, as well as professions and any physical descriptions that might be used to identify the sources mentioned in this chapter, have been changed to ensure that they remain anonymous. In the 2012 World's Most Repressive Societies ranking produced by the organization Freedom House, which measures the state of civil and political liberties across the world, Turkmenistan was vying with Burma, Sudan

and North Korea for the lowest places. Repression is common currency in Turkmenistan.

3. These figures were provided by a Western diplomat and a Western expat, both of whom have lived in Turkmenistan for several years.

4. A diplomat living in Ashgabat confirmed that a place at the Turkmen State University costs between $20,000 and $80,000 depending on the area of study. Degrees in the arts and humanities are cheaper, as careers available to graduates in these subjects are not very well paid. Engineering degrees are the most expensive, as jobs, especially in the oil and gas industries, are better paid and these graduates can make money quickly. Getting a job always involves paying some kind of fee in advance: prostitutes have to pay a bribe to the local police, while anyone looking for a job sweeping roads in the relentless 50-degree heat first has to pay a $200 fee.

5. 'Les Rapports secrets du Département d'État Américain. Le meilleur de WikiLeaks' ('The secret relations of the US State Department: the best of WikiLeaks'), Le Monde Hors-Série, March 2011, pp. 71–4.

6. High-ranking members of the Communist Party of China often lead official visits to foreign countries in which Chinese government officials take part, despite the fact that these visits technically represent the state institutions and not any one political party. This fact highlights the subordinate role played by state institutions in the mechanism of Chinese politics, compared to the dominant role of the country's only political party – the CPC.

7. BP's 2012 annual report on world energy reserves suggests that the amount of proven gas reserves in Turkmenistan is close to 25 trillion cubic metres. BP Statistical Review of World Energy, June 2012; 'Turkmenistan foreign policy', Richard Pomfret, China and Eurasia Forum Quarterly, 6 (4), 2008, pp. 19–34.

8. Saparmurat Niyazov, the first president of Turkmenistan who led the country from its independence in 1991 until his sudden death in 2006 (probably caused by diabetes), was succeeded by Gurbanguly Berdymukhammedov, the country's former minister of health, a role that he gained after working as a dentist. The great physical resemblance between the two men has led to a string of speculations, including rumours that Berdymukhammedov is in fact Niyazov's illegitimate son.

Expat residents in Ashgabat tell all kinds of incredible stories about daily life in the country. For example, one source described the surreal nature of presidential visits to other provinces in the country: 'I was invited to attend the inauguration of a new town to the east of Ashgabat, which President Berdymukhammedov would be attending. When I got there, I was astonished to find a dazzling white marble town where the hospitals were fully stocked with state-of-the-art equipment and the children in the nurseries spoke English. The president's visit was celebrated with dancing and chanting by thousands of people who had headed out into the streets, and the president visited facilities throughout the town which wouldn't have been out of place in the most highly developed countries of the world. For logistical reasons I had to spend the night in the area, and so I went back to the same town the next day. I found that the streets were deserted and the shops and public buildings were all closed. I didn't understand what was happening, until one of the locals explained that everything that had happened the day before was just one big set up. They had brought children from Ashgabat and trained them for months for this show. The hospital equipment had also been brought there from the capital. It had all just been one big work of fiction orchestrated by the state.'

This same source explained that the president's visits abroad also have their elements of fiction. The state-owned Turkmen television company apparently edited images taken from a speech by the president to the United Nations (easily done as a result of the rotary nature of operations at the UN) to demonstrate that Turkmenistan's head of state constantly receives enthusiastic applause from his foreign counterparts. 'Is it true that all the world's presidents invited our head of state to give a speech and then wouldn't stop clapping? That's what we see on television,' a Turkmen friend asked our source, who will remain anonymous here for obvious reasons.

9. Getting a press visa for Turkmenistan is practically impossible. Getting a tourist visa is equally arduous and expensive and, among other things, involves the traveller having to provide detailed information about his or her route weeks in advance, as well as having to rely on a local guide throughout the visit to the country. As the authors had not mentioned their trip to Turkmenabat to their appointed guide (to avoid raising any suspicion), the trip to the town was technically 'illegal', as the guide himself assured the authors, threateningly, by phone.

10. The authors met Lei Li (not his real name) through a Chinese online chat room. They made contact with him from Beijing, and after months of conversations in cyberspace he agreed to meet the authors in this remote corner of Turkmenistan.

11. The Chinese CNPC is the only foreign company exploiting Turkmenistan's onshore gas reserves. The other foreign corporations in the country

are only exploring the offshore reserves of hydrocarbons in the Caspian Sea.

12. *World Energy Outlook 2011*, International Energy Agency (OECD/IEA, 2011).

13. Between the initial opening of the gas pipeline in December 2009 and June 2012, China imported 30 billion cubic metres (m³) of gas from Turkmenistan, according to figures from CNPC. On the basis of the bilateral agreements signed in June 2012, this figure should reach 65 billion m³ per year by 2015. Nevertheless, experts see Turkmenistan as an unreliable business partner in terms of supplying the amount of gas it promises to supply, as some sources doubt that the country can really achieve supplies of this volume.

   The International Energy Agency (IEA) estimates that by 2015 China's demand for gas will reach 165 billion m³ per year. Meanwhile, BP's 2012 energy report stated that China consumed 130.7 billion m³ of gas in 2011 and produced 102.5 billion m³ of gas. Sources: 'PetroChina pipeline turns on gas supply', *China Daily*, 5 June 2012; 'China turns to Turkmenistan for gas amid Gazprom pipe talks', Bloomberg, 4 March 2011; *World Energy Outlook 2011*, op. cit.; *BP Statistical Review of World Energy*, op. cit.

14. Although there is little information available on these agreements in the public domain, published sources state that the CDB lent Turkmengaz $4 billion in 2009 in order to begin developing several gas deposits, including those in South Yolotan and Osman. In 2011, the CDB supplied an extra $4.1 billion loan to be repaid over ten years after a three-year grace period. The loans are guaranteed with the country's hydrocarbons and, according to some sources, will be repaid with supplies of gas. Sources: 'China boosts gas imports from Turkmenistan', Vladimir Socor, *Asia Times*, 2 July 2009; 'China lends $4.1 billion to gas-rich Turkmenistan', Reuters, 27 April 2011.

15. China currently has three policy banks: the China Development Bank (CBD), the Export-Import Bank (the Exim Bank) and Agricultural Bank of China (ABC). These banks were established to support China's infrastructure development (CBD), trade promation (Exim Bank) and agriculture (ABC). Out of the three, the Exim Bank is the one with the clearest political leanings. It is the only Chinese institution qualified to offer 'concessional loans' and 'preferential export buyer's credit', loans which offer much lower rates of interest than the market rate and highly favourable repayment conditions, which serve to provide aid and investment for developing countries. The loans serve the double purpose of

facilitating Chinese exports and supporting Chinese diplomacy. The Exim Bank, an impenetrable institution which acts directly on the orders of the State Council, does not publish any data in its annual report detailing the amount of credit it has granted or identifying who has received these loans. In a surreal interview which the authors finally secured with the institution in 2010, described in this book's introduction (p.13), Yan Qifa, deputy director of the bank's department of economic research, told the authors that he did not know 'how many concessional loans China grants each year'.

On the other hand, the CDB, which was established in 1994, is also government-owned and its control falls under the State Council. Domestically, it supports government-led infrastructure projects, while internationally it follows Chinese SOEs in their ventures abroad. The CDB has an extensive international presence, and is the largest provider of international financing among China's banks under China's 'go-out' investment policy. The CDB seems to be adopting a more commercially oriented business approach, and is perceived to be following a strategy aiming to transform it into a universal banking conglomerate. However, given its business nature and ownership structure, it is unlikely that the government would withdraw its support.

16. The Brookings Institute expert Erica Downs argues that the Chinese state-owned oil companies and the CDB have managed to acquire a certain degree of independence from the government over recent years. This does not mean, however, that they do not ultimately have to submit to the rule of the party state (which is in charge of naming the presidents of these corporations, among other things). Nevertheless, Downs argues that 'China Inc.' is not a 'monolithic' entity which makes its decisions 'from the top down'. Analysts Julie Jiang and Jonathan Sinton put forward a similar argument in their recent report for the International Energy Agency. In this regard, it is important to point out that, while Chinese state-owned corporations and banks try to pursue a balance between the country's national interests and the profitability of the projects they carry out, it is impossible to separate the state or the characteristics of its financial system from China's expansion across the world. This is particularly true if we take into account the fact that the technology owned by these companies lags 'several decades' behind that of Western companies, according to various experts who spoke to the authors on the subject. In the words of the academic Ricardo Soares de Oliveira, 'While still lagging behind Western companies in most areas, Chinese NOCs [National Oil Companies] bring to the table the weight

of the Chinese state, a willingness to pay for long-term engagements that would not be viable if perceived in the short term, and cheap finance to secure deals.'

Probably the best example is the agreement made in February 2009 between the Russian companies Rosneft and Transneft, on the one hand, and the CDB and CNPC, on the other. On the basis of this agreement, the CDB committed to granting the two Russian companies a $25 billion loan at an annual interest rate of 5.69 per cent (a highly favourable rate considering the economic situation at the time). In return, the Russian companies committed to providing the CNPC with a daily supply of 300,000 barrels of oil at the market price. This caused Russia to change its original plans, after fifteen years of negotiations, and finally consent to build a Chinese branch of the Eastern Siberia Pacific Ocean (ESPO) pipeline, which originally only aimed to provide a link between the Siberian oil reserves and Japan.

Sources: *Inside China, Inc.: China Development Bank's Cross-Border Energy Deals*, Erica Downs (Brookings Institute, 2011); *Overseas Investments by Chinese National Oil Companies: Assessing the Drivers and Impacts*, Julie Jiang and Jonathan Sinton (IEA, February 2011). Quote by Soares de Oliveira taken from 'Making sense of Chinese oil investment in Africa', in *China Returns to Africa: A Rising Power and a Continent Embrace*, eds. Chris Alden, Daniel Large and Ricardo Soares de Oliveira, (Hurst, 2008), p. 98.

17. China's currency reserves, which represented a total of $3.2 trillion at the close of 2011, stem primarily from four different sources: direct foreign investment in the country, China's trade surplus, tourism and the so-called 'sterilization' process of its currency (China buys in dollars to maintain a fixed exchange rate). The SAFE (State Administration of Foreign Exchange) manages the funds using various different types of investment, basing its decisions on the degree of risk involved, strategic requirements and profitability. Up until the 2008 crisis, China used to invest a significant amount of its currency in US Treasury bonds, but risk perception and the fact that its assets might be losing purchasing power has since led Beijing to diversify its investments. The use of part of its currency reserves to finance projects carried out by Chinese businesses abroad is perfectly in line with this strategy. As such, China's currency reserves also serve to make its businesses more international, making a decisive contribution to China's conquest of foreign markets.

18. Despite its much noted signs of illiteracy, the 'Book of the Soul' was apparently written by Niyazov 'with the help of the inspiration which

God sent to his heart'. The two-volume work outlines a family tree linking the president back to the very beginnings of humanity. It also provides instruction about how to behave in public and at home. The book is compulsory reading at schools and universities in Turkmenistan, and knowledge of the work is a necessary requirement to get a job as a government employee, and even when applying for a driving licence. There are over forty foreign translations of the *Ruhnama*, all of them commissioned by entrepreneurs who have followed the lead of Turkish businessman Ahmet Çalik by translating the work into languages including French, English and Chinese. Arto Halonen's documentary film, *Shadow of the Holy Book*, provides more information on the subject.

19. Evidence of this relationship can be seen in *Édition Spécial*, the documentary made by TF1 – a private television channel owned by Bouygues – to celebrate the dictator's visit to France in September 1996. Niyazov, Martin Bouygues and the presidents of TF1, Gas de France and Électricité de France (EDF) all took part in the programme, which was directed by the journalist Jean-Claude Narcy. The group of French businessmen are seen singing Turkmenbashi's praises over the course of the forty-minute programme, never daring to contradict or question him on subjects such as corruption, human rights or civil liberties. The programme, which was broadcast in Turkmenistan but never shown in France, is available to view at: http://www.dailymotion.com/video/xiouw_tf1-bouygues-et-le-turkmenistan; last accessed 22 August 2012.

   For more information about the rising price of business in Turkmenistan as a result of corruption, see '*Les Rapports secrets du Département d'État Américain: Le meilleur de WikiLeaks*', op. cit.

20. The only exception is a pipeline connecting Turkmenistan with neighbouring Iran. According to the World Bank, Ashgabat will use this pipeline to transport an annual supply of 20 billion m^3 of gas to the Islamic republic over the coming years.

21. *Inside China, Inc.: China Development Bank's Cross-Border Energy Deals*, op. cit.

22. Within the framework of the peace agreements signed in 2005, a referendum took place between January and February 2011 in the south of Sudan in which 99 per cent of the population voted for independence and the creation of a new state of South Sudan, which came into effect on 9 July 2011. However, tensions remain on the border and war once more threatens the region.

23. When the authors visited Khartoum in July 2010, the CNPC's local office was based in the Hotel Sudan, a building with 260 rooms and five

floors where the company's main Chinese employees sleep and work. By virtue of being Chinese, the authors' assistant was able to spend a night in one of the hotel's spacious rooms and enjoyed a selection of thirty dishes from Sichuan and other regions cooked each day by fifteen Chinese chefs. As well as the Hotel Sudan, situated half way between the Presidential Palace and the Ministry of Oil on Khartoum's main road, CNPC had also acquired two more buildings as a result of its expansion in the country. The company was also putting the final touches to a new skyscraper to fulfil the needs of its staff in Sudan.

24. Thanks to colossal investments estimated to exceed $15 billion, China is certainly the key player in the Sudanese oil sector, although it is not the only one. CNPC owns 40 per cent of shares in the Greater Nile Petroleum Operating Company (GNPOC), the consortium in charge of exploiting several oil wells in the country and constructing the 1,500-kilometre oil pipeline that carries crude oil from the south of the country to Port Sudan on the coast of the Red Sea. CNPC also owns a further 41 per cent of shares in the country's second largest consortium, Petrodar Operating Company, where the Chinese Sinopec (a company in which the Chinese state is the majority shareholder) owns an additional 6 per cent. The Malaysian state-owned company Petronas and the Indian state-owned Oil and Natural Gas Corporation Limited (ONGC) are also present in the Sudanese oil sector through shares in these consortia, although to a lesser extent than China. Source: 'From non-interference to constructive engagement?', Daniel Large, in *China Returns to Africa: A Rising Power and a Continent Embrace*, eds. Chris Alden, Daniel Large and Ricardo Soares de Oliveira, (Hurst, 2008), pp. 280–84.

25. Since then and until 2011, Sudan has held a place on the list of China's main oil suppliers. Over a decade later, Sudan is still an important oil supplier for China, providing 5.3 per cent of China's total oil imports in 2010. This is despite the limited production of oil in the Arab country, the poor quality of its crude oil and China's growing demand. China is in turn the biggest buyer of Sudanese oil, purchasing 12.59 million tons of crude oil in 2010 (around 50 per cent of the country's total output for the year). The current production rate varies between 500,000 and 750,000 barrels of oil each day, according to a Sudanese expert interviewed for this book. Source: Chinese customs office, http://www.customs.gov.cn/publish/portal0/tab7841/module24699/info292637.htm.

26. Sudan's economy grew at a rate of over 10 per cent in 2006 and 2007 and at around 5 per cent during the years following the 2008 financial crisis.

27. The conflict in Darfur, a region in western Sudan, broke out in 2003 between Arab tribes (with funding and weapons provided by Khartoum's Arab regime) and the black population, who accused the Arab political elite of racial oppression. This racial conflict between Arabs and the region's black population has led to 300,000 deaths and forced over 2.5 million people to leave their homes. The United States has classified the events as 'genocide'. Between 2009 and 2010, the International Criminal Court (ICC) of the United Nations issued international arrest warrants against President al-Bashir for alleged war crimes and five other crimes against humanity in Darfur. China has used its power of abstention at the UN Security Council to reduce the international pressure on al-Bashir's regime on several occasions, and has also publicly voiced its opposition to the arrest of the Sudanese president. Al-Bashir travelled to China in June 2011 and was received with great ceremony by President Hu Jintao, angering human rights groups and United Nations' officials.

28. 'China's growing role in African peace and security', *SAFERWORLD*, January 2011, pp. 49–53.

29. China tried unsuccessfully to stop this information from filtering through to the press in October 2010. 'China tries to block Darfur weapons report', Ewan MacAskill, *Guardian*, 21 October 2010.

30. *BP Statistical Review of World Energy*, op. cit.

31. The tactic used by some Western oil companies is to stay in Iran 'finishing off old contracts', but nobody dares to start working on any new projects. 'It's a strategic way of staying in the country in case the situation improves,' a source working in the sector told the authors.

32. The US State Department places the total value of investments cancelled in Iran's oil sector as a result of American sanctions at between $50 and $60 billion. 'Iran's Chinese Energy Partners', Mark Dubovitz and Laura Grossman, Foundation for Defense of Democracies, September 2010, p. 3.

33. According to experts consulted on the subject, Chinese oil technology is rudimentary. One of its weaker areas is the production of liquefied natural gas (LNG). This is the process of converting natural gas into liquid gas, allowing it to be transported for long distances in shipping tankers in the absence of a gas pipeline. Tehran urgently needs to exploit its offshore South Pars gas field because Iran 'shares' gas with neighbouring Qatar, a country that is currently exploiting this gas on a greater scale. Despite the fact that experts estimate that China will take 'several years or even decades' to catch up with its Western rivals, CNPC took over

from Total at South Pars 11 in 2009 after the French company, which had originally secured the contract to exploit these resources, pulled out of the project. Some sources argue that Total was forced to pull out as a result of pressure from the United States.

34. From its internationally isolated position, Iran's official figures regarding foreign investment tend to exaggerate the real amount of capital flowing into the country. For example, the Iranian press estimated the value of energy contracts signed by Chinese companies since 2005 at $120 billion. However, experts reject this figure. The real value of Chinese investments in Iran's energy sector is likely to be closer to the $40 billion announced by Iran's deputy oil minister, Hossein Noqrehkar Shirazi. As for China, the usual lack of transparency is at work. When the authors contacted the three Chinese oil companies (CNPC, Sinopec and CNOOC), none of them was prepared to give an interview or provide any information about their operations in Iran. Source: 'China invests $40 billion in Iran's energy sector', *Tehran Times*, 1 August 2010.

35. 'The Impact of Iran Sanctions Six Months In', Trevor Houser, Rhodium Group, 27 June 2012.

36. Iran currently produces around 4 million barrels of oil each day. However, it is estimated that unless the Islamic Republic invests $120 billion by 2015 this figure could fall to 2.7 million barrels. 'Iran's Chinese Energy Partners', op. cit., p. 6.

37. The preamble to resolution 1929 of the UN Security Council, which was supported by China's vote, admits 'the potential connection between Iran's revenues derived from its energy sector and the funding of Iran's proliferation-sensitive nuclear activities'.

38. 'US embassy cables: China and US compare notes on how to handle Iran', *Guardian*, 29 November 2010.

39. 'Iran's Chinese Energy Partners', op. cit., p.3.

40. 'How do you deal toughly with your banker?' the US Secretary of State is said to have asked the then prime minister of Australia Kevin Rudd, according to WikiLeaks. Here Hillary Clinton is referring to China's influence at the White House as a result of being the largest foreign holder of American debt, with an estimated total of $1.1 trillion in US Treasury bonds. In spite of this, in January 2012 the United States imposed sanctions on the Chinese state-owned petrochemical company Zhuhai Zhenrong, which Washington says is the largest supplier of refined petroleum products to Iran. Although a small player compared to the big Chinese majors, Beijing reacted angrily to the sanctions. Sources: 'WikiLeaks: Hillary Clinton's question: how can we stand up to Beijing?',

Ewen MacAskill, *Guardian*, 4 December 2010; 'China seen as risk as holdings surpass $1 trillion', Reuters, 1 March 2011.

41. In 2012 Luanda was placed second, after Tokyo, as the most expensive capital city in the world, according to the consulting firm Mercer. An expat employee at an international organization in Luanda told us that despite a US$10,000 monthly corporate budget to subsidize the rent on his home, 'I still have to pay out at least 15,000 dollars to get access to an apartment that meets international standards, with hot water and 24-hour electricity.' When the authors visited the capital, they were unable to find any accommodation for less than $300 per night for a double room. This is all down to the country's economic boom caused by the development of the oil industry (including its more harmful effects), the limited services on offer and the absence of any local manufacturing industry – the legacy of twenty-seven years of war – which means that Angola is forced to import all of its goods.

42. Angola produced 1.7 million barrels of crude oil a day in 2011, exceeded only by Nigeria. *BP Statistical Review of World Energy*, June 2012. The information on Angola's oil income is taken from the article 'The new imperialism: China in Angola', by Rafael Marques de Morais, *World Affairs Journal*, March/April 2011.

43. Dos Santos has been in power for over thirty years. In Angola's last elections in 2010, he won a landslide victory with 82 per cent of the votes.

44. The model used by China in Angola and throughout the rest of Africa is copied from Japan, which carried out numerous projects in China in the 1970s and 1980s in return for Chinese oil.

45. In her book on China's role in Africa, *The Dragon's Gift*, Deborah Brautigam argues that Germany was the first country to lift the pressure on Angola, by unilaterally writing off the country's debt in 2003. *The Dragon's Gift: The Real History of China in Africa* (Oxford University Press, 2009), p. 275.

46. 'Thirst for African Oil: Asian National Oil Companies in Nigeria and Angola', Alex Vines, Lillian Wong, Markus Weimer and Indira Campos, Chatham House Report, August 2009.

47. The Angolan state-owned oil company Sonangol used its right to veto in order to grant the block to Sinopec, despite the fact that Shell had selected as a successor the Indian state-owned Oil and Natural Gas Corporation Limited (ONGC) to take up 50 per cent of the shares. 'China in Angola: an emerging energy partnership', Paul Hare, *China Brief*, 6, May 2007.

48. 'The main factor in the success of the strategies used by Chinese oil companies in Angola is the interconnection between business and diplomacy',

argues one of the best reports written on bilateral relations between the two countries. 'Thirst for African Oil', op. cit. Figures provided by the Chinese ambassador in Luanda, Zhang Bolun. Source: 'China lends Angola $15 bn but creates few jobs', Agence France-Presse, 9 March 2011.

49. Based on publicly announced figures, experts estimate that CIF has lent a total of between $2.9 and $9 billion to Luanda in credit to be repaid with oil. 'Thirst for African Oil', op. cit.

50. For a detailed diagram showing the composition of the conglomerate and its associates, see 'Thirst for African Oil', op. cit., p. 86.

51. CSIH and SSI (a company which is part-owned by a subsidiary of the Chinese state-owned company Sinopec) own shares in eight out of the twenty-nine oil blocks which Luanda has put out to international tender since June 2011. Source: www.sonangol.co.ao.

52. Many African experts see Guinea as a 'narco-state', acting as a bridge on the drugs route between Latin America and Europe. It is here that CIF and CSIH have jointly signed a contract with the military junta led by Captain Moussa Dadis Camara to build infrastructure worth $7 billion in return for exploiting the country's mineral reserves. The agreement was made on 28 September 2009, just days after Camara's troops killed over 150 civilians and raped dozens of women while suppressing a demonstration at Conakry's main stadium. In Zimbabwe, the two companies jointly signed an agreement with Robert Mugabe's regime in November 2009 to exploit the country's platinum and gold mines and oil resources, in exchange for an $8 billion investment in infrastructure. In both cases, the Chinese state-owned company South Locomotive and Rolling Stock Corporation (CSR) participated in the agreements by supplying material. Source: 'CIF, Beijing's stalking horse', *Africa-Asia Confidential*, 3 (7), May 2010.

53. 'The Chinese government has nothing to do with the business [carried out by CIF], and does not know any details about the company,' the spokesperson for the Chinese Foreign Office Ma Zhaoxu said on 19 October 2010. In an interview in Beijing, ambassador Liu Guijin, China's special representative on African affairs, assured the authors that 'CIF is definitely a Hong Kong-based private business company. I don't think the government can have any kind of relationship with it or ask the CIF to front the interests of the Chinese government. There is no such understanding or links ... The CIF is a headache for me and my [government] colleagues because there are so many negative comments and reports ... I am also trying to understand why they are so influential in Angola or Guinea. Maybe it's because they are a private company and

can use all kinds of measures to try to get contracts from the governments there. But [Chinese state-owned oil companies] based in mainland China are restricted by government regulations and cannot act freely . . . They have to consider the impact on relations between the two countries.' Source: 'CIF, Beijing's stalking horse', op. cit.

54. Born in Algeria, Pierre Falcone is an influential middleman who in the past has lent his services, via his various companies, in the negotiation of oil and arms contracts. He can currently be found in a French prison after being sentenced to six years' imprisonment for his role, along with the son of the former French president François Mitterrand, in the sale of illegal arms to Angola in the 1990s. He is linked to the binomial CIF-CSIH through his consultancy company, Pierson Asia.

55. 'Data reveal huge sums spirited out of Angola', Reuters, 4 April 2011.

56. This is the address of both the Ministry of Public Security and the headquarters of the Chinese foreign intelligence services. Source: 'The 88 Queensway Group: A Case Study in Chinese Investors' Operations in Angola and Beyond', Lee Levkovitz et al., U.S.–China Economic & Security Review Commission, 10 July 2009.

57. As well as the presence of Sonangol's president, Manuel Vicente, on the board of directors for various companies linked to CIF, the Angolan president's son, José Filomeno 'Zenu' Dos Santos, is CSIH's representative in Angola.

58. 'CIF, Beijing's stalking horse', op. cit.

59. Venezuela possesses the world's greatest crude oil reserves, particularly in the Orinoco Belt area to the south-east of the country. *BP Statistical Review of World Energy*, op. cit.

60. *El Poder y el Delirio* [Power and Delirium], Enrique Krauze (Tusquets, 2008).

61. Ibid., p. 278.

62. As is often the case in Venezuela, the conditions of these loans are somewhat opaque. The authors managed to gain access to part of the contract and confirmed that half of CDB's $20 billion loan is provided in dollars while the rest is provided in yuan. The repayment is to be made with oil over a ten-year period and represents 'the first time that Venezuela seems to be making a long-term commitment in terms of its oil', according to experts consulted by the authors on the subject.

Beatriz de Majo, an expert on relations between the two countries, explained to the authors that China has tied its loan to the purchase of its own products: this is partly done by granting half of the total amount in yuan, which must be spent entirely on Chinese products and services.

In terms of the remaining $10 billion, de Majo asserted that '40 per cent will go towards Sino-Venezuelan projects while China will control the remaining 60 per cent'. In other words, Beijing will decide what this money will be spent on.

In terms of arms sales, China has managed to sell eighteen K-8 fighter aircraft to Venezuela, a country that has embarked on an arms race worth billions of dollars in recent years, with invaluable support from Russia.

63. Venezuela's oil reserves are the largest on the planet. Experts estimate that the reserves are 'infinite', in the sense that by the time the world stops using oil as its main energy source as a result of the development and pre-eminence of alternative forms of energy, Venezuela will still possess reserves of crude oil in the Orinoco Belt. It costs the same to fill a car's petrol tank for a year in Venezuela as it does to fill it just once in Europe.

64. Sales of Venezuelan crude oil to the United States have fallen significantly in recent years. Although Washington still buys an estimated 45 per cent of Venezuela's crude oil, or around a million barrels per day, this figure has been known to reach 1.5 million barrels per day in the past.

Caracas argues that it wants to diversify its markets in order to become less dependent on the United States, although some former collaborators close to Chávez told the authors that 'it would be a crime to lose the United States with its premium market just to give it all up to another country [China] at a discounted rate'. The reason behind this argument is the cost of transporting the oil, which is usually paid for by the supplier. These costs are much smaller when transporting oil to the United States (where it takes five days to arrive) than to China (forty-five days). Other countries selected by Chávez's government to help reduce dependency on the West include Belarus, Iran and Russia.

65. As well as the January 2010 investment, China has other oil supply contracts in Venezuela. These contracts relate to certifying oil reserves in the Orinoco Belt, buying residues and other marginal investments or investments that were made before Chávez came to power.

66. Crude oil production has fallen dramatically over recent years. Before Chávez came to power, Venezuela produced 3.6 barrels of oil per day; according to official figures, that figure has now dropped to 3.1 million barrels. However, the International Energy Agency and other secondary sources believe that the real production figure is closer to 2.7 million barrels per day. This decline in production has dramatic implications for Venezuela's economy because of its great dependency on the oil sector.

The productive sector has been hit very hard by *chavista* policies, including the expropriation of 3 million hectares of land and over 400 companies. 'Venezuela, a good deal from China?', *Financial Times*, 16 March 2011.

67. China currently imports around half its oil supplies from the Middle East. Beijing has been working hard to diversify its energy sector, travelling to every corner of the planet with the aim of ensuring that the instability of the Middle East will not be able to damage China's energy security.

    Despite its second-rate technology, China has made a dramatic entry into Venezuela's Orinoco Belt. As such, CNCP is an associate of PDVSA in Junín 4 block, where the oil company will invest $16 billion to extract 400,000 barrels per day. Sinopec, meanwhile, is an associate of PDVSA in the exploitation of Junín 1 and Junín 8, where it aims to extract 200,000 barrels per day.

    The progress made by Chinese – and Russian – oil companies in Venezuela is a result of the reluctance shown by Western companies to invest in the country because of the legal insecurity caused by Chávez's regime. This is particularly true since the wave of nationalizations in 2007, when American companies such as ExxonMobil and Conoco-Phillips decided to leave the country. The limited interest shown in the tenders by other nations has led Caracas to turn to Russia and China for new investments in the oil sector, according to two former presidents of PDVSA interviewed for this book.

68. In 2011 PDVSA generated an income over $124 billion while its total investments in 2010 exceeded $11 billion.

69. Orimulsion is a technique used to mix low-quality extra-heavy crude oil – which dominates Venezuela's oil reserves – with water, allowing it to be transported in cargo ships. This type of oil can be used to generate electricity and is sold at the same price as coal, because of its extremely low quality and because the costs of refining it into a high-quality product are very high.

70. Enrique Krauze estimates that 'the gifts given by Chávez to the world amounted to 33 billion dollars between 1999 and 2007': *El Poder y el Delirio*, op. cit., p. 294.

71. Source: '*Cuba y China consolidan su alianza estratégica*' ['Cuba and China consolidate their strategic alliance'], Mauricio Vicent, *El País*, 8 June 2011.

72. In July 2011 Hugo Chávez announced that he had been diagnosed with cancer, which left the country's political future in a state of obvious uncertainty. Citing medical records provided by unnamed intelligence sources, Spain's *ABC* newspaper reported in January 2012 that Chávez's

cancer had metastasized and that his life expectancy was only nine months.

5 THE FOUNDATIONS OF THE CHINESE WORLD

1. Led by the president's right-hand man, Osama Abdullah, the DIU is a highly powerful organization in Sudan. It handles enormous budgets, manages infrastructure projects and has its own security forces, which have been accused of carrying out massacres linked to protests led by people affected by the dams. Recently elevated to form the Ministry of Electricity and Dams, the organization continues to operate under the direct supervision of President al-Bashir. Sources: 'Black Gold for Blue Gold? Sudan's Oil, Ethiopia's Water and Regional Integration', Harry Verhoeven, Chatham House Report, June 2011; 'Climate change, conflict and development in Sudan: neo-Malthusian global narratives and local power struggles', Harry Verhoeven, *Development and Change*, 42 (3), 2011.

2. The authors originally approached Sinohydro, the main contractor for the Merowe Dam, to request a permit allowing them to visit the dam's facilities. However, the words of Peng, the head of the Chinese company in Sudan, to the authors' Chinese guide made it perfectly clear how he felt about helping them: 'I don't like foreigners. The Americans and the English say lots of bad things about China. It's a shame that you've come here with foreigners, because if you had come alone we would definitely have taken you to Merowe,' he said, right in front of the authors, in his office in Khartoum. After he refused permission, the authors applied for a permit from the DIU.

3. The analyst Harry Verhoeven argues that Khartoum is committing to the development of dams and the rebirth of agriculture for two purposes: first, to bring electricity to the capital and northern Sudan in order to fuel industrial projects; and, secondly, to facilitate the agricultural irrigation that will allow Sudan to become involved in 'the global food crisis debate', providing the regime with new opportunities and agro-dollars from Islamic countries interested in this type of investment. The real beneficiaries of this model will most likely be Khartoum's Islamic elite.

4. Between 2004 and 2007, clashes between the people affected by the dam and the security forces led to an unspecified number of deaths and injuries as well as frequent confrontations, imprisonments and repressive measures, according to activists working in the area. In 2006, an Amri village was flooded with no prior warning, 'so that the people had to run

out of their houses like rats', according to a local leader. It is also rumoured that there were fresh outbreaks of violence in 2009.

5. In his 2007 presentation 'Lethal Partnership: China Investment Destroying African Communities: The Case of the Merowe Dam, Sudan', the activist Ali Askouri argued that the poverty rate among the affected communities had risen from 10 per cent to 60 per cent. This was four years after work on the dam began and two years before its conclusion. When the authors interviewed him in Khartoum, Askouri assured them that many of the younger displaced people had migrated to the cities, and particularly to the capital, where they were forced to beg in order to survive.

6. Other sources interviewed in Sudan estimated that the number of people affected was actually between 70,000 and 74,000. In the summer of 2010, around 600 families were still refusing to be relocated.

7. The lack of clarity surrounding the Merowe Dam prevented the authors from finding out precise details about the project. However, it is common knowledge that China has played a decisive role in both its financing and construction. During the authors' visit to the area, Awad told them that 'the Chinese are involved in the new infrastructure and the villages for the relocated people and in the new hospital project.'

8. The fact that Chinese companies carry out their foreign construction projects using their own contingent of employees who work extremely long hours and rarely leave the building site has fuelled the myth that China is using prisoners as free labour. Some critics have even publicly denounced this practice, without providing any evidence whatsoever. Over the course of their investigation on the ground, the authors did not come across any proof to support this accusation.

9. One of the most important of the nine new dams that the Chinese are helping to build is the Kajbar Dam based on the Nile's third waterfall. In this project, the Exim Bank is providing 75 per cent of the funding, while Sinohydro will carry out the construction work in a project that is expected to cost $800 million. Furthermore, a Chinese company will be the main contractor in another controversial project, the Roseires Dam on the Blue Nile.

10. At the beginning of the project, the dam had an official budget of $1.8 billion, $519 million of which would be financed by the Exim Bank. But the project's official website states that China has provided $608 million out of the $2.381 billion which the dam has actually cost. The website also says that the Sudanese government financed another $550 million, while various Arab funds from the Persian Gulf provided the remainder of the total costs. However, in December 2010 the Sudanese minister of finance

publicly announced that the total cost of Merowe had reached $3.5 billion, while sources consulted by the authors in Khartoum estimated that the actual amount could exceed $5 billion. Amid such a tangle of figures and lack of transparency, it is difficult to tell whether or not China has actually contributed a greater amount of funding than it officially admits to providing.

11. http://www.internationalrivers.org/campaigns/sinohydro-corporation.

12. A report carried out by the *Financial Times* showed that the two Chinese development banks granted loans worth at least $110 billion in 2009 and 2010, while the World Bank granted $100 billion between mid-2008 and mid-2010. Source: 'China's lending hits new heights', Geoff Dyer and Jamil Anderlini, *Financial Times*, 17 January 2011.

13. There is no denying the fact that the Three Gorges Dam has had a positive impact in terms of the volume of electricity generated, flood control and the navigability of the river. However, the project has been fiercely criticized for its environmental impact, the destruction of a cultural legacy and the traumatic forced relocation of 1.7 million people. A report published by Chinese scientists in 2010 demonstrated that the number of earthquakes in the regions close to the dam had multiplied by thirty since 2003, when work began on filling the dam's 600 square kilometre reservoir. Some sources have linked the dam to the effects of the powerful earthquake that devastated the Chinese region of Sichuan in May 2008, causing the deaths of almost 90,000 people. Source: 'China's admission spotlights Three Gorges woes', Dan Martin, Agence France-Presse, 29 June 2011.

14. In May 2010, Ali Askouri and the European Centre for Constitutional and Human Rights (ECCHR) presented a lawsuit at a court in Frankfurt against various executives from the German company Lahmeyer International. Like the French company Alstom and the Swiss ABB, the company was involved in the Merowe Dam project. The lawsuit, which is still pending resolution (the hearing of witnesses is due to start at the end of 2012), was presented as a result of the German company's alleged role in the flooding of villages close to Merowe which forced thousands of families to lose their homes and caused the death of hundreds of thousands of cattle. In 2006, the German company was also excluded from receiving World Bank contracts during a seven-year period as a result of corruption.

15. According to several sources consulted in Sudan, the opaqueness and the immunity from scrutiny enjoyed by Chinese companies make them ideal associates in the web of corruption which allegedly lies behind the

Merowe project. Ali Askouri argued that 'the whole point of the dam was to make room for corruption', while environmental expert Asim al-Moghrabi made the following statement: 'Why has this dam been built? The answer is plain and simple: because of corruption. The Chinese are corrupt and we're corrupt. We can't hold the Chinese responsible for having been contracted to do a job, but we can hold them responsible for being corrupt.' The lack of transparency in terms of the total cost of the project, which was budgeted at $1.8 billion but ran to an estimated final cost of around $5 billion, clearly supports the hypothesis that Merowe was in fact a front for a money laundering network. An American diplomatic cable published by WikiLeaks referred to evidence of corruption which the International Criminal Court's Chief Prosecutor, Luis Moreno Ocampo, was said to have against President al-Bashir, who allegedly possesses $9 billion in savings stashed away in secret foreign bank accounts. Source: 'WikiLeaks: Sudanese president "stashed $9bn in UK banks"', Afua Hirsch, *Guardian*, 17 December 2010.

16. Out of all the Chinese dam projects at the eye of the storm in 2011, the most striking of all is the Gibe III Dam in Ethiopia. The Industrial and Commercial Bank of China (ICBC) agreed to finance $500 million to provide equipment to build this dam, which will affect half a million people as well as impacting on areas classified as World Heritage sites by UNESCO. The World Bank, the African Development Bank and the European Investment Bank all refused to take part in a project considered to be 'the most destructive' of all the dams under construction across the world, according to International Rivers.

17. Source: '李福胜: 海外投资要关切当地抱怨' ['Li Fusheng: Overseas investment should care about the local complaint'], *Global Times*, 11 January 2011 [in Mandarin].

18. According to various interviews carried out in Ecuador, the loan consisted of $1.682 billion to be repaid over fifteen years with a five-and-a-half-year deferral period and a 6.9 per cent interest rate. This figure represents 85 per cent of the budgeted cost of the dam, as the Chinese side demanded that the Ecuadorian state should fund the other 15 per cent. However, Quito was able to provide the $300 million needed thanks to a previous loan agreed between the two countries for $1 billion, which means that China effectively financed 100 per cent of the dam.

19. Ecuador's strategic sectors minister, Jorge Glas, announced that there are currently fifteen planned projects in which China may soon be participating with its companies and funding. In September 2010 a consortium led by China Gezhouba Group closed a $672 million contract to build a

mine in the Latin American country, which would be partially financed by the Chinese Exim Bank. Meanwhile, Rafael Quintero, the Ecuadorian under secretary of foreign affairs responsible for Asia, Africa and Oceania, told the authors that 'Ecuador needs infrastructure in order to diversify our industry, and so we are interested in Chinese investments in hydroelectric power stations, petrochemical complexes and the modernization of our ports.' Quito and Beijing are reportedly in conversations over the partial financing of the country's biggest infrastructure project to date, the so-called Pacific Refinery, an installation which requires an investment of $12.5 billion.

20. 'China has an enormous capacity for investments, which is what our country needs. Furthermore, we need investments which don't make us overly dependent, and which don't come with too many conditions. We are working to ensure that the investments that come into our country aren't reliant on the support of the IMF or the World Bank, which have restricted the development of our country over recent decades,' said Ricardo Patiño, the chancellor of Correa's government, when the authors interviewed him in Quito.

A combination of two factors risks leading Ecuador into a dangerous position of international isolation: first, the country's refusal to ask for help from traditional financial institutions and, secondly, its dependency on China. 'While Chinese financing in infrastructure projects has played an important role given the lack of [Ecuador's own] public funds, it also highlights the lack of alternative financing available', argues the *Ecuador Infrastructure Report Q4 2010* by Business Monitor International.

21. *Ecuador Infrastructure Report Q4 2010*, op. cit.

22. The Ecuadorian mining sector has an enormous amount of potential but is 'frozen' pending the approval of an appropriate legal framework. Nevertheless, in 2011 the Canada-based mining company Ecuacorriente, controlled by China Railway Construction Corporation and another Chinese company, Tongling Nonferrous Metals Group, announced its plans to invest $2.8 billion in a copper project in Ecuador. This investment will include the construction of a hydroelectric plant, several bridges and roads as well as a port. Source: 'DJ Ecuacorriente plans to invest $2.8 b in Ecuador up to 2016', Dow Jones, 29 March 2011.

Furthermore, the $2 billion loan was granted by the China Development Bank. The total amount of Chinese loans granted to Ecuador amounts to around $7 billion. Source: 'China, Ecuador sign $2 billion loan deal', *Wall Street Journal*, 28 June 2011.

23. This is a reference to the 'go out strategy', the official directive given by the Chinese government to its companies in order to encourage them to go out to foreign markets.

24. 'China's Foreign Aid', Information Office of the State Council of the People's Republic of China, April 2011.

    The 2,025 projects mentioned in the report are included under the title 'Complete Projects', one of eight categories of foreign aid. 'Complete projects' refers to 'productive or civil projects constructed in recipient countries with the help of financial resources provided by China ... The Chinese side is responsible for the whole or part of the process, from studies and surveys to design and construction, provides all or part of the equipment and building materials, and sends engineers and technical personnel to organize and guide the construction, installation and trial production of these projects. After a project is completed, China hands it over to the recipient country.' According to the report, this type of project makes up 40 per cent of China's total expenditure on foreign aid. Among other projects mentioned in the document, the most striking involve the construction of 85 sporting complexes, 201 transport infrastructure projects and 236 scientific, educational or health complexes.

    Beijing anticipates three types of financial resources for foreign aid: subsidies, which are mainly put towards humanitarian aid and the construction of hospitals, schools, low-cost housing and water-supply projects; interest-free loans, which are planned for developing countries and which normally include five years of use, a five-year deferral period and a ten-year repayment period; and concessional loans, which are awarded by the Exim Bank with low interest rates and a repayment period of between fifteen and twenty years. Beijing had granted concessional loans for 325 projects in 76 countries by 2009, according to the report.

25. Sources differ on the total number of stadiums that China has built in Africa. A note from the Agence France-Presse agency in 2010 stated that fifty-two stadiums had been built in Africa with Chinese financing, basing its estimate on sources taken from the Chinese media. During their travels, the authors witnessed the construction of Chinese stadiums in Ndola (Zambia), Luanda (Angola) and Maputo (Mozambique). Source: http://www.elmercurio.com.ec/240591-china-levanta-las-infraestructuras-depor tivas-de-africa.html, accessed 27 May 2010.

26. The name of Anhui Wai Jing's subsidiary company in Costa Rica is Chinafecc Central America.

27. The authors came across another example of this attitude at the National Stadium in Maputo, which was also built by Anhui Wai Jing. The academics Jorgen Carling and Heidi Ostbo Haugen describe a similar matter involving Chinese construction companies in Cape Verde in 'Mixed fates of a popular minority: Chinese migrants in Cape Verde', in *China Returns to Africa: A Rising Power and a Continent Embrace*, eds. Chris Alden, Daniel Large and Ricardo Soares de Oliveira (Hurst, 2008), p. 327.

28. Source: http://www.diariolasamericas.com/noticia/102566/o/o/empresa-china-abandona-proyecto-inmobiliario-privado-tras. The news item is based on a note from the EFE agency.

29. In 2011, Argentina ranked 113 out of 183 in the World Bank's index measuring how easy it is to do business around the world. Source: World Bank, Doing Business project (http://www.doingbusiness.org/).

30. Argentina, a country roughly the size of India with a population of barely 40 million people, is the world's third largest soya producer after the United States and Brazil. It is also the world's largest exporter of soybean oil and soya flour, the last of which is a very important component in animal feed for pigs and chickens, as well as other animals.

     When the authors interviewed Darío Genua and Guillermo Villagra, the directors of Open Agro, an Argentinian consultancy specializing in agricultural investments in the Latin American country, they said that Argentina has the clear potential to become the breadbasket of China, as the country currently 'only develops 73 per cent of its productive land. With that it produces enough food for between 350 and 400 million people, but this amount could be increased.' According to Open Agro, Argentina annually produces 50 million tons of soya, 30 million tons of corn and 10 million tons of wheat, as well as sunflowers, rapeseed and other types of crop. Argentina currently exports 90 per cent of its total produce.

31. The food price index produced by the Food and Agriculture Organization of the United Nations reached 238 points in February 2011, the highest level since the FAO began measuring the growth of food prices. While the authors were updating this chapter in August 2012, international prices were still very close to their all-time high. International observers and analysts suggest that the 2011 uprisings in the Arab world were partly due to dissatisfaction among the middle classes as a result of the rise in food prices. Source: 'How much is enough?', *The Economist*, 24 February 2011; 'Drought forces reductions in U.S. crop forecasts', *New York Times*, 10 August 2012.

32. According to this source, food products make up 70 per cent of Argentina's total exports to China, with soya and soya derivatives as the most important products. This situation was affected by a dispute between the two countries after Beijing decided to ban imports of Argentinian soya in 2010, claiming that the product was of low quality. However, this was China's reprisal for the numerous anti-dumping actions that Argentina had made against China at the World Trade Organization. Consequently, Argentina's exports of soya and soya derivatives dropped sharply: in 2009, Argentina exported 1.9 million tons of soybean oil to the Asian country (77 per cent of its total imports), a figure which fell abruptly to 224,000 tons in 2010. Argentina has made up for this drop in exports by increasing sales to India, although India pays a lower price for the produce. The impact on Argentina is highly significant as soya makes up 30 per cent of Argentina's fiscal income, and is known as 'Argentina's fiscal miracle' in the country.

33. China is currently self-sufficient in 95 per cent of its food supplies. Experts place the 'red line' for food security at a minimum of 120 million hectares; in other words, this is the minimum amount of Chinese arable land necessary to feed the Chinese people. However, sources such as Professor Zheng suspect that this line has already been crossed, as provincial governments do not pass on accurate figures to Beijing regarding the amount of arable land, as the countryside is becoming increasingly urbanized each year. Corruption and the provincial governments' prioritization of economic growth play a vital role in this issue.

34. China's National Bureau of Statistics announced in January 2012 that urban population had surpassed that of rural areas for the first time. The urbanization process is far from over, as a mass exodus of rural workers to the towns is currently taking place as a result of the significant difference in income between the towns and the countryside. Recent studies suggest that over 250 million rural workers live currently in Chinese cities. Professor Zheng estimates that an urban worker earns on average 3.3 times more than a rural worker. This is partly due to the control of food prices carried out by the Chinese government through its state-owned companies: the companies exercise an almost monopolistic control over the initial stages of the sector, thereby guaranteeing stable supplies of rice, wheat, soya, pork and other types of food. 'Chinese state-owned companies buy produce from the rural workers when the prices are very low. They store this produce, and when the prices rise they inject the market with the necessary quantity for the prices to drop

again,' explained Professor Zhou Deyi of the Agricultural University of Huazhong when the authors met him in Beijing.

In this way, the government can fight inflation hitting the Chinese food sector, which could potentially lead to protests that could threaten the survival of the government authorities. This is a very real danger, as is shown as much by past social tensions in China as by the 2010 and 2011 uprisings in the Arab world. Beijing is hitting rural workers hard in order to control food prices, as rural workers have seen a reduction in their income, Zheng tells us. 'The government has decided to prioritize the demands of China's urban population, which wants low prices, at the expense of the rural workers.'

35. *Il Nuovo Colonialism: Caccia Alle Terre Coltivabili* [The New Colonialism: A Hunt for Arable Land], Franca Roiatti (Egea, 2010), p. 11.

36. The ecologist Lester Brown, founder and president of the Earth Policy Institute, estimates that 130 million Chinese people are being fed today thanks to the overexploitation of freshwater resources, such as underground waters. He further estimates that each time the Earth's temperature increases by one centigrade as a result of global warming, the world's grain harvests fall by 10 per cent. Source: 'The new geopolitics of food', Lester Brown, *Foreign Policy*, May–June 2011.

37. As well as buying land in north-east Brazil, China is currently carrying out other initiatives to gain a certain amount of control over the Latin American food chain. Chinese companies have therefore reacted to the government's limits on the acquisition of arable land by making investments, such as the one in Rio Negro, which allow them to improve infrastructure in order to boost the food supply chain, especially in terms of soya production.

The state-owned Chinese companies are reportedly in discussion with at least six Brazilian states (Bahía, Goiás, Santa Catarina, Rio Grande do Sul, Tocantins and Mato Grosso) to guarantee their ability to buy soya directly from the producers in order to avoid the volatile and insecure market. The biggest investment so far is being carried out by the Chinese state-owned company Sanhe Hopeful, which is reportedly prepared to invest $7.6 billion over the next decade in order to boost agriculture and logistics in the Goiás state in return for guaranteeing an annual supply of 6 million tons of soya. Source: '*Chineses investem na soja brasileira*' ['Chinese invest in Brazilian soya'], *Folha de São Paulo*, 3 April 2011.

38. The Golden Triangle Special Economic Zone required an investment of 3 billion yuan, or 300 million euros, which was used to build hotels and

casinos throughout the 3,000-hectare area. A jetty on the Mekong river was also built in order to welcome customers to the zone. A second phase is scheduled to include the construction of a golf course, swimming pools, shopping centres, karaoke bars, massage centres and other leisure hubs. The concession is granted for ninety-nine years and the total investment for the project's various phases is predicted to rise to $2.25 billion by 2020, the equivalent of double the Laotian government's national budget. The UN has expressed its fears that the SEZ will become an epicentre of money laundering for drug traffickers as a result of its proximity to the Golden Triangle. Source: 'High stakes as Laos turns to casinos', *South China Morning Post*, 23 January 2011.

6 THE NEW VICTIMS OF THE 'FACTORY OF THE WORLD'

1. The company's full name in *pinyin* is Anhui Wai Jing She Ji Tuan; its English translation is Anhui Foreign Economic Construction (Group) Co. Created in 1992, the company undertakes infrastructure projects throughout the world and has offices in fourteen countries in Asia, Africa, Europe, the Caribbean and the South Pacific. For more information, see http://www.afecc.com/.

2. In a tender with other Chinese companies, the state-owned Anhui Wai Jing was awarded the contract to build Maputo's National Stadium, a project with an initial cost of 400 million yuan (42 million euros). Work began in November 2008 and was completed two years later. The authors visited the site in August 2010 when Anhui Wai Jing was also involved in other projects in the country, such as the airport in the capital city. Sources in the country consulted by the authors pointed out that the stadium was a gift from China as a result of Mozambique's enormous potential in the agribusiness, timber, mining and oil sectors.

3. Jiang Ning said that, as well as the 260 Chinese employees working at the stadium, the number of Mozambican workers on Anhui Wai Jing's payroll has fluctuated between 150 and 250 over the course of the two-year building project, according to the company's needs. For companies with over 100 employees, article 31 of Mozambique's labour law fixes the maximum quota of foreign workers at 5 per cent of the workforce, a proportion which the Chinese have systematically sidestepped thanks to the exception made by the law when the work is classified as 'in the public interest'. João Feijó, a sociologist who was just completing a comparative study on labour conditions in Mozambique when the

authors met him in August 2010, stated that he has not come across any Chinese companies where 'at least 30 per cent of the workforce wasn't Chinese'.

4. According to João Feijó, a sociologist and labour expert based in Maputo, 'a Portuguese, Italian or South African company would pay at least 6,000 meticais, or around 130 euros for the same role.'

5. This figure is provided by a Mozambican union which based its calculations on the costs incurred by a family of five over the course of one month. These costs include transport, coal, water, rice, cooking oil, tomatoes and other vegetables. The list does not include costs which are non-essential for survival, such as meat, fish, clothes, medical treatment and schooling.

6. Based on the authors' numerous interviews with Chinese employers and officials, pay discrimination in favour of Chinese workers over local workers seems to be justified in the eyes of Chinese companies as compensation for the personal cost of having to leave their country, environment and family for several years. It also stems from the practically unanimous opinion that Chinese employees work harder, better, faster and with more discipline than the locals, therefore making them more productive. This line of reasoning, which many times is backed up by reality, is often expressed using arguments that incorporate racist connotations, as the authors confirmed during their interviews with these sources.

7. Telephone conversation with a representative of Anhui Wai Jing at the company's headquarters in China, 26 October 2010.

8. The 'China–Africa Friendship Award – Top 10 Chinese Enterprises in Africa' was granted to Anhui Wai Jing in January 2011. The prize is awarded by China's Ministry of Foreign Affairs and the Chinese–African People's Friendship Association, among other organizations.

9. While in Mozambique, the authors listened to the complaints of local workers on other Chinese building sites in the country. For example, on the 95-kilometre road that the state-owned China Henan International Co-operation Group is building between Xai-Xai and Chisbuka in southern Mozambique, several workers complained of low salaries (25 cents for each hour worked), the lack of contracts and insurance, the company's refusal to pay travel expenses to help their employees get to work, their bosses' harsh treatment, and the lack of adequate equipment. When the authors spoke to the company, they denied that there were any problems at the site.

10. João Feijó, 'Relações sino-moçambicanas em context organizacional: uma análise de empresas em Maputo' ['Sino-Mozambican relations in

the context of organizations: an analysis of companies in Maputo'], in *A construção Social do Outro: perspectivas cruzadas sobre estrangeiros e moçambicanos* [The Social Construction of the Other: Mixed Perspectives on Foreigners and Mozambicans], ed. Carlos Serra (Imprensa Universitária, Maputo, 2010), pp. 245–316. The study includes thirty-four interviews with Chinese and Mozambican workers at eight Chinese companies in the Mozambican capital.

11. The 'Copperbelt' is the official name of Zambia's mining province, which harbours one of the word's largest reserves of copper and cobalt.

12. The TAZARA project (Tanzania-Zambia Railway Authority), which began in 1970 and was completed five years later, required an enormous amount of effort on the part of the 25,000 Chinese and additional 50,000 Tanzanian and Zambian workers involved. The project included building 300 bridges, 23 tunnels and 147 stations along the length of the route. In its day, TAZARA was seen as the biggest Chinese co-operation project ever carried out on foreign territory, and Beijing and many African countries still see the project as a symbol of the good relations and 'win-win co-operation' between China and Africa.

13. The Special Economic Zone (SEZ) in Chambishi is one of seven such zones that China plans to implement in the continent with the agreement of the respective African governments. Built in the image of the SEZs that China has been creating in its own territory since 1979, these zones are aimed at attracting foreign investment using tempting fiscal conditions and attractive land prices as bait. So far, the zones have not proved to be very effective; in fact, they are almost a total failure. In *African Shenzhen: China's special economic zones in Africa* (Cambridge University Press, 2011), Deborah Brautigam and Tang Xiaoyang point out that the only zones that are currently functioning are the ones in Zambia and Egypt, while those in Mauritius, Ethiopia, Algeria and Nigeria (where two zones have been established) have either been under construction for years or suspended altogether. While carrying out research for this book, the authors visited the SEZ in Suez in Egypt, where there is only a modest Chinese presence, and the zone in Chambishi, which will eventually have a secondary base in Lusaka. According to the magazine *Zambia Review 2010*, this will involve an investment of $900 million and will boast between 50 and 60 companies employing 6,000 Zambians by 2014. According to the interviews carried out by the authors, there are currently only seven companies operating in the area. Police officers and security guards refused to let the authors into a site full of security cam-

NOTES

eras. The spokesman for China Nonferrous Mining Group, the promoter of the project, declined to grant them an interview.

14. The fatal explosion which took place on 20 April 2005 was blamed on the inexperience of the workers, who were mostly on temporary contracts and had no training or experience, as well as the lack of adequate equipment and negligent attention to even the most basic security practices. The dead workers, who were all aged between eighteen and twenty-three, had been earning between $15 and $25 each month, according to the report *Zambian Mining Labour: Modernity, Casualization and Other Forms of Precariousness*, Grace-Edward Galabuzi (Ryerson University, 2005). Each family received $10,000 in compensation.

15. The four workers assured the authors that the conditions offered by other foreign companies are 'much better', but there are few opportunities to work for these firms as the majority of companies in Chambishi are Chinese. The study 'Chinese Investments in Africa: A Labour Perspective' by the African Labour Research Institute in 2009 states that Chinese mining companies in Zambia pay around 30 per cent less than their competitors. When the authors contacted Fifteen Metallurgical Construction Company in Beijing, representatives of the company denied that there was any controversy over working conditions in Zambia.

16. According to NUMAW, the only exception is the mine run by China Nonferrous Metal Mining Group in Luanshya, located between Kitwe and Ndola, where working conditions are 'standard'. This is due to the fact that the company was obliged to uphold the pre-existing working conditions offered by the previous owner when it invested in the mine. In employment terms, the Luanshya mine is the only Chinese-financed mine offering optimum working conditions in the whole of the Copperbelt, according to NUMAW.

17. Hundreds of the 800 miners employed by the Chinese-owned Collum Coal Mine took part in the protest on 15 October 2010 against the unsafe working conditions in the mining installation. The two foremen opened fire, wounding eleven miners. The case was officially dismissed because of a lack of witnesses, which does seem somewhat surprising given the circumstances. The local and foreign press speculated that political pressures and the release from prison of two Zambian women accused of drug trafficking in China may have been the real cause of the dismissal.

18. China invested $400 million in Zambia's mining sector in 2009, at the height of the global crisis. According to the Chinese vice minister of commerce, Li Jinzao, cumulative investment flows from China to Zambia

322

reached $5.6 billion in early 2012. Bilateral trade reached $3.4 billion in 2011.

19. China's most vocal critic on the continent, Zambia's President Michael Sata, met with the Chinese ambassador in Lusaka in his first official appointment after winning the presidency. He made the point that Chinese companies are still welcome in the country, but insisted that they have to obey national laws. A few months into his presidency, Sata now seems to have toned down his criticism and a bilateral agreement was signed in March 2012 in which China guaranteed further grants, technical co-operation and investments.

20. See Chapter 3 for a description of the equally insecure working conditions experienced by local workers in Chinese mines in Peru and Burma.

21. In November 2011, Human Rights Watch's report 'You'll Be Fired If You Refuse: Labor Abuses in Zambia's Chinese State-owned Copper Mines' detailed the persistent abuses in Chinese-run mines in Zambia, including poor health and safety conditions. This report is in line with what the authors witnessed on their field research in Zambia.

22. *Chinese Investments in Africa: A Labour Perspective*, op. cit.

23. China, the world's second largest economy with hopes of overtaking the United States by 2020, is still setting a third-world minimum wage through its local governments: around 1,400 yuan (160 euros) in towns and cities and 900 yuan (100 euros) in rural areas, as of 2013. Since the beginning of the process of 'opening and reform', Beijing has been reluctant to improve working conditions among its working classes, conscious that low costs are the key to the success and longevity of the 'factory of the world'. For example, the first central government regulation on minimum wages wasn't issued until 2003. However, since 2009–10 the Chinese government seems to have decided to change a model which is unsustainable in the long term as a result of the enormous inequalities that it generates. This has led the government to tighten its employment legislation, enforce a greater observance of these commitments, and to significantly increase the minimum wage in the hope of putting an end to this inequality, at least in the towns to the east of the country where social unrest is more likely to happen. In 2012 about fifteen provinces increased their minimum wage, most noticeably in Shenzhen, where the minimum wage is now 1,500 yuan per month, and Shanghai, where it is 1,450 yuan. The authorities are also experimenting with collective wage negotiations between the Communist Party's trade union and employers as a means of boosting wages. The Chinese government hopes that these measures will also promote the creation of a middle

class, allowing China to move towards an economic model based on consumption.

24. To explain their whole story from beginning to end, the four workers arrived in Beijing by train in May 2010, at the authors' own request and expense. They brought with them various types of documents that backed up their version of events (contracts, pay slips, tables indicating future payments, plane tickets, visas, etc.). The authors intervened in their case in order to make sure that they would have access to legal representation at their upcoming trial.

25. The documents which the men brought with them to Beijing reflected the complexity of the salary-paying system for migrant workers. The salary is paid in various instalments and to various recipients (employees on the one hand, and their families on the other), in a labyrinthine system aimed at preventing the workers from spending all their money and depriving their family of support, and also ensuring that the worker will not abandon his commitment to the company before the end of his contract. While this system is technically legal, in practice it denies the worker the right to resign. Although this practice is not unique to China, the severe application of these contracts by the Chinese has no equal in our day and age. Some companies go even further: they take away the workers' passports to prevent them from renouncing their salaries and leaving the project, effectively making them hostages of the company. Sources: 'Hired on Sufferance: China's Migrant Workers in Singapore', Aris Chan, China Labour Bulletin, February 2011, and interviews with Zhang Zhiqiang, a Chinese lawyer and expert in migrant labour issues.

26. When the authors contacted him by telephone, Lei Youbin denied all the accusations and refused to give any convincing explanation for them, before abruptly hanging up.

27. At least a dozen Chinese workers have resigned as a result of precarious working conditions and mistreatment at the hands of Aolong's bosses, who are still using violence and threats to keep their workers in line. The last incident of this kind occurred on the eve of the Chinese New Year of the Rabbit in February 2011, when employers beat a worker after he complained about working conditions at the camp. The ineffectiveness of the Gabonese legal system and the half-heartedness of the Chinese legal system – which is demonstrated by the sentence in this case, which only required the company to pay the workers' salaries without any other compensation – have allowed Aolong to continue imposing its own law in Africa. These primitive labour conditions have also affected Gabonese workers hired by CCCC, who in April 2012 threatened to go

on strike to denounce unfair deductions from their payments. Source: '*Les employés de Construction Companyltd menacent de rentrer en grève*', *Gaboneco*, 14 April 2012.

28. In the absence of any official figures, various estimates place the number of Chinese workers in Angola at between 70,000 and 300,000.

29. Sources: 'Hired on Sufferance: China's Migrant Workers in Singapore', op. cit., and the authors' own interview with China Labour Bulletin in Hong Kong.

30. The authors were able to gain access to the model contract used by the Meilian agency, which includes clauses such as one specifying that the cost of food in the canteen will be shared on a fifty-fifty basis between employer and employee, and another specifying that the employer has the right to deduct the worker's salary for work-related errors or for damages to material. The contract also anticipates fines of between 5,000 and 10,000 yuan for certain types of behaviour or the failure to comply with certain work-related aspects of the role. Furthermore, the contract authorizes the employers to terminate the agreement if the employee 'causes trouble or takes part in strikes', or if he 'disobeys the bosses . . . or carries out inadequate work causing a loss to the company', among other reasons. Translated from the original Chinese document.

31. This leading NGO based in Hong Kong has spent years following and denouncing labour abuses committed in China. For more information, see http://www.china-labour.org.hk/en/.

32. Since the collapse of Maoism, the mantra of the Chinese regime has been 'economic growth and political stability'. Unemployment is therefore one of the government's obsessions, and it will spare no effort to reduce it and thereby avoid unrest that could endanger the Communist Party's hegemony in terms of national power. As well as Beijing's initiatives to encourage employment at all costs, such as the $586 billion fiscal stimulus package approved in 2008 to help combat the financial crisis, local government representatives are given free rein to adopt policies on a local level. For example, the Qingzhou county government in the province of Shandong, one of the focal points of the labour export industry, has promoted emigration to 'earn foreign money' and fight unemployment. A study carried out by Chinese experts reflected the urgency of the situation in the area, where 700,000 rural workers had to share a stretch of arable land barely 62,800 hectares in size. To help combat this problem, the local government created a labour export company that has already sent over 50,000 workers to other provinces and to countries such as Russia, Japan and South Korea.

33. Lei Lin of the Meilian agency partly attributes this excess of labourers to the impact of the Three Gorges Dam, which has caused the relocation of 1.5 million workers to date. The dam has led to the creation of large numbers of displaced people, who have not only lost their homes but have also had to abandon their traditional livelihoods. The local government has carried out various initiatives to prevent the potential build-up of tension as a result of the poverty this has caused. For example, between 1999 and 2009 the local government promoted the exportation of labour to other countries by offering fiscal discounts and improved credit access to companies prepared to send at least 100 workers abroad. Source: '重庆市鼓励扩大对外劳务合作规模若干优惠政策(试行)' ['The preferential policy on encouraging labour co-operation in Chongqing'], provided by the government of Chongqing in 1999, and available at http://www.pccqpc.com.cn/office/law.nsf/7dec3d01d2b5 eb6448256aef00066148/2 b3a1f0376ad7e3b48256862002bba1f?OpenDocument&Click=.

34. The law stipulates that the commission which the agency charges the worker for its services must not exceed 12.5 per cent of the total agreed in the contract. However, in practice it is common for the agencies to charge more than this, according to China Labour Bulletin.

7 THE CHINESE MIRACLE DEFIES THE PLANET

1. *Logging in the Wild East: China and the Forest Crisis in the Russian Far East*, Charlie Pye-Smith (Forest Trends, 2006).
2. In September 1998, the Chinese government announced a draconian plan banning logging across much of China's territory as a consequence of the constant flooding that took the lives of 3,600 people in central China that year, causing economic losses to the value of $30 billion. Experts attributed the floods – which were concentrated around the Yangtze river – to excessive logging and the poor quality of the dams built on the riverbanks, a consequence of corruption. 'Forests, floods, and the environmental state in China', Graeme Lang, *Organization and Environment*, June 2002.
3. 'The Russian–Chinese Timber Trade: Export, Supply Chains, Consumption, and Illegal Logging', WWF Forest Programme, 2007.
4. If logging is carried out selectively, as is the case with Siberia's rare species, the Primorsky region's average forestry production is between 1 and 1.5 cubic metres per hectare. Consequently, 10 million cubic metres is equivalent to between 8 and 10 million forest hectares, according to Anatoly Lebedev.

5. 'Collectively, Chinese importers control the timber trade and set prices, and it is very difficult for Russian timber exporters ... to do business directly with the end-users of their timber. There are no avenues for Russian exporters to enter the NE China timber market directly. At present, Russian exporters cannot supply timber to China without a Chinese trading company being involved.' 'The Russian–Chinese Timber Trade', op. cit., p. 13.

6. These were the prices in place when the authors visited the area in April 2010.

7. *Russian Logs in China: the Softwood Commodity Chain and Economic Development in China*, Song Weiming et al. (Forest Trends, 2007).

8. *Logging in the Wild East*, op. cit. and 'The Russian–Chinese Timber Trade', op. cit.

9. Estimates suggest that 95 per cent of the wood that Russia exports to China consists of tree trunks that have not undergone any type of industrial processing. *Logging in the Wild East*, op. cit., p.2.

10. 'China does not have legislation that makes it illegal to place illegally sourced wood products on the market, and nor does it have in place due diligence systems, such as the US or Europe, or public procurement policies like Europe or Japan. There are likely to be many and complex reasons why China [does not have these policies in place], having to do with legal structures and history ... and its very strong commitment to the national sovereignty of other countries, etc. I do note, however, that China is making strong strides on some supply chain and environmental issues,' Kerstin Canby from the organization Forest Trends explained in an email interview.

11. *Russian Logs in China*, op. cit.

12. When the authors interviewed Zhu Changling, director of the China National Furniture Association, he estimated that there were over 50,000 companies operating in the sector on Chinese territory, providing employment to 5 million people.

13. Between 40 and 60 per cent of the businesses involved in exporting Mozambican wood to China are run by Chinese state-owned companies. *Tristezas Tropicais: More Sad Stories from the Forests of Zambézia*, Catherine Mackenzie and Daniel Ribeiro (Maputo, 2009), p. 34. In Russia, the majority of these businesses are private companies.

14. As Ana Alonso explains, there are two ways of carrying out logging in Mozambique: by obtaining a simple licence that can be renewed annually and can only be held by Mozambicans; or by obtaining a forestry concession. These concessions are open to everybody, but obtaining them

through the legal channels involves investing over a million dollars and dealing with several years of complicated bureaucracy.

According to Alonso, the Chinese companies do not own forestry concessions in the provinces of Sofala, Zambezia and Nampula. However, they do participate indirectly in logging in these regions, as they often use local people to gain access to a simple licence. In Alonso's words, this is a 'malicious system because the Chinese company piles the Mozambican with debt and ensures that the wood that is felled is sold directly to the company under the conditions it names'. One of the tricks that is commonly used in the sector involves the way in which the quality and quantity of the wood is recorded. This enables the licence-holder to exceed the annual limit for legal logging (500 tons of top quality wood with a cost of around $8,000) so that they can repay the loan.

On this subject, the expert Catherine Mackenzie estimates that 'the majority of small operators are only able to enter the sector by obtaining credit from the Asian timber buyers', *Mozambique: Chinese Takeaway!* Catherine Mackenzie (FONGZA, 2006), p. 13.

15. In the absence of any official statistics, we can multiply the 7,500 tons of wood that Zheng annually exports to China by fifty, which is the number of Chinese companies estimated to be working in the area. The amount of unprocessed wood annually exported by Chinese companies in the province of Sofala alone would therefore exceed 375,000 tons.

16. 'Mozambique: resistance forms to illegal logging', UN Integrated Regional Information Networks, 20 April 2007.

17. 'Between 1997 and 2007, the volume of [China's] manufactured wood product exports – mainly plywood and furniture – skyrocketed more than eight-fold from 5.1 to 48.5 million m³', *Recent Developments in Forest Products Trade Between Russia and China: Potential Production, Processing, Consumption and Trade Scenarios*, Steve Northway et al. (Forest Trends, 2009), p. 2.

18. In 2011 China imported 42.3 million cubic metres of logs, a 23 per cent increase in volume from 2010. Russia was the largest supplier of logs to China in 2011, with a 33.2 per cent share by volume. The National Development and Reform Commission (NDRC), China's main economic planning body, estimates that the country will face a deficit of between 140 and 150 million cubic metres of timber for industrial use by 2015. Sources: 'The Forest Industry Snapshot', MFLNRO, British Columbia, February 2012; *Recent Developments In Forest Products Trade Between Russia and China*, op. cit., p. 2.

19. *State of the World's Forests 2011*, Food and Agriculture Organization of the United Nations (FAO).

20. This represents a 34.4 per cent increase on 2009. Source: 2010 年全国林产品进出口额 962.7亿美元增 37.1 per cent, available at http://www.wood168.net/woodnews/20625.html.

21. *Sharing the Blame: Global Consumption and China's Role in Ancient Forest Destruction* (Greenpeace, 2006), p. 42.

22. 'Investigation into the Global Trade in Malagasy Precious Woods: Rosewood, Ebony and Pallisander', Global Witness and the Environmental Investigation Agency (US), October 2010, p. 11.

23. In spring 2010, southern China suffered its worst drought in six decades, which affected over 50 million people. Source: 'China says drought now affecting 50 million people', Ben Blanchard, Reuters, 19 March 2010.

24. China has already built four dams on the Mekong: Manwan, Daochaoshan, Jinghong and Xiaowan. At 292 metres high, the last is the tallest in the world with the capacity to store 15,000 cubic metres of water (enough to regulate the water levels of the river). A total of 70,000 people have been relocated in China as a result of these hydroelectric projects, a figure that will rise to 130,000 over the course of this decade as the rest of the dams on the Chinese side of the river are completed, according to Yu Xiaogang, director of Green Watershed. Sources who prefer not to be named told the authors that significant outrages had taken place in terms of compensation paid to the people affected by the dams (including compensation lower than the established rate and relocation to seismic hazard zones or areas with no drinking water). However, the victims 'are afraid of talking to the press because this may include informers for the Chinese authorities'. China is ranked 171 out of 178 in the list produced in 2010 by Reporters without Borders (RSF) measuring the degree of freedom of the press throughout the world. Source: 'Mekong Tipping Point: Hydropower Dams, Human Security and Regional Stability', Richard Cronin and Timothy Hamlin, The Henry L. Stimson Center, 2010, p. 29.

25. Most of the electricity generated by the dams built on the Chinese section of the Mekong is sold to Canton, Thailand and Laos, according to Yu Xiaogang.

26. 'Dams in China Turn the Mekong into a River of Discord', Michael Richardson, Yale Center for the Study of Globalization, 2009.

27. Estimates suggest that Lake Tonle Sap in Cambodia and the Mekong Delta in Vietnam are the areas that have been hardest hit by the end of the natural cycle of the Mekong river. In the case of Tonle Sap, activists

and experts fear that more species will become extinct in an ecosystem that is already threatened by pollution and excessive fishing, and which provides 70 per cent of the protein consumption of Cambodia's 15 million inhabitants. In Vietnam, the dams are blamed for low water levels which have allowed the sea to win territory over the freshwater Mekong Delta, a region which is fundamental to Vietnam's food security because of its high levels of rice production. Sources: *Freshwater Under Threat, South East Asia*, United Nations Environment Programme (UNEP), 2009; 'China hydropower dams in Mekong River give shocks to 60 million', Lee Yoolim, *Bloomberg Markets Magazine*, 26 October 2010.

28. At the time of writing in 2012, China is the only country that has built dams on the main Mekong river. The other countries in the region have been carrying out studies into the construction of hydroelectric projects on the river since the 1970s, and these studies have increased in recent years. The most advanced project is the Xayabouri Dam, an infrastructure project planned for northern Laos with a capacity to generate 1,260 megawatts. Other studies are underway into the construction of eleven more dams along the river in Laos, Vietnam and Cambodia. Viability reports indicate that the impact of these projects would be disastrous, leading experts to request a ten-year moratorium on the construction of any new dams on the river.

China also plays an important role in the dams that have been planned downstream. On the one hand, the construction of Chinese dams has broken the taboo that once surrounded the development of any projects on such an important river. On the other hand, Beijing is an important investor, as it is estimated that, if the plans are approved, around 40 per cent of the hydroelectric projects downstream on the Mekong and its tributaries would be undertaken by Chinese companies. Sources: 'Strategic Environmental Assessment of Hydropower on the Mekong Mainstream, Final Report', International Centre for Environmental Management, October 2010; 'Cascade Effect', Philip Hirsch, Australian Mekong Resource Centre: http://www.chinadialogue.net/article/show/single/en/4093-Cascade-effect.

29. China has built at least twenty dams and plans to construct another forty on the eight main rivers which begin in the Himalayan mountains. Source: 'Water wars? Thirsty, energy-short China stirs fear', Denis Gray, Associated Press, 16 April 2011.

30. *A Sino-Indian River War: How Serious is the Threat?* Jonathan Holslag, (BICCS, 2008).

31. China has built fifteen reservoirs on the tributaries of the Ili river and a 22-metre-wide, 300-kilometre-long channel on the Irtysh river to supply water to its oil industry located in Karamay in Xinjiang province. Source: 'The upstream superpower: China's international rivers', E. James Nickum, in *Management of Transboundary Rivers and Lakes*, eds. Olli Varis, Cecilia Tortajada and Asit K. Biswas (Springer, 2008), p. 239.

32. Less than 1 per cent of China's total water resources originate outside the country's borders. Ibid., p. 230.

33. Ibid.

34. Approved in 1997 by 103 votes in favour, 27 abstentions and 3 votes against, the Convention attempts to lay the foundations for the resolution of potential water conflicts. He Deming explained to the authors why China continues to oppose this agreement, to which it still refuses to subscribe: 'It is an unfair text because it considers the priorities of downstream regions. It establishes restrictions on hydroelectric projects further upstream in order to protect the environment, but by doing so it restricts the development of "upstream" countries.' See also 'The upstream superpower: China's international rivers', op. cit., p. 231.

35. It is only fair to point out that this environmental sensibility is improving in China. This is mostly a consequence of the pressing need to reverse a catastrophic and unsustainable environmental situation caused by thirty years of brutal development.

36. The industrialization of China, which began in 1949 when the Communist Party came to power and gained momentum after the economic reforms of 1978, has had a profound impact on the environment. While China's transformation into the world's factory – a result of the relocation of Western industry – has played a very important role, it is important not to underestimate the effect of the authorities' lack of attention to protecting the environment over the last six decades.

    Consequently, China is home to twenty of the thirty most contaminated cities in the world as well as thousands, or even tens of thousands, of so-called 'cancer villages', where unrestrained industrial dumping in lakes and rivers has sent levels of the illness rocketing among the local population. Furthermore, estimates suggest that 26 per cent of the water in Chinese rivers and lakes is unsuitable for human use, while the remaining 62 per cent is barely drinkable. Only 1 per cent of the 560 million Chinese city-dwellers breathe safe air, according to European Union standards.

    In a report published in 2007 – which was rumoured to have been censored by the Chinese government, who demanded a reduction to its shocking figures – the World Bank estimated that 760,000 Chinese people die annually as a result of pollution. Sources: *Cost of Pollution in China: Economic Estimates of Physical Damages* (World Bank, 2007); 'Transboundary water pollution management: lessons learned from river basin management in China, Europe and the Netherlands', Xia Yu, *Utrecht Law Review*, 7 (1), January 2011.

37. In Chapter 3 we saw how Shougang Hierro Peru, a company operating in Peru's Marcona mines amid grave criticism of their environmental standards, was considered one of the most polluting companies in China.

38. In May 2011, a court in Fujian gave Zijing Mining Group, one of China's biggest gold producers, a $4.62 billion fine in response to toxic dumping that poisoned thousands of fish in a river in Fujian and left 60,000 people without their water supply.

39. Erdos took over the rights to exploit bauxite in the mining concessions in the eastern Mondulkiri region after announcing an investment of $3 billion, which included the construction of two (carbon energy) power stations and the running of a controversial project on Boeng Kak lake in Phnom Penh. Approximately 3,000 families were forced from their homes beside the lake in return for very little compensation so that the company could build lucrative luxury housing with the support of the local political elite. Sources: Interviews with sources who asked not to be named; 'Thousands displaced as Chinese investment moves into Cambodia', Prak Chan Thul, *South China Morning Post*, 7 April 2011.

8 THE *PAX SINICA* OF THE MIDDLE KINGDOM

1. In autumn 1950, a year after the foundation of the People's Republic of China, Mao Zedong sent thousands of troops into Tibet to suppress its people. Resistance to the invader reached its peak in March 1959, when a cruelly repressed uprising in Lhasa led the Dalai Lama to flee and seek exile in India, where he remains to this day. Since then, Dharamsala has been the headquarters of the Tibetan government in exile.

2. According to the Tibetan government in exile, there are approximately 100,000 Tibetan people living in India, with 12,000 of them based in Dharamsala. Nepal is home to the second biggest Tibetan community outside Tibet, with at least 20,000 Tibetan immigrants.

3. A WikiLeaks cable from the American embassy in New Delhi showed that a total of 87,096 Tibetan refugees were registered at the Reception Centre in Dharamsala between 1980 and 2009. For years the annual

influx of refugees was around 3,000. Out of these, approximately 600 were children whose parents had forced them to escape to prevent them from being educated under Chinese rule. For these parents, getting their children out of Tibet means investing around $1,000 – their life savings – to pay for Nepalese guides over the Himalayas. Many of these children never see their parents again.

4. On 14 March 2008, just months before the celebration of the Beijing Olympic Games, a protest led by monks in Lhasa against Chinese domination and the lack of religious liberties spread into other areas and monasteries across Tibet over the following days. Many Tibetan people took part in the violence, which involved attacking people of Han Chinese ethnicity and their businesses. The response of the Chinese police and army was ruthless, both in suppressing the uprising and in the repression that followed. The Western press was not authorized to cover the events, and the official version therefore differs significantly from the Tibetan sources. According to these sources, at least 220 Tibetans died and another 7,000 were arrested. Meanwhile, Beijing assured the world that the Tibetan violence had resulted in just nineteen deaths, all of them Chinese. Human Rights Watch chronicles the abuse carried out by Chinese security forces in Tibet between 2008 and 2010 in the report 'I Saw It With My Own Eyes', published in 2010.

5. Lobsang Sangay, who was born in India and studied law at Harvard, was elected as the Tibetan prime minister in April 2011 after securing 55 per cent of the votes of Tibetan people living abroad. He will take on the political role which was previously carried out by the Dalai Lama, who will continue as the Tibetan spiritual leader.

6. In an interview with the Chinese academic Ma Jiali, a leading expert in China–India relations as well as deputy director of the think tank China Reform Forum, he pointed out that in the 'probable' event of a radicalization of the Tibetan movement after the death of the Dalai Lama, 'China will ask India not to allow exiled Tibetans to carry out political activities against China, because Tibet is the most sensitive issue for the Chinese government.' When the authors asked him whether Beijing hoped that India would co-operate as Nepal is currently doing, he answered, 'Yes, exactly, like in Nepal.' This could potentially cause conflict in democratic India where the Tibetans are popular with public opinion, the media and the political classes. If the Indian government has to try to accommodate this feeling with Chinese demands, this could lead to tensions between China and India.

7. This is a reference to the direct relationship between the Tibet issue and India's dispute with Pakistan, a traditional ally of Beijing. The pacification of Tibet – or, alternatively, the escalation of tensions in the area – would have related repercussions for India in Pakistan.

8. During a visit to Delhi in 1956, Zhou Enlai, the Chinese prime minister during the Maoist era, warned Nehru of the consequences of giving asylum to the Dalai Lama. In 1959, in the midst of disagreements between the two countries over the demarcation of the border, including China's construction of a strategic road uniting Xinjiang with Tibet through the disputed region of Aksai Chin, Nehru gave asylum to the Tibetan spiritual leader and granted permission for Dharamsala to become the headquarters of the Tibetan government in exile. In Beijing's eyes, Nehru had crossed the line.

9. After the exile of the Tibetan people, the CIA supported and financed the guerrilla operations of hundreds of Tibetans who were trained in camps in Nepal and India to undermine Beijing's power in Tibet. United States' support of this secret guerrilla army lasted until the 1970s, when China and the United States established diplomatic relations. Source: *La Actualidad de China* [China Today], Rafael Poch-de-Feliu (Critica, 2009), pp. 538 ff.

10. 'The fact that China's leaders saw Indian efforts as attempts to "grab Tibet", to turn Tibet into "a buffer zone", to return Tibet to its pre-1949 status, to "overthrow China's sovereignty", or to cause Tibet to "throw off the jurisdiction of China's central government", does not necessarily mean that those perceptions were accurate. In fact, this core Chinese belief was wrong. This belief which Chinese analysts explain underpinned China's decision for war in 1962 was, in fact, inaccurate. It was a deeply pernicious Chinese misperception that contributed powerfully to the decision for war in 1962.' 'China's decision for war with India in 1962', John W. Garver, in *New Directions in the Study of Chinese Foreign Policy*, eds. Robert S. Ross and Alastair Iain Johnston (Stanford University Press, 2006).

11. Nehru was naively convinced that China would not react to the border incursions of his troops and, therefore, that there would be no large-scale Chinese offensive. When this did in fact occur, the Indian troops were consequently not expecting the attack and were not duly prepared. China's advance was therefore unstoppable.

12. Relations continued to deteriorate after the war as a result of China's support of Pakistan during the 1965 Indo-Pakistani conflict, as well as the signing of a co-operation treaty with the Soviet Union in 1971 which

brought New Delhi under Soviet influence, and several border skirmishes which lasted well into the 1980s.

13. Co-operation between India and China has gone beyond matters of trade. For example, the two countries tend to agree on multilateral issues, whether at the G20 or on questions of climate change or the so-called 'South–South co-operation'. However, the two countries still do not see eye to eye on other matters: the issue of shared water resources, the frequent anti-dumping actions which India has filed against China at the World Trade Organization, India's trade deficit, Beijing's lack of enthusiasm in supporting New Delhi's aspirations to a seat on the UN Security Council, and China's provocative policy on visa concessions in the disputed border zones, which India sees as an insult, among other issues.

14. India has claimed an area the size of Switzerland from China for the Ladakh region on its northern border. To the east of the country, China has claimed an area three times as large from India, including much of Arunachal Pradesh, an area of great significance for Tibetan Buddhists. Beijing does not recognize the so-called 'McMahon Line' marking the border between India and Tibet, which was established in 1914 by the British colonial power and the leaders of a de facto independent Tibet. This dispute overlaps with the dispute between India and Pakistan over the state of Jammu and Kashmir, in which Beijing has openly given its support to Islamabad.

15. While there is widespread support for the Tibetan cause in India, there is no shortage of commentators who question New Delhi's policy on the region. One of these is Madhav Das Nalapat, a professor at Manipal University and a highly influential expert in the country, who, despite being openly critical of China's policy towards India, told the authors that 'India has paid a very high price in geopolitical terms for its support of the Dalai Lama and the Tibetan people'.

16. As well as the six divisions currently in position, India has also deployed its border police and is apparently forming two more divisions of mountain troops to reinforce Arunachal Pradesh. Meanwhile, estimates suggest that China has deployed 500,000 men in Tibet, where it has the capacity to mobilize twelve divisions in less than a month, thanks to infrastructure it has built in the region to facilitate the movement of troops. These include the railway running to Lhasa across the roof of the world, five airports and a network of roads covering a distance of 41,000 kilometres. 'Consolidating Control: Chinese Infrastructure Development in Tibet', Monika Chansoria, CLAWS, Spring 2011.

17. The planned schedule included an interview with the Chinese directors of Huawei's Indian headquarters in New Delhi and a visit to the company's R&D Centre in Bangalore. Despite the cancellation of the meeting in Delhi, the authors' appointment in Bangalore still went ahead. All the executives interviewed in Bangalore were Indian nationals. The authors were not able to interview a single Chinese executive at the company.

18. That year Huawei became the second biggest world player in the sector after Ericsson. Source: http://www.chinadaily.com.cn/bizchina/2011-02/01/content_11953774.htm.

    According to sources at the company, 10 per cent of its turnover is reinvested in R&D Centres, where the company has 51,000 employees (46 per cent of its total staff). A 'Telco' professional with ten years' experience earns an annual salary of around $40,000 at Huawei India, which is three to four times less than a professional with the same profile would earn in the United States or Europe.

19. In theory, the ban was extended to all providers of foreign equipment, but the government's action was clearly directed towards Chinese companies. Sources at Huawei told the authors that the circular 'was relaxed' in August 2010 when the company agreed to demonstrate its transparency by revealing its source-code, the so-called DNA of its technology. Huawei's competitors refused to do the same, leading the Indian government to limit the effects of its security measure, explained those same sources.

    In April 2012 the Indian intelligence agency Research and Analysis Wing (RAW) asked New Delhi to be cautious in its dealings with the Chinese firm Huawei, in the belief that the company has links with the Chinese Army. Suspicions about Huawei's links with China's State-security agencies seem also to explain why, in March 2012, the Australian government blocked the Shenzhen-based company from bidding for contracts, valued at $38 billion, to improve the broadband network of the country.

20. With respect to the composition of its shareholders, Huawei will only say that the company 'is 100 per cent the property of its employees and nobody holds more than 2 per cent'. Until the publication of its 2010 annual report, practically nothing at all was known about who was who in the company's executive team. Ren Zhengfei does not grant interviews to the press and the company has no plans to list itself on the stock exchange, which would oblige it to become more transparent.

21. In August 2010 the *New York Times* revealed that Beijing had deployed between 7,000 and 11,000 men in the strategic Gilgit-Baltistan region in

Pakistan-administered Kashmir with the aim of securing the overland route that would connect Xinjiang to the Indian Ocean. India claims this territory as its own.

22. In accordance with a bilateral agreement signed in July 2010, China will build another two nuclear reactors for civilian use in Pakistan, at a cost of $2.4 billion. China had previously built two other reactors at the same plant. The agreement represents a violation of the Nuclear Suppliers Group directives, which prohibit nuclear trade with countries that have not signed the Nuclear Non-Proliferation Treaty, as is the case with Pakistan. To justify its involvement, China has suggested that its nuclear sales will contribute to stability in southern Asia, echoing Pakistan's claims that the nuclear pact between India and the United States has caused a nuclear imbalance in the region.

    Several experts interviewed by the authors in India showed their concern about the 'inappropriate use' that Pakistan may be making of the dual-purpose nuclear technology supplied by China. These suspicions are not only based on Islamabad's desire to achieve balance in the region by keeping the nuclear threat alive, but also on China's historical role in Pakistan's nuclear programme. The invaluable assistance offered by Beijing to Islamabad in the 1980s and subsequent years became evident after the revelation of the nuclear trade plot masterminded by the famous Pakistani scientist Abdul Qadeer Khan, who provided details of China's connection to Pakistan's military nuclear programme. China's assistance played an invaluable role in helping Pakistan to quickly gain access to the atomic bomb. Beijing has never admitted its involvement in this proliferation. 'The Americans have turned a blind-eye to China's nuclear proliferation,' claimed a former Indian diplomat in Pakistan.

23. '千刀万剐' is an expression that appeared for the first time in a work written during the Yuan dynasty. It literally means 'use 10,000 daggers, make 10,000 cuts'. The phrase is used in New Delhi to describe the tactic that Beijing is allegedly employing in order to weaken its neighbour.

24. A further two experts told the authors that Chinese academics are incapable of answering questions about why China does not use its influence over Pakistan to try to put an end to the terrorism. 'China collaborates in the war against terror, but only if it represents a threat to its territorial integrity or to its people. Terrorism has many faces in Pakistan. If it doesn't affect them, it doesn't bother them,' one of them told us.

25. China plans to transform Gwadar into an energy hub and would therefore need to build an oil pipeline across Pakistan as far as Xinjiang in order to transport oil from Africa and the Middle East. In spring 2011 it

was announced that China would be in charge of administering the port, but the Beijing government denied that it had further asked Islamabad to host a Chinese naval base.

26. 'China and India: A Rivalry Takes Shape – Analysis', Harsh V. Pant, Foreign Policy Research Institute, June 2011.

27. The Russian-bought *Admiral Gorshkov* aircraft carrier will be operational by 2013. It is further expected that a homemade aircraft carrier will be completed by 2015. Source: 'China and India: A Rivalry Takes Shape – Analysis', Harsh V. Pant, op. cit.; Pant is an expert in security and defence in the Asia Pacific at King's College, London.

28. China, Taiwan and Vietnam all claim sovereignty over the Spratly Islands while Malaysia, Brunei and the Philippines claim parts of the archipelago. In 2002 these countries signed the Declaration on the Conduct of Parties in South China Sea, which, although it does not represent a step forward in terms of resolving the problem, was approved with the aim of avoiding military escalation in the region by committing the parties to following certain guidelines. The Declaration enjoins the claimants not to occupy any islet which was not previously inhabited. Since then, China, Vietnam and Malaysia have reinforced their presence on the previously occupied islets by building landing strips, barracks, watch towers and the necessary infrastructure to take in fishing communities of between 200 and 300 people. This is being done with the legal aim of demonstrating the 'effective administration' of the territory which would be a key factor under the unlikely circumstances of the dispute being resolved at an international tribunal.

29. China occupied the Paracel Islands in 1974, taking advantage of the weakness of the Saigon government just before the end of the Vietnam War. Given the close ties between Moscow and Hanoi the aim was to take over the islands which Beijing feared could harbour a Soviet naval base in the future, dangerously close to the Chinese island of Hainan. The current stance of Chinese diplomats with respect to Vietnam's claim on the islands is inflexible: 'The Chinese position is: that's it, it's over, we don't talk about it. It's closed, finished, over,' according to Ian Storey, of the Institute of Southeast Asian Studies (ISEAS), who the authors interviewed in Singapore.

30. The last major military conflict in the South China Sea was in 1988, when seventy Vietnamese sailors were killed in a clash with the PLA-Navy. Since then, a handful of fishermen have been killed, mostly in accidents.

31. China's military budget for 2012 officially increased by 11.2 per cent in comparison with 2011, reaching 670.3 billion yuan ($106 billion). While this figure is still a far cry from the United States' military expenditure, which is placed at around $614 billion, experts criticize the opaqueness surrounding China's military plans and argue that the real expenditure is likely to be far greater than official figures suggest, possibly two or three times greater. Beijing allegedly does not include its expenditure on the development and modernization of fighter aircraft and an aircraft carrier in this total, among other items. In 1994, China's military budget barely exceeded $6 billion.

32. In the past, China has used ballistic-missile testing alongside – or even inside – Taiwan's territorial waters to warn the island's leaders against crossing what Beijing sees as a red line: a declaration of independence, for example. Proof of this can be seen in the launching of several Chinese missiles in 1995 and 1996 in Taiwan's territorial waters, on the route of a significant part of its commercial naval traffic. This led to a response from the United States, whose president at the time, Bill Clinton, ordered the greatest American military deployment in Asia since the end of the Vietnam War. The United States government used the 'Taiwan Reaction Act' to guarantee the defensive security of the island in the event of any future attack, which explains why the United States is Taiwan's main supplier of arms. Source: 'New China missile unit near Taiwan: spy chief', Agence France-Presse, 26 May 2011.

33. Just twenty-three countries currently recognize the Republic of China ('Taiwan's official name) as a sovereign nation, independent from the People's Republic of China. The majority of these countries (twelve) are found in Central America, South America and the Caribbean. Most other nations, including all the big international players, subscribe to the 'one-China' principle and support the continuance of the current status quo. In other words, they believe that Taiwan – like Tibet – is part of the People's Republic of China.

34. Despite signing the ECFA, China has continued to boycott and put pressure on other nations to stop Taiwan from participating as a 'country' in the international community. This has made it impossible for Taiwan to begin negotiations or sign commercial agreements with countries or regions of interest, such as the European Union or Japan. Contrary to the expectations of the Taiwanese government, this has led to a greater economic isolation of the island. Critics of the ECFA argue that China is using the process of regional economic integration to marginalize Taiwan by forcing the island to channel its relations with the rest of the

world through Beijing. Source: 'Taiwan risks trade isolation, group warns', *Wall Street Journal*, 25 May 2011.

34. During a conversation in May 2009 with the US deputy secretary of state, James Steinberg, Lee insisted that Beijing was in no hurry to integrate the island into Chinese territory and said that China is following the same economic strategy in Taiwan that it adopted with Hong Kong: investments, buying assets and increasing its economic influence to fit its long-term political objectives. 'Senior Singapore leader says China's leader has patience for Taiwan: WikiLeaks', *Want China Times*, 8 December 2010.

36. President Chen's former colleague, Tao Liu, also told the authors that 'after Chen was elected he began to receive an enormous amount of pressure from Japan, the United States and the European Union. They told him that even though he had won the elections, he couldn't declare independence; he couldn't change the status quo.'

37. According to a poll carried out by the Taiwanese television station TVBS which was broadcast on 12 November 2008, 15 per cent of the respondents thought that Chen had been arrested for political reasons.

38. The most controversial issue surrounding the aid package was China's act of buying Costa Rican debt. Although it was announced that China would buy Costa Rican bonds when the relationship was first established, the details of the matter were not made public. The newspaper *La Nación*, which Arias described as a 'little shit' during his interview with the authors, resorted to legal means to force the conditions of the deal to be published: a 2 per cent interest rate and a repayment period of twelve years. China did not want the interest rate to be published 'because it didn't lend money at that interest rate to every country', Arias told us in justification of the lack of transparency.

    Several authoritative sources in San José who asked to remain anonymous assured us that the secrecy was really connected to another issue. Although the buying of bonds represented an acquisition by the Chinese state using its foreign currency reserves, and should therefore have been carried out via the State Administration of Foreign Exchange (SAFE), it was actually carried out through Bo An Investment Company, a business registered in Hong Kong. According to these sources, this company served to allow somebody from Arias's former government to pocket the 2 per cent interest, which would never end up in the coffers of the Chinese State.

39. 'China refused Panama offer to drop Taiwan: WikiLeaks', Agence France-Presse, 14 May 2011.

EPILOGUE

1. According to the Venezuela Violence Observatory (OVV), 155,577 homicides took place in the country between Chávez's appointment as president in 1999 and 2011. This means that the number of homicides has almost quadrupled since he came to power and this trend is far from over: 2011 was the most violent year in Venezuela's history. The so-called 'breach of impunity' also reveals the dramatic nature of the situation: out of the total number of murders mentioned, 91 per cent remained unpunished. Source: the authors' interviews with the sociologist Roberto Briceño-León, director of the OVV.

2. *The Rise and Fall of the Great Powers*, Paul Kennedy (Vintage, 1989).

3. The quintessential example is seen in the automobile sector, which was declared strategic by the government with the aim of transforming China into one of the world's heavyweights in the sector, like the United States, Germany or Japan. In order to do this, Beijing obliged foreign brands operating in the Chinese market to go into partnership with a Chinese manufacturer, with the aim of forcing a transfer of technology which would eventually allow China to achieve its objectives. Three decades later, Beijing is reaping the fruits of its labours: Shanghai has become the new Detroit and Chinese brands are aspiring to become global players in the medium term.

4. Chinese companies are accused of paying extremely low taxes in some African countries, either because of doubts surrounding the actual volume of exported products (which is what tax is paid on) or as a result of the tax holidays offered by the governments of these countries.

5. Qin defended China's presence and modus operandi in Africa using a string of figures which were mostly taken from the report 'China's Foreign Aid', published by the State Council in 2011. He specifically referred to the case of Zambia, which is presented as a model of Sino-African co-operation, explaining that China has invested $6 billion and created 6,000 jobs in the country. These figures are certainly impressive for anybody who has not, like the authors, had the chance to see for themselves the precarious working conditions offered to those 6,000 employees (described in Chapter 6) and the conflicts surrounding Chinese investments in Zambia.

6. A good example that highlights the importance of side effects is Nigeria. The risk of focusing only on development without paying any attention to justice or corruption has led the country into a climate of great violence. The report *Illicit Financial Flows from Developing Countries:*

2000–2009 published by Global Financial Flows points out that a total of $130 billion was lost in Nigeria as a result of corruption between 2000 and 2008. This represents an average of $15 billion per year, or between 4 and 9 per cent of the country's GDP.

7. 'China's Policy and its Effects in Africa', presented at the European Parliament on 28 March 2008.

8. 'China blocks Nam on Internet', Jo-Maré Duddy, *The Namibian*, 30 July 2009.

9. Various Chinese state departments are in charge of controlling the press (newspapers, radio and television) as well as internet content (blogs, news pages, chat rooms). The Central Department of Propaganda is the highest-ranking organization in terms of controlling cultural and journalistic content to ensure that they are in line with the official version stipulated by the Communist Party of China and its interests. However, the State Council Information Office and provincial and local governments also take charge of supervising news content.

The media and websites regularly receive what is known among Chinese journalists as the 'Directives from the Ministry of Truth' (in reference to George Orwell's *1984*), according to the respected news website China Digital Times. Written in authoritative language and sent to the people in charge of editorial departments, these orders are used by the Chinese government to lay down the rules about what is publishable and what should be kept off the radar. After spending several months analysing these directives, the authors began to understand that this paranoid control of the media spans every topic and format and – contrary to what is commonly believed in the West – also applies to topics which go beyond issues connected to human rights or democracy. Cases of corruption involving government officials, for example, are kept quiet, as are news stories covering the salary increases of China's military, violent incidents against the authorities or genetic research projects.

The control of information goes beyond simply banning or eliminating content. Some experts such as David Bandurski, an analyst working on the China Media Project at Hong Kong University, point out that Beijing has 30,000 cyber-police officers at its disposal, who spend day and night trawling the internet and blocking web pages, comments and other web content. As if that were not enough, the government has access to approximately 280,000 commentators who have been recruited to influence contributions to chat rooms, online forums and other sites of internet debate and to make these look spontaneous. Many of these 'red shirts', or '50 cent communists' as Bandurski calls them, are students who earn half a yuan (five euro cents) for each comment that contributes to influencing the dominant direction in forums for debate in order to steer these towards favourable positions from the point of view of the authorities. This technique aims to neutralize undesirable public opinion by spreading the views of the Communist Party, according to this specialist. Source: 'China's guerrilla war for the web', David Bandurski, *Far Eastern Economic Review*, July 2008.

10. China's expansion is causing these institutions to gradually adapt or give way to the new Chinese logic and criteria. In 2010 the Export-Import Bank of the United States made the unprecedented decision to match the financial terms offered by the Exim Bank of China so that General Electric would be able to gain a supply contract for 150 locomotives in Pakistan. Japan has also made its financial demands more flexible in order to compete with China on the world stage. Source: 'Western nations match China's game', John Pomfret, *Washington Post*, 12 January 2011.

11. *When China Rules the World*, Martin Jacques (Allen Lane, 2009).

12. *The China Fantasy: How Our Leaders Explain Away Chinese Repression*, James Mann (Viking Penguin, 2007).

13. In March 2012, China approved a law which 'legalized' disappearances or, in other words, the barely legal detentions which the police were enforcing at that point in time against dissidents and lawyers. This law eliminates many of the guarantees offered – at least on paper – by the former law, granting the police new and extraordinary powers. For example, it allows suspects to be detained for a period of up to six months in secret locations. Within the CPC, one year of debate was needed to reach consensus on the law. By comparison, China's private property law, passed in 2007, needed about fifteen years, as it was vigorously resisted by the Communist Party's old guard.

Index